DISNEY MASTERS

MICKEY MOUSE: THE RIDDLE OF BRIGABOOM

by Romano Scarpa

FANTAGRAPHICS | SEATTLE

Publisher: GARY GROTH
Editor: DAVID GERSTEIN
Design: RYAN McCARDLE and DAVID GERSTEIN
Production: PAUL BARESH and C HWANG
Associate Publisher: ERIC REYNOLDS

Fantagraphics Books, Inc. | 7563 Lake City Way NE | Seattle WA 98115 | (800) 657-1100

Visit us at fantagraphics.com. Follow us on Twitter at @fantagraphics and on Facebook at facebook.com/fantagraphics.

First printing: January 2024 | ISBN 978-1-68396-880-1 | Printed in China | Library of Congress Control Number: 2017956971

The stories in this volume were originally published in the following magazines:

"The Famed Jumping Frog of Queen Zenobia" ("Topolino e l le rane saltatrici") in Italian *Topolino* #1468-1469, January 15 and 23, 1984 (I TL 1468-AP)
"The Unsinkable Kildare Coot" ("Sgrizzo il più balzano papero del mondo") in Italian *Topolino* #465, October 25, 1964 (I TL 465-B)
"The Riddle of Brigaboom" ("Topolino e l'enigma di Brigaboom") in Italian *Topolino* #1779-1791, December 31, 1989 to March 25, 1990 (I TL 1779-BP)
"Remotely Impossible" in Danish *Anders And & Co.* #2000-47, November 20, 2000 (D 98474)

TITLES IN THIS SERIES

Mickey Mouse: The Delta Dimension (Romano Scarpa) (*Disney Masters* Vol. 1)
Donald Duck: Uncle Scrooge's Money Rocket (Luciano Bottaro) (*Disney Masters* Vol. 2)
Mickey Mouse: The Case of the Vanishing Bandit (Paul Murry) (*Disney Masters* Vol. 3)
Donald Duck: The Great Survival Test (Daan Jippes and Freddy Milton) (*Disney Masters* Vol. 4)
Mickey Mouse: The Phantom Blot's Double Mystery (Romano Scarpa) (*Disney Masters* Vol. 5)
Uncle Scrooge: King of the Golden River (Giovan Battista Carpi) (*Disney Masters* Vol. 6)
Mickey Mouse: The Pirates of Tabasco Bay (Paul Murry) (*Disney Masters* Vol. 7)
Donald Duck: Duck Avenger Strikes Again (Romano Scarpa with Carl Barks) (*Disney Masters* Vol. 8)
Mickey Mouse: The Ice Sword Saga Book 1 (Massimo De Vita) (*Disney Masters* Vol. 9)
Donald Duck: Scandal on the Epoch Express (Mau and Bas Heymans) (*Disney Masters* Vol. 10)
Mickey Mouse: The Ice Sword Saga Book 2 (Massimo De Vita) (*Disney Masters* Vol. 11)
Donald Duck: The Forgetful Hero (Giorgio Cavazzano) (*Disney Masters* Vol. 12)
Mickey Mouse: The Sunken City (Paul Murry) (*Disney Masters* Vol. 13)
Donald Duck: Follow the Fearless Leader (Dick Kinney and Al Hubbard) (*Disney Masters* Vol. 14)
Mickey Mouse: New Adventures of the Phantom Blot (Paul Murry) (*Disney Masters* Vol. 15)
Donald Duck: Jumpin' Jupiter! (Luciano Bottaro) (*Disney Masters* Vol. 16)
Mickey Mouse: The Man From Altacraz (Romano Scarpa) (*Disney Masters* Vol. 17)
Uncle Scrooge: Pie in the Sky (William Van Horn) (*Disney Masters* Vol. 18)
Mickey Mouse: Trapped in the Shadow Dimension (Andrea "Casty" Castellan) (*Disney Masters* Vol. 19)
Donald Duck: 20,000 Leaks Under the Sea (Dick Kinney and Al Hubbard) (*Disney Masters* Vol. 20)
Mickey Mouse: The Monster of Sawtooth Mountain (Paul Murry) (*Disney Masters* Vol. 21)
Uncle Scrooge: Operation Galleon Grab (Giorgio Cavazzano) (*Disney Masters* Vol. 22)
Mickey Mouse: The Riddle of Brigaboom (Romano Scarpa) (*Disney Masters* Vol. 23)

COMING SOON

Uncle Scrooge: World Wide Witch (Daniel Branca) (*Disney Masters* Vol. 24)

ALSO AVAILABLE

Adventures of the Gummi Bears: A New Beginning (Bobbi JG Weiss, Doug Gray, Anibal Uzál, Rubén Torreiro, and others) (*The Disney Afternoon Adventures* Vol. 4)
Disney One Saturday Morning Adventures (40+ creators including Daan Jippes, Laura McCreary, and Scott Gimple)
Mickey and Donald Fantastic Futures (Francesco Artibani, Lorenzo Pastrovicchio, Claudio Sciarrone and others)
Scrooge McDuck: The Dragon of Glasgow (Joris Chamblain and Fabrizio Petrossi)
Uncle Scrooge and Donald Duck in Les Misérables and War and Peace (Giovan Battista Carpi)
Walt Disney's Donald Duck: "Maharajah Donald" (Carl Barks)
Walt Disney's Silly Symphonies 1935-1939 Starring Donald Duck and the Big Bad Wolf (Al Taliaferro with Carl Barks, Merrill De Maris, and Ted Osborne)

WALT DISNEY

MICKEY MOUSE

The RIDDLE of BRIGABOOM

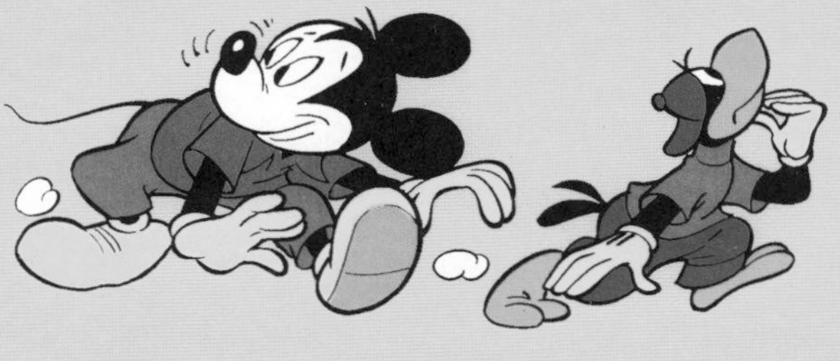

CONTENTS

This content has been reprinted in its entirety as first created from 1964-2000.

This title includes negative depictions and mistreatment of people or cultures. These stereotypes were wrong then and are wrong now. Rather than remove this content, we want to acknowledge its harmful impact, learn from it and spark conversation to create a more inclusive future together. Disney is committed to creating stories with inspirational and aspirational themes that reflect the rich diversity of the human experience around the globe. To learn more about how stories have impacted society, please visit www.disney.com/StoriesMatter.

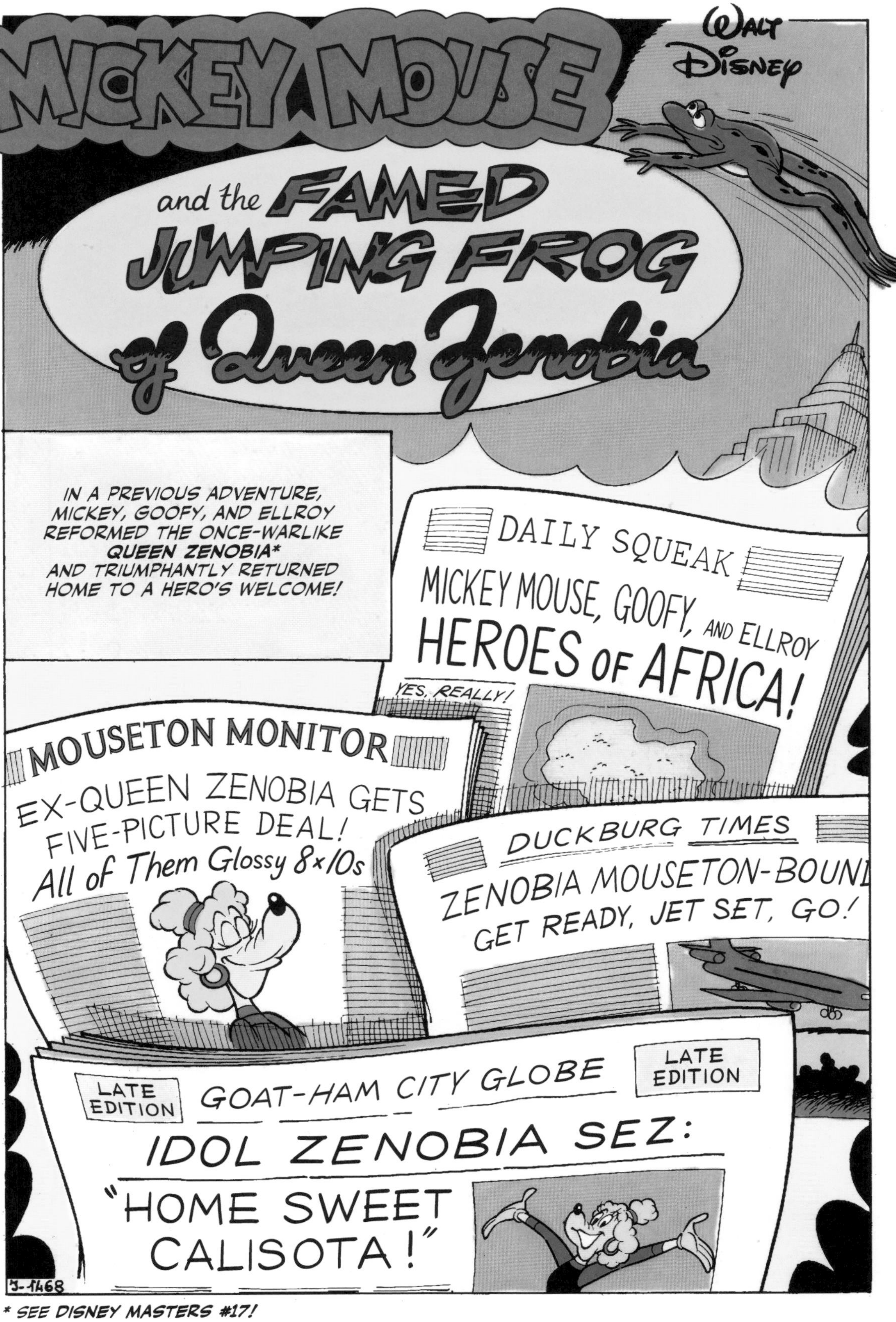
MICKEY MOUSE
WALT DISNEY
and the FAMED JUMPING FROG of Queen Zenobia
IN A PREVIOUS ADVENTURE, MICKEY, GOOFY, AND ELLROY REFORMED THE ONCE-WARLIKE QUEEN ZENOBIA* AND TRIUMPHANTLY RETURNED HOME TO A HERO'S WELCOME!
DAILY SQUEAK
MICKEY MOUSE, GOOFY, AND ELLROY HEROES OF AFRICA!
YES, REALLY!
MOUSETON MONITOR
EX-QUEEN ZENOBIA GETS FIVE-PICTURE DEAL!
All of Them Glossy 8×10s
DUCKBURG TIMES
ZENOBIA MOUSETON-BOUNI
GET READY, JET SET, GO!
LATE EDITION
GOAT-HAM CITY GLOBE
LATE EDITION
IDOL ZENOBIA SEZ:
"HOME SWEET CALISOTA!"
I-1468

* SEE DISNEY MASTERS #17!

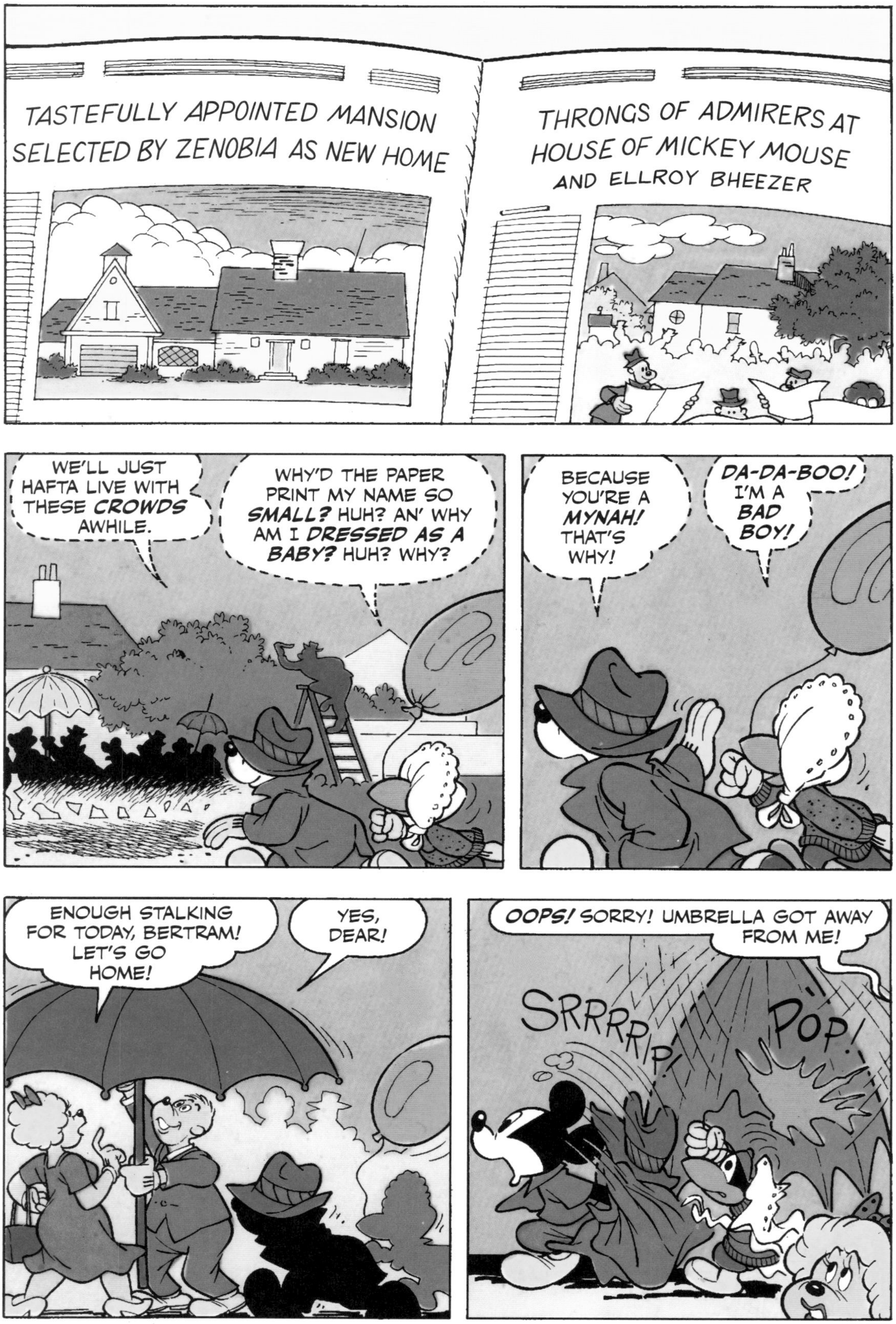
TASTEFULLY APPOINTED MANSION SELECTED BY ZENOBIA AS NEW HOME
THRONGS OF ADMIRERS AT HOUSE OF MICKEY MOUSE AND ELLROY BHEEZER
WE'LL JUST HAFTA LIVE WITH THESE CROWDS AWHILE.
WHY'D THE PAPER PRINT MY NAME SO SMALL? HUH? AN' WHY AM I DRESSED AS A BABY? HUH? WHY?
BECAUSE YOU'RE A MYNAH! THAT'S WHY!
DA-DA-BOO! I'M A BAD BOY!
ENOUGH STALKING FOR TODAY, BERTRAM! LET'S GO HOME!
YES, DEAR!
OOPS! SORRY! UMBRELLA GOT AWAY FROM ME!
SRRRRRIP!
POP!

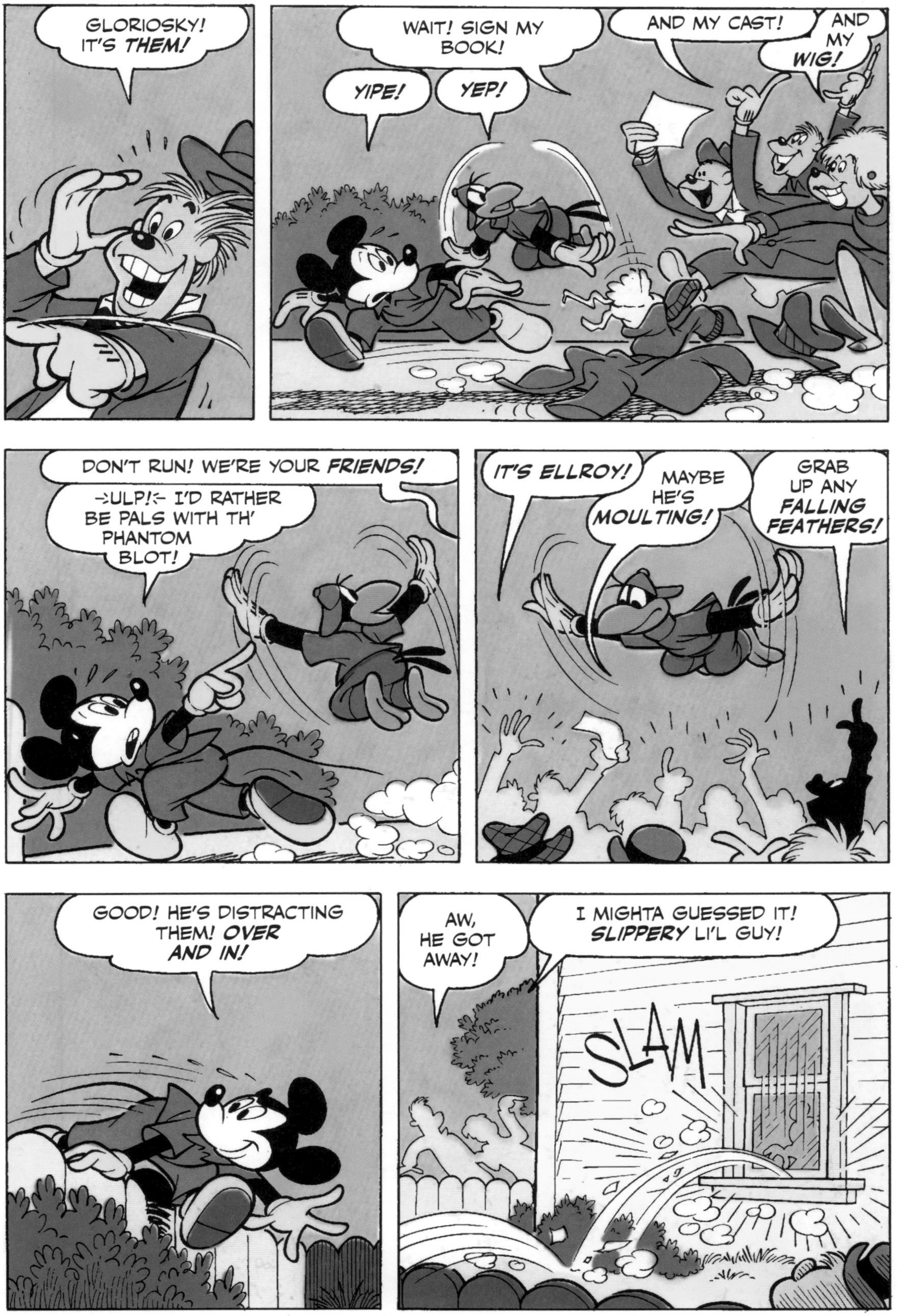
GLORIOSKY! IT'S THEM!
WAIT! SIGN MY BOOK!
YIPE!
YEP!
AND MY CAST!
AND MY WIG!
DON'T RUN! WE'RE YOUR FRIENDS!
-ULP!- I'D RATHER BE PALS WITH TH' PHANTOM BLOT!
IT'S ELLROY!
MAYBE HE'S MOULTING!
GRAB UP ANY FALLING FEATHERS!
GOOD! HE'S DISTRACTING THEM! OVER AND IN!
AW, HE GOT AWAY!
I MIGHTA GUESSED IT! SLIPPERY LI'L GUY!
SLAM

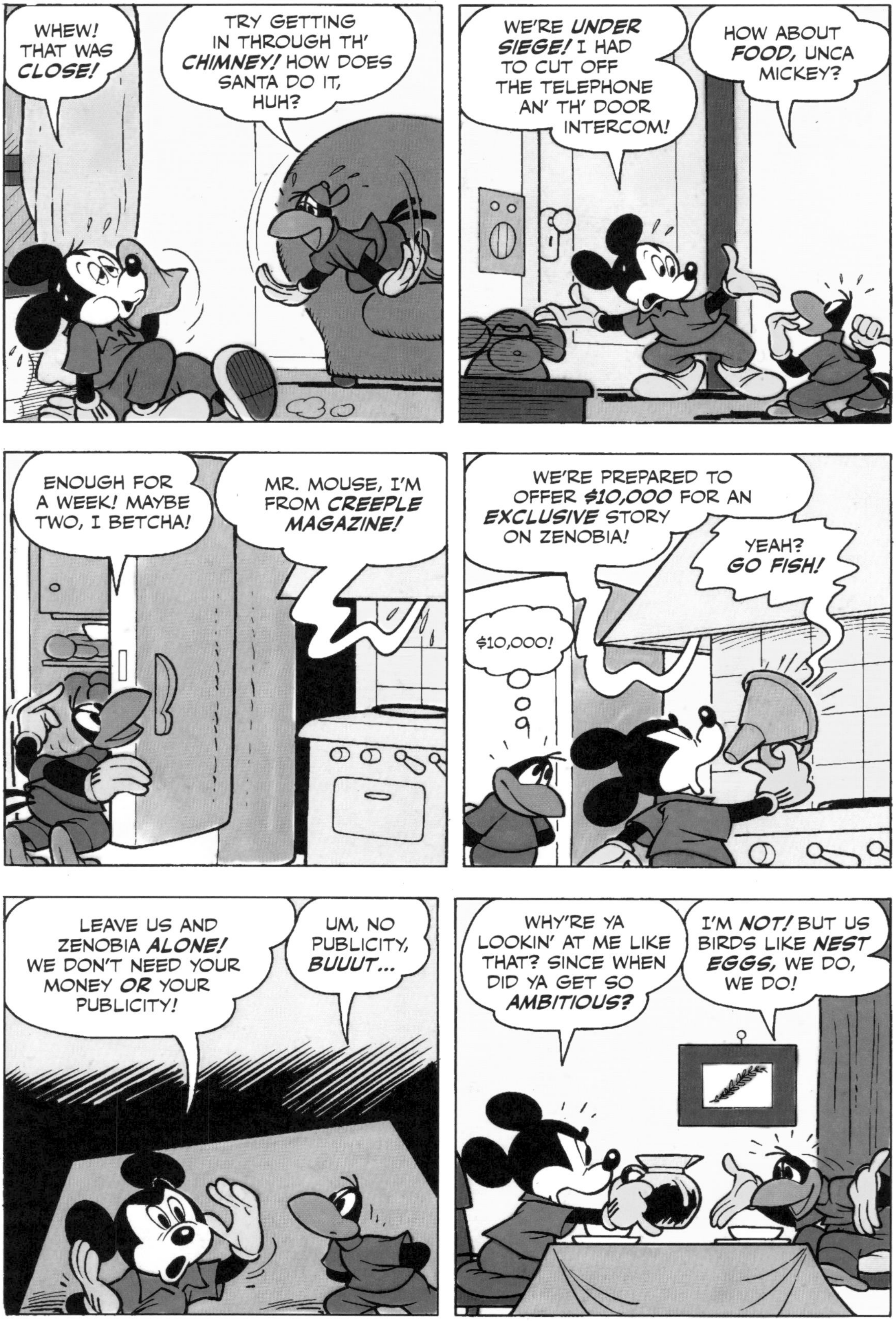
WHEW! THAT WAS CLOSE!
TRY GETTING IN THROUGH TH' CHIMNEY! HOW DOES SANTA DO IT, HUH?
WE'RE UNDER SIEGE! I HAD TO CUT OFF THE TELEPHONE AN' TH' DOOR INTERCOM!
HOW ABOUT FOOD, UNCA MICKEY?
ENOUGH FOR A WEEK! MAYBE TWO, I BETCHA!
MR. MOUSE, I'M FROM CREEPLE MAGAZINE!
WE'RE PREPARED TO OFFER $10,000 FOR AN EXCLUSIVE STORY ON ZENOBIA!
YEAH? GO FISH!
$10,000!
LEAVE US AND ZENOBIA ALONE! WE DON'T NEED YOUR MONEY OR YOUR PUBLICITY!
UM, NO PUBLICITY, BUUUT...
WHY'RE YA LOOKIN' AT ME LIKE THAT? SINCE WHEN DID YA GET SO AMBITIOUS?
I'M NOT! BUT US BIRDS LIKE NEST EGGS, WE DO, WE DO!

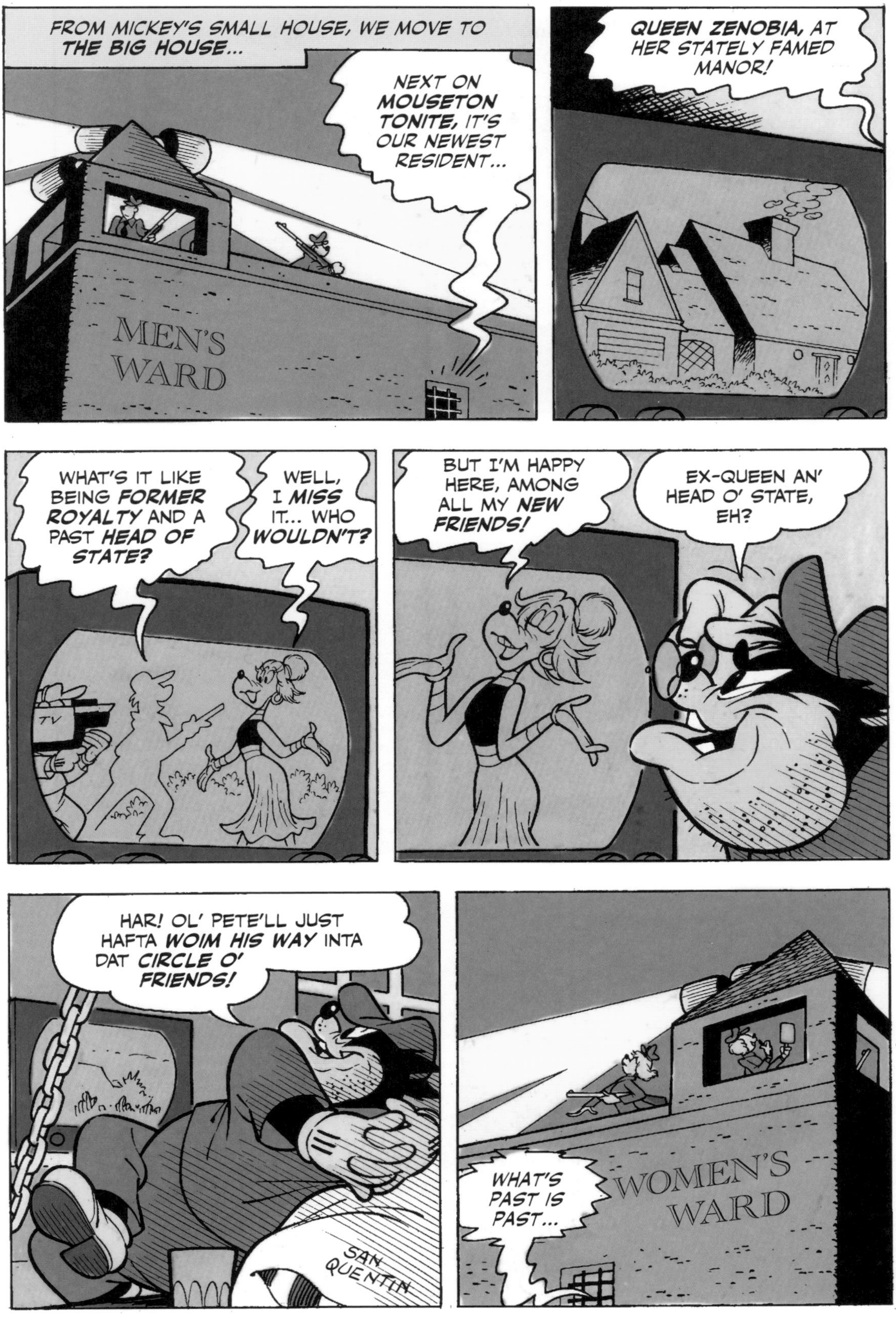
FROM MICKEY'S SMALL HOUSE, WE MOVE TO THE BIG HOUSE...
NEXT ON MOUSETON TONITE, IT'S OUR NEWEST RESIDENT...
MEN'S WARD
QUEEN ZENOBIA, AT HER STATELY FAMED MANOR!
WHAT'S IT LIKE BEING FORMER ROYALTY AND A PAST HEAD OF STATE?
WELL, I MISS IT... WHO WOULDN'T?
TV
BUT I'M HAPPY HERE, AMONG ALL MY NEW FRIENDS!
EX-QUEEN AN' HEAD O' STATE, EH?
HAR! OL' PETE'LL JUST HAFTA WOIM HIS WAY INTA DAT CIRCLE O' FRIENDS!
SAN QUENTIN
WHAT'S PAST IS PAST...
WOMEN'S WARD

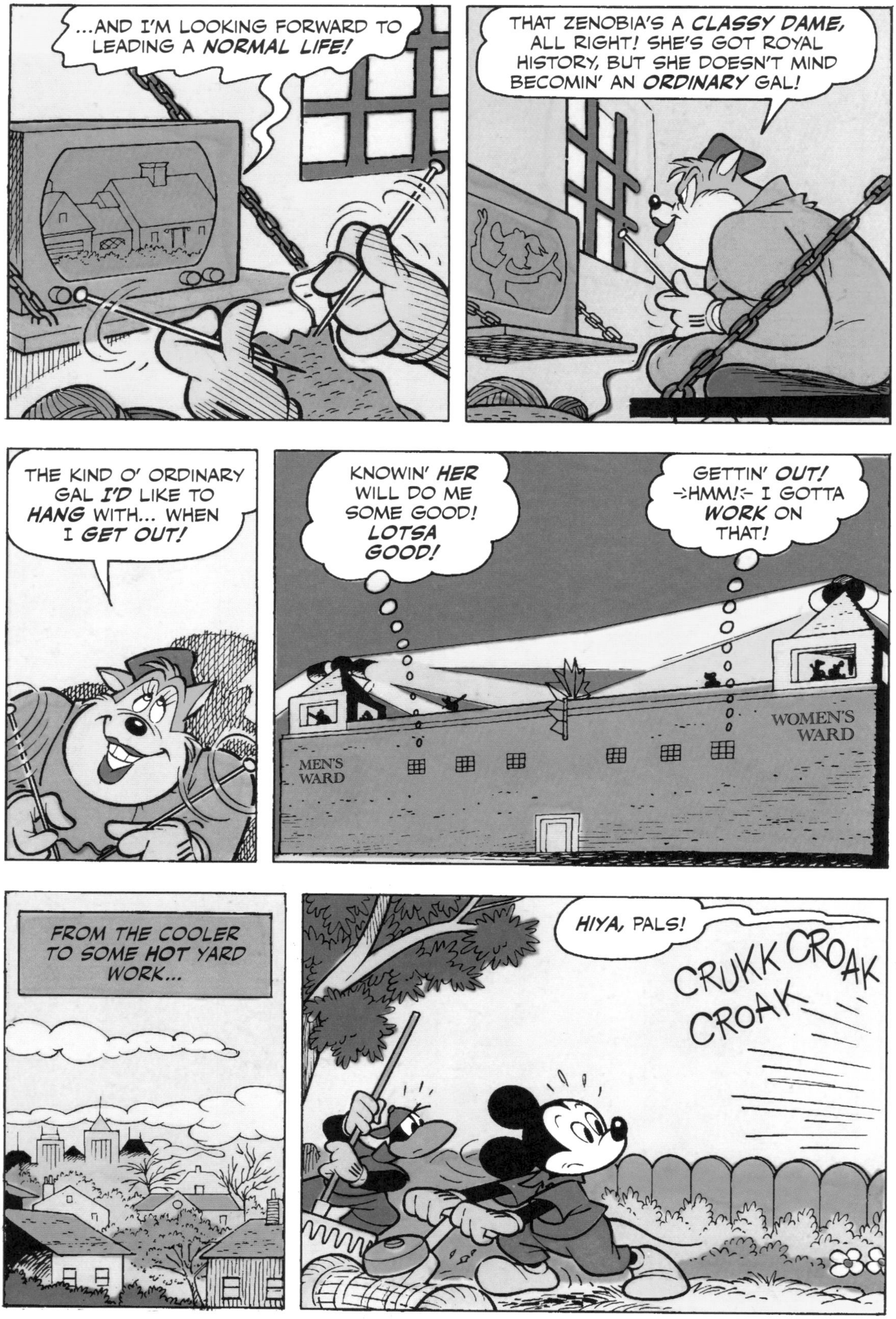
...AND I'M LOOKING FORWARD TO LEADING A NORMAL LIFE!
THAT ZENOBIA'S A CLASSY DAME, ALL RIGHT! SHE'S GOT ROYAL HISTORY, BUT SHE DOESN'T MIND BECOMIN' AN ORDINARY GAL!
THE KIND O' ORDINARY GAL I'D LIKE TO HANG WITH... WHEN I GET OUT!
KNOWIN' HER WILL DO ME SOME GOOD! LOTSA GOOD!
GETTIN' OUT! ~HMM!~ I GOTTA WORK ON THAT!
MEN'S WARD
WOMEN'S WARD
FROM THE COOLER TO SOME HOT YARD WORK...
HIYA, PALS!
CRUKK CROAK CROAK

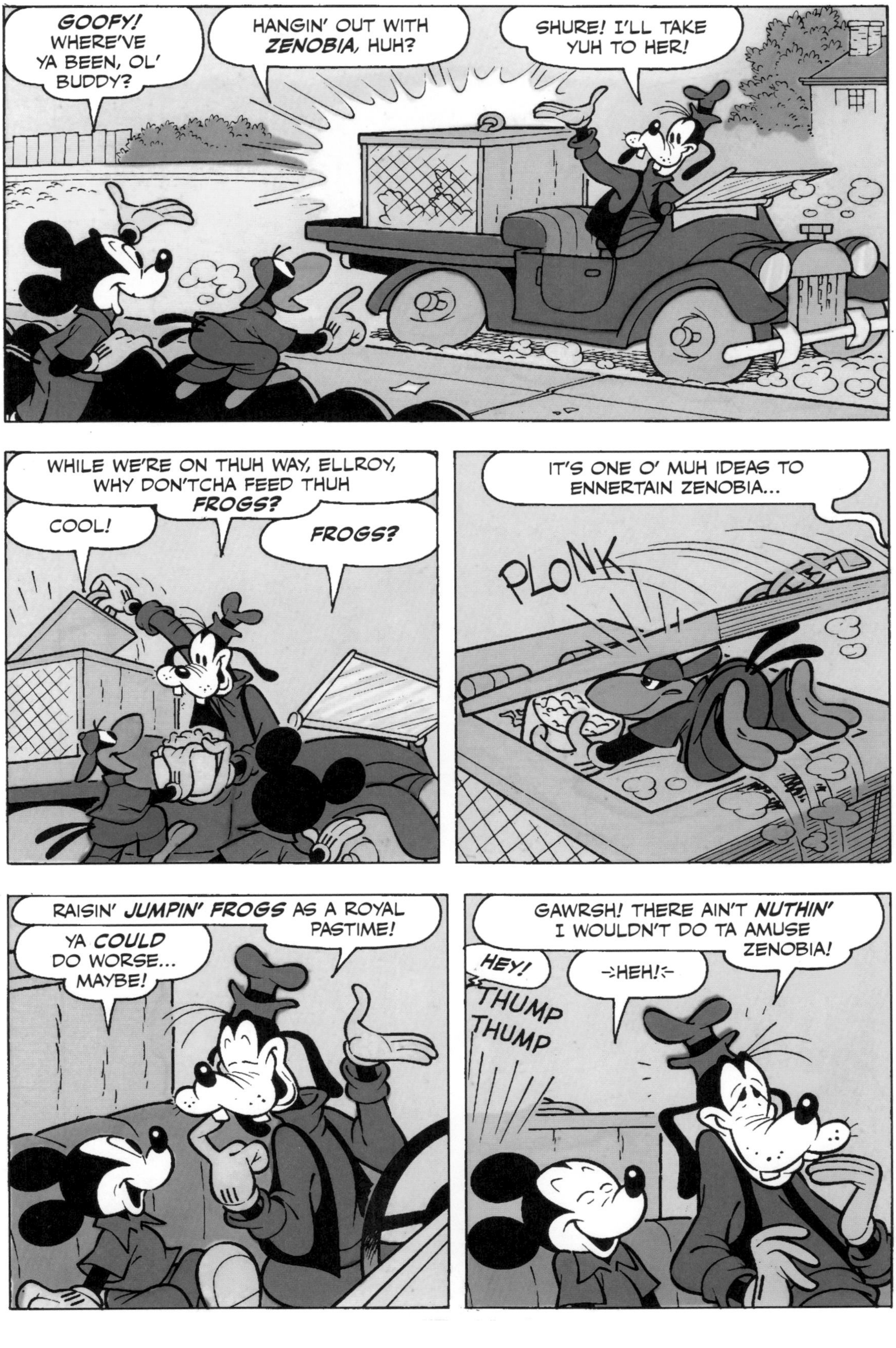
GOOFY! WHERE'VE YA BEEN, OL' BUDDY?
HANGIN' OUT WITH ZENOBIA, HUH?
SHURE! I'LL TAKE YUH TO HER!
WHILE WE'RE ON THUH WAY, ELLROY, WHY DON'TCHA FEED THUH FROGS?
COOL!
FROGS?
IT'S ONE O' MUH IDEAS TO ENNERTAIN ZENOBIA...
PLONK
RAISIN' JUMPIN' FROGS AS A ROYAL PASTIME!
YA COULD DO WORSE... MAYBE!
GAWRSH! THERE AIN'T NUTHIN' I WOULDN'T DO TA AMUSE ZENOBIA!
HEY!
HEH!
THUMP THUMP

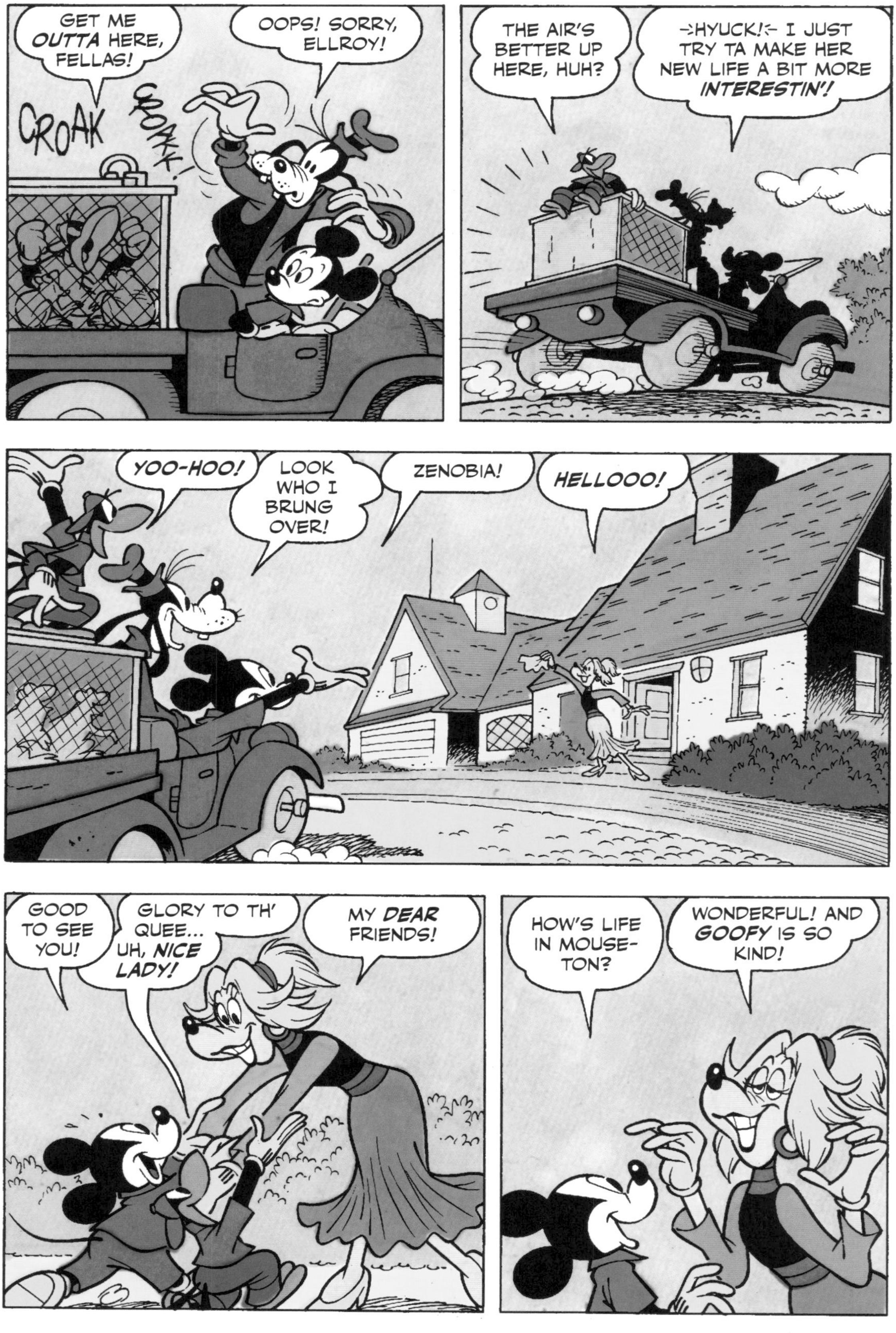
GET ME *OUTTA* HERE, FELLAS!
OOPS! SORRY, ELLROY!
CROAK
CROAK
THE AIR'S BETTER UP HERE, HUH?
–HYUCK!– I JUST TRY TA MAKE HER NEW LIFE A BIT MORE *INTERESTIN'!*
YOO-HOO!
LOOK WHO I BRUNG OVER!
ZENOBIA!
HELLOOO!
GOOD TO SEE YOU!
GLORY TO TH' QUEE... UH, *NICE LADY!*
MY *DEAR* FRIENDS!
HOW'S LIFE IN MOUSE-TON?
WONDERFUL! AND *GOOFY* IS SO KIND!

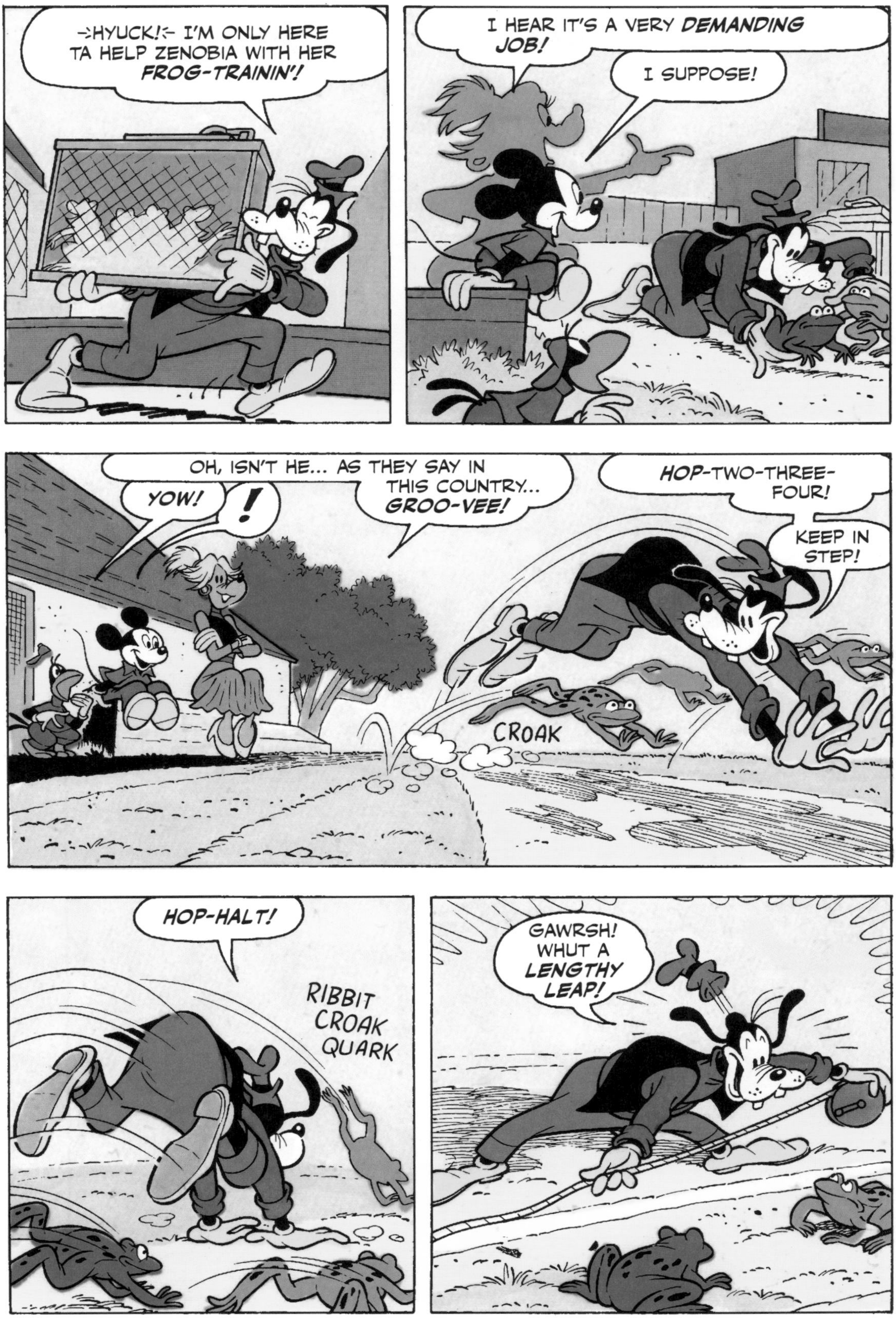

-HYUCK!- I'M ONLY HERE TA HELP ZENOBIA WITH HER FROG-TRAININ'!
I HEAR IT'S A VERY DEMANDING JOB!
I SUPPOSE!
OH, ISN'T HE... AS THEY SAY IN THIS COUNTRY... GROO-VEE!
YOW!
!
HOP-TWO-THREE-FOUR!
KEEP IN STEP!
CROAK
HOP-HALT!
RIBBIT
CROAK
QUARK
GAWRSH! WHUT A LENGTHY LEAP!

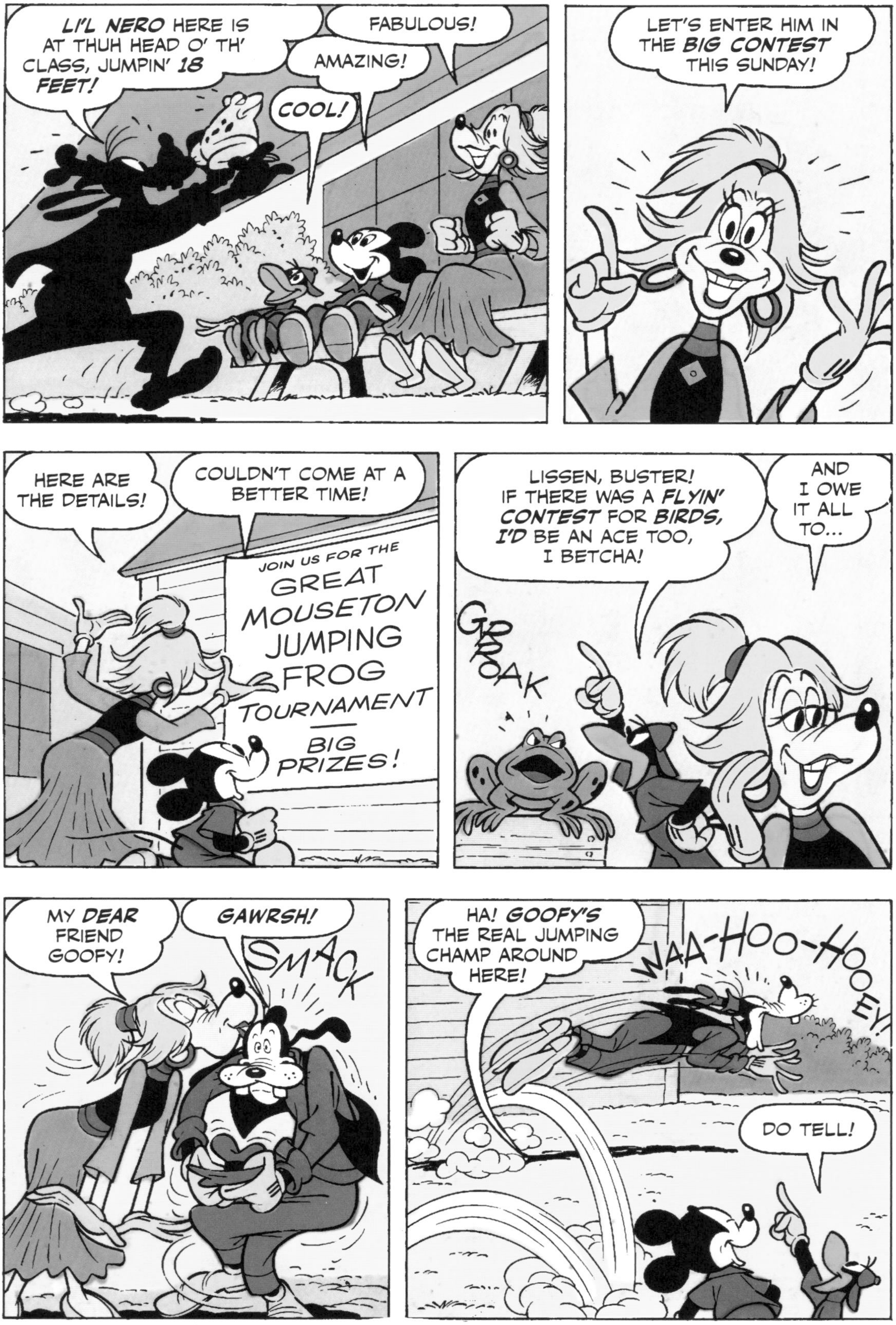
LI'L NERO HERE IS AT THUH HEAD O' TH' CLASS, JUMPIN' 18 FEET!
FABULOUS!
AMAZING!
COOL!
LET'S ENTER HIM IN THE BIG CONTEST THIS SUNDAY!
HERE ARE THE DETAILS!
COULDN'T COME AT A BETTER TIME!
JOIN US FOR THE GREAT MOUSETON JUMPING FROG TOURNAMENT — BIG PRIZES!
LISSEN, BUSTER! IF THERE WAS A FLYIN' CONTEST FOR BIRDS, I'D BE AN ACE TOO, I BETCHA!
AND I OWE IT ALL TO...
GRROAK
MY DEAR FRIEND GOOFY!
GAWRSH!
SMACK
HA! GOOFY'S THE REAL JUMPING CHAMP AROUND HERE!
WAA-HOO-HOOEY!
DO TELL!

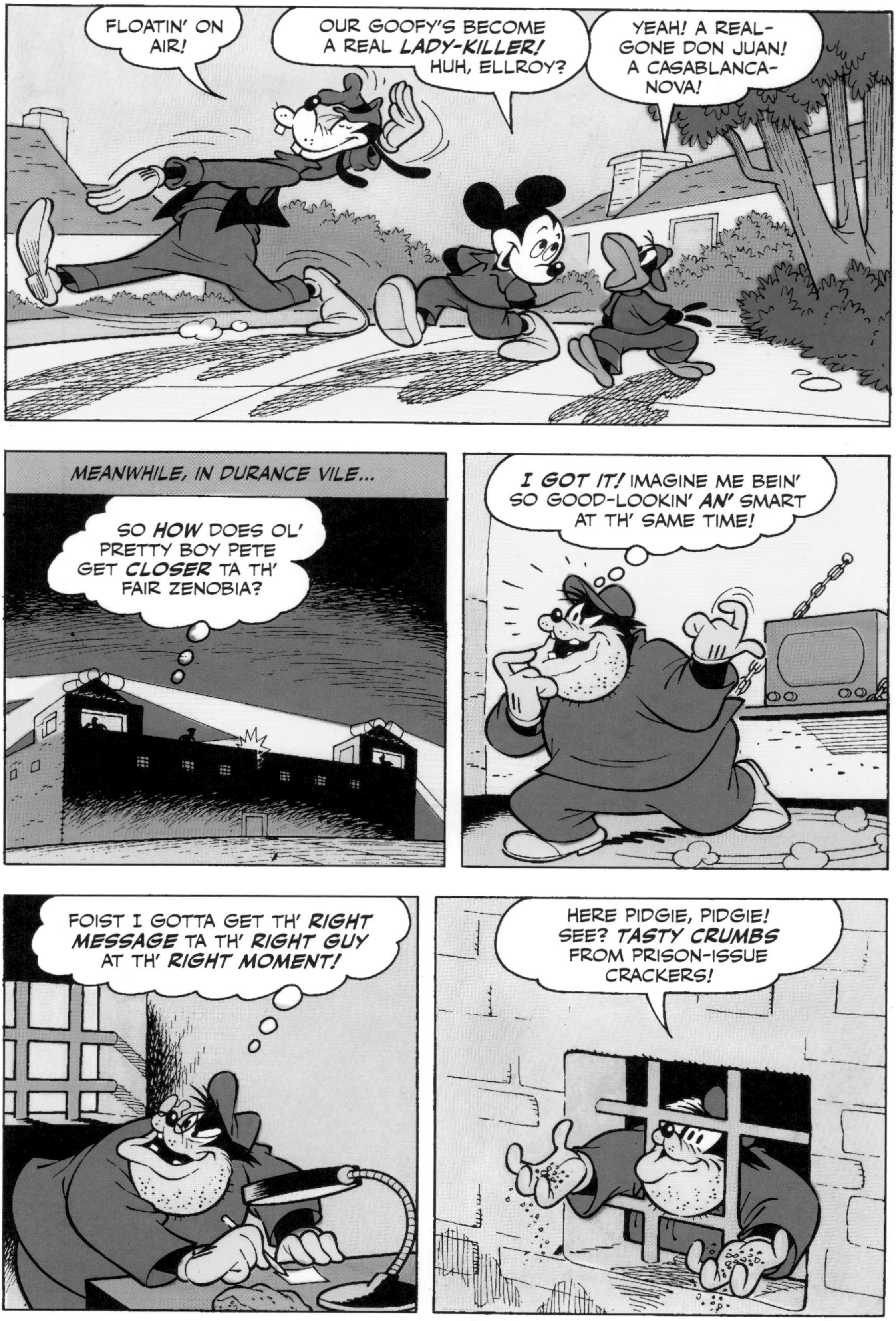
FLOATIN' ON AIR!
OUR GOOFY'S BECOME A REAL LADY-KILLER! HUH, ELLROY?
YEAH! A REAL-GONE DON JUAN! A CASABLANCA-NOVA!
MEANWHILE, IN DURANCE VILE...
SO HOW DOES OL' PRETTY BOY PETE GET CLOSER TA TH' FAIR ZENOBIA?
I GOT IT! IMAGINE ME BEIN' SO GOOD-LOOKIN' AN' SMART AT TH' SAME TIME!
FOIST I GOTTA GET TH' RIGHT MESSAGE TA TH' RIGHT GUY AT TH' RIGHT MOMENT!
HERE PIDGIE, PIDGIE! SEE? TASTY CRUMBS FROM PRISON-ISSUE CRACKERS!

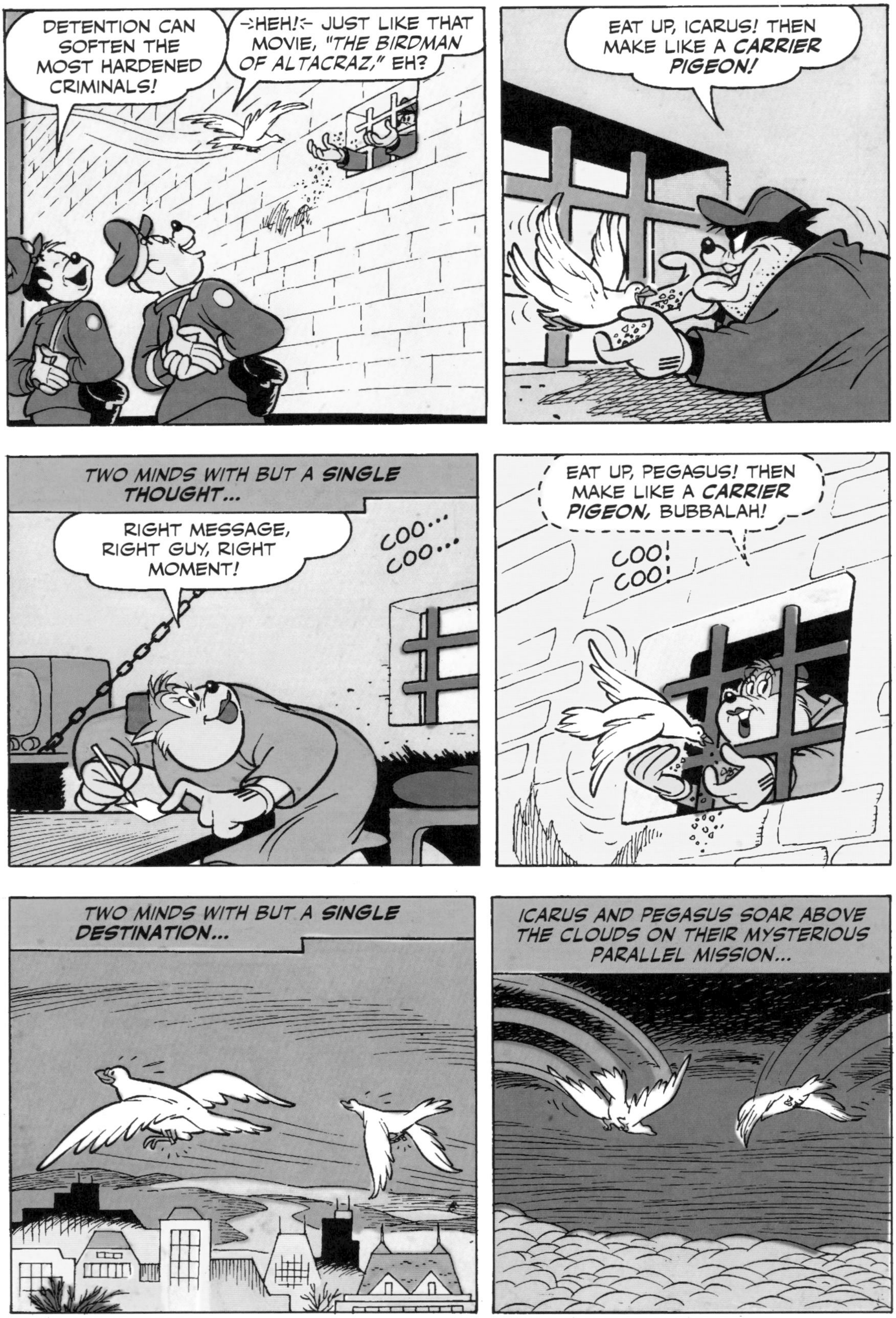
DETENTION CAN SOFTEN THE MOST HARDENED CRIMINALS!
–HEH!– JUST LIKE THAT MOVIE, "THE BIRDMAN OF ALTACRAZ," EH?
EAT UP, ICARUS! THEN MAKE LIKE A CARRIER PIGEON!
TWO MINDS WITH BUT A SINGLE THOUGHT...
RIGHT MESSAGE, RIGHT GUY, RIGHT MOMENT!
COO... COO...
EAT UP, PEGASUS! THEN MAKE LIKE A CARRIER PIGEON, BUBBALAH!
COO! COO!
TWO MINDS WITH BUT A SINGLE DESTINATION...
ICARUS AND PEGASUS SOAR ABOVE THE CLOUDS ON THEIR MYSTERIOUS PARALLEL MISSION...

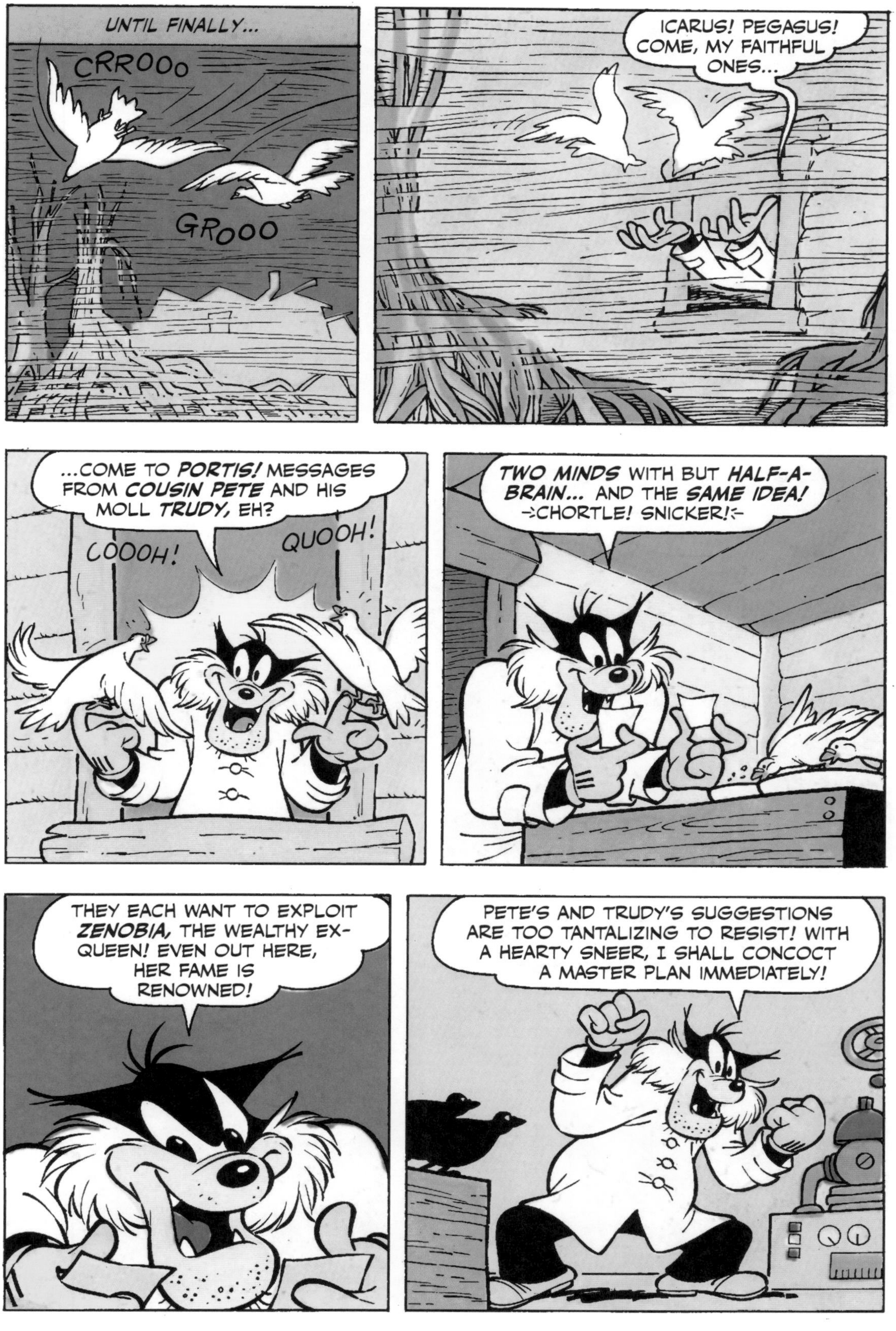
UNTIL FINALLY...
CRROOo
GROOO
ICARUS! PEGASUS! COME, MY FAITHFUL ONES...
...COME TO PORTIS! MESSAGES FROM COUSIN PETE AND HIS MOLL TRUDY, EH?
COOOH!
QUOOH!
TWO MINDS WITH BUT HALF-A-BRAIN... AND THE SAME IDEA! -CHORTLE! SNICKER!-
THEY EACH WANT TO EXPLOIT ZENOBIA, THE WEALTHY EX-QUEEN! EVEN OUT HERE, HER FAME IS RENOWNED!
PETE'S AND TRUDY'S SUGGESTIONS ARE TOO TANTALIZING TO RESIST! WITH A HEARTY SNEER, I SHALL CONCOCT A MASTER PLAN IMMEDIATELY!

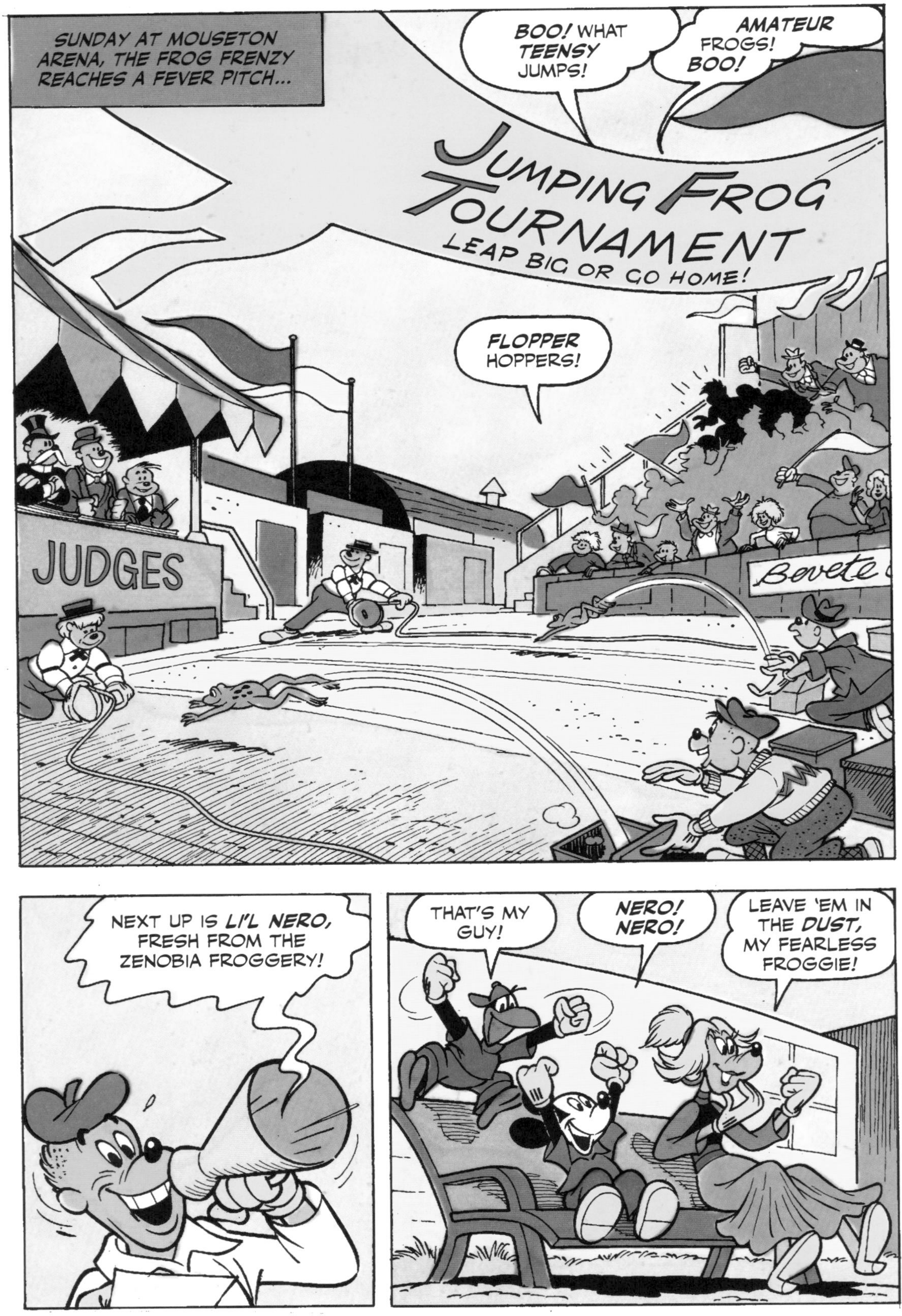

SUNDAY AT MOUSETON ARENA, THE FROG FRENZY REACHES A FEVER PITCH...
BOO! WHAT TEENSY JUMPS!
AMATEUR FROGS! BOO!
JUMPING FROG TOURNAMENT
LEAP BIG OR GO HOME!
FLOPPER HOPPERS!
JUDGES
Bevete
NEXT UP IS LI'L NERO, FRESH FROM THE ZENOBIA FROGGERY!
THAT'S MY GUY!
NERO! NERO!
LEAVE 'EM IN THE DUST, MY FEARLESS FROGGIE!

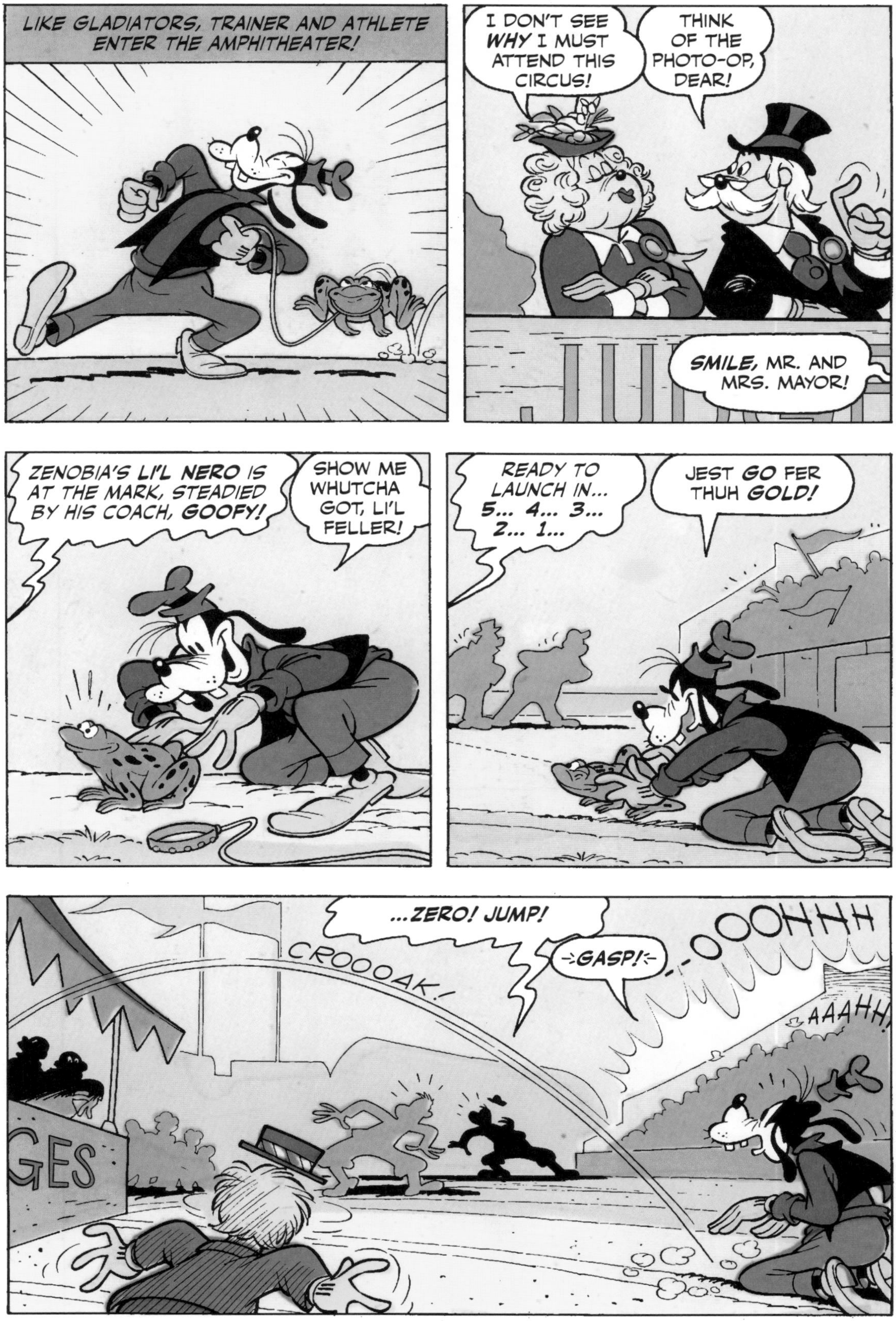
LIKE GLADIATORS, TRAINER AND ATHLETE ENTER THE AMPHITHEATER!
I DON'T SEE WHY I MUST ATTEND THIS CIRCUS!
THINK OF THE PHOTO-OP, DEAR!
SMILE, MR. AND MRS. MAYOR!
ZENOBIA'S LI'L NERO IS AT THE MARK, STEADIED BY HIS COACH, GOOFY!
SHOW ME WHUTCHA GOT, LI'L FELLER!
READY TO LAUNCH IN... 5... 4... 3... 2... 1...
JEST GO FER THUH GOLD!
...ZERO! JUMP!
CROOOOAK!
GASP!
OOOHHHH
AAAHH!
GES

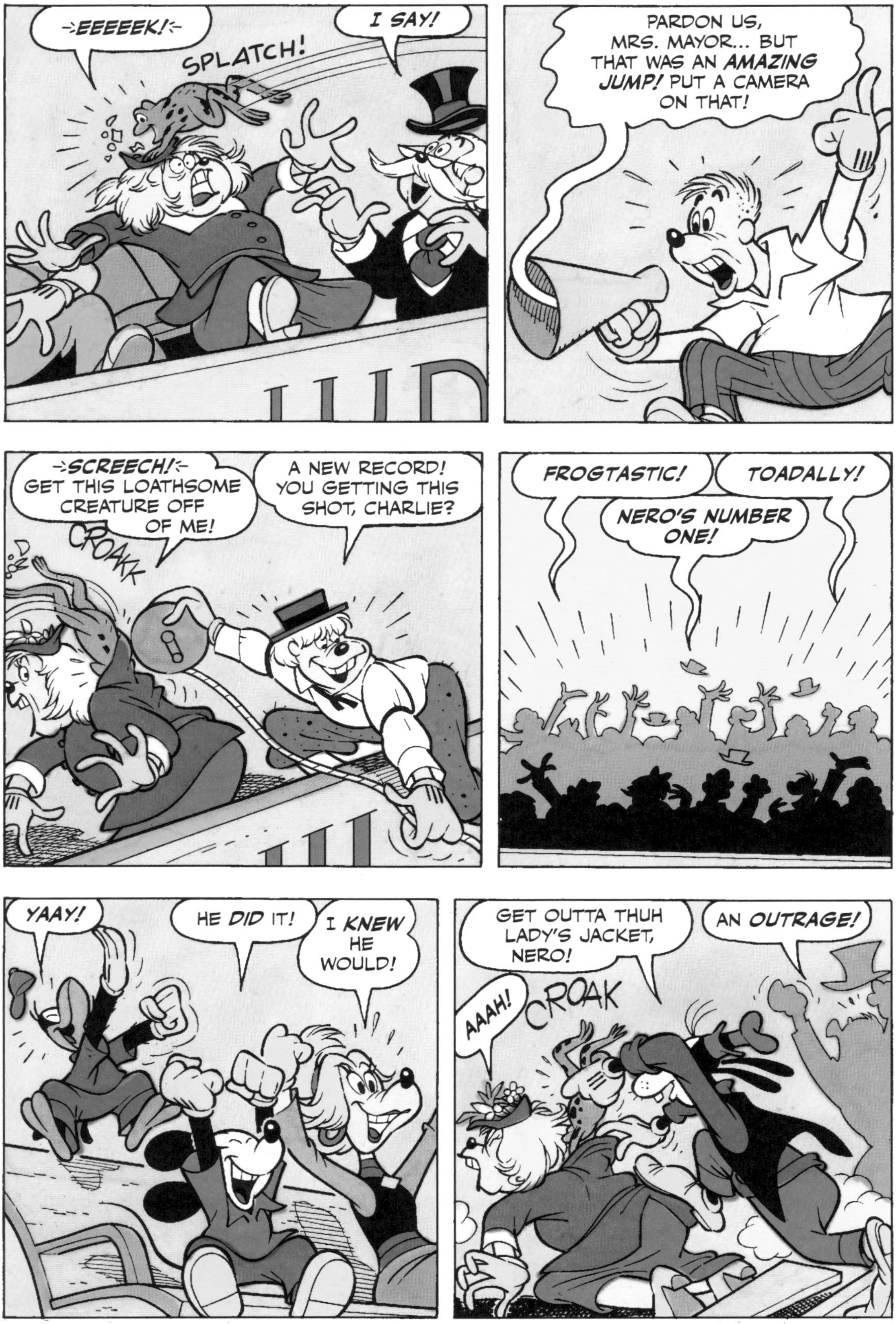
-EEEEEK!-
I SAY!
SPLATCH!
PARDON US, MRS. MAYOR... BUT THAT WAS AN AMAZING JUMP! PUT A CAMERA ON THAT!
-SCREECH!- GET THIS LOATHSOME CREATURE OFF OF ME!
A NEW RECORD! YOU GETTING THIS SHOT, CHARLIE?
CROAKK
FROGTASTIC!
TOADALLY!
NERO'S NUMBER ONE!
YAAY!
HE DID IT!
I KNEW HE WOULD!
GET OUTTA THUH LADY'S JACKET, NERO!
AN OUTRAGE!
AAAH!
CROAK

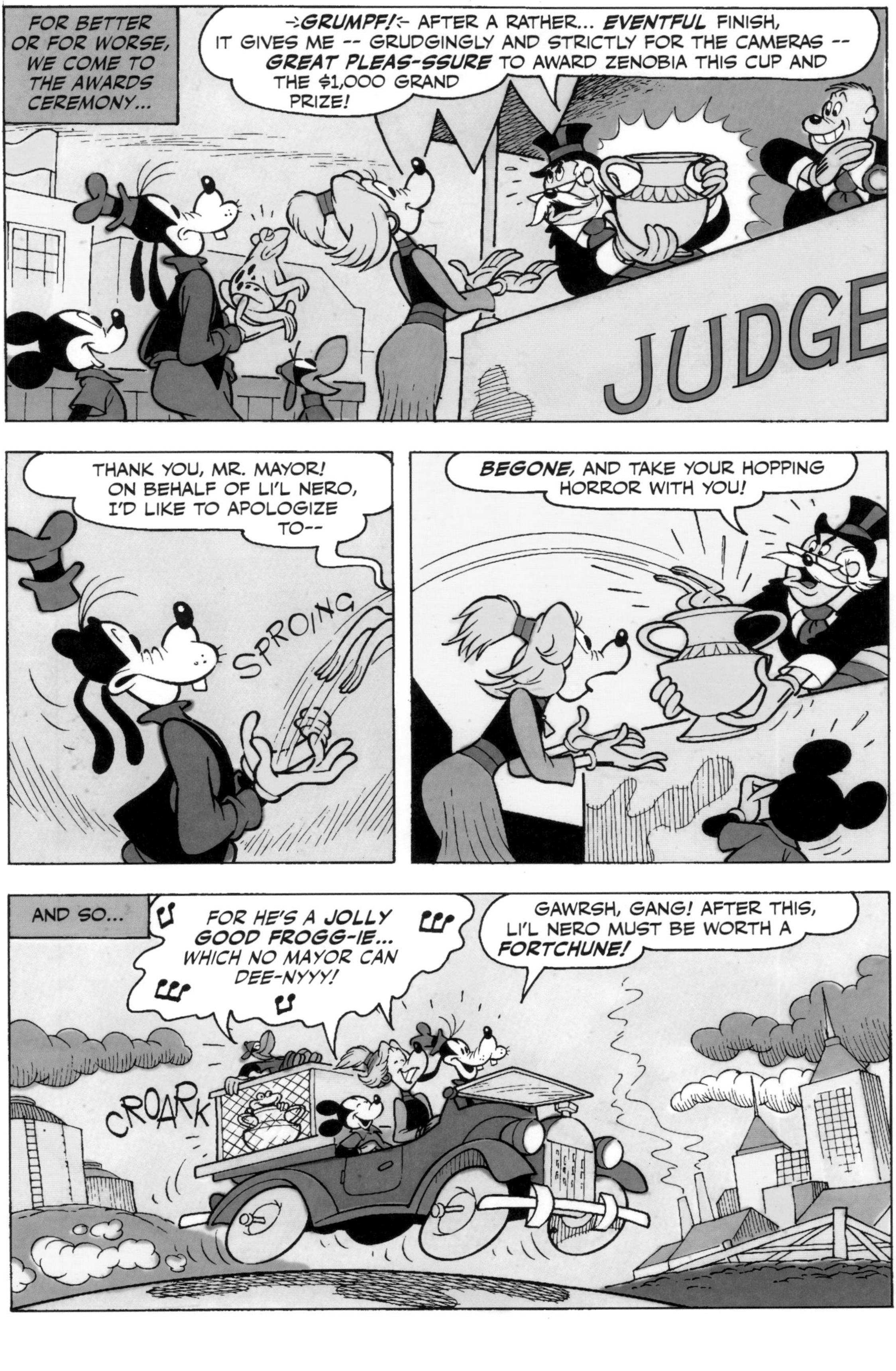
FOR BETTER OR FOR WORSE, WE COME TO THE AWARDS CEREMONY...
-GRUMPF!- AFTER A RATHER... EVENTFUL FINISH, IT GIVES ME -- GRUDGINGLY AND STRICTLY FOR THE CAMERAS -- GREAT PLEAS-SSURE TO AWARD ZENOBIA THIS CUP AND THE $1,000 GRAND PRIZE!
JUDGE
THANK YOU, MR. MAYOR! ON BEHALF OF LI'L NERO, I'D LIKE TO APOLOGIZE TO--
SPROING
BEGONE, AND TAKE YOUR HOPPING HORROR WITH YOU!
AND SO...
FOR HE'S A JOLLY GOOD FROGG-IE... WHICH NO MAYOR CAN DEE-NYYY!
GAWRSH, GANG! AFTER THIS, LI'L NERO MUST BE WORTH A FORTCHUNE!
CROARK

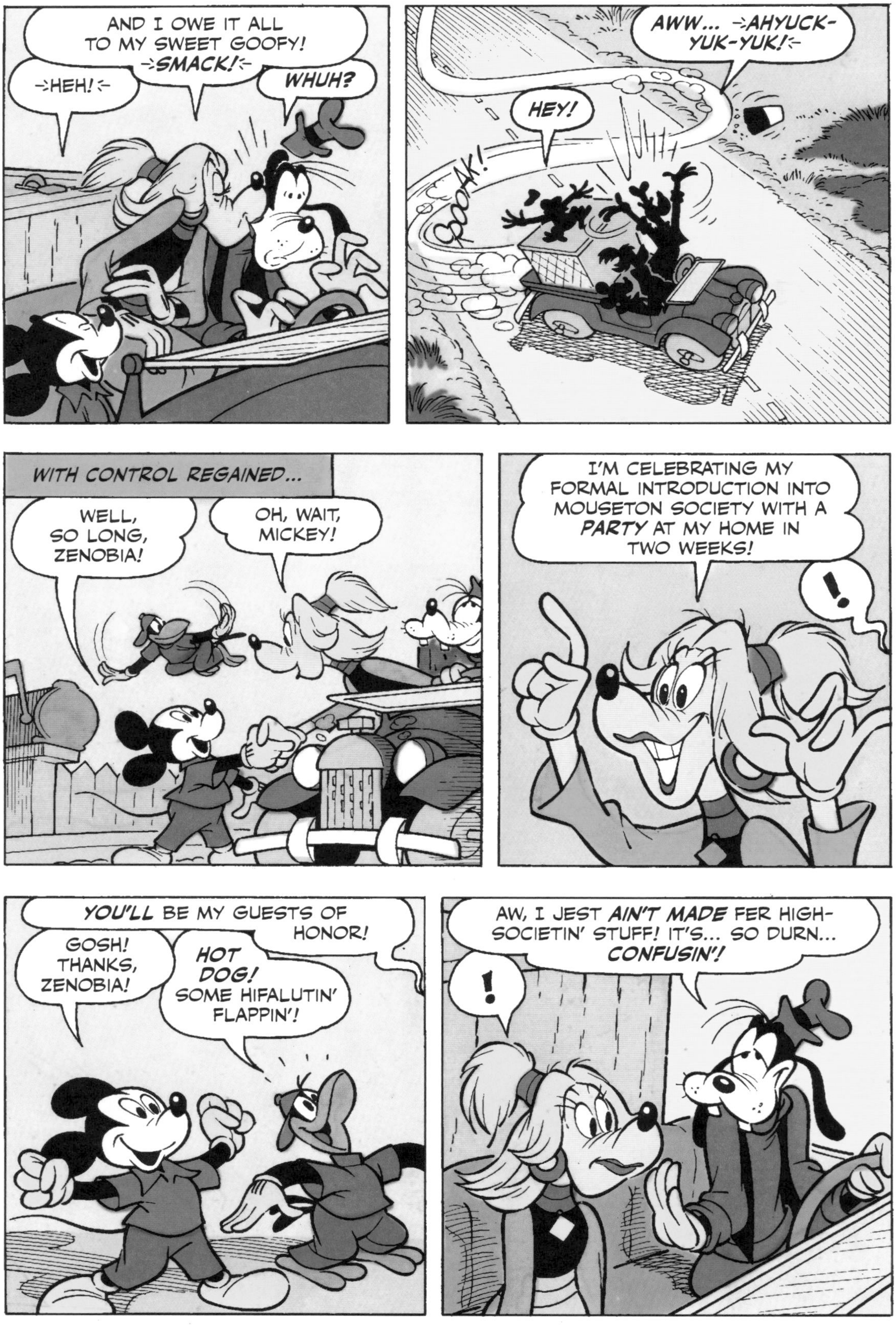
AND I OWE IT ALL TO MY SWEET GOOFY! SMACK!
HEH!
WHUH?
AWW... AHYUCK-YUK-YUK!
HEY!
BOOOAK!
WITH CONTROL REGAINED...
WELL, SO LONG, ZENOBIA!
OH, WAIT, MICKEY!
I'M CELEBRATING MY FORMAL INTRODUCTION INTO MOUSETON SOCIETY WITH A PARTY AT MY HOME IN TWO WEEKS!
!
YOU'LL BE MY GUESTS OF HONOR!
GOSH! THANKS, ZENOBIA!
HOT DOG! SOME HIFALUTIN' FLAPPIN'!
AW, I JEST AIN'T MADE FER HIGH-SOCIETIN' STUFF! IT'S... SO DURN... CONFUSIN'!
!

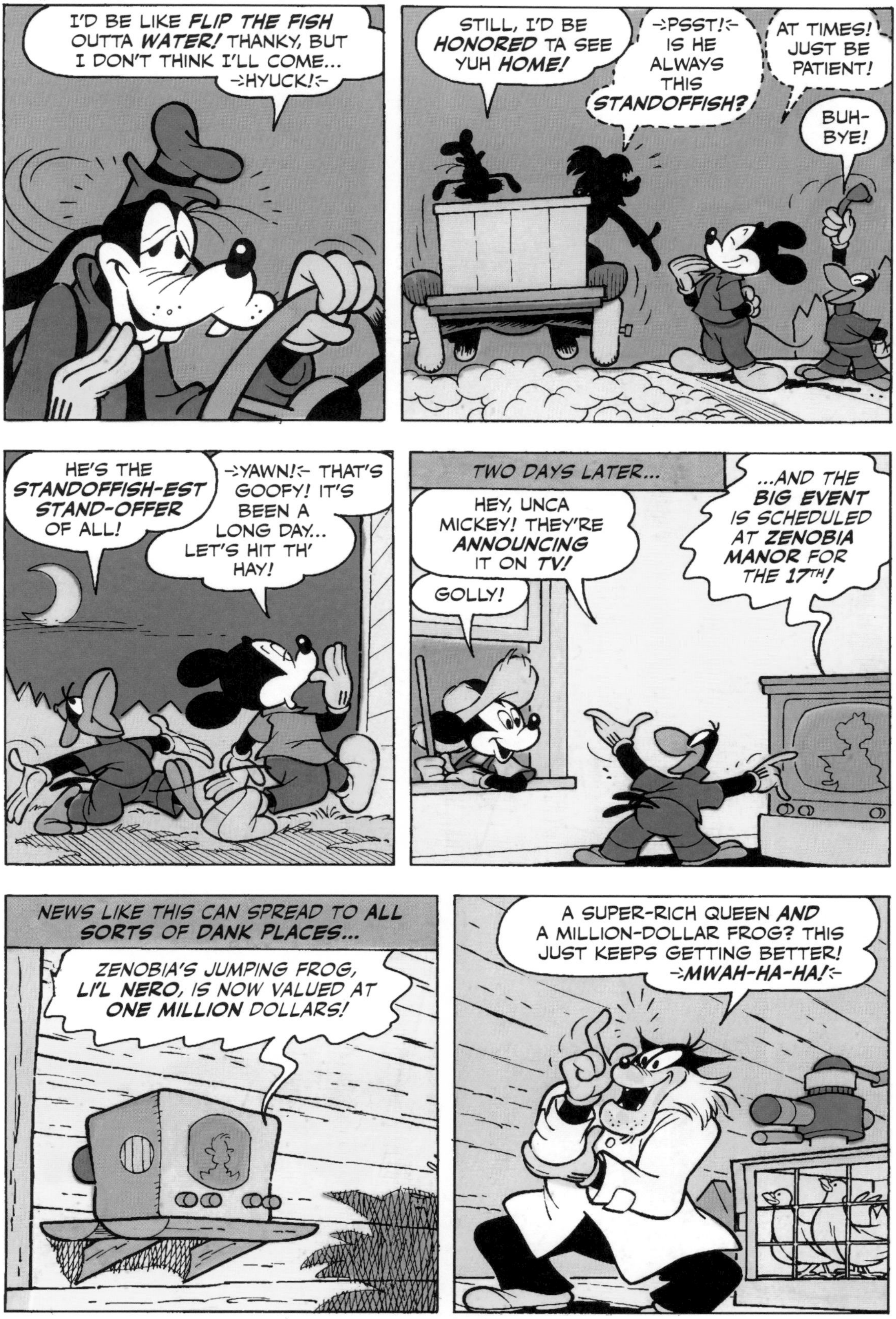
I'D BE LIKE FLIP THE FISH OUTTA WATER! THANKY, BUT I DON'T THINK I'LL COME... ~HYUCK!~
STILL, I'D BE HONORED TA SEE YUH HOME!
~PSST!~ IS HE ALWAYS THIS STANDOFFISH?
AT TIMES! JUST BE PATIENT!
BUH-BYE!
HE'S THE STANDOFFISH-EST STAND-OFFER OF ALL!
~YAWN!~ THAT'S GOOFY! IT'S BEEN A LONG DAY... LET'S HIT TH' HAY!
TWO DAYS LATER...
HEY, UNCA MICKEY! THEY'RE ANNOUNCING IT ON TV!
...AND THE BIG EVENT IS SCHEDULED AT ZENOBIA MANOR FOR THE 17TH!
GOLLY!
NEWS LIKE THIS CAN SPREAD TO ALL SORTS OF DANK PLACES...
ZENOBIA'S JUMPING FROG, LI'L NERO, IS NOW VALUED AT ONE MILLION DOLLARS!
A SUPER-RICH QUEEN AND A MILLION-DOLLAR FROG? THIS JUST KEEPS GETTING BETTER! ~MWAH-HA-HA!~

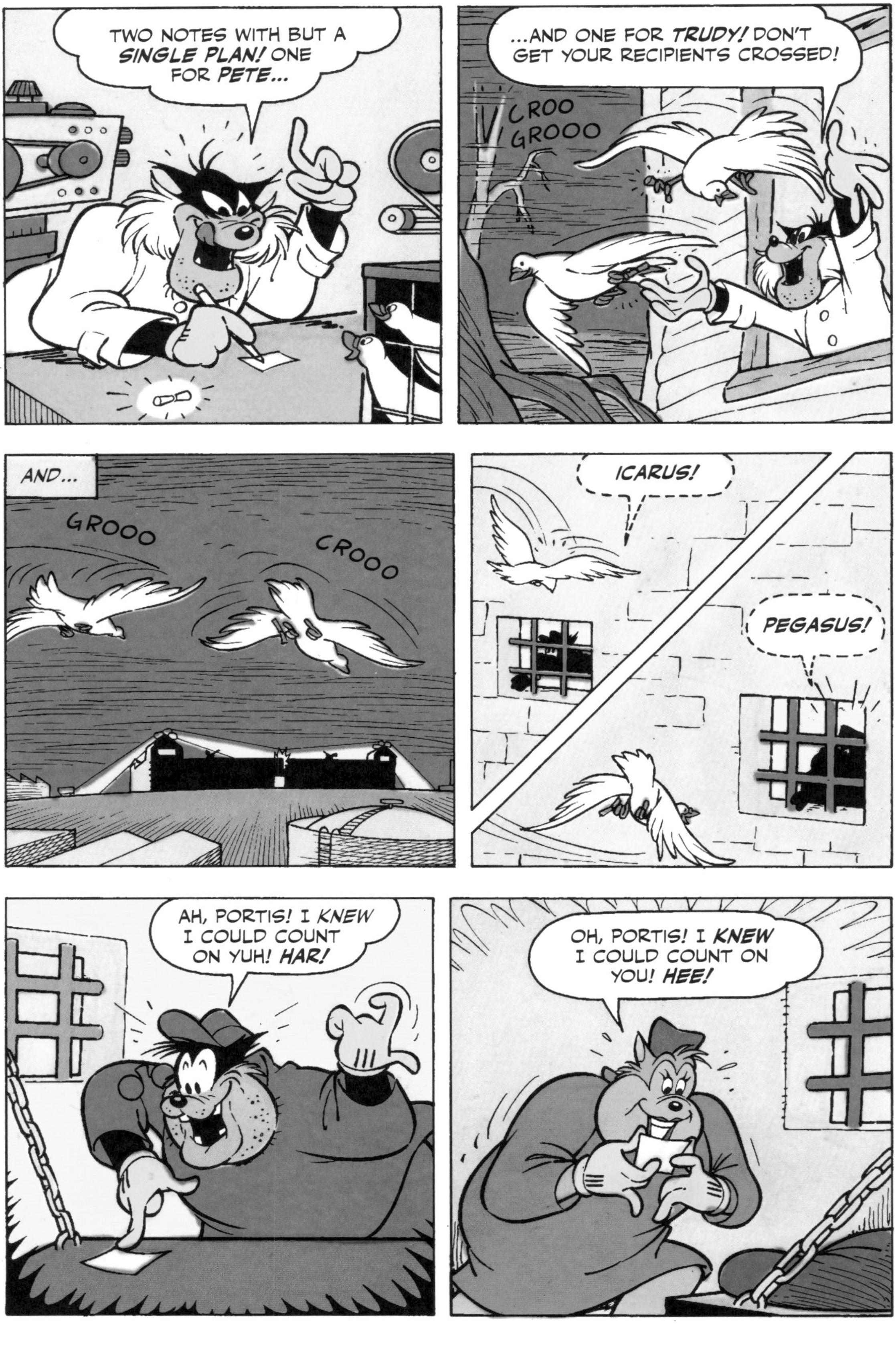
TWO NOTES WITH BUT A SINGLE PLAN! ONE FOR PETE...
...AND ONE FOR TRUDY! DON'T GET YOUR RECIPIENTS CROSSED!
CROO GROOO
AND...
GROOO
CROOO
ICARUS!
PEGASUS!
AH, PORTIS! I KNEW I COULD COUNT ON YUH! HAR!
OH, PORTIS! I KNEW I COULD COUNT ON YOU! HEE!

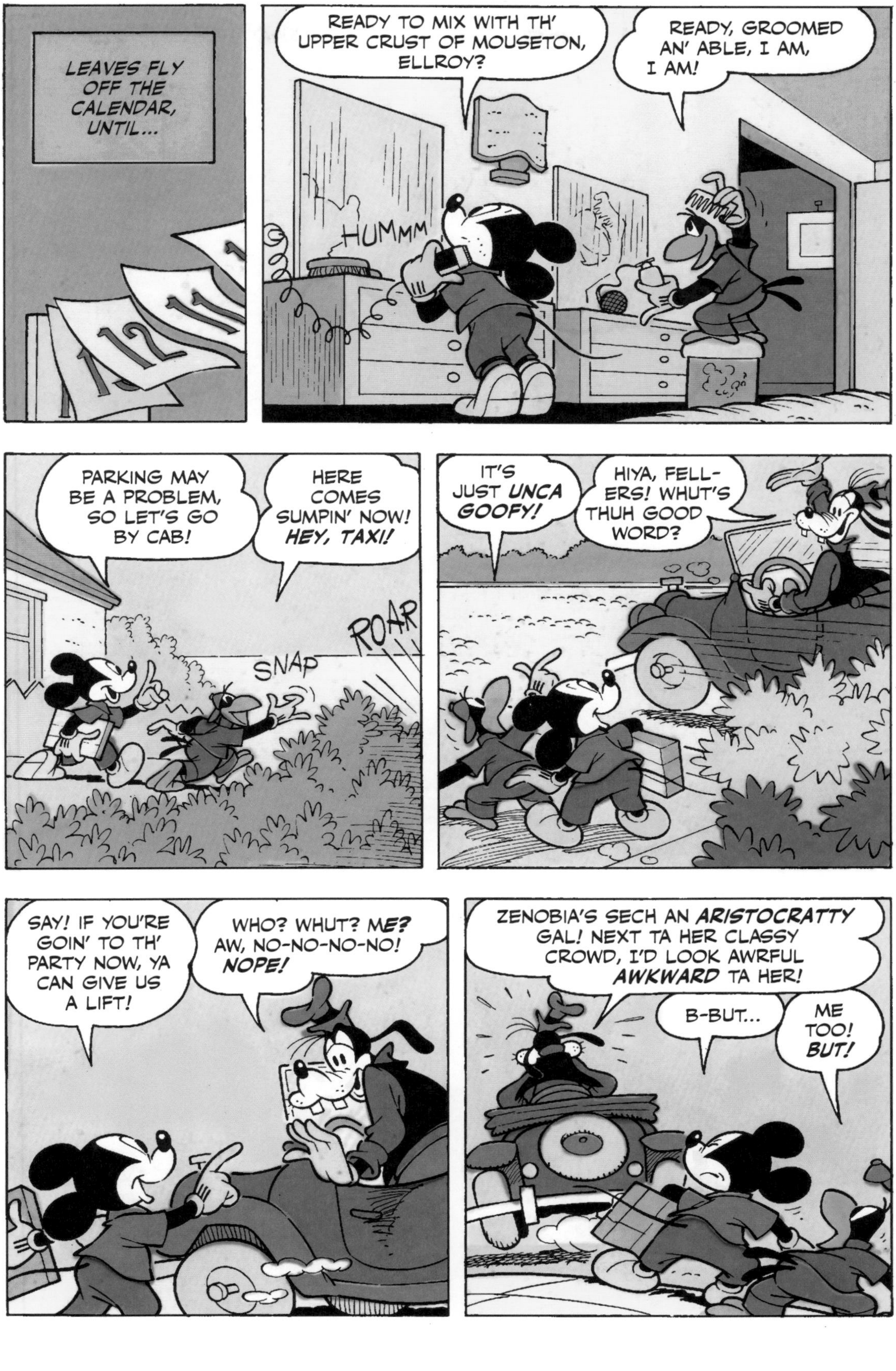
LEAVES FLY OFF THE CALENDAR, UNTIL...
READY TO MIX WITH TH' UPPER CRUST OF MOUSETON, ELLROY?
READY, GROOMED AN' ABLE, I AM, I AM!
HUMMM
PARKING MAY BE A PROBLEM, SO LET'S GO BY CAB!
HERE COMES SUMPIN' NOW! HEY, TAXI!
SNAP
ROAR
IT'S JUST UNCA GOOFY!
HIYA, FELL-ERS! WHUT'S THUH GOOD WORD?
SAY! IF YOU'RE GOIN' TO TH' PARTY NOW, YA CAN GIVE US A LIFT!
WHO? WHUT? ME? AW, NO-NO-NO-NO! NOPE!
ZENOBIA'S SECH AN ARISTOCRATTY GAL! NEXT TA HER CLASSY CROWD, I'D LOOK AWRFUL AWKWARD TA HER!
B-BUT...
ME TOO! BUT!

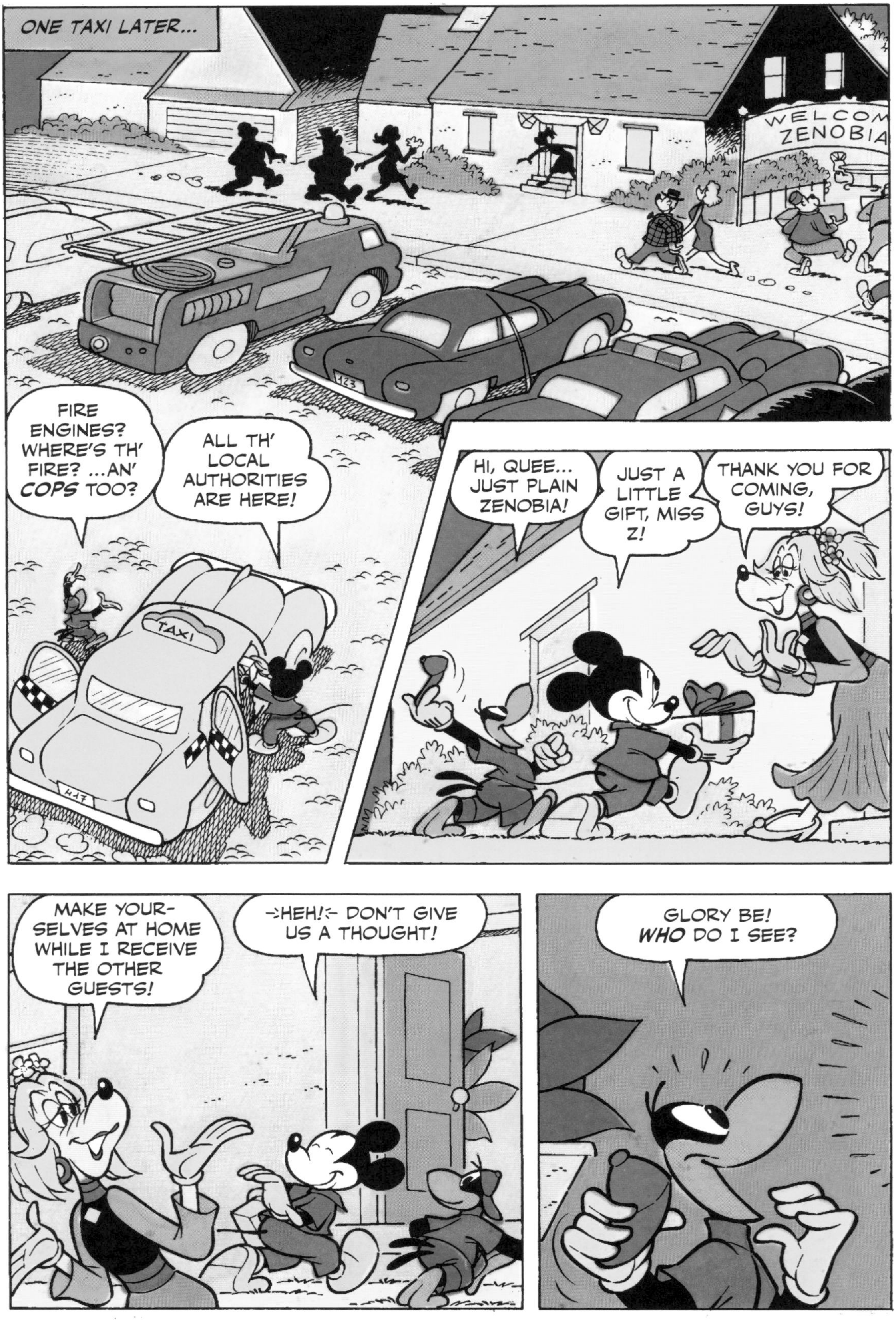
ONE TAXI LATER...
WELCOM
ZENOBIA
FIRE ENGINES? WHERE'S TH' FIRE? ...AN' COPS TOO?
ALL TH' LOCAL AUTHORITIES ARE HERE!
TAXI
HI, QUEE... JUST PLAIN ZENOBIA!
JUST A LITTLE GIFT, MISS Z!
THANK YOU FOR COMING, GUYS!
MAKE YOURSELVES AT HOME WHILE I RECEIVE THE OTHER GUESTS!
-HEH!- DON'T GIVE US A THOUGHT!
GLORY BE! WHO DO I SEE?

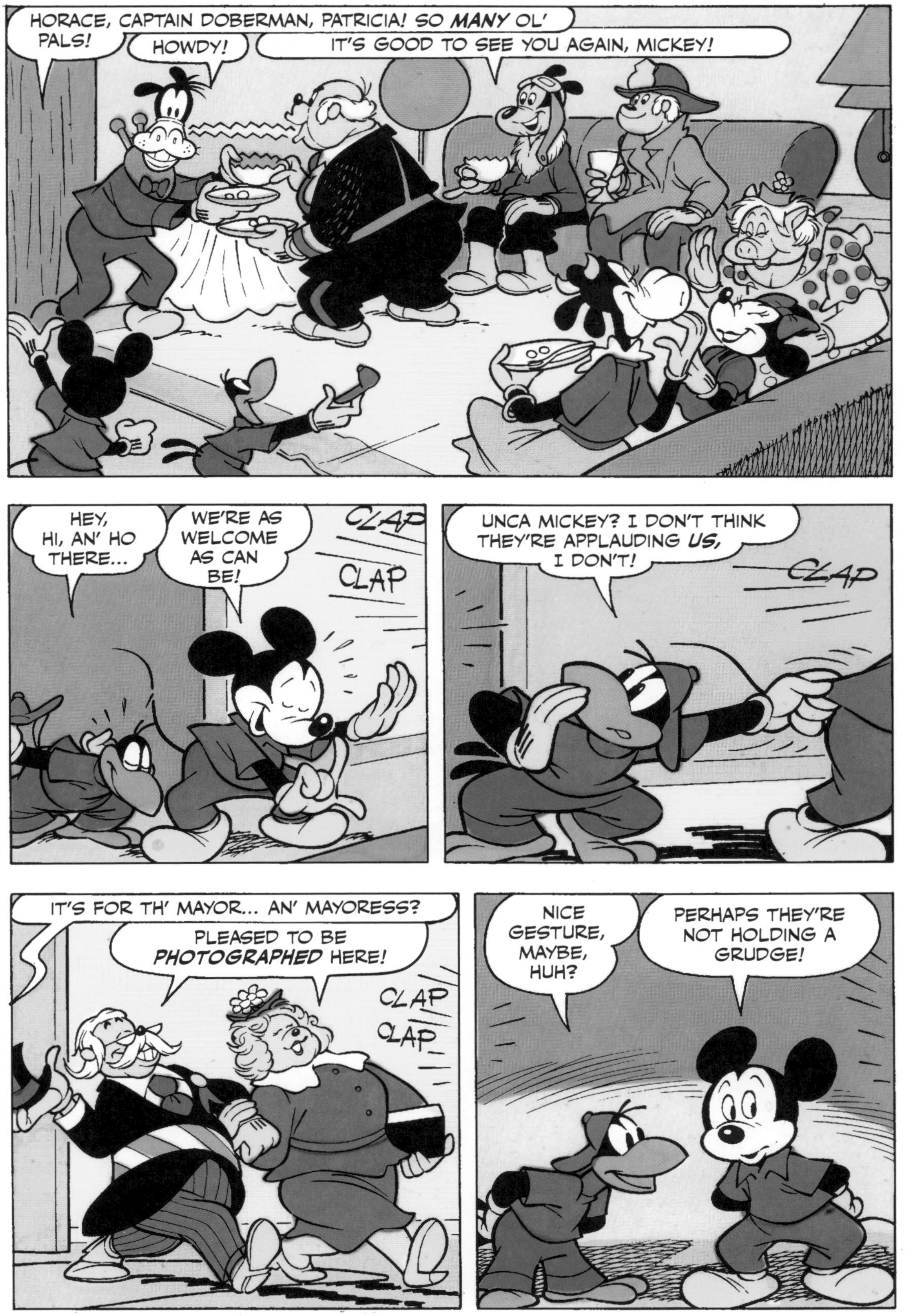
HORACE, CAPTAIN DOBERMAN, PATRICIA! SO MANY OL' PALS!
HOWDY!
IT'S GOOD TO SEE YOU AGAIN, MICKEY!
HEY, HI, AN' HO THERE...
WE'RE AS WELCOME AS CAN BE!
CLAP
CLAP
UNCA MICKEY? I DON'T THINK THEY'RE APPLAUDING US, I DON'T!
CLAP
IT'S FOR TH' MAYOR... AN' MAYORESS?
PLEASED TO BE PHOTOGRAPHED HERE!
CLAP
CLAP
NICE GESTURE, MAYBE, HUH?
PERHAPS THEY'RE NOT HOLDING A GRUDGE!

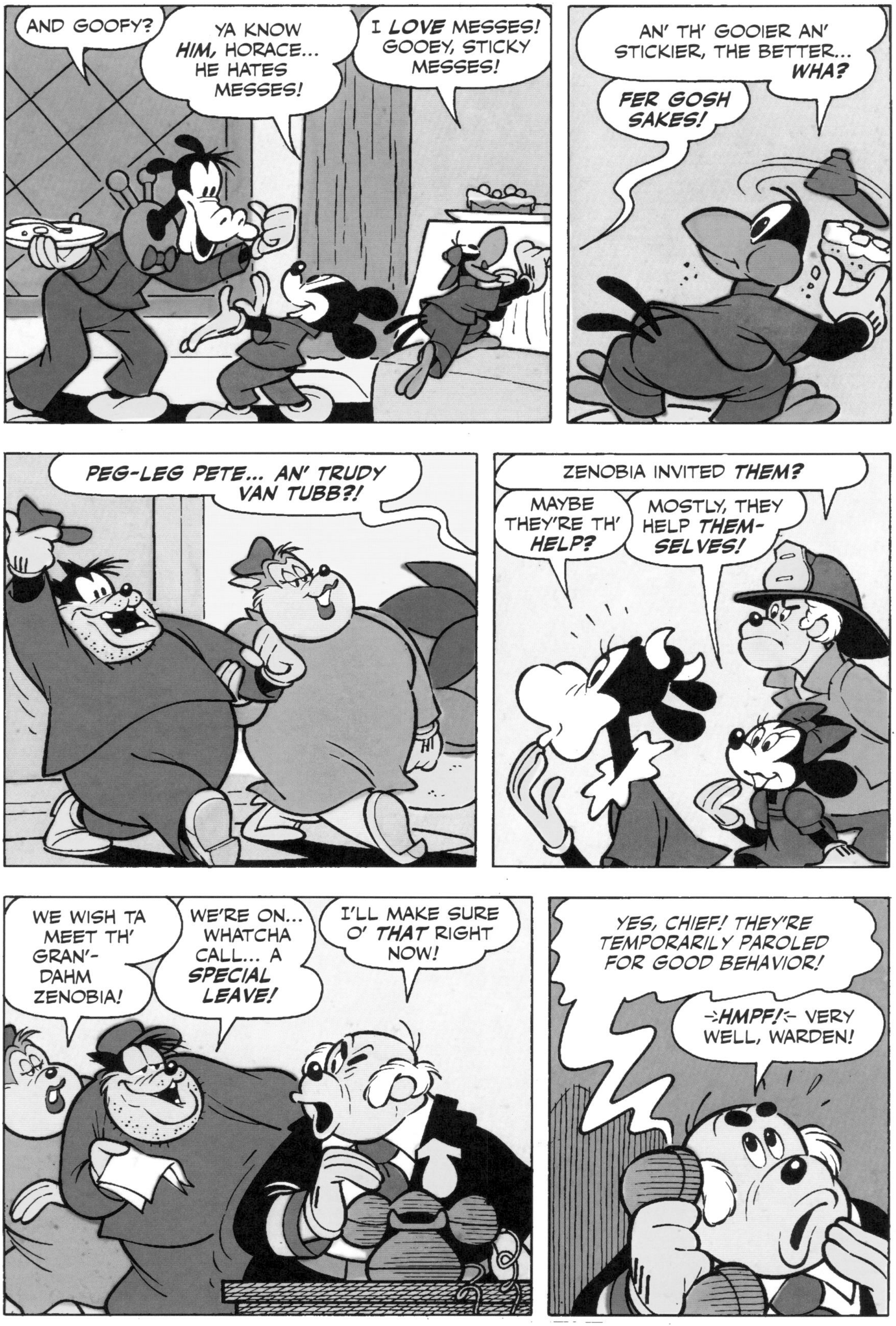
AND GOOFY?
YA KNOW HIM, HORACE... HE HATES MESSES!
I LOVE MESSES! GOOEY, STICKY MESSES!
AN' TH' GOOIER AN' STICKIER, THE BETTER... WHA?
FER GOSH SAKES!
PEG-LEG PETE... AN' TRUDY VAN TUBB?!
ZENOBIA INVITED THEM?
MAYBE THEY'RE TH' HELP?
MOSTLY, THEY HELP THEM-SELVES!
WE WISH TA MEET TH' GRAN'-DAHM ZENOBIA!
WE'RE ON... WHATCHA CALL... A SPECIAL LEAVE!
I'LL MAKE SURE O' THAT RIGHT NOW!
YES, CHIEF! THEY'RE TEMPORARILY PAROLED FOR GOOD BEHAVIOR!
HMPF! VERY WELL, WARDEN!

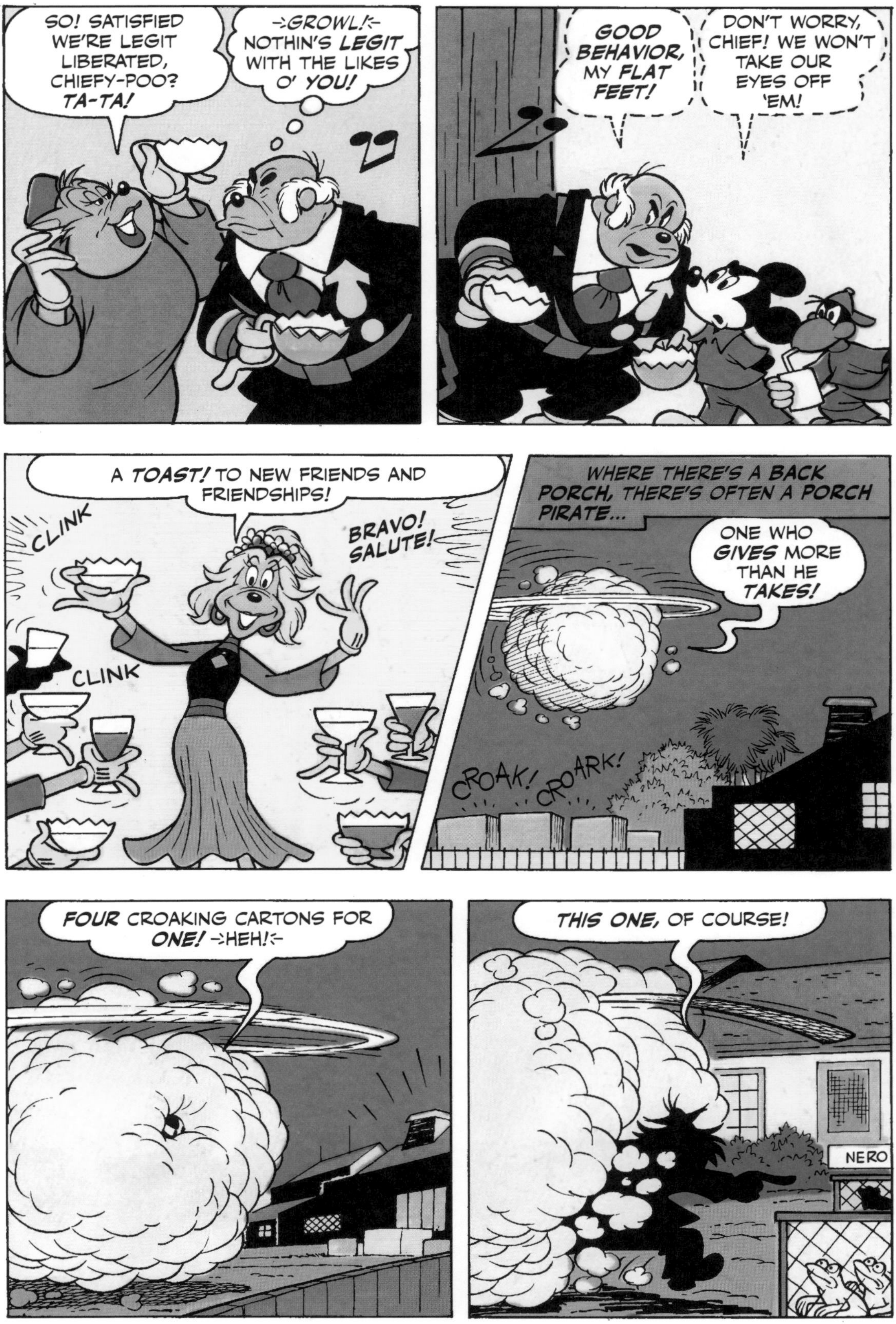
SO! SATISFIED WE'RE LEGIT LIBERATED, CHIEFY-POO? TA-TA!
-GROWL!- NOTHIN'S LEGIT WITH THE LIKES O' YOU!
GOOD BEHAVIOR, MY FLAT FEET!
DON'T WORRY, CHIEF! WE WON'T TAKE OUR EYES OFF 'EM!
A TOAST! TO NEW FRIENDS AND FRIENDSHIPS!
CLINK
BRAVO! SALUTE!
CLINK
WHERE THERE'S A BACK PORCH, THERE'S OFTEN A PORCH PIRATE...
ONE WHO GIVES MORE THAN HE TAKES!
CROAK! CROARK!
FOUR CROAKING CARTONS FOR ONE! -HEH!-
THIS ONE, OF COURSE!
NERO

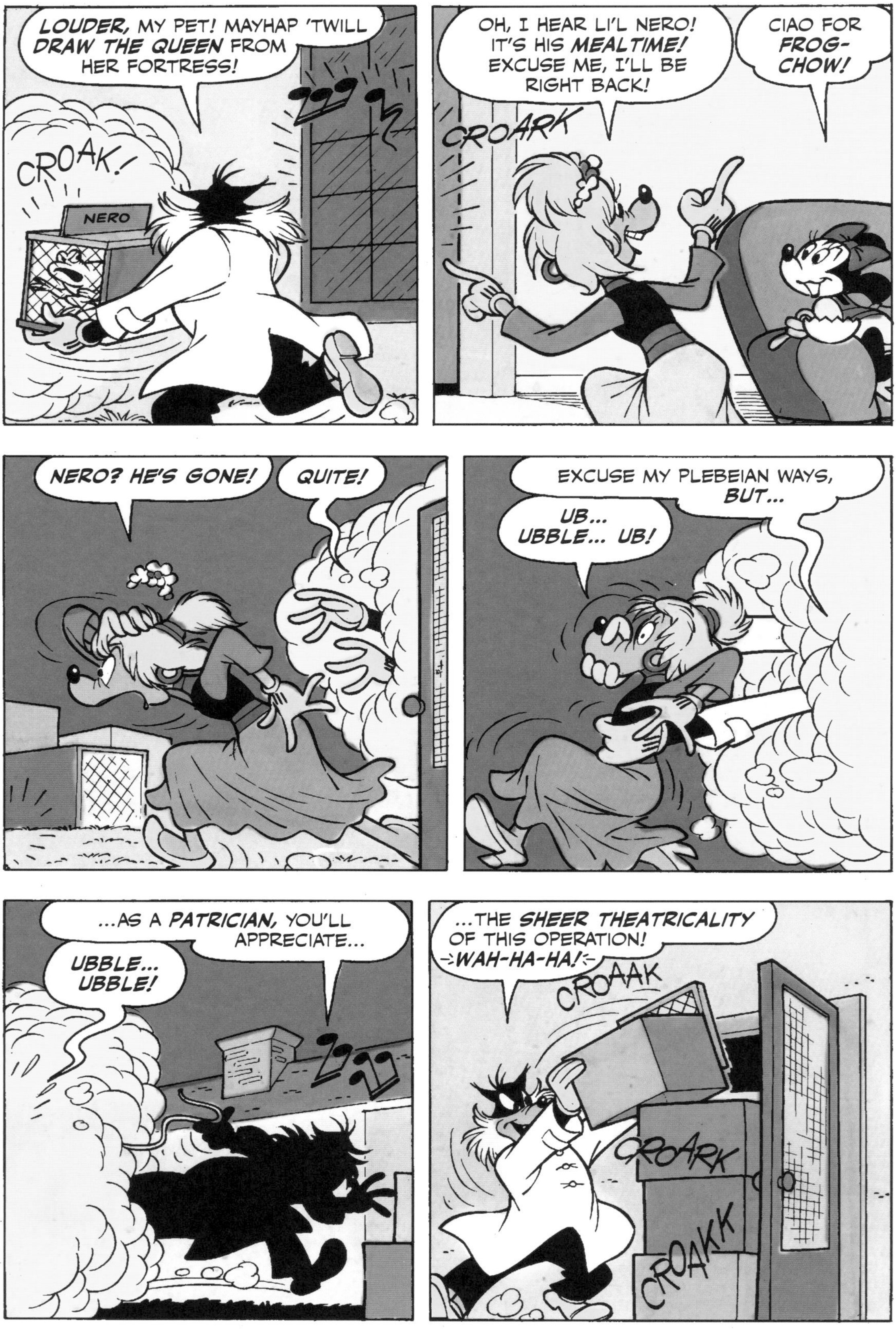
LOUDER, MY PET! MAYHAP 'TWILL DRAW THE QUEEN FROM HER FORTRESS!
CROAK!
NERO
OH, I HEAR LI'L NERO! IT'S HIS MEALTIME! EXCUSE ME, I'LL BE RIGHT BACK!
CIAO FOR FROG-CHOW!
CROARK
NERO? HE'S GONE!
QUITE!
EXCUSE MY PLEBEIAN WAYS, BUT...
UB... UBBLE... UB!
...AS A PATRICIAN, YOU'LL APPRECIATE...
UBBLE... UBBLE!
...THE SHEER THEATRICALITY OF THIS OPERATION!
WAH-HA-HA!
CROAAK
CROARK
CROAKK

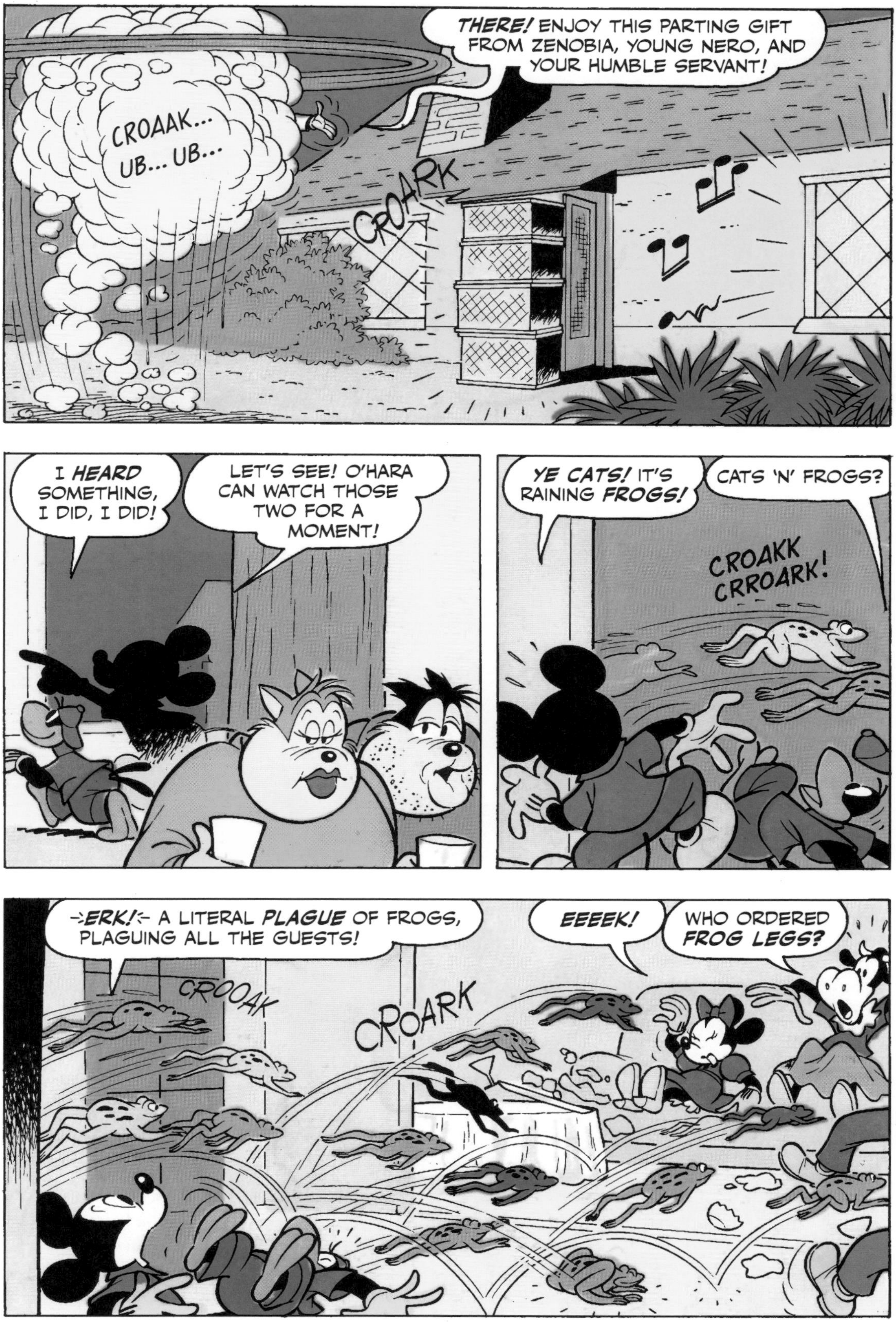
THERE! ENJOY THIS PARTING GIFT FROM ZENOBIA, YOUNG NERO, AND YOUR HUMBLE SERVANT!
CROAAK... UB... UB...
CROARK
I HEARD SOMETHING, I DID, I DID!
LET'S SEE! O'HARA CAN WATCH THOSE TWO FOR A MOMENT!
YE CATS! IT'S RAINING FROGS!
CATS 'N' FROGS?
CROAKK CRROARK!
-ERK!- A LITERAL PLAGUE OF FROGS, PLAGUING ALL THE GUESTS!
EEEEK!
WHO ORDERED FROG LEGS?
CROOAK
CROARK

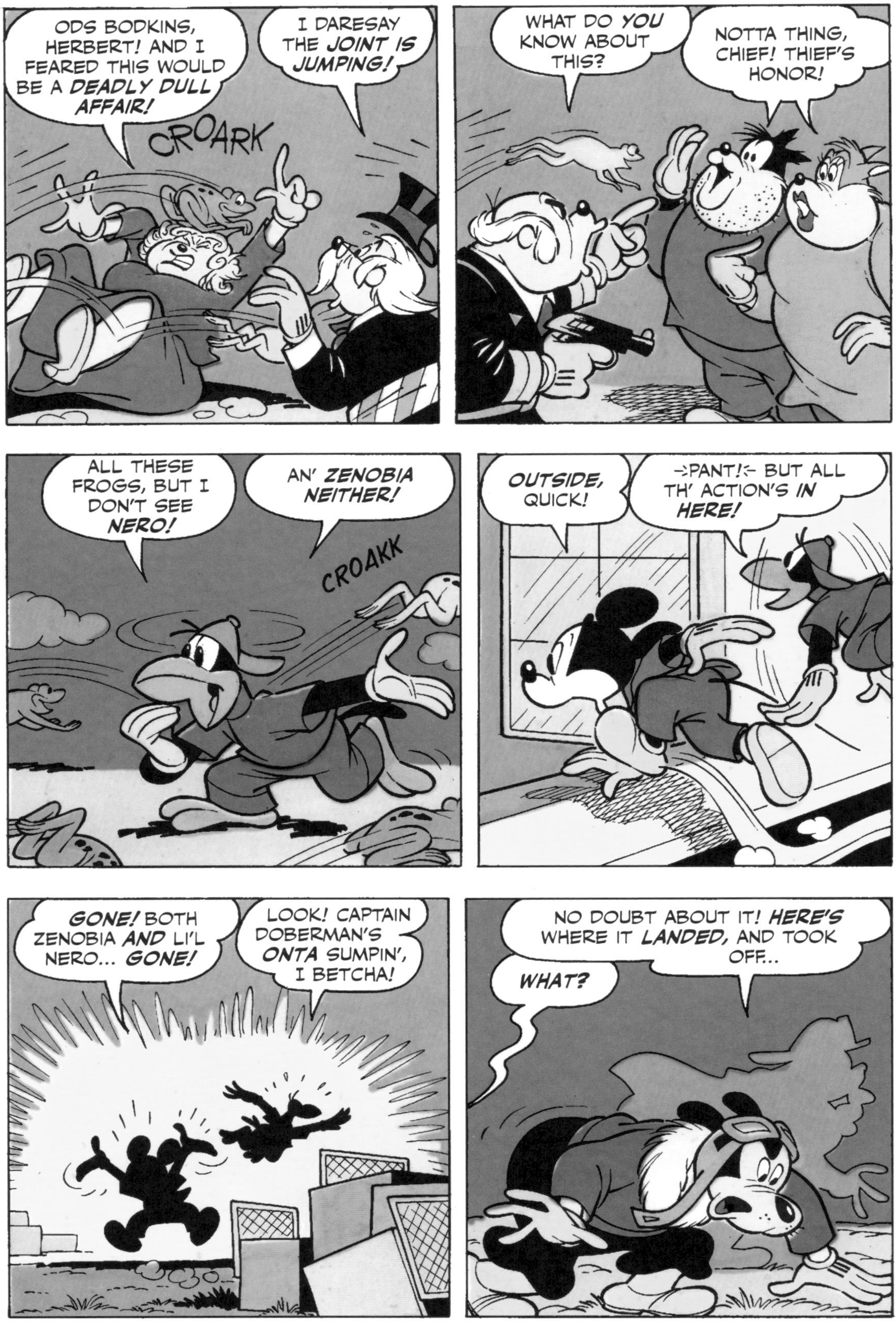
ODS BODKINS, HERBERT! AND I FEARED THIS WOULD BE A DEADLY DULL AFFAIR!
I DARESAY THE JOINT IS JUMPING!
CROARK
WHAT DO YOU KNOW ABOUT THIS?
NOTTA THING, CHIEF! THIEF'S HONOR!
ALL THESE FROGS, BUT I DON'T SEE NERO!
AN' ZENOBIA NEITHER!
CROAKK
OUTSIDE, QUICK!
-PANT!- BUT ALL TH' ACTION'S IN HERE!
GONE! BOTH ZENOBIA AND LI'L NERO... GONE!
LOOK! CAPTAIN DOBERMAN'S ONTA SUMPIN', I BETCHA!
NO DOUBT ABOUT IT! HERE'S WHERE IT LANDED, AND TOOK OFF...
WHAT?

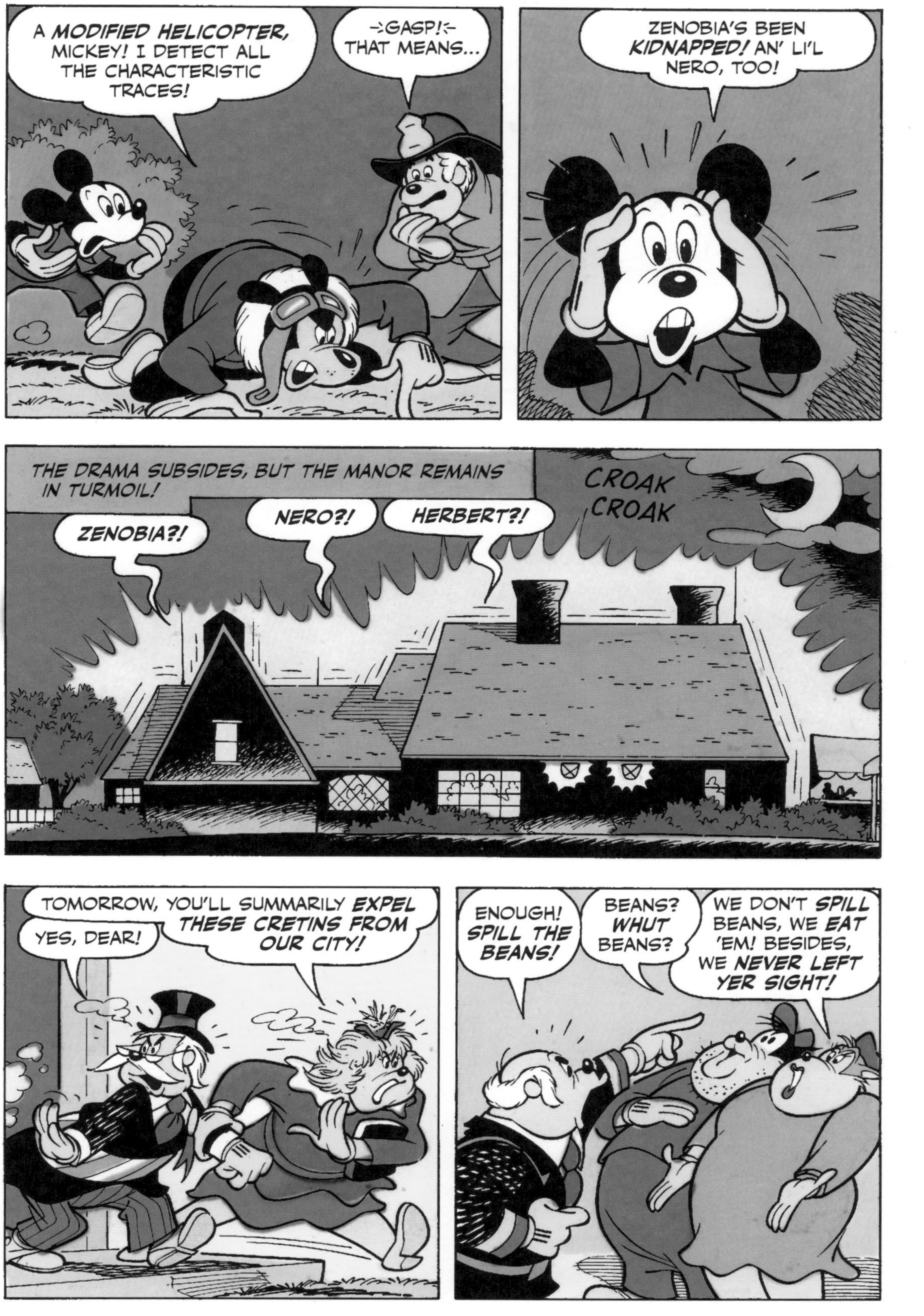
A MODIFIED HELICOPTER, MICKEY! I DETECT ALL THE CHARACTERISTIC TRACES!
-GASP!- THAT MEANS...
ZENOBIA'S BEEN KIDNAPPED! AN' LI'L NERO, TOO!
THE DRAMA SUBSIDES, BUT THE MANOR REMAINS IN TURMOIL!
ZENOBIA?!
NERO?!
HERBERT?!
CROAK CROAK
TOMORROW, YOU'LL SUMMARILY EXPEL THESE CRETINS FROM OUR CITY!
YES, DEAR!
ENOUGH! SPILL THE BEANS!
BEANS? WHUT BEANS?
WE DON'T SPILL BEANS, WE EAT 'EM! BESIDES, WE NEVER LEFT YER SIGHT!

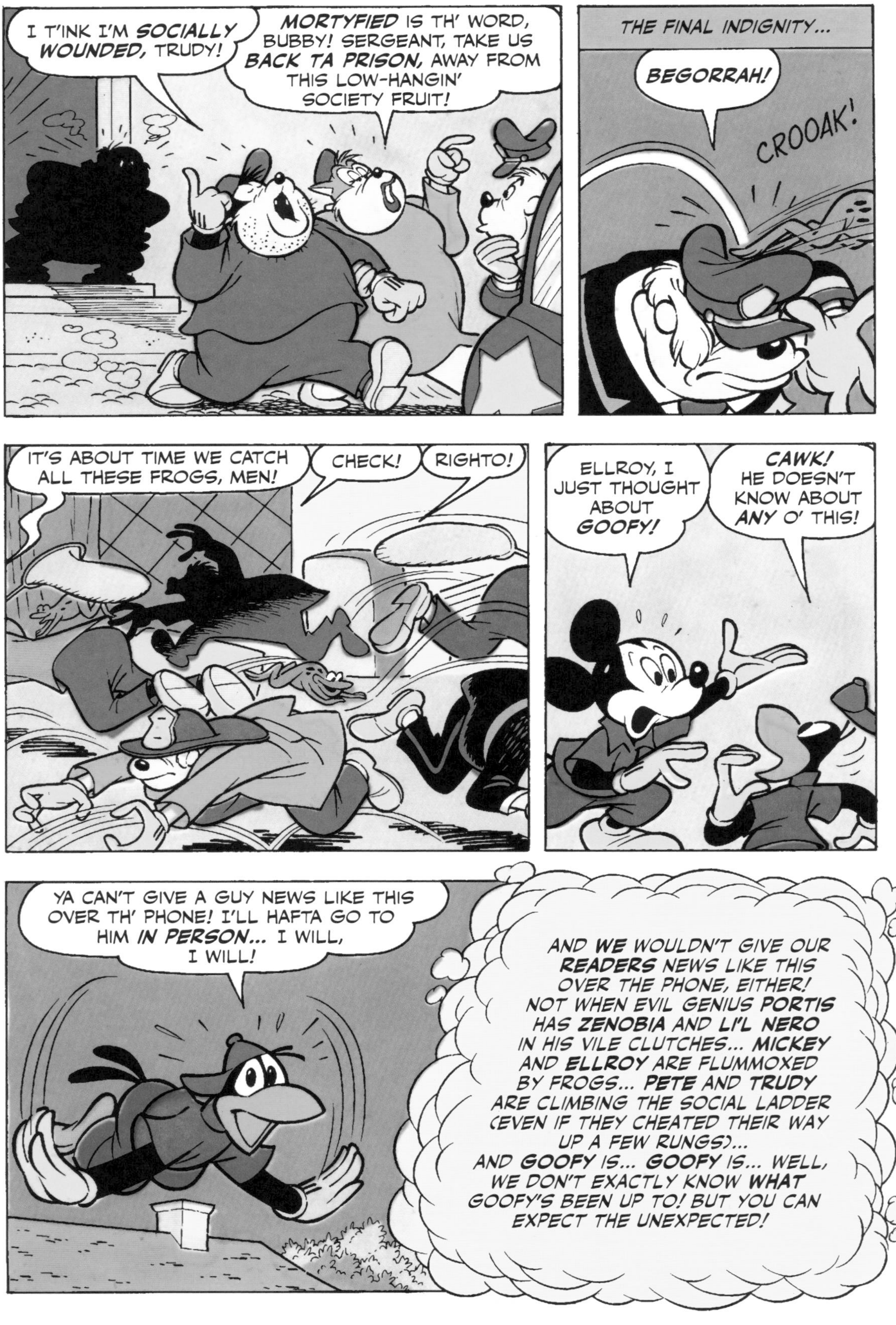

I T'INK I'M SOCIALLY WOUNDED, TRUDY!
MORTYFIED IS TH' WORD, BUBBY! SERGEANT, TAKE US BACK TA PRISON, AWAY FROM THIS LOW-HANGIN' SOCIETY FRUIT!
THE FINAL INDIGNITY...
BEGORRAH!
CROOAK!
IT'S ABOUT TIME WE CATCH ALL THESE FROGS, MEN!
CHECK!
RIGHTO!
ELLROY, I JUST THOUGHT ABOUT GOOFY!
CAWK! HE DOESN'T KNOW ABOUT ANY O' THIS!
YA CAN'T GIVE A GUY NEWS LIKE THIS OVER TH' PHONE! I'LL HAFTA GO TO HIM IN PERSON... I WILL, I WILL!
AND WE WOULDN'T GIVE OUR READERS NEWS LIKE THIS OVER THE PHONE, EITHER! NOT WHEN EVIL GENIUS PORTIS HAS ZENOBIA AND LI'L NERO IN HIS VILE CLUTCHES... MICKEY AND ELLROY ARE FLUMMOXED BY FROGS... PETE AND TRUDY ARE CLIMBING THE SOCIAL LADDER (EVEN IF THEY CHEATED THEIR WAY UP A FEW RUNGS)... AND GOOFY IS... GOOFY IS... WELL, WE DON'T EXACTLY KNOW WHAT GOOFY'S BEEN UP TO! BUT YOU CAN EXPECT THE UNEXPECTED!

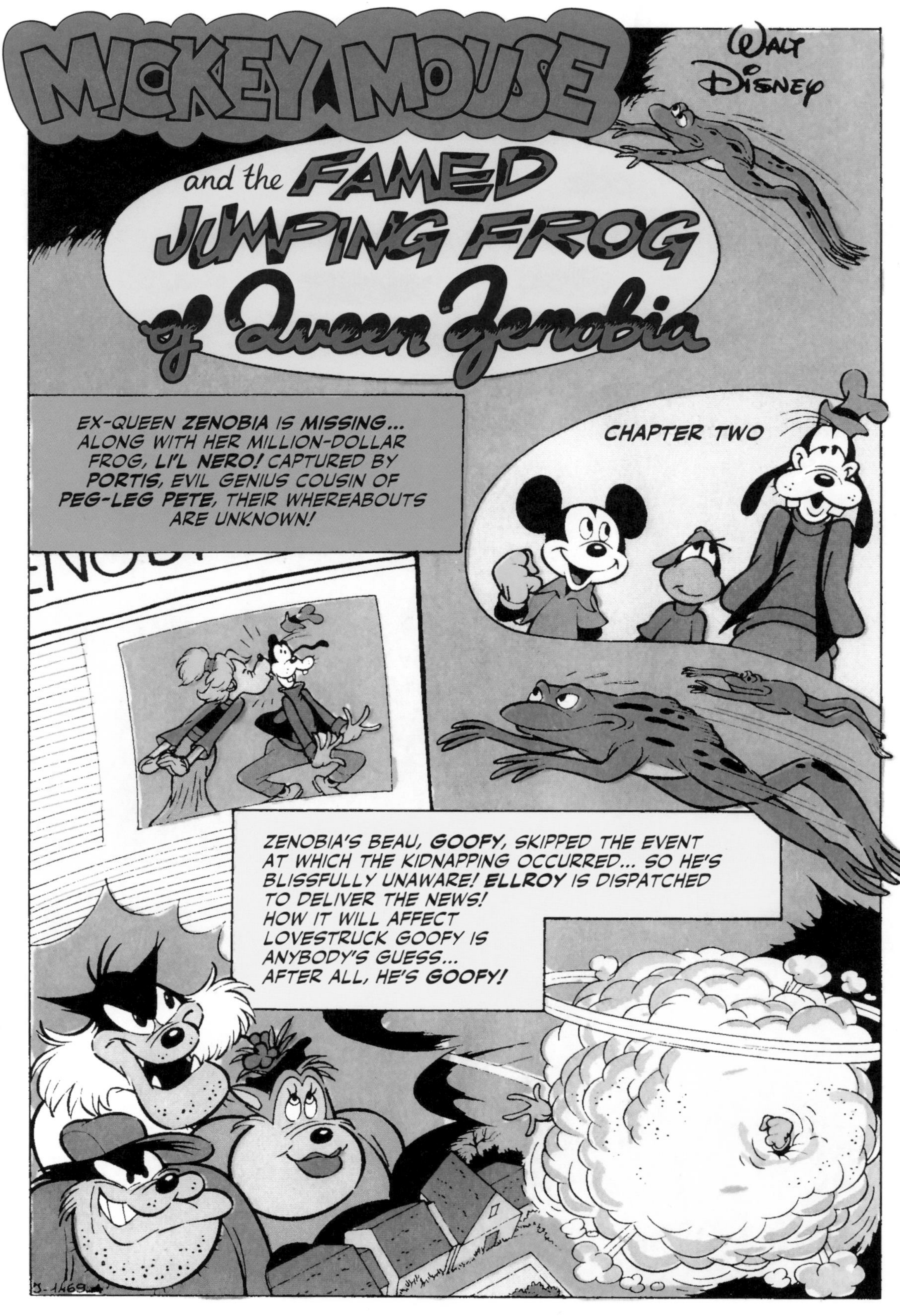
MICKEY MOUSE
WALT DISNEY
and the FAMED JUMPING FROG of Queen Zenobia
EX-QUEEN ZENOBIA IS MISSING... ALONG WITH HER MILLION-DOLLAR FROG, LI'L NERO! CAPTURED BY PORTIS, EVIL GENIUS COUSIN OF PEG-LEG PETE, THEIR WHEREABOUTS ARE UNKNOWN!
CHAPTER TWO
ZENOBIA'S BEAU, GOOFY, SKIPPED THE EVENT AT WHICH THE KIDNAPPING OCCURRED... SO HE'S BLISSFULLY UNAWARE! ELLROY IS DISPATCHED TO DELIVER THE NEWS! HOW IT WILL AFFECT LOVESTRUCK GOOFY IS ANYBODY'S GUESS... AFTER ALL, HE'S GOOFY!
J-1469

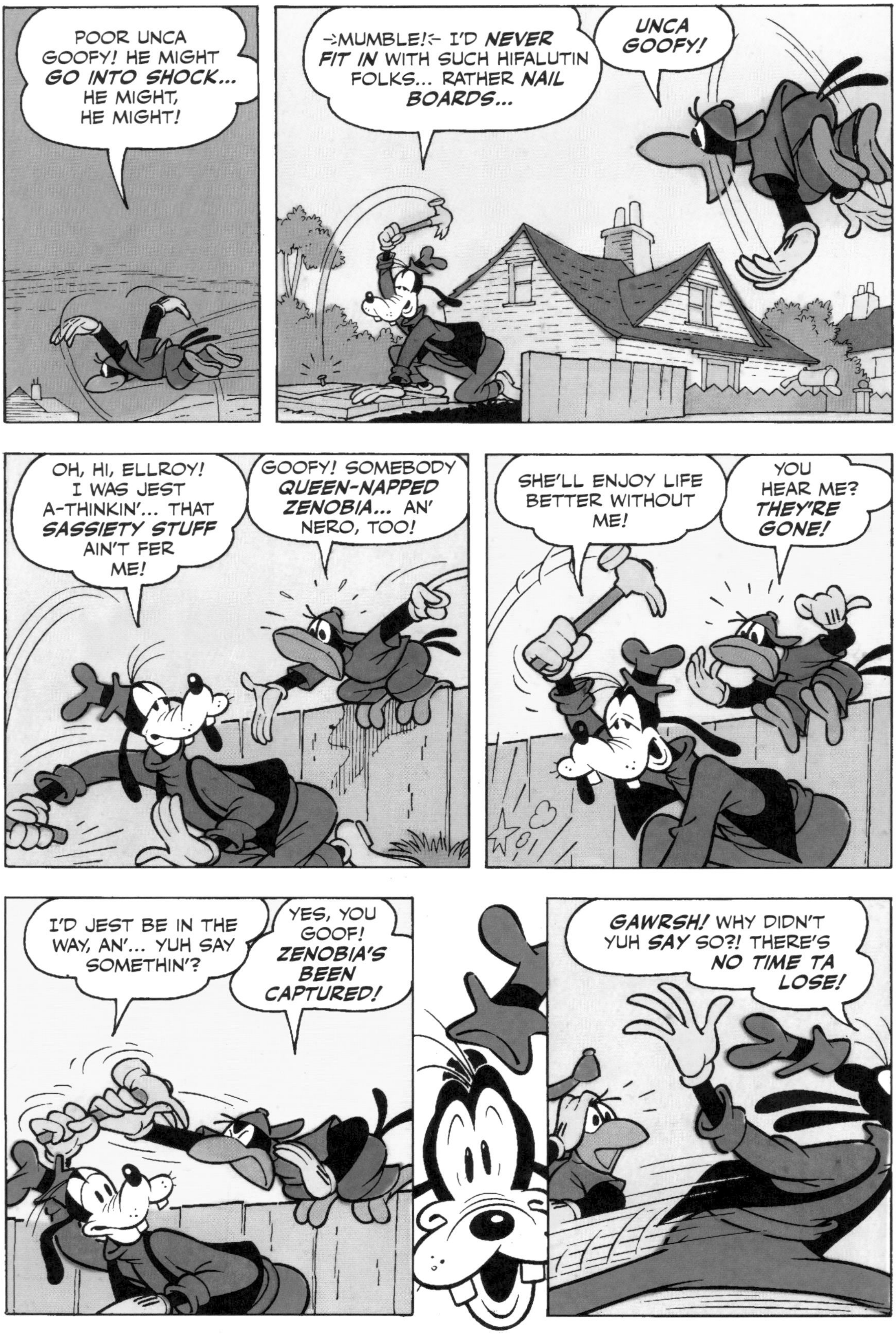
POOR UNCA GOOFY! HE MIGHT GO INTO SHOCK... HE MIGHT, HE MIGHT!
-MUMBLE!- I'D NEVER FIT IN WITH SUCH HIFALUTIN FOLKS... RATHER NAIL BOARDS...
UNCA GOOFY!
OH, HI, ELLROY! I WAS JEST A-THINKIN'... THAT SASSIETY STUFF AIN'T FER ME!
GOOFY! SOMEBODY QUEEN-NAPPED ZENOBIA... AN' NERO, TOO!
SHE'LL ENJOY LIFE BETTER WITHOUT ME!
YOU HEAR ME? THEY'RE GONE!
I'D JEST BE IN THE WAY, AN'... YUH SAY SOMETHIN'?
YES, YOU GOOF! ZENOBIA'S BEEN CAPTURED!
GAWRSH! WHY DIDN'T YUH SAY SO?! THERE'S NO TIME TA LOSE!

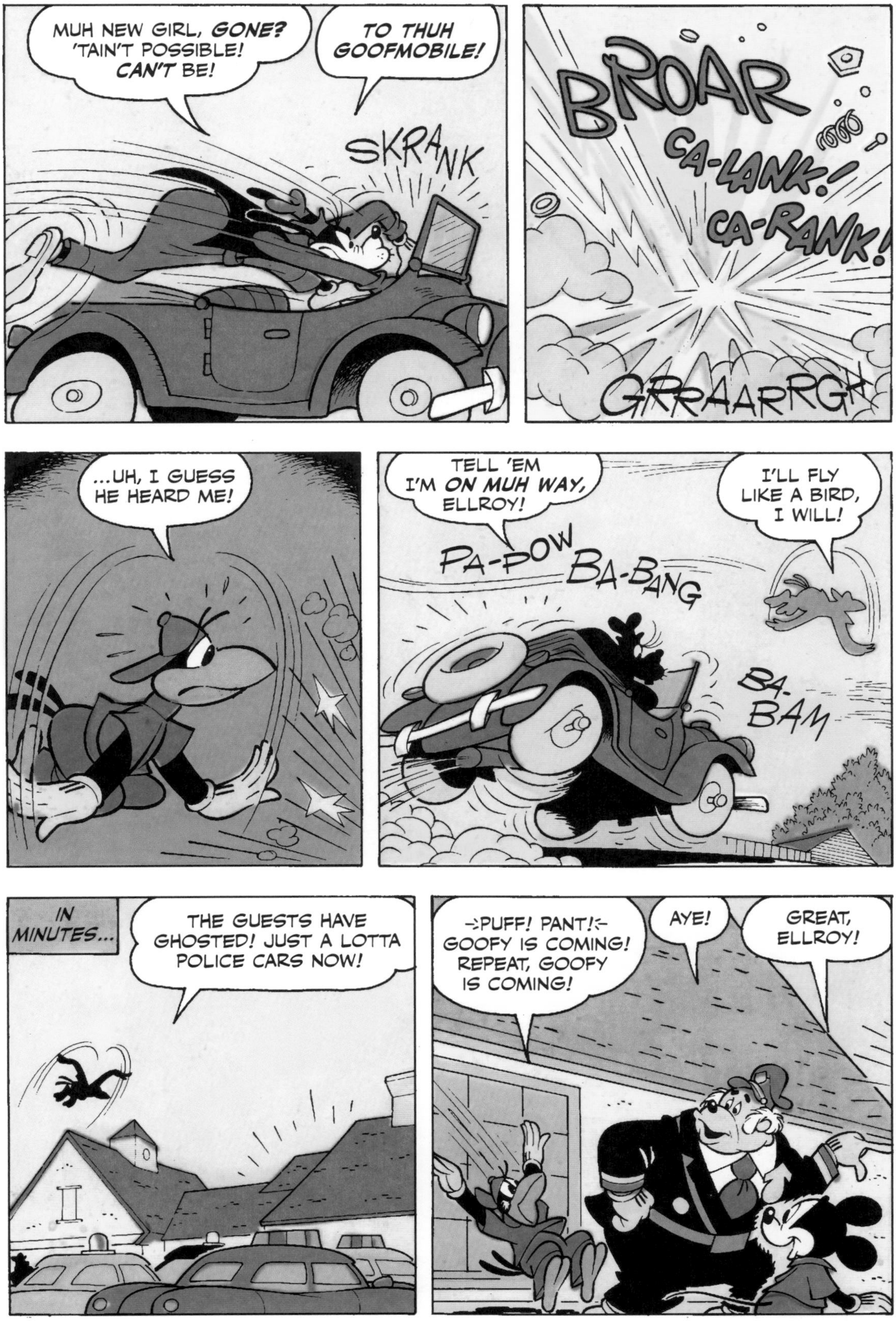
MUH NEW GIRL, GONE? 'TAIN'T POSSIBLE! CAN'T BE!
TO THUH GOOFMOBILE!
SKRANK
BROAR
CA-LANK!
CA-RANK!
GRRAARRGH
...UH, I GUESS HE HEARD ME!
TELL 'EM I'M ON MUH WAY, ELLROY!
PA-POW
BA-BANG
I'LL FLY LIKE A BIRD, I WILL!
BA-BAM
IN MINUTES...
THE GUESTS HAVE GHOSTED! JUST A LOTTA POLICE CARS NOW!
PUFF! PANT! GOOFY IS COMING! REPEAT, GOOFY IS COMING!
AYE!
GREAT, ELLROY!

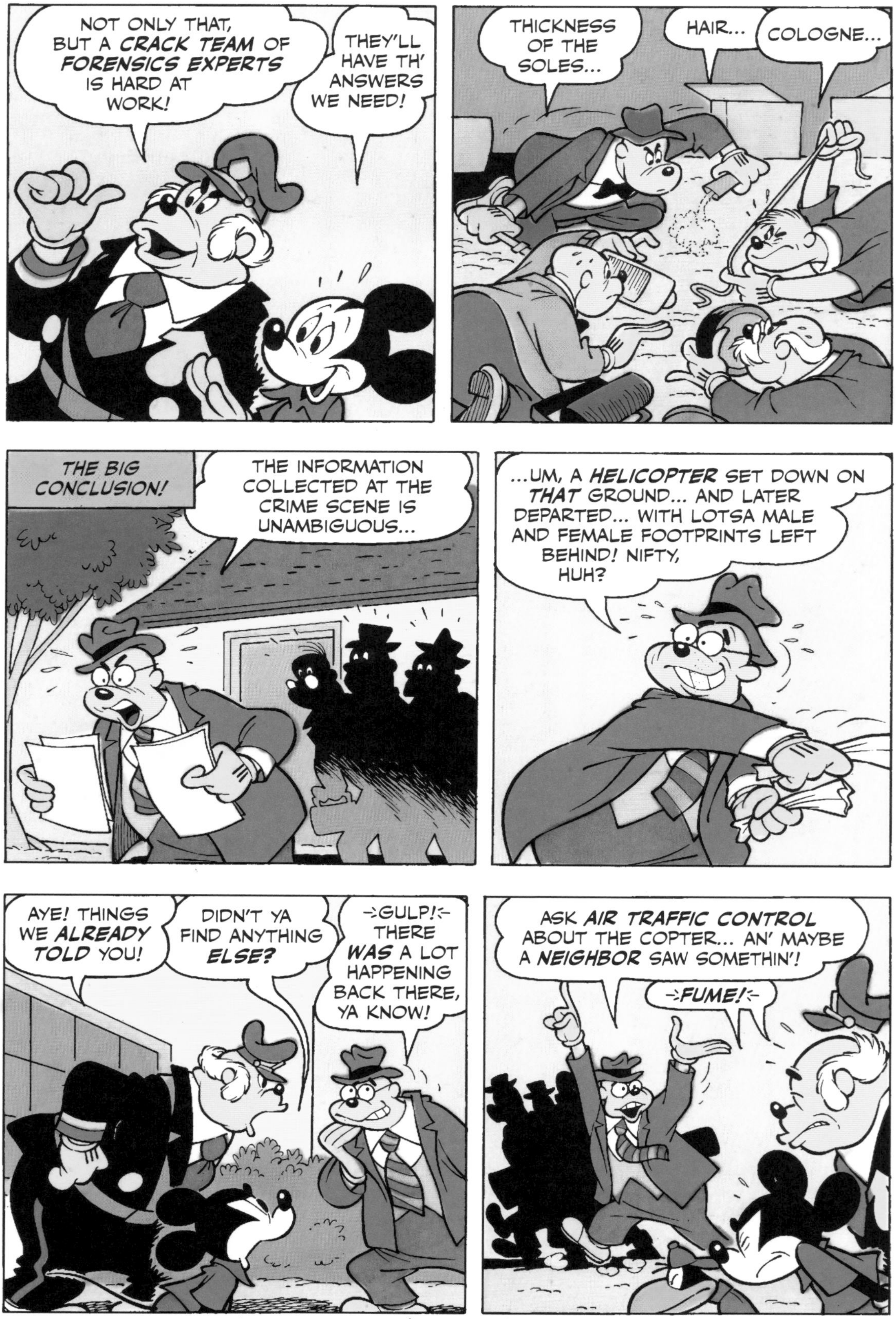
NOT ONLY THAT, BUT A CRACK TEAM OF FORENSICS EXPERTS IS HARD AT WORK!
THEY'LL HAVE TH' ANSWERS WE NEED!
THICKNESS OF THE SOLES...
HAIR...
COLOGNE...
THE BIG CONCLUSION!
THE INFORMATION COLLECTED AT THE CRIME SCENE IS UNAMBIGUOUS...
...UM, A HELICOPTER SET DOWN ON THAT GROUND... AND LATER DEPARTED... WITH LOTSA MALE AND FEMALE FOOTPRINTS LEFT BEHIND! NIFTY, HUH?
AYE! THINGS WE ALREADY TOLD YOU!
DIDN'T YA FIND ANYTHING ELSE?
GULP! THERE WAS A LOT HAPPENING BACK THERE, YA KNOW!
ASK AIR TRAFFIC CONTROL ABOUT THE COPTER... AN' MAYBE A NEIGHBOR SAW SOMETHIN'!
FUME!

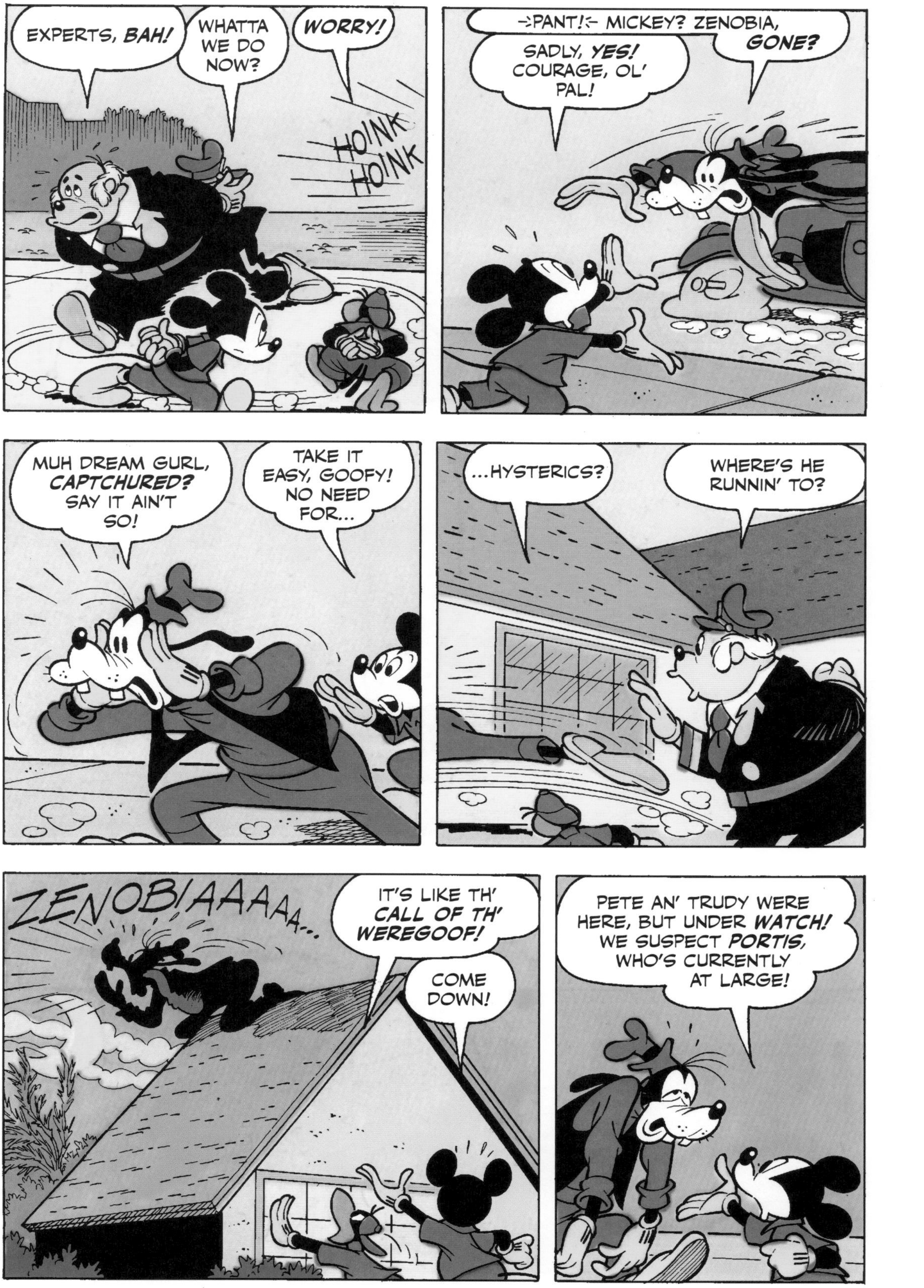

EXPERTS, BAH!
WHATTA WE DO NOW?
WORRY!
HOINK HOINK
-PANT!- MICKEY? ZENOBIA, GONE?
SADLY, YES! COURAGE, OL' PAL!
MUH DREAM GURL, CAPTCHURED? SAY IT AIN'T SO!
TAKE IT EASY, GOOFY! NO NEED FOR...
...HYSTERICS?
WHERE'S HE RUNNIN' TO?
ZENOBIAAAAA...
IT'S LIKE TH' CALL OF TH' WEREGOOF!
COME DOWN!
PETE AN' TRUDY WERE HERE, BUT UNDER WATCH! WE SUSPECT PORTIS, WHO'S CURRENTLY AT LARGE!

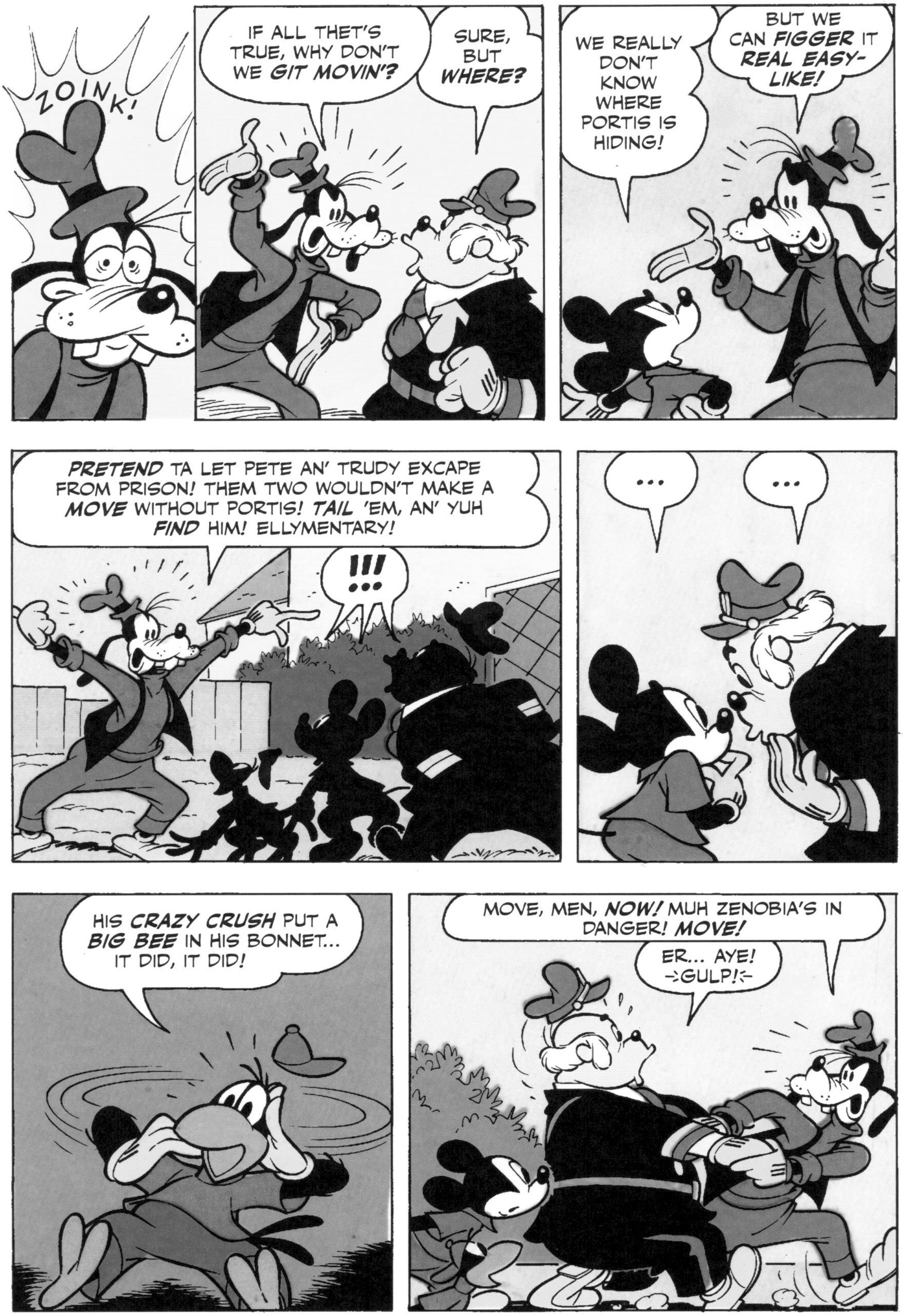
ZOINK!
IF ALL THET'S TRUE, WHY DON'T WE *GIT MOVIN'?*
SURE, BUT *WHERE?*
WE REALLY DON'T KNOW WHERE PORTIS IS HIDING!
BUT WE CAN *FIGGER* IT *REAL EASY-LIKE!*
PRETEND TA LET PETE AN' TRUDY EXCAPE FROM PRISON! THEM TWO WOULDN'T MAKE A *MOVE* WITHOUT PORTIS! *TAIL* 'EM, AN' YUH *FIND* HIM! ELLYMENTARY!
!!! ...
...
...
HIS *CRAZY CRUSH* PUT A *BIG BEE* IN HIS BONNET... IT DID, IT DID!
MOVE, MEN, *NOW!* MUH ZENOBIA'S IN DANGER! *MOVE!*
ER... AYE! -GULP!-

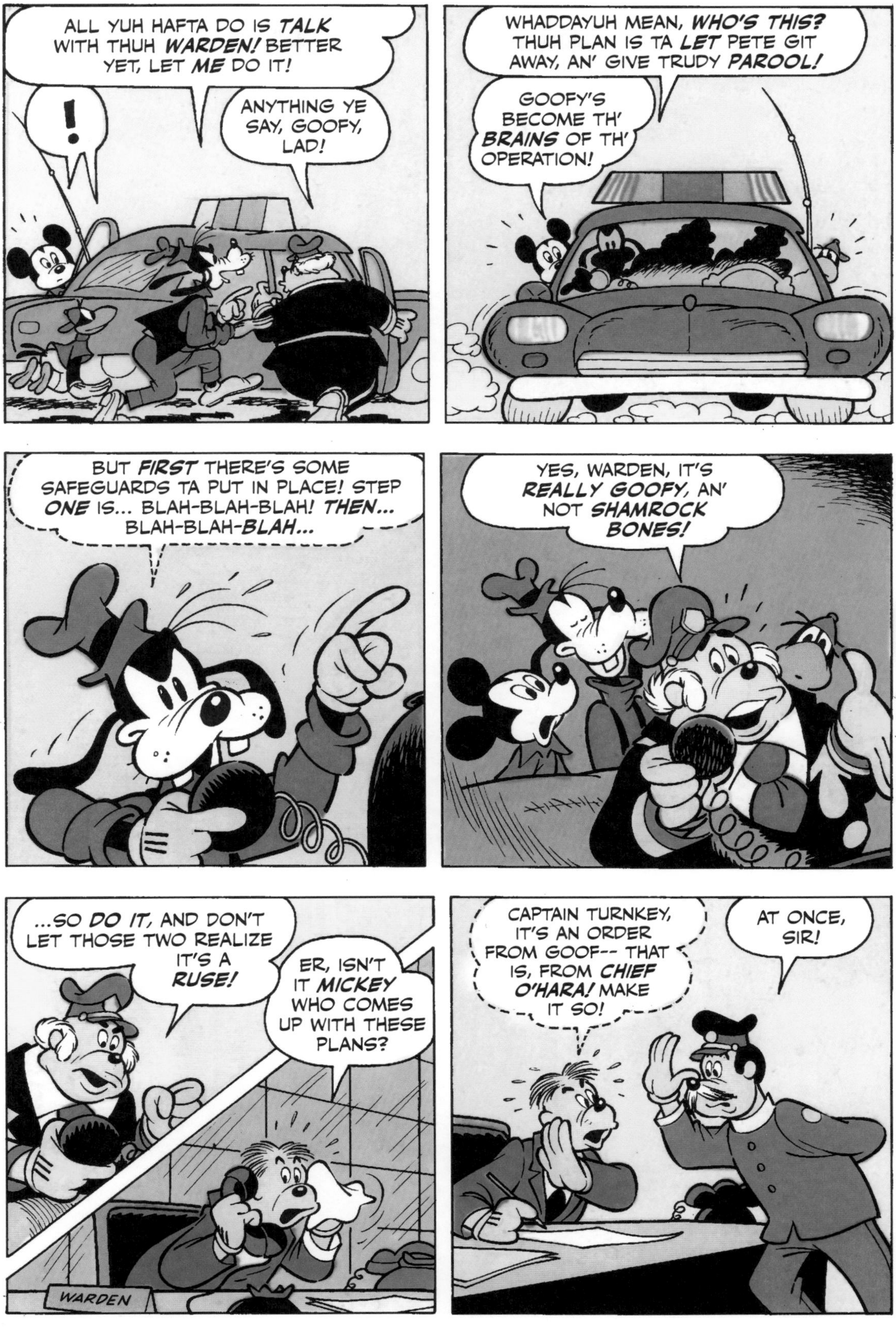
ALL YUH HAFTA DO IS TALK WITH THUH WARDEN! BETTER YET, LET ME DO IT!
!
ANYTHING YE SAY, GOOFY, LAD!
WHADDAYUH MEAN, WHO'S THIS? THUH PLAN IS TA LET PETE GIT AWAY, AN' GIVE TRUDY PAROOL!
GOOFY'S BECOME TH' BRAINS OF TH' OPERATION!
BUT FIRST THERE'S SOME SAFEGUARDS TA PUT IN PLACE! STEP ONE IS... BLAH-BLAH-BLAH! THEN... BLAH-BLAH-BLAH...
YES, WARDEN, IT'S REALLY GOOFY, AN' NOT SHAMROCK BONES!
...SO DO IT, AND DON'T LET THOSE TWO REALIZE IT'S A RUSE!
ER, ISN'T IT MICKEY WHO COMES UP WITH THESE PLANS?
WARDEN
CAPTAIN TURNKEY, IT'S AN ORDER FROM GOOF-- THAT IS, FROM CHIEF O'HARA! MAKE IT SO!
AT ONCE, SIR!

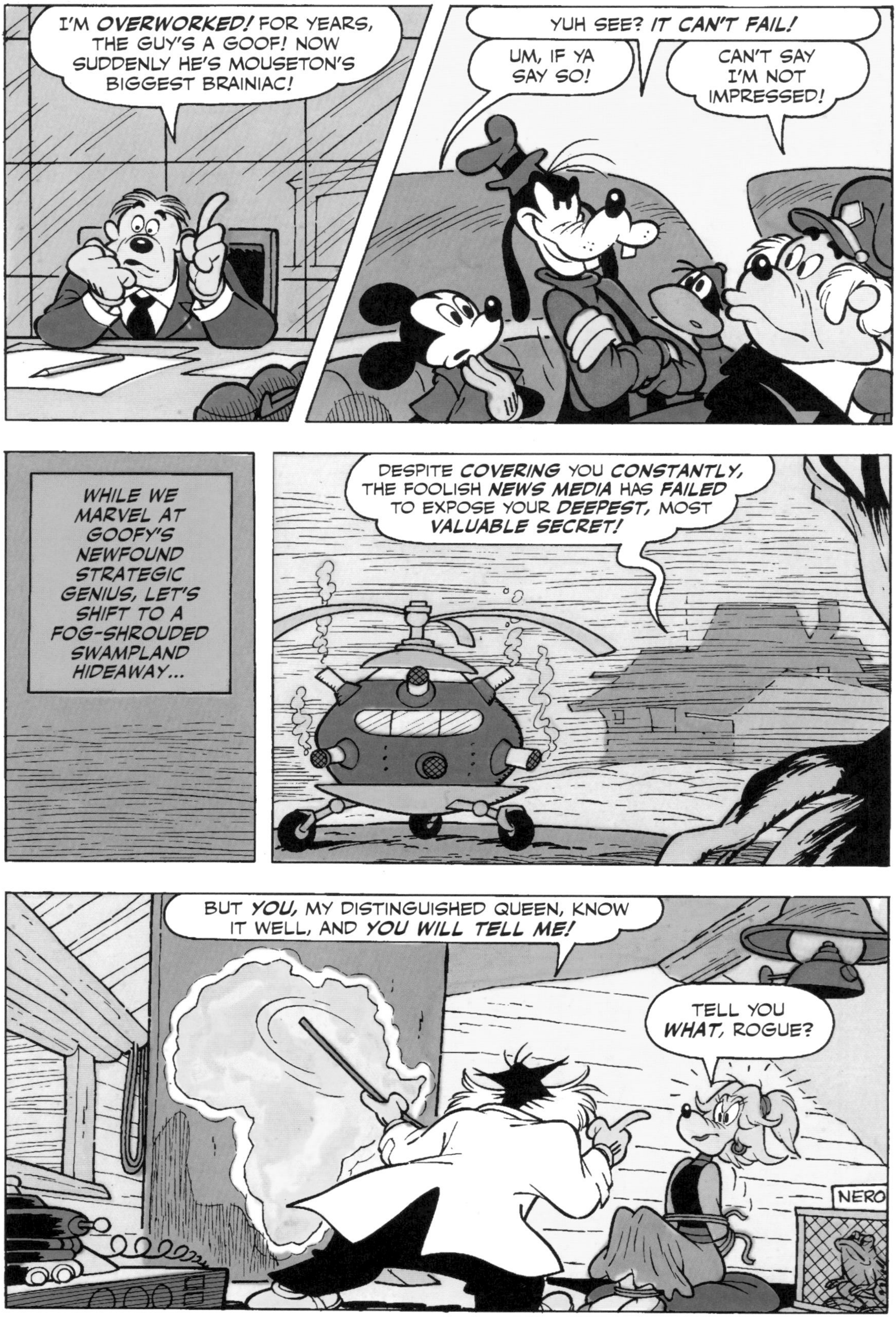
I'M OVERWORKED! FOR YEARS, THE GUY'S A GOOF! NOW SUDDENLY HE'S MOUSETON'S BIGGEST BRAINIAC!
YUH SEE? IT CAN'T FAIL!
UM, IF YA SAY SO!
CAN'T SAY I'M NOT IMPRESSED!
WHILE WE MARVEL AT GOOFY'S NEWFOUND STRATEGIC GENIUS, LET'S SHIFT TO A FOG-SHROUDED SWAMPLAND HIDEAWAY...
DESPITE COVERING YOU CONSTANTLY, THE FOOLISH NEWS MEDIA HAS FAILED TO EXPOSE YOUR DEEPEST, MOST VALUABLE SECRET!
BUT YOU, MY DISTINGUISHED QUEEN, KNOW IT WELL, AND YOU WILL TELL ME!
TELL YOU WHAT, ROGUE?
NERO

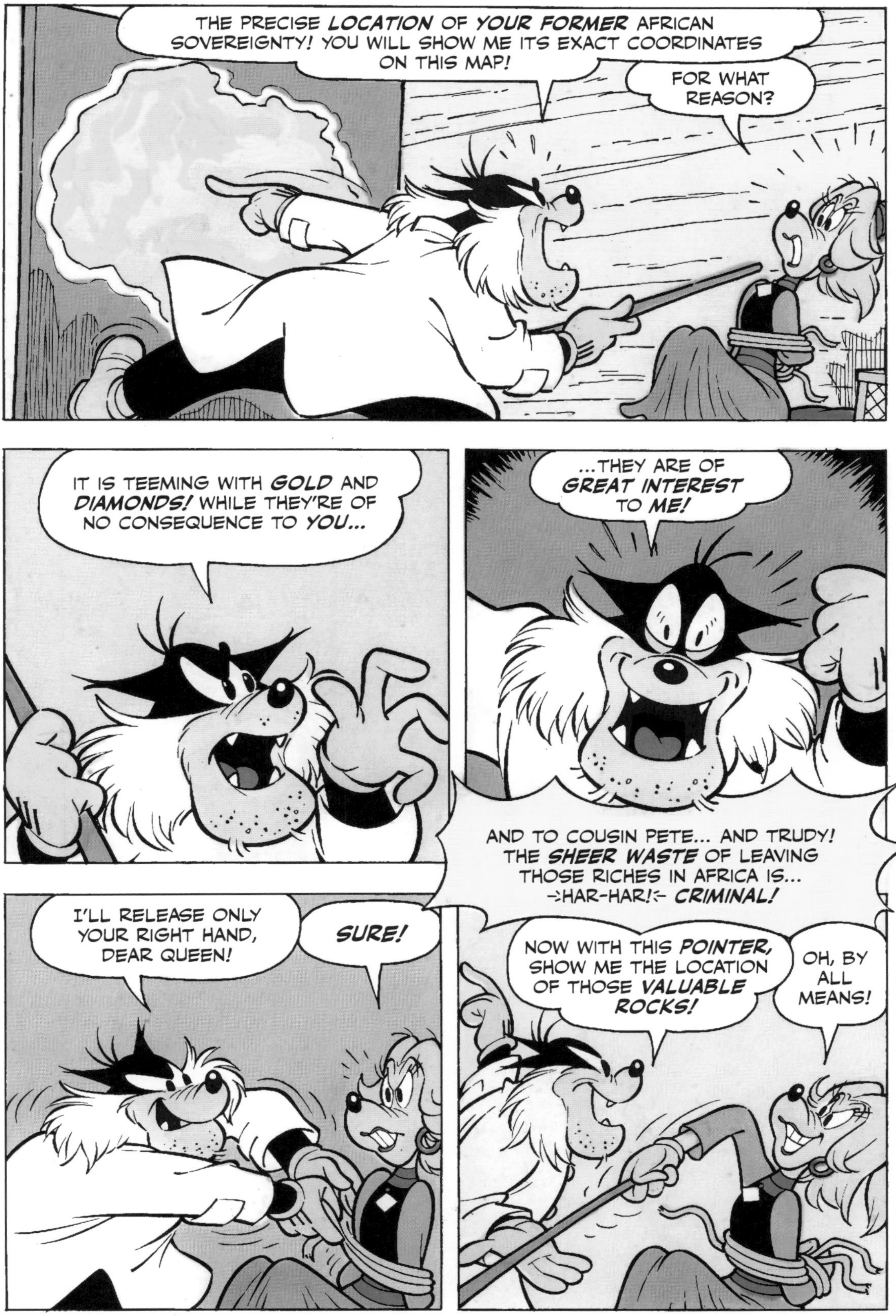
THE PRECISE LOCATION OF YOUR FORMER AFRICAN SOVEREIGNTY! YOU WILL SHOW ME ITS EXACT COORDINATES ON THIS MAP!
FOR WHAT REASON?
IT IS TEEMING WITH GOLD AND DIAMONDS! WHILE THEY'RE OF NO CONSEQUENCE TO YOU...
...THEY ARE OF GREAT INTEREST TO ME!
AND TO COUSIN PETE... AND TRUDY! THE SHEER WASTE OF LEAVING THOSE RICHES IN AFRICA IS... →HAR-HAR!← CRIMINAL!
I'LL RELEASE ONLY YOUR RIGHT HAND, DEAR QUEEN!
SURE!
NOW WITH THIS POINTER, SHOW ME THE LOCATION OF THOSE VALUABLE ROCKS!
OH, BY ALL MEANS!

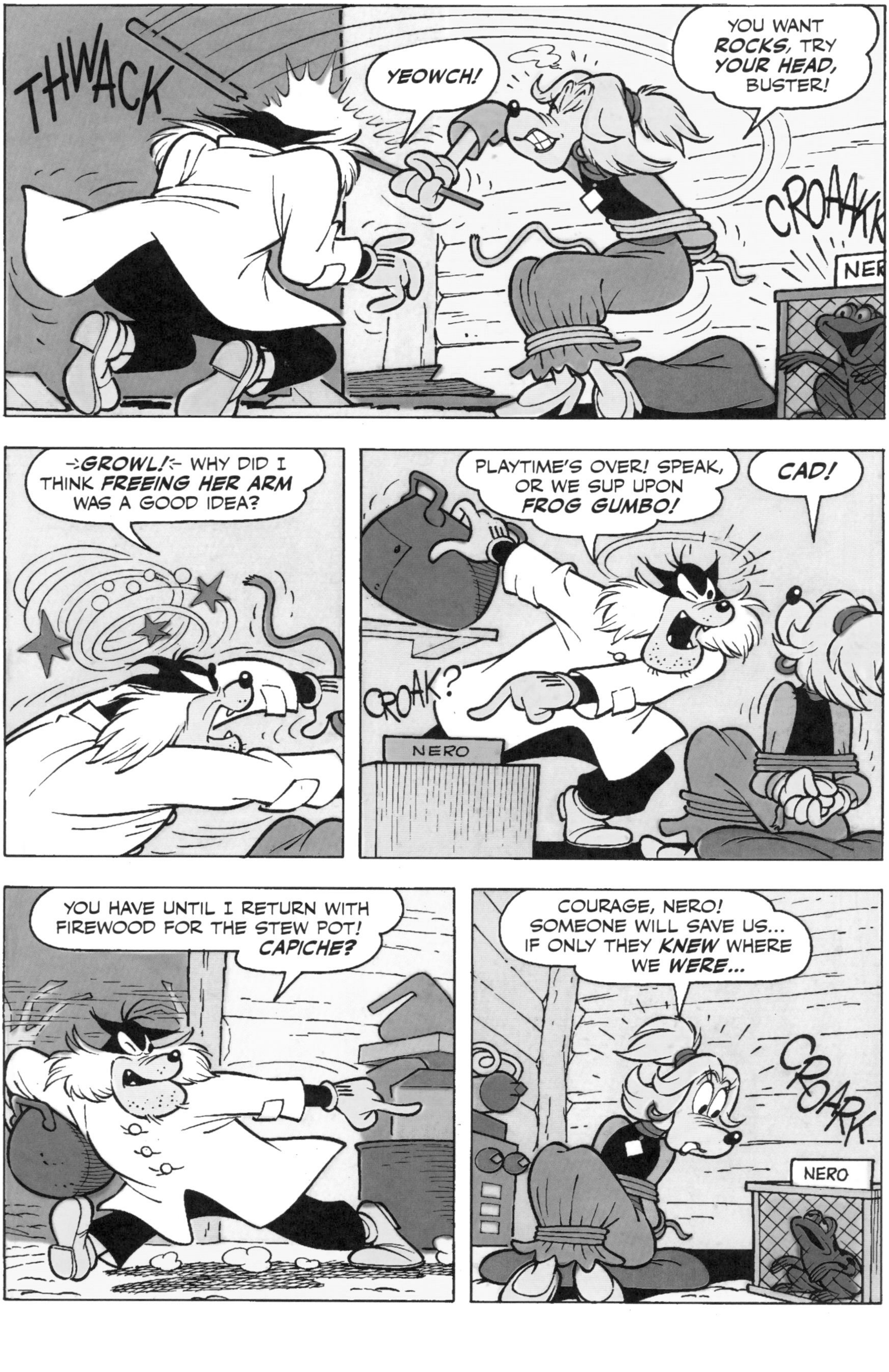
THWACK
YEOWCH!
YOU WANT ROCKS, TRY YOUR HEAD, BUSTER!
CROAAKK
NER
-GROWL!- WHY DID I THINK FREEING HER ARM WAS A GOOD IDEA?
PLAYTIME'S OVER! SPEAK, OR WE SUP UPON FROG GUMBO!
CAD!
CROAK?
NERO
YOU HAVE UNTIL I RETURN WITH FIREWOOD FOR THE STEW POT! CAPICHE?
COURAGE, NERO! SOMEONE WILL SAVE US... IF ONLY THEY KNEW WHERE WE WERE...
CROARK
NERO

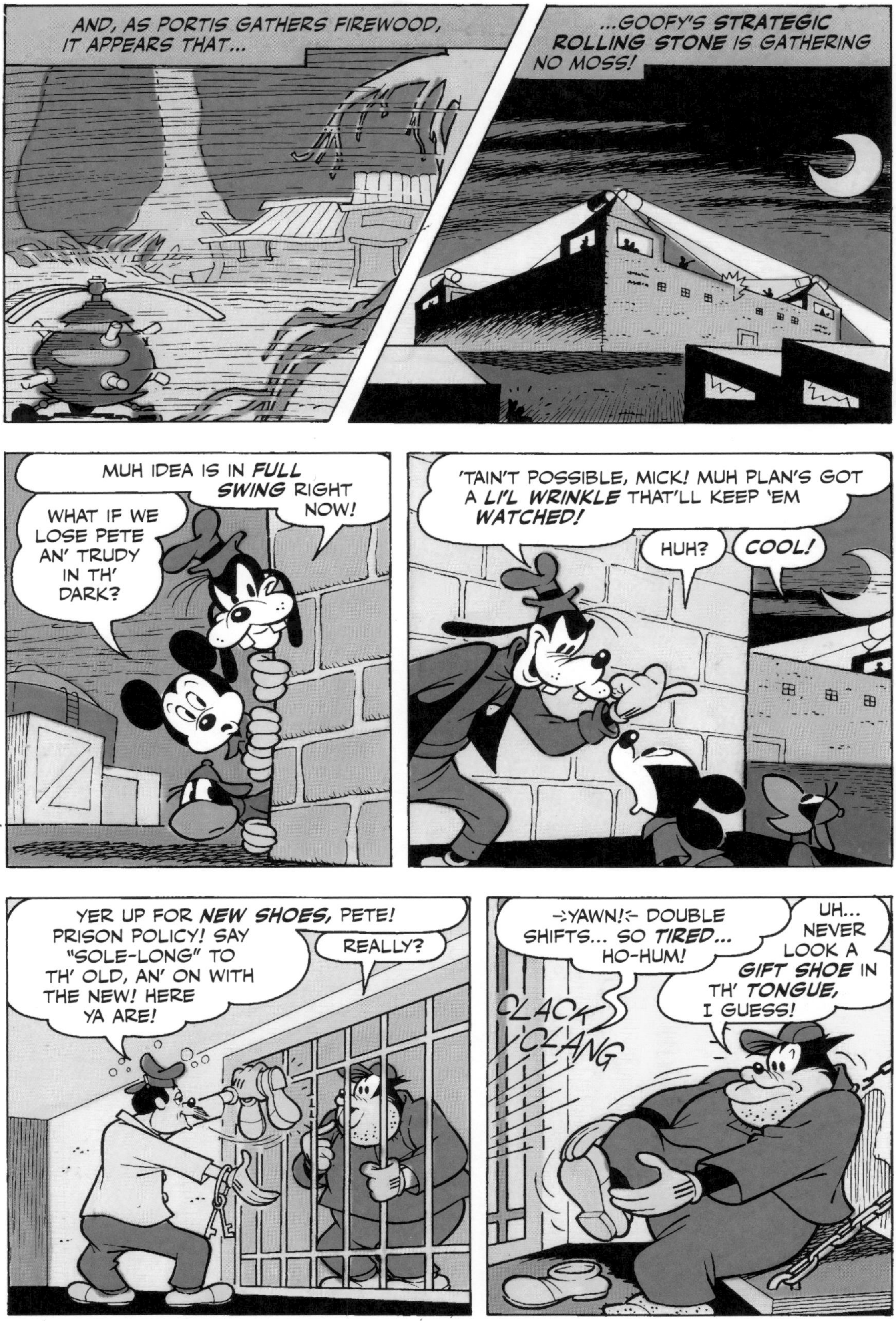
AND, AS PORTIS GATHERS FIREWOOD, IT APPEARS THAT...
...GOOFY'S STRATEGIC ROLLING STONE IS GATHERING NO MOSS!
MUH IDEA IS IN FULL SWING RIGHT NOW!
WHAT IF WE LOSE PETE AN' TRUDY IN TH' DARK?
'TAIN'T POSSIBLE, MICK! MUH PLAN'S GOT A LI'L WRINKLE THAT'LL KEEP 'EM WATCHED!
HUH?
COOL!
YER UP FOR NEW SHOES, PETE! PRISON POLICY! SAY "SOLE-LONG" TO TH' OLD, AN' ON WITH THE NEW! HERE YA ARE!
REALLY?
->YAWN!<- DOUBLE SHIFTS... SO TIRED... HO-HUM!
UH... NEVER LOOK A GIFT SHOE IN TH' TONGUE, I GUESS!
CLACK
CLANG

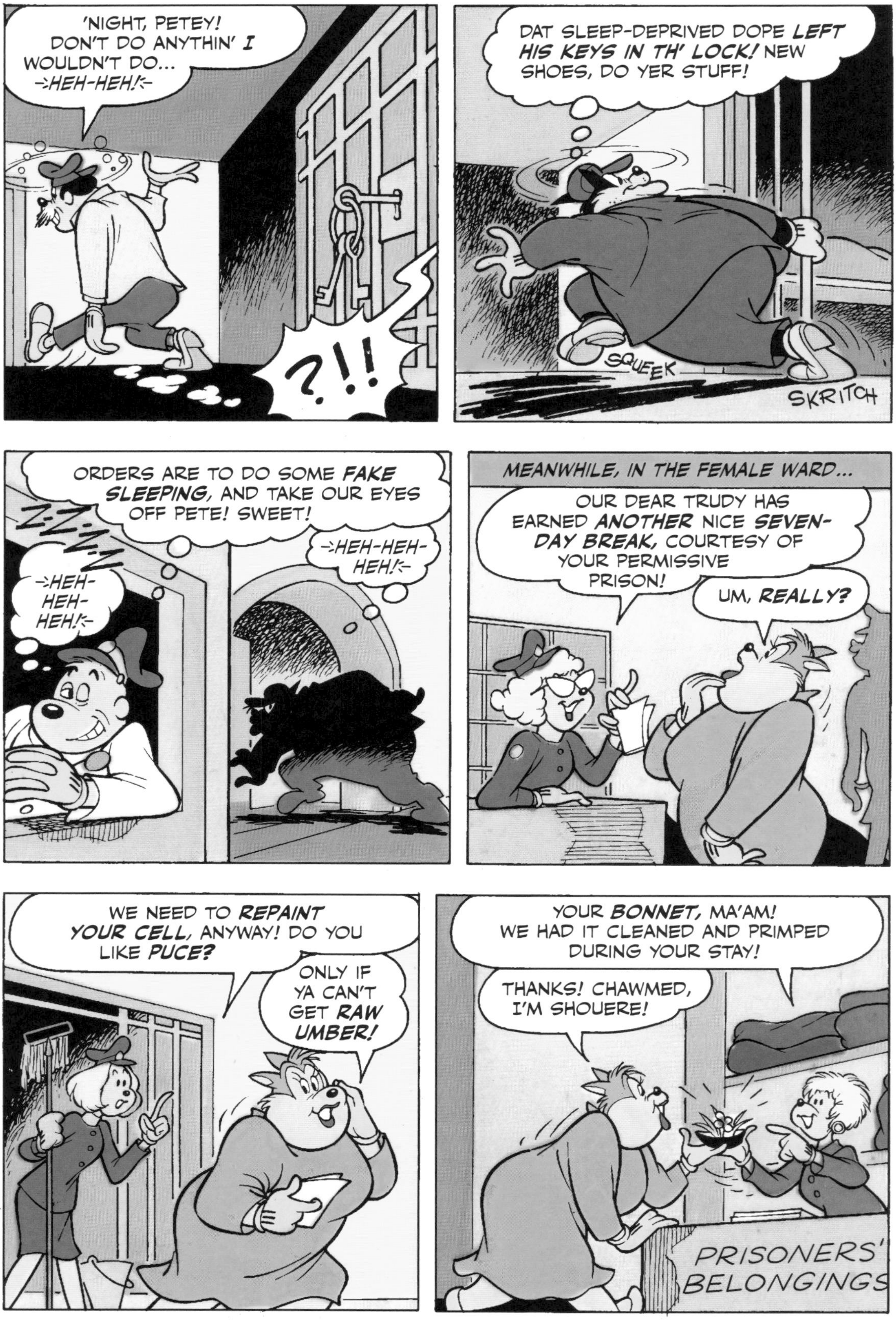
'NIGHT, PETEY! DON'T DO ANYTHIN' I WOULDN'T DO... -HEH-HEH!-
?!!
DAT SLEEP-DEPRIVED DOPE LEFT HIS KEYS IN TH' LOCK! NEW SHOES, DO YER STUFF!
SQUEEK
SKRITCH
ORDERS ARE TO DO SOME FAKE SLEEPING, AND TAKE OUR EYES OFF PETE! SWEET!
-HEH-HEH-HEH!-
-HEH-HEH-HEH!-
MEANWHILE, IN THE FEMALE WARD...
OUR DEAR TRUDY HAS EARNED ANOTHER NICE SEVEN-DAY BREAK, COURTESY OF YOUR PERMISSIVE PRISON!
UM, REALLY?
WE NEED TO REPAINT YOUR CELL, ANYWAY! DO YOU LIKE PUCE?
ONLY IF YA CAN'T GET RAW UMBER!
YOUR BONNET, MA'AM! WE HAD IT CLEANED AND PRIMPED DURING YOUR STAY!
THANKS! CHAWMED, I'M SHOUERE!
PRISONERS' BELONGINGS

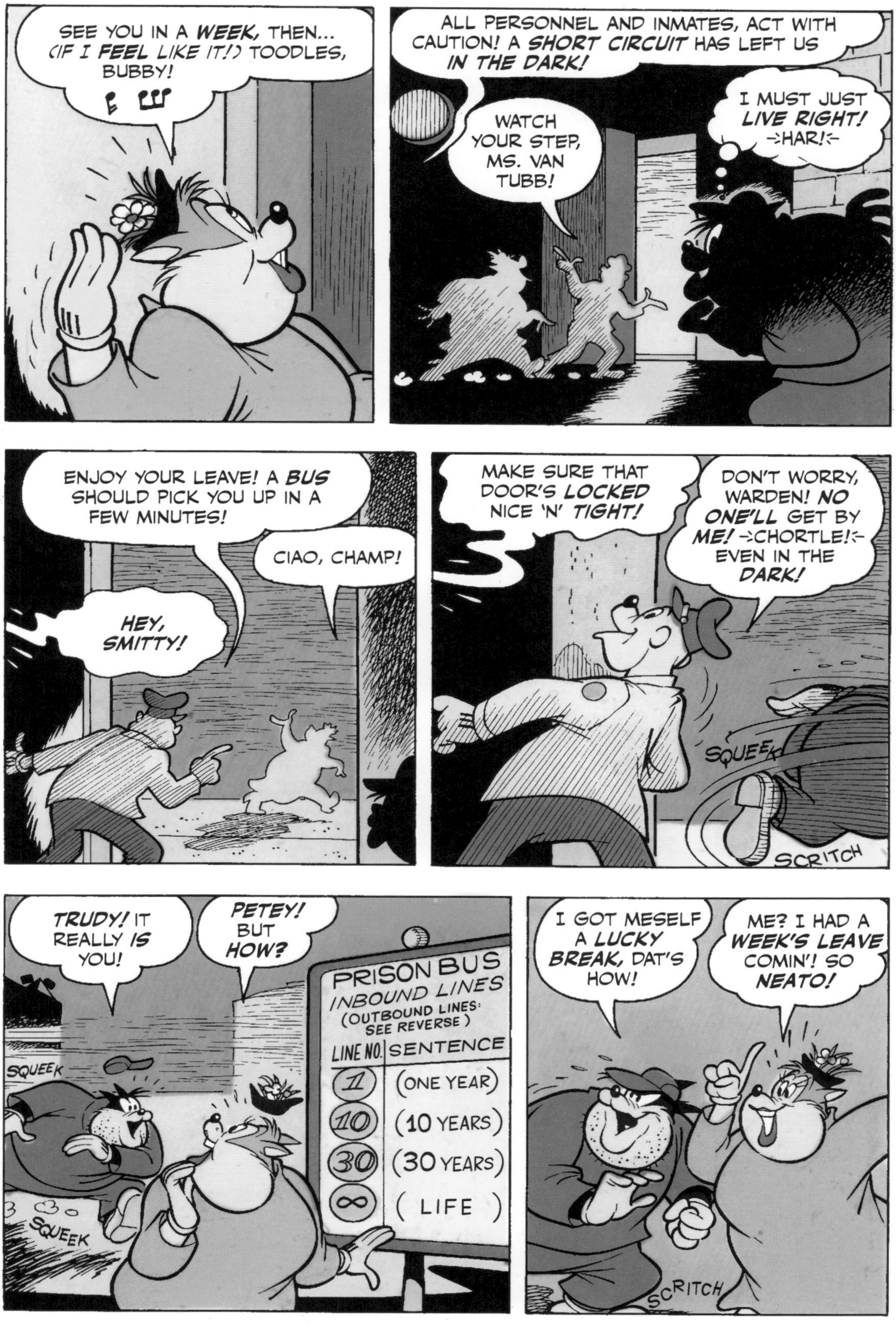

SEE YOU IN A WEEK, THEN... (IF I FEEL LIKE IT!) TOODLES, BUBBY!
ALL PERSONNEL AND INMATES, ACT WITH CAUTION! A SHORT CIRCUIT HAS LEFT US IN THE DARK!
WATCH YOUR STEP, MS. VAN TUBB!
I MUST JUST LIVE RIGHT! -HAR!-
ENJOY YOUR LEAVE! A BUS SHOULD PICK YOU UP IN A FEW MINUTES!
CIAO, CHAMP!
HEY, SMITTY!
MAKE SURE THAT DOOR'S LOCKED NICE 'N' TIGHT!
DON'T WORRY, WARDEN! NO ONE'LL GET BY ME! -CHORTLE!- EVEN IN THE DARK!
SQUEEK
SCRITCH
TRUDY! IT REALLY IS YOU!
PETEY! BUT HOW?
PRISON BUS
INBOUND LINES
(OUTBOUND LINES: SEE REVERSE)
LINE NO. SENTENCE
1 (ONE YEAR)
10 (10 YEARS)
30 (30 YEARS)
∞ (LIFE)
SQUEEK
SQUEEK
I GOT MESELF A LUCKY BREAK, DAT'S HOW!
ME? I HAD A WEEK'S LEAVE COMIN'! SO NEATO!
SCRITCH

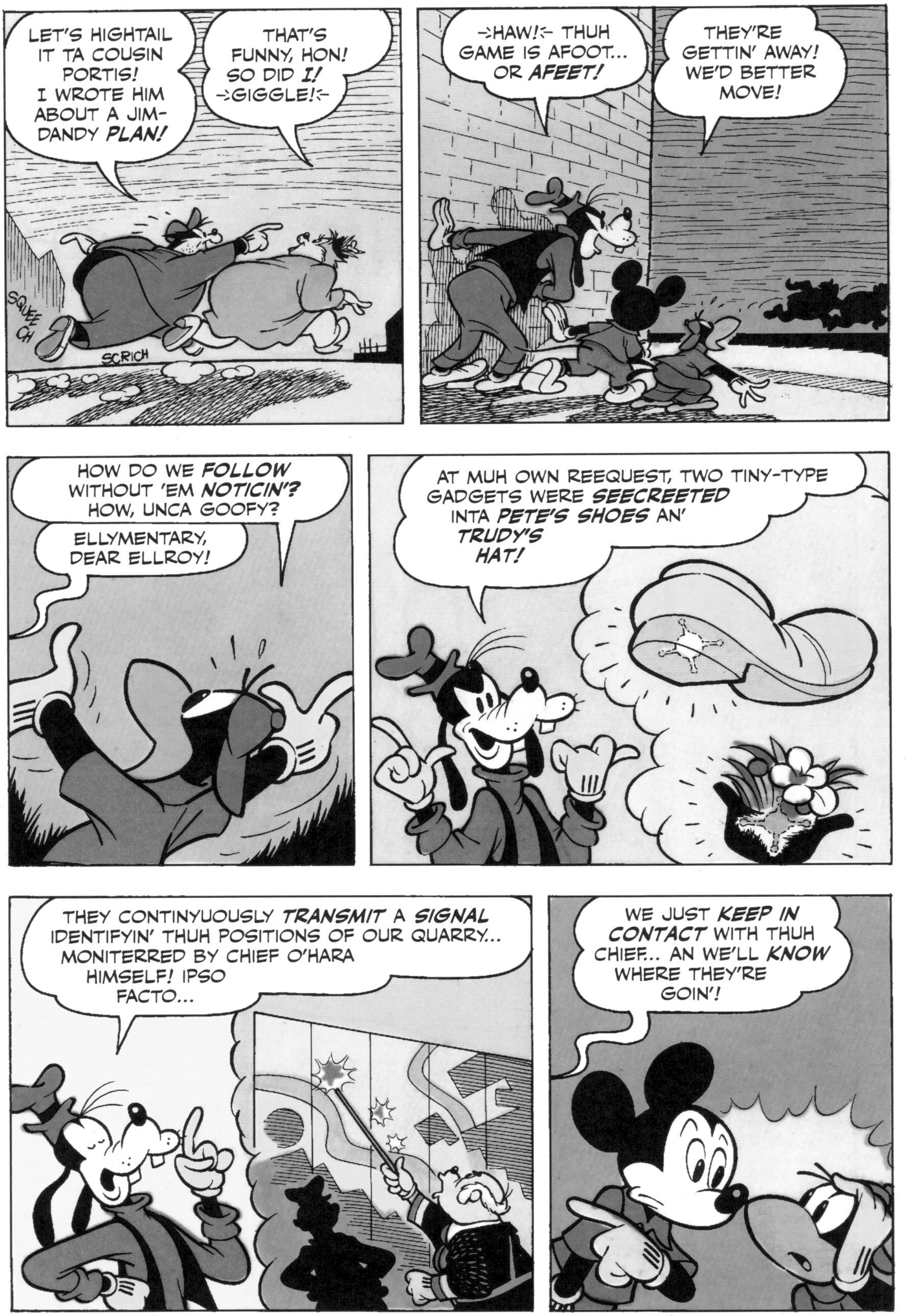

LET'S HIGHTAIL IT TA COUSIN PORTIS! I WROTE HIM ABOUT A JIM-DANDY *PLAN!*
THAT'S FUNNY, HON! SO DID *I!* ->GIGGLE!<-
SQUEECH
SCRICH
->HAW!<- THUH GAME IS AFOOT... OR *AFEET!*
THEY'RE GETTIN' AWAY! WE'D BETTER MOVE!
HOW DO WE *FOLLOW* WITHOUT 'EM *NOTICIN'?* HOW, UNCA GOOFY?
ELLYMENTARY, DEAR ELLROY!
AT MUH OWN REEQUEST, TWO TINY-TYPE GADGETS WERE *SEECREETED* INTA *PETE'S SHOES* AN' *TRUDY'S HAT!*
THEY CONTINYUOUSLY *TRANSMIT* A *SIGNAL* IDENTIFYIN' THUH POSITIONS OF OUR QUARRY... MONITERRED BY CHIEF O'HARA HIMSELF! IPSO FACTO...
WE JUST *KEEP IN CONTACT* WITH THUH CHIEF... AN WE'LL *KNOW* WHERE THEY'RE GOIN'!

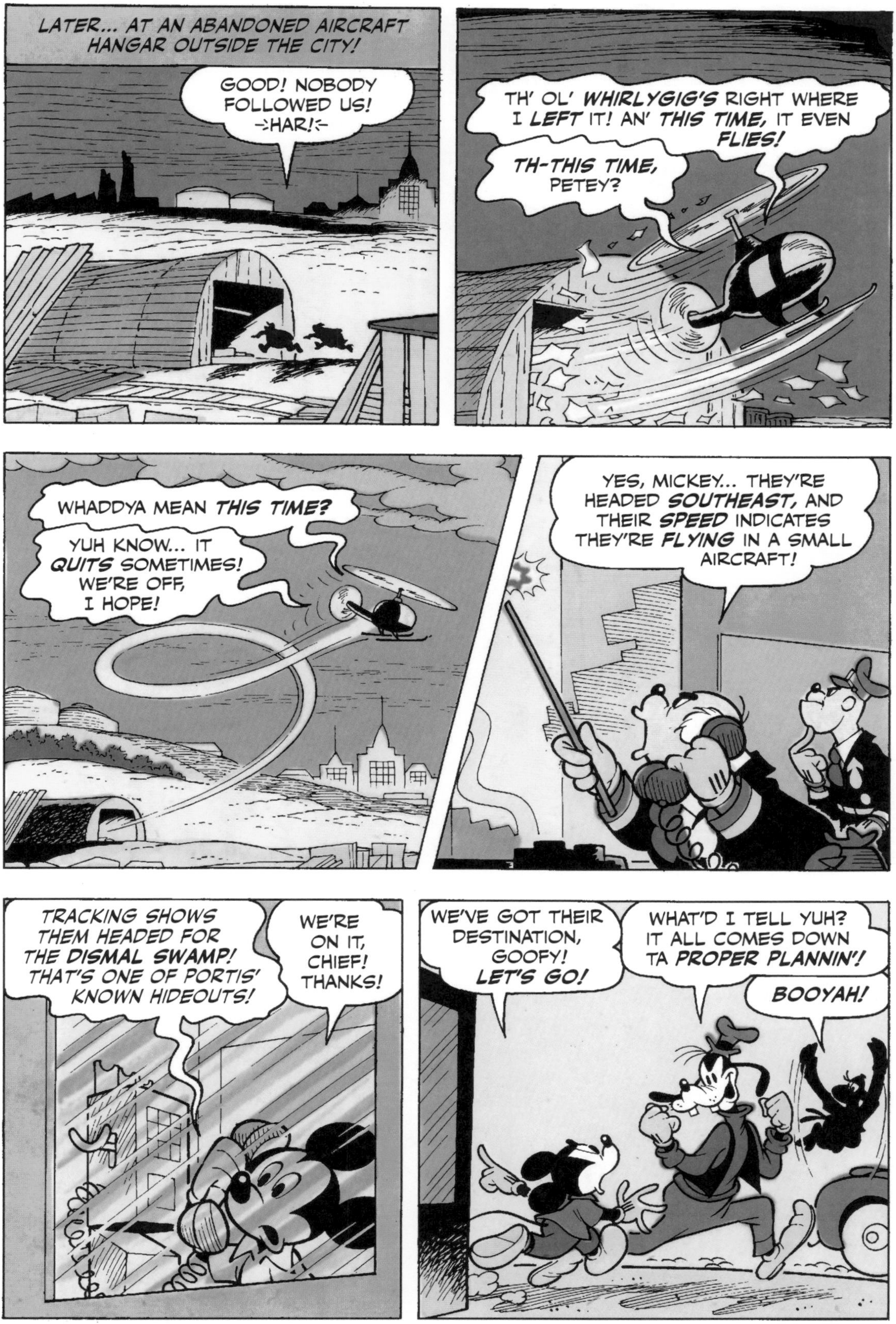
LATER... AT AN ABANDONED AIRCRAFT HANGAR OUTSIDE THE CITY!
GOOD! NOBODY FOLLOWED US! -HAR!-
TH' OL' WHIRLYGIG'S RIGHT WHERE I LEFT IT! AN' THIS TIME, IT EVEN FLIES!
TH-THIS TIME, PETEY?
WHADDYA MEAN THIS TIME?
YUH KNOW... IT QUITS SOMETIMES! WE'RE OFF, I HOPE!
YES, MICKEY... THEY'RE HEADED SOUTHEAST, AND THEIR SPEED INDICATES THEY'RE FLYING IN A SMALL AIRCRAFT!
TRACKING SHOWS THEM HEADED FOR THE DISMAL SWAMP! THAT'S ONE OF PORTIS' KNOWN HIDEOUTS!
WE'RE ON IT, CHIEF! THANKS!
WE'VE GOT THEIR DESTINATION, GOOFY! LET'S GO!
WHAT'D I TELL YUH? IT ALL COMES DOWN TA PROPER PLANNIN'!
BOOYAH!

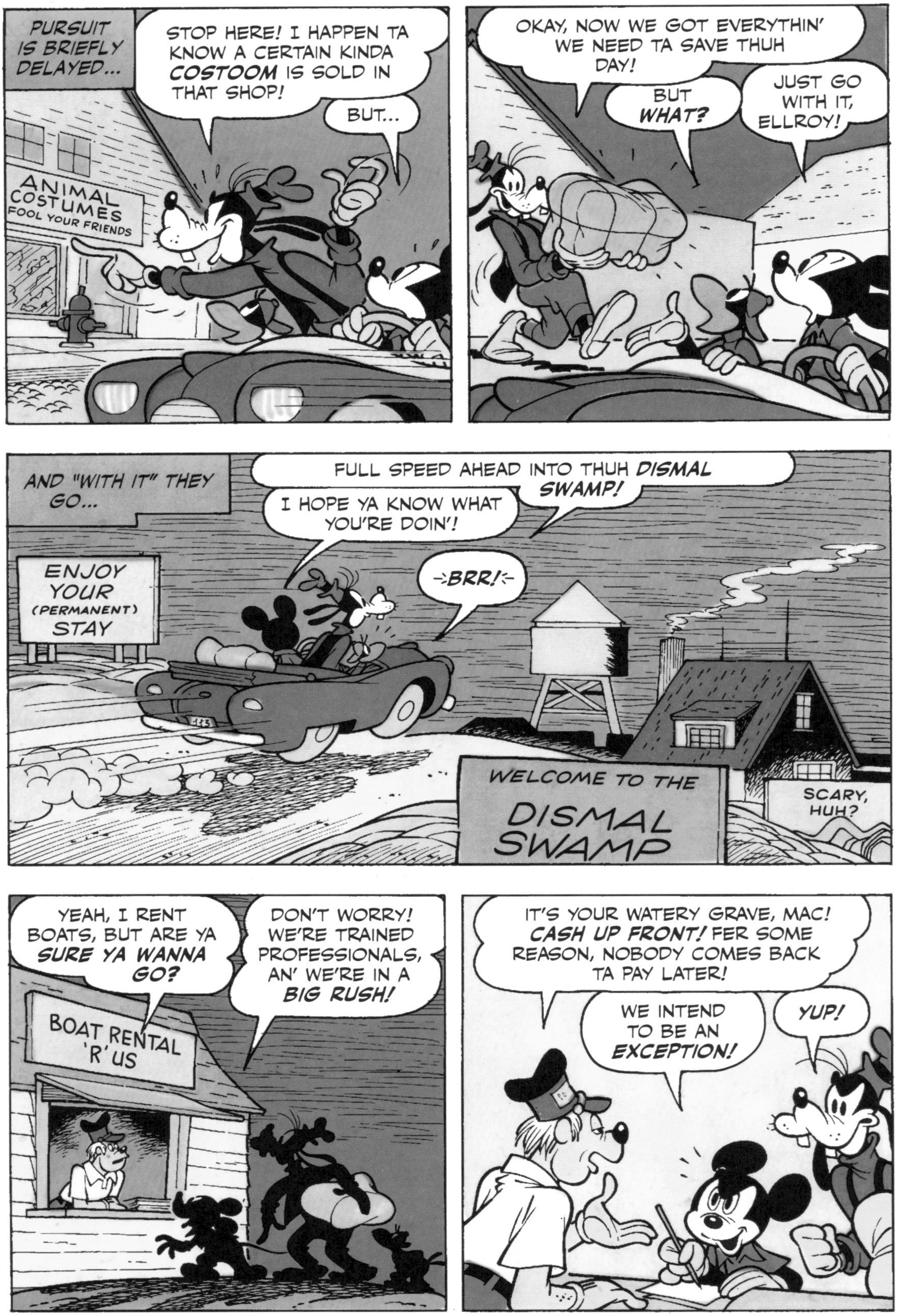
PURSUIT IS BRIEFLY DELAYED...
STOP HERE! I HAPPEN TA KNOW A CERTAIN KINDA COSTOOM IS SOLD IN THAT SHOP!
BUT...
ANIMAL COSTUMES FOOL YOUR FRIENDS
OKAY, NOW WE GOT EVERYTHIN' WE NEED TA SAVE THUH DAY!
BUT WHAT?
JUST GO WITH IT, ELLROY!
AND "WITH IT" THEY GO...
FULL SPEED AHEAD INTO THUH DISMAL SWAMP!
I HOPE YA KNOW WHAT YOU'RE DOIN'!
BRR!
ENJOY YOUR (PERMANENT) STAY
WELCOME TO THE DISMAL SWAMP
SCARY, HUH?
YEAH, I RENT BOATS, BUT ARE YA SURE YA WANNA GO?
DON'T WORRY! WE'RE TRAINED PROFESSIONALS, AN' WE'RE IN A BIG RUSH!
BOAT RENTAL 'R' US
IT'S YOUR WATERY GRAVE, MAC! CASH UP FRONT! FER SOME REASON, NOBODY COMES BACK TA PAY LATER!
WE INTEND TO BE AN EXCEPTION!
YUP!

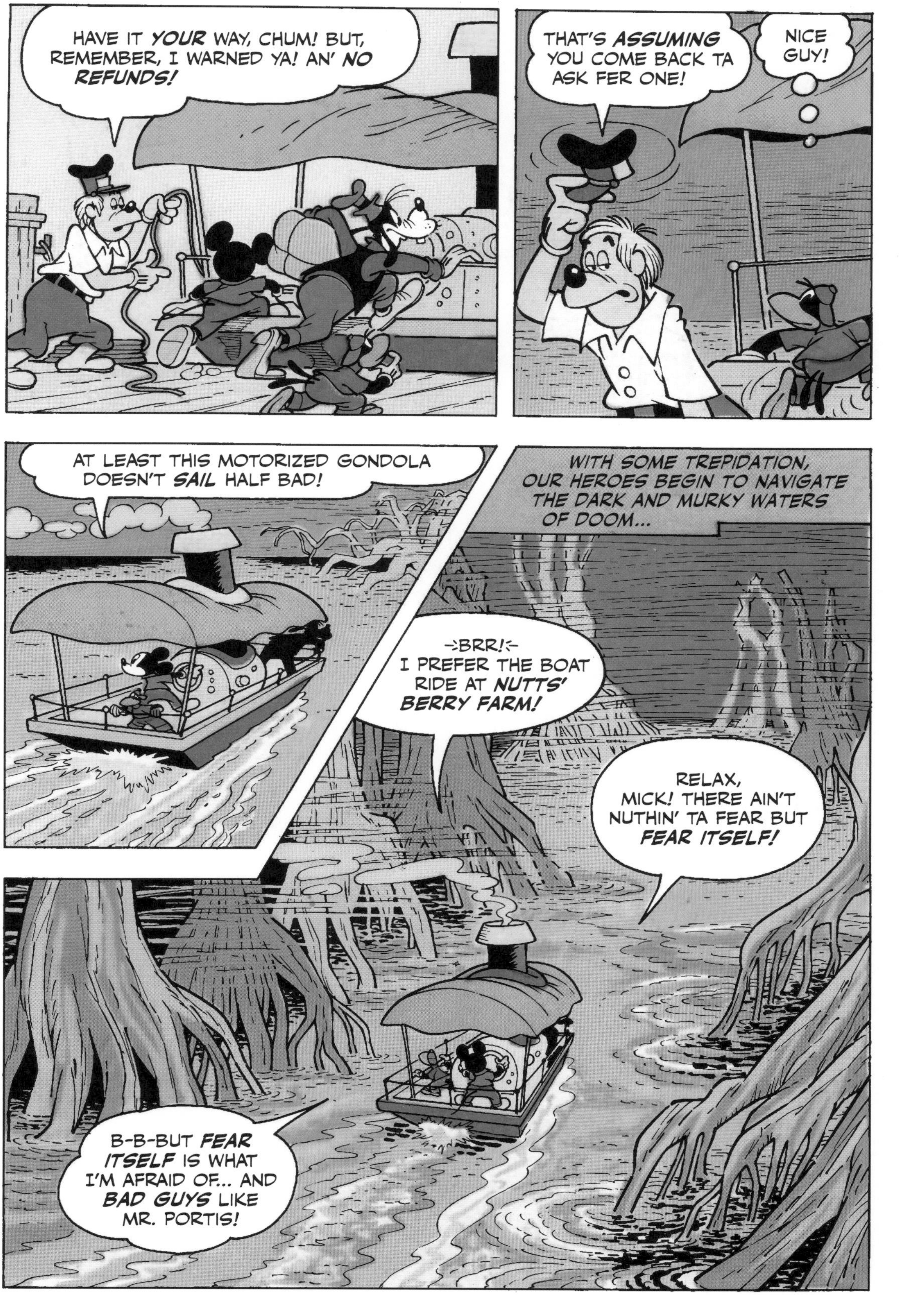
HAVE IT YOUR WAY, CHUM! BUT, REMEMBER, I WARNED YA! AN' NO REFUNDS!
THAT'S ASSUMING YOU COME BACK TA ASK FER ONE!
NICE GUY!
AT LEAST THIS MOTORIZED GONDOLA DOESN'T SAIL HALF BAD!
WITH SOME TREPIDATION, OUR HEROES BEGIN TO NAVIGATE THE DARK AND MURKY WATERS OF DOOM...
-BRR!- I PREFER THE BOAT RIDE AT NUTTS' BERRY FARM!
RELAX, MICK! THERE AIN'T NUTHIN' TA FEAR BUT FEAR ITSELF!
B-B-BUT FEAR ITSELF IS WHAT I'M AFRAID OF... AND BAD GUYS LIKE MR. PORTIS!

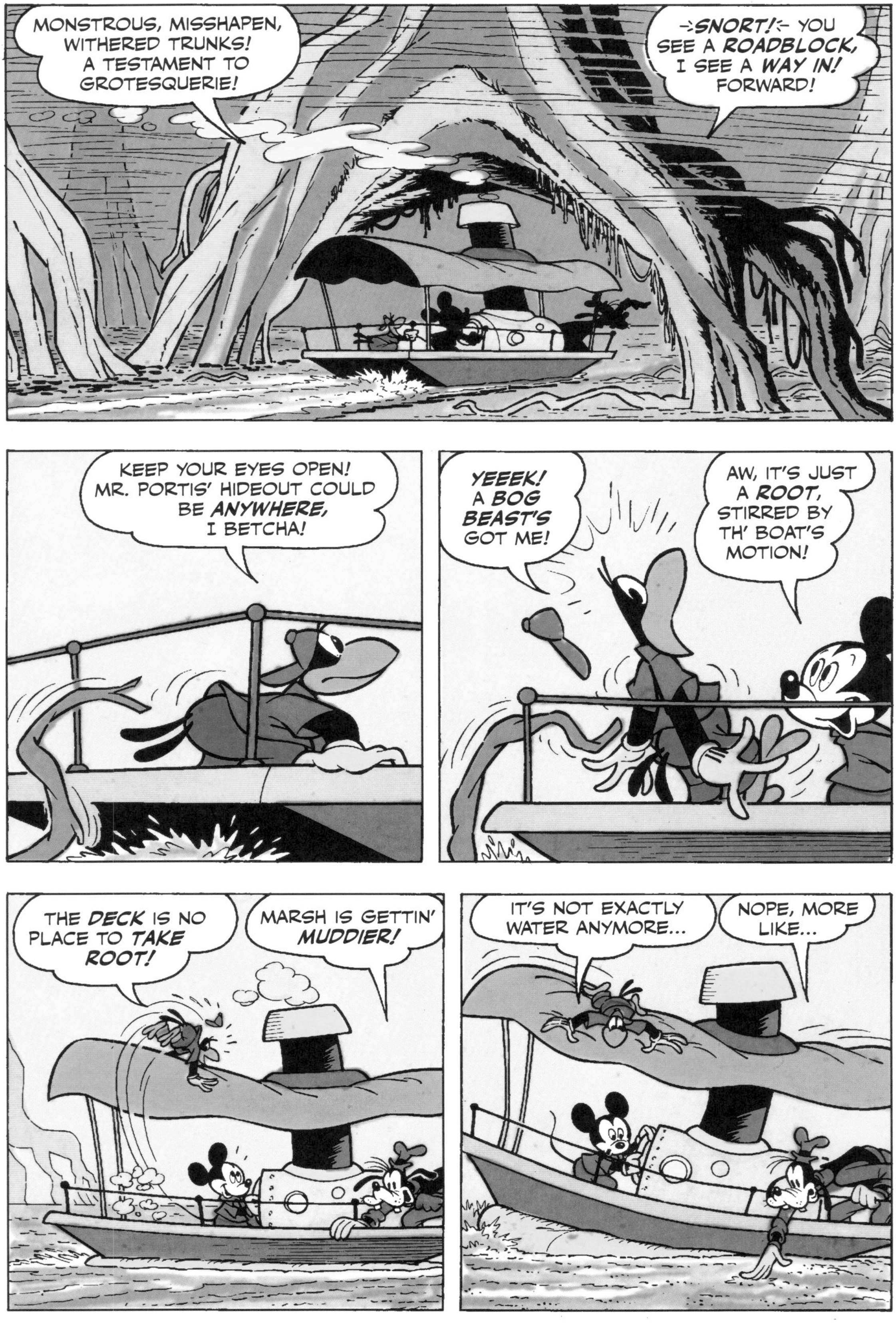
MONSTROUS, MISSHAPEN, WITHERED TRUNKS! A TESTAMENT TO GROTESQUERIE!
-SNORT!- YOU SEE A ROADBLOCK, I SEE A WAY IN! FORWARD!
KEEP YOUR EYES OPEN! MR. PORTIS' HIDEOUT COULD BE ANYWHERE, I BETCHA!
YEEEK! A BOG BEAST'S GOT ME!
AW, IT'S JUST A ROOT, STIRRED BY TH' BOAT'S MOTION!
THE DECK IS NO PLACE TO TAKE ROOT!
MARSH IS GETTIN' MUDDIER!
IT'S NOT EXACTLY WATER ANYMORE...
NOPE, MORE LIKE...

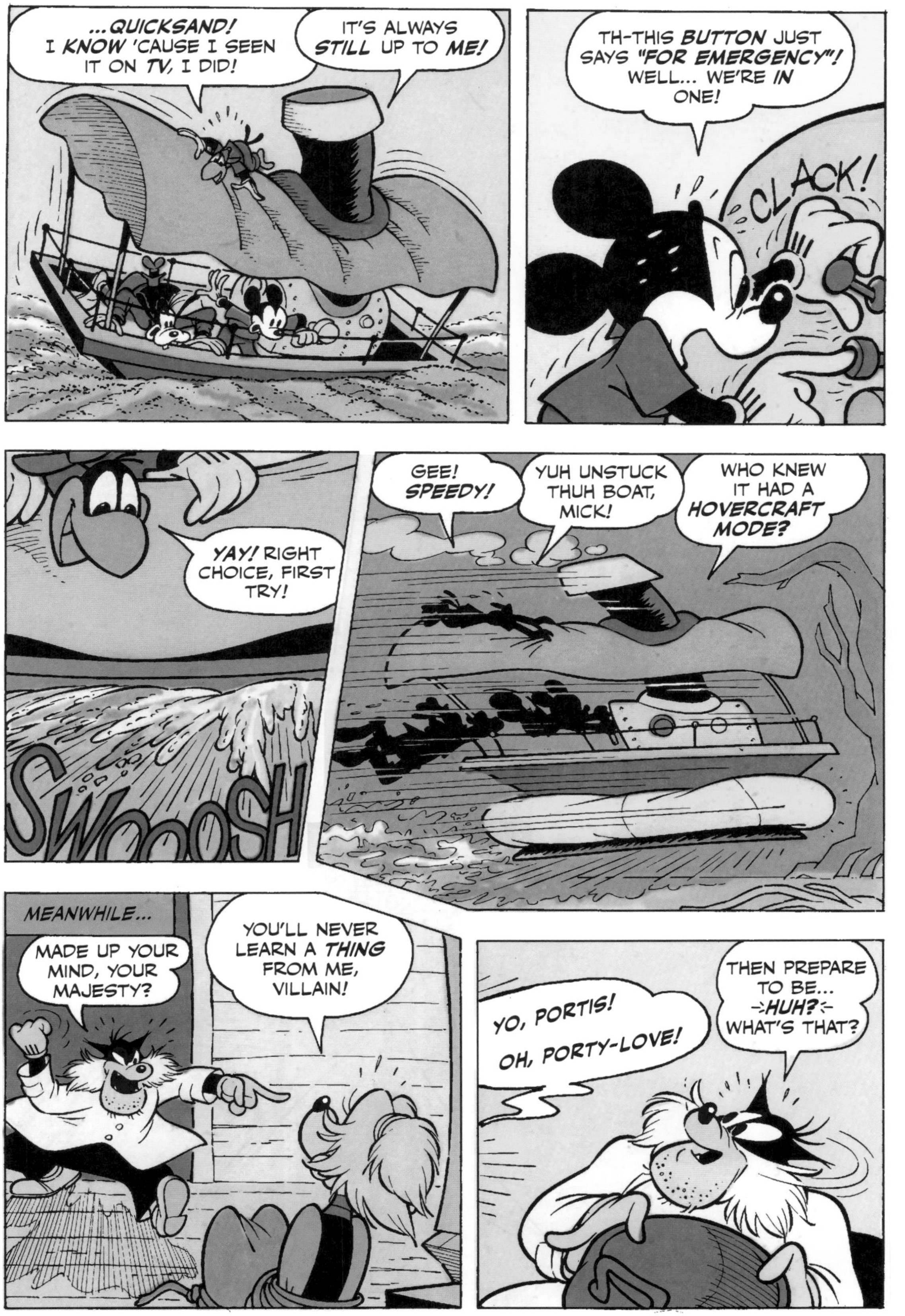
...QUICKSAND! I KNOW 'CAUSE I SEEN IT ON TV, I DID!
IT'S ALWAYS STILL UP TO ME!
TH-THIS BUTTON JUST SAYS "FOR EMERGENCY"! WELL... WE'RE IN ONE!
CLACK!
YAY! RIGHT CHOICE, FIRST TRY!
SWOOOSH
GEE! SPEEDY!
YUH UNSTUCK THUH BOAT, MICK!
WHO KNEW IT HAD A HOVERCRAFT MODE?
MEANWHILE...
MADE UP YOUR MIND, YOUR MAJESTY?
YOU'LL NEVER LEARN A THING FROM ME, VILLAIN!
YO, PORTIS!
OH, PORTY-LOVE!
THEN PREPARE TO BE... HUH? WHAT'S THAT?

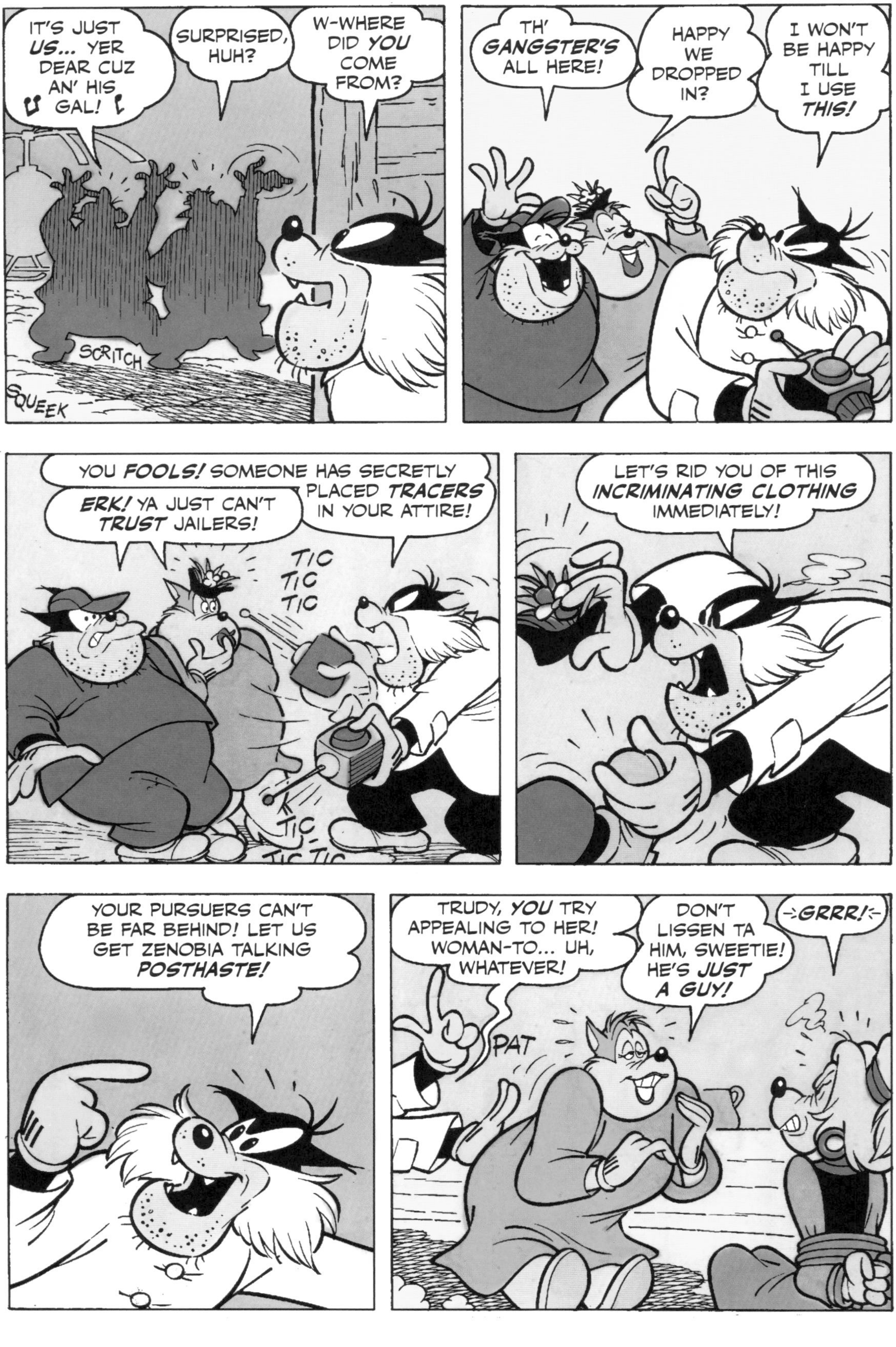
IT'S JUST US... YER DEAR CUZ AN' HIS GAL!
SURPRISED, HUH?
W-WHERE DID YOU COME FROM?
SCRITCH
SQUEEK
TH' GANGSTER'S ALL HERE!
HAPPY WE DROPPED IN?
I WON'T BE HAPPY TILL I USE THIS!
YOU FOOLS! SOMEONE HAS SECRETLY PLACED TRACERS IN YOUR ATTIRE!
ERK! YA JUST CAN'T TRUST JAILERS!
TIC TIC TIC
TIC
LET'S RID YOU OF THIS INCRIMINATING CLOTHING IMMEDIATELY!
YOUR PURSUERS CAN'T BE FAR BEHIND! LET US GET ZENOBIA TALKING POSTHASTE!
TRUDY, YOU TRY APPEALING TO HER! WOMAN-TO... UH, WHATEVER!
DON'T LISSEN TA HIM, SWEETIE! HE'S JUST A GUY!
GRRR!
PAT

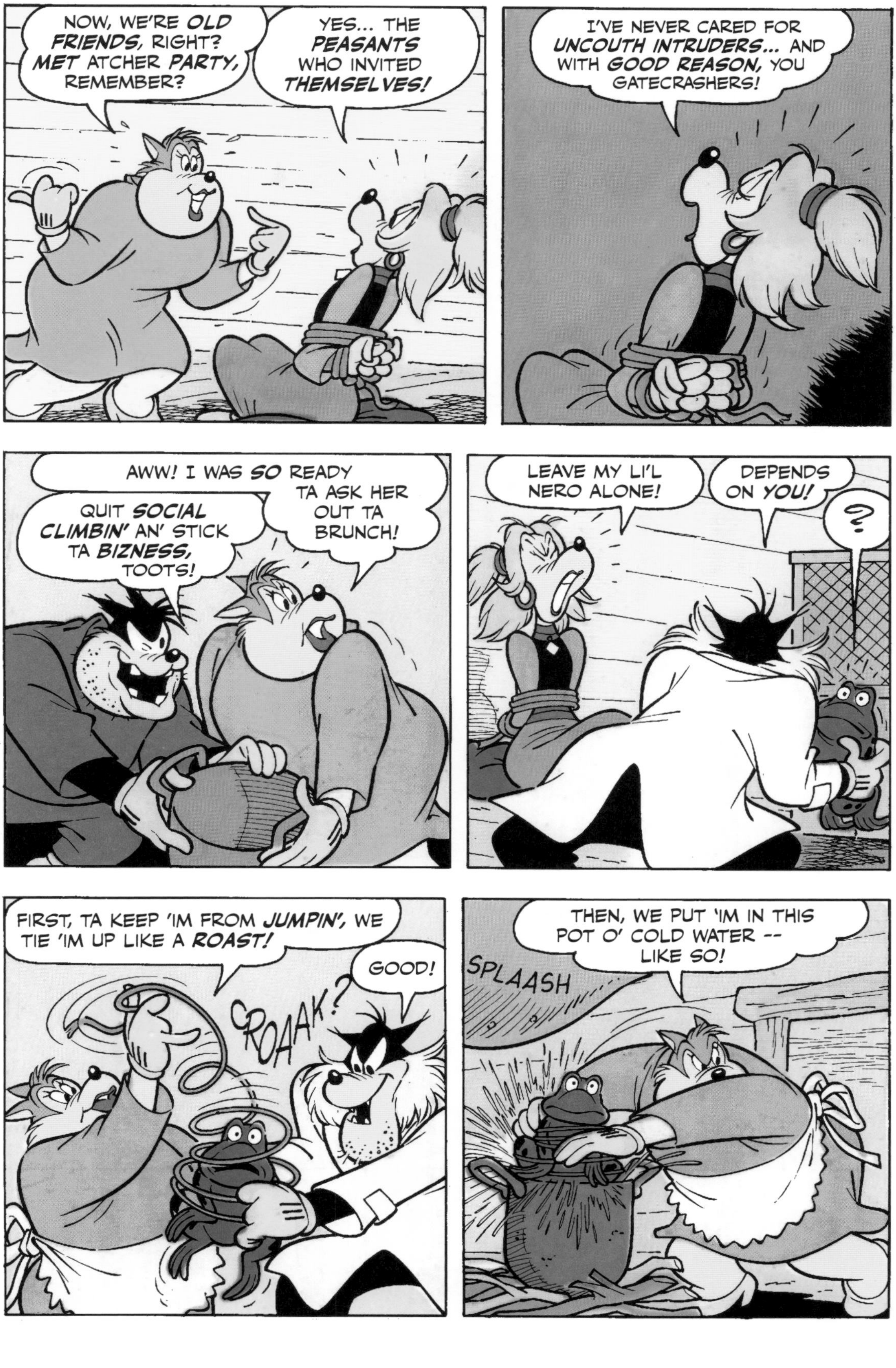
NOW, WE'RE OLD FRIENDS, RIGHT? MET ATCHER PARTY, REMEMBER?
YES... THE PEASANTS WHO INVITED THEMSELVES!
I'VE NEVER CARED FOR UNCOUTH INTRUDERS... AND WITH GOOD REASON, YOU GATECRASHERS!
AWW! I WAS SO READY TA ASK HER OUT TA BRUNCH!
QUIT SOCIAL CLIMBIN' AN' STICK TA BIZNESS, TOOTS!
LEAVE MY LI'L NERO ALONE!
DEPENDS ON YOU!
?
FIRST, TA KEEP 'IM FROM JUMPIN', WE TIE 'IM UP LIKE A ROAST!
CROAAK?
GOOD!
THEN, WE PUT 'IM IN THIS POT O' COLD WATER -- LIKE SO!
SPLAASH

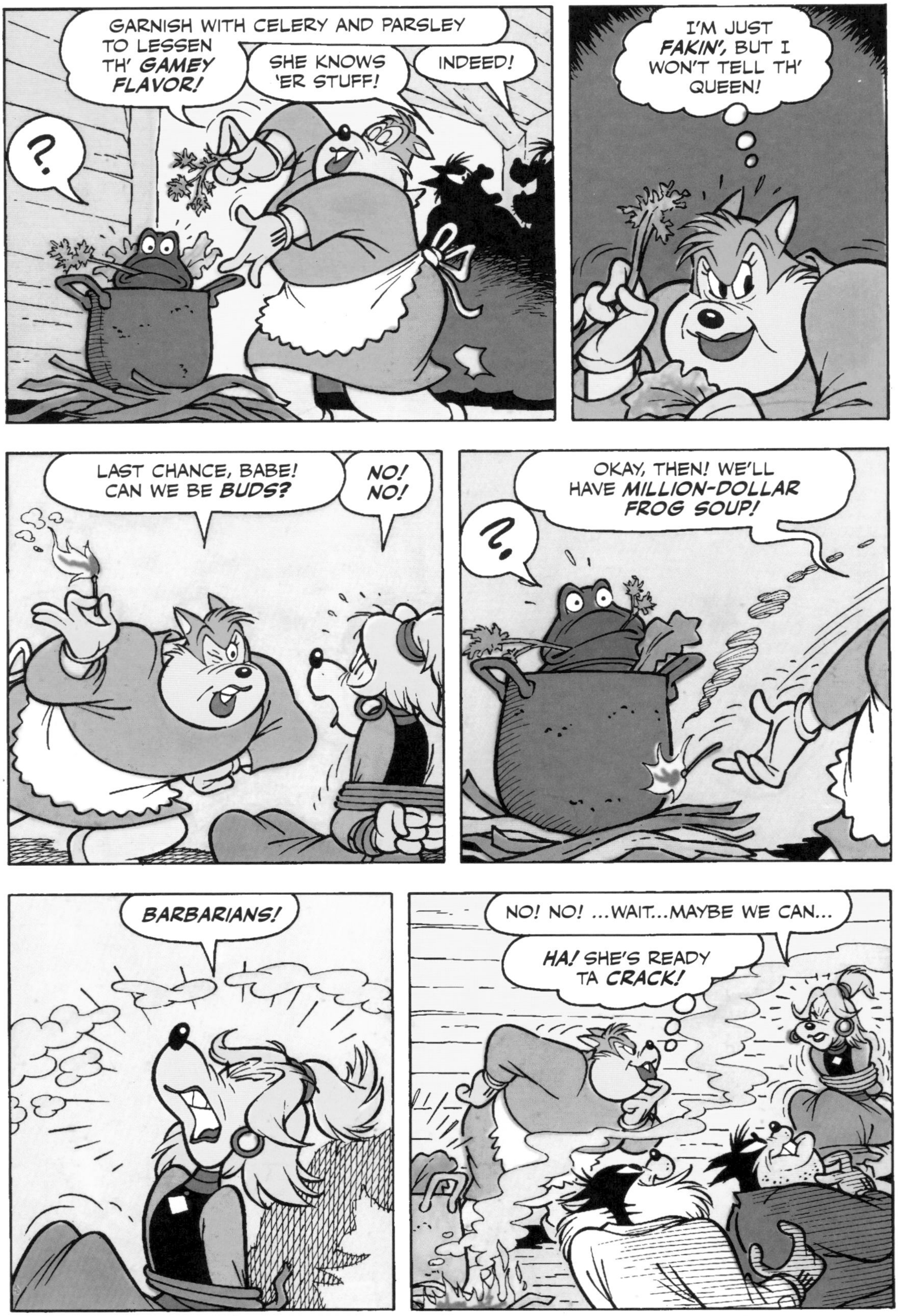
GARNISH WITH CELERY AND PARSLEY TO LESSEN TH' GAMEY FLAVOR!
SHE KNOWS 'ER STUFF!
INDEED!
?
I'M JUST FAKIN', BUT I WON'T TELL TH' QUEEN!
LAST CHANCE, BABE! CAN WE BE BUDS?
NO! NO!
OKAY, THEN! WE'LL HAVE MILLION-DOLLAR FROG SOUP!
?
BARBARIANS!
NO! NO! ...WAIT...MAYBE WE CAN...
HA! SHE'S READY TA CRACK!

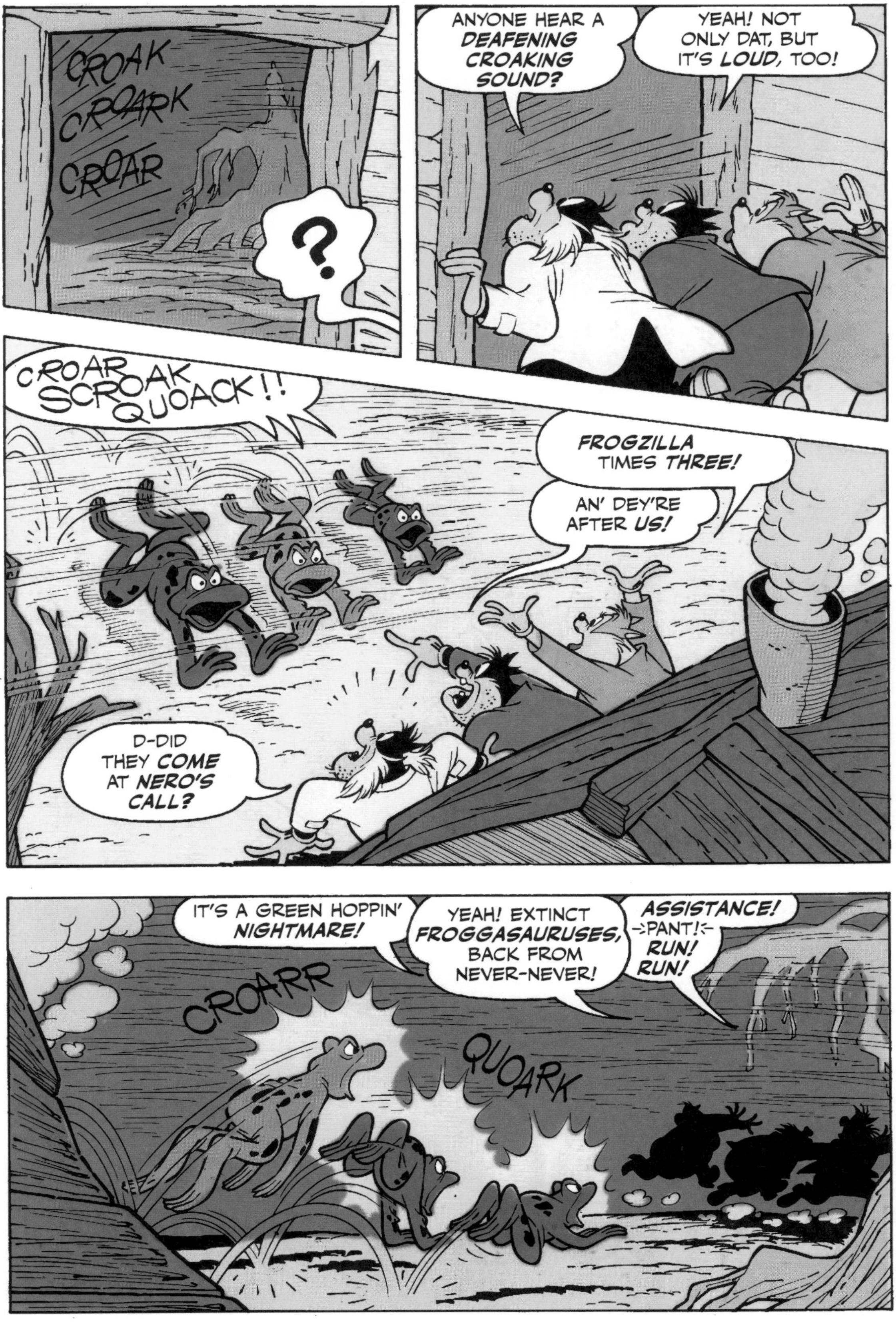

CROAK
CROARK
CROAR
?
ANYONE HEAR A DEAFENING CROAKING SOUND?
YEAH! NOT ONLY DAT, BUT IT'S LOUD, TOO!
CROAR SCROAK QUOACK!!
FROGZILLA TIMES THREE!
AN' DEY'RE AFTER US!
D-DID THEY COME AT NERO'S CALL?
IT'S A GREEN HOPPIN' NIGHTMARE!
YEAH! EXTINCT FROGGASAURUSES, BACK FROM NEVER-NEVER!
ASSISTANCE! -PANT!- RUN! RUN!
CROARR
QUOARK

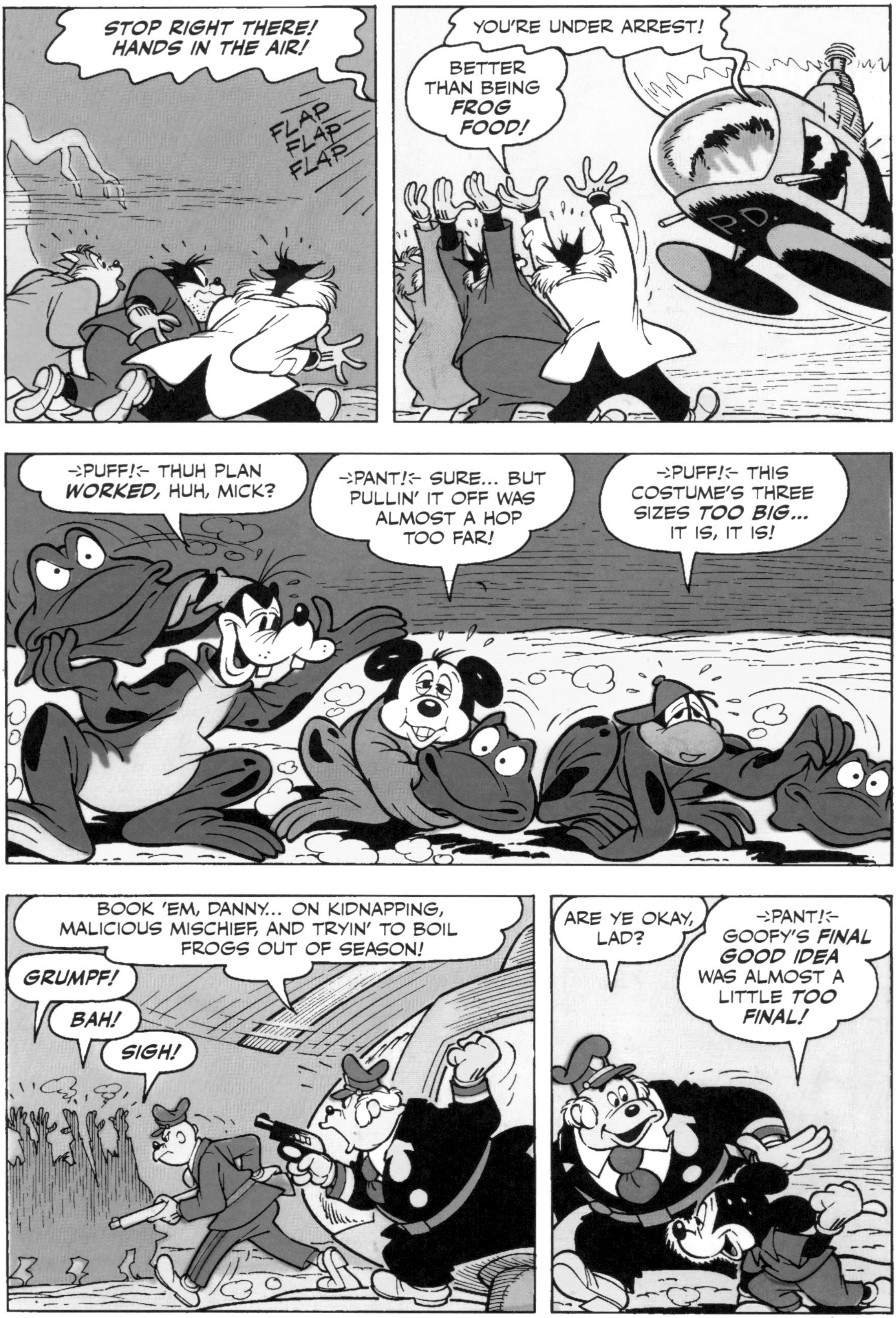
STOP RIGHT THERE! HANDS IN THE AIR!
FLAP FLAP FLAP
YOU'RE UNDER ARREST!
BETTER THAN BEING FROG FOOD!
P.D.
-PUFF!- THUH PLAN WORKED, HUH, MICK?
-PANT!- SURE... BUT PULLIN' IT OFF WAS ALMOST A HOP TOO FAR!
-PUFF!- THIS COSTUME'S THREE SIZES TOO BIG... IT IS, IT IS!
BOOK 'EM, DANNY... ON KIDNAPPING, MALICIOUS MISCHIEF, AND TRYIN' TO BOIL FROGS OUT OF SEASON!
GRUMPF!
BAH!
SIGH!
ARE YE OKAY, LAD?
-PANT!- GOOFY'S FINAL GOOD IDEA WAS ALMOST A LITTLE TOO FINAL!

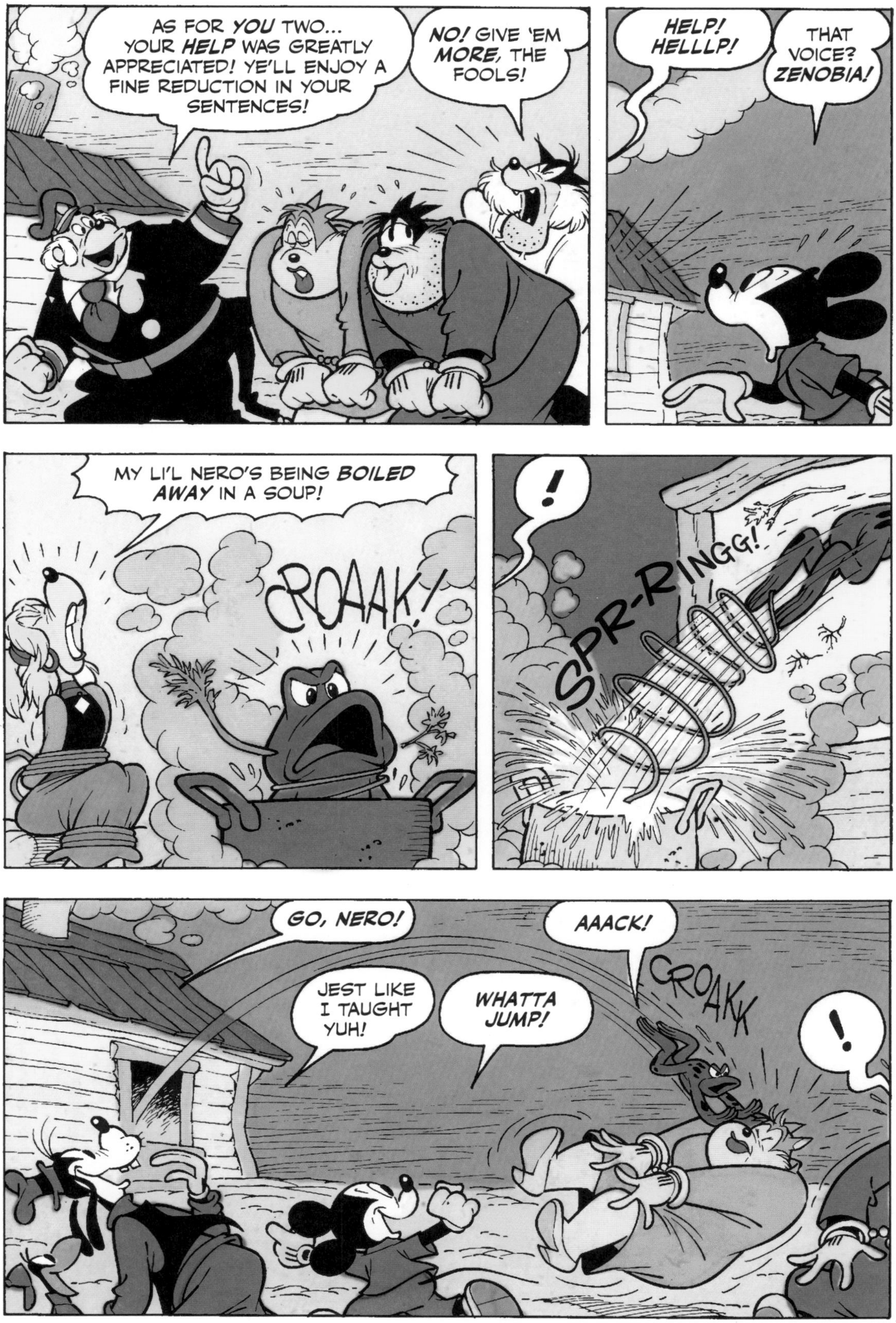
AS FOR YOU TWO... YOUR HELP WAS GREATLY APPRECIATED! YE'LL ENJOY A FINE REDUCTION IN YOUR SENTENCES!
NO! GIVE 'EM MORE, THE FOOLS!
HELP! HELLLP!
THAT VOICE? ZENOBIA!
MY LI'L NERO'S BEING BOILED AWAY IN A SOUP!
CROAAK!
!
SPR-RINGG!
GO, NERO!
AAACK!
JEST LIKE I TAUGHT YUH!
WHATTA JUMP!
CROAKK
!

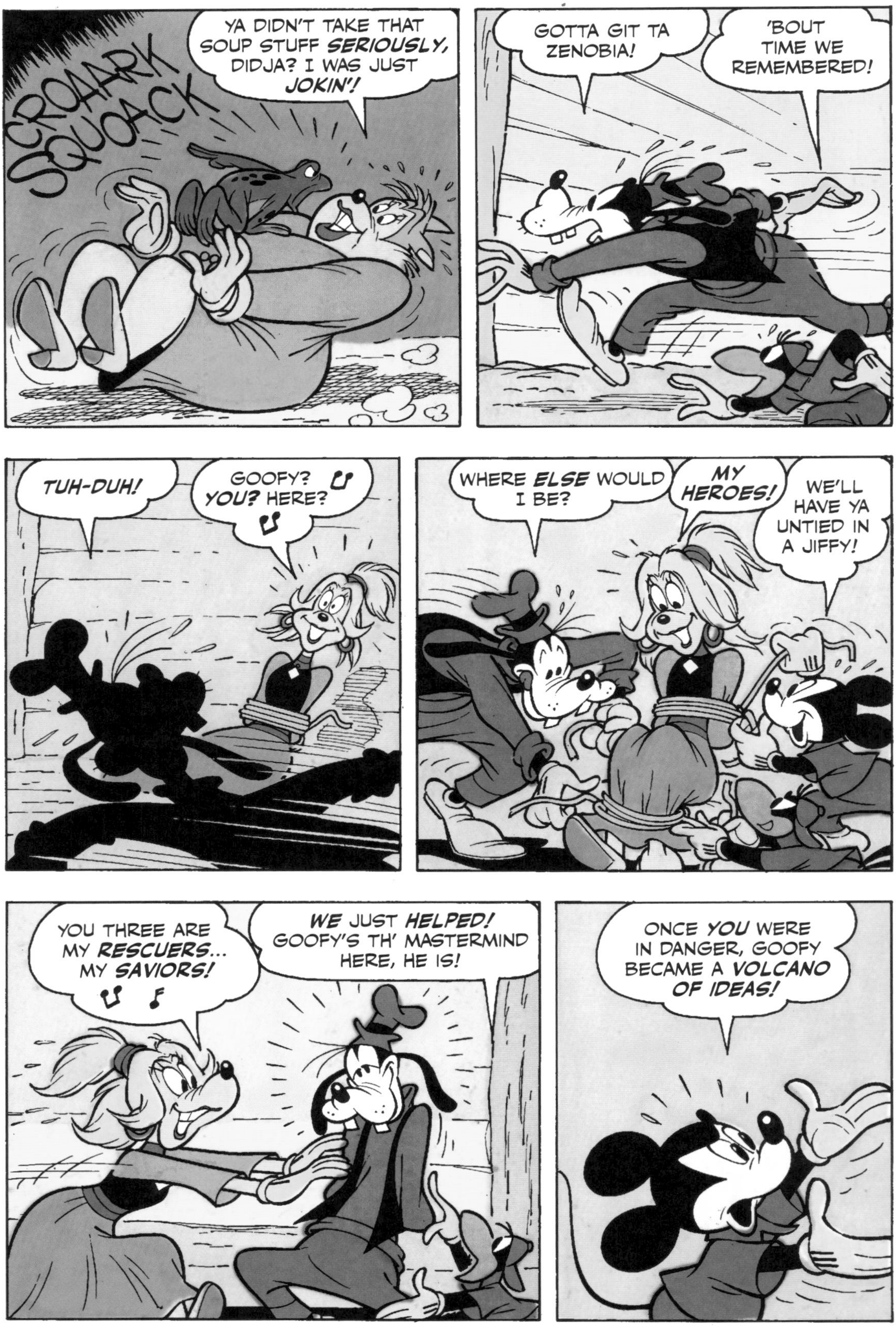
CROAARK SQUOACK
YA DIDN'T TAKE THAT SOUP STUFF SERIOUSLY, DIDJA? I WAS JUST JOKIN'!
GOTTA GIT TA ZENOBIA!
'BOUT TIME WE REMEMBERED!
TUH-DUH!
GOOFY? YOU? HERE?
WHERE ELSE WOULD I BE?
MY HEROES!
WE'LL HAVE YA UNTIED IN A JIFFY!
YOU THREE ARE MY RESCUERS... MY SAVIORS!
WE JUST HELPED! GOOFY'S TH' MASTERMIND HERE, HE IS!
ONCE YOU WERE IN DANGER, GOOFY BECAME A VOLCANO OF IDEAS!

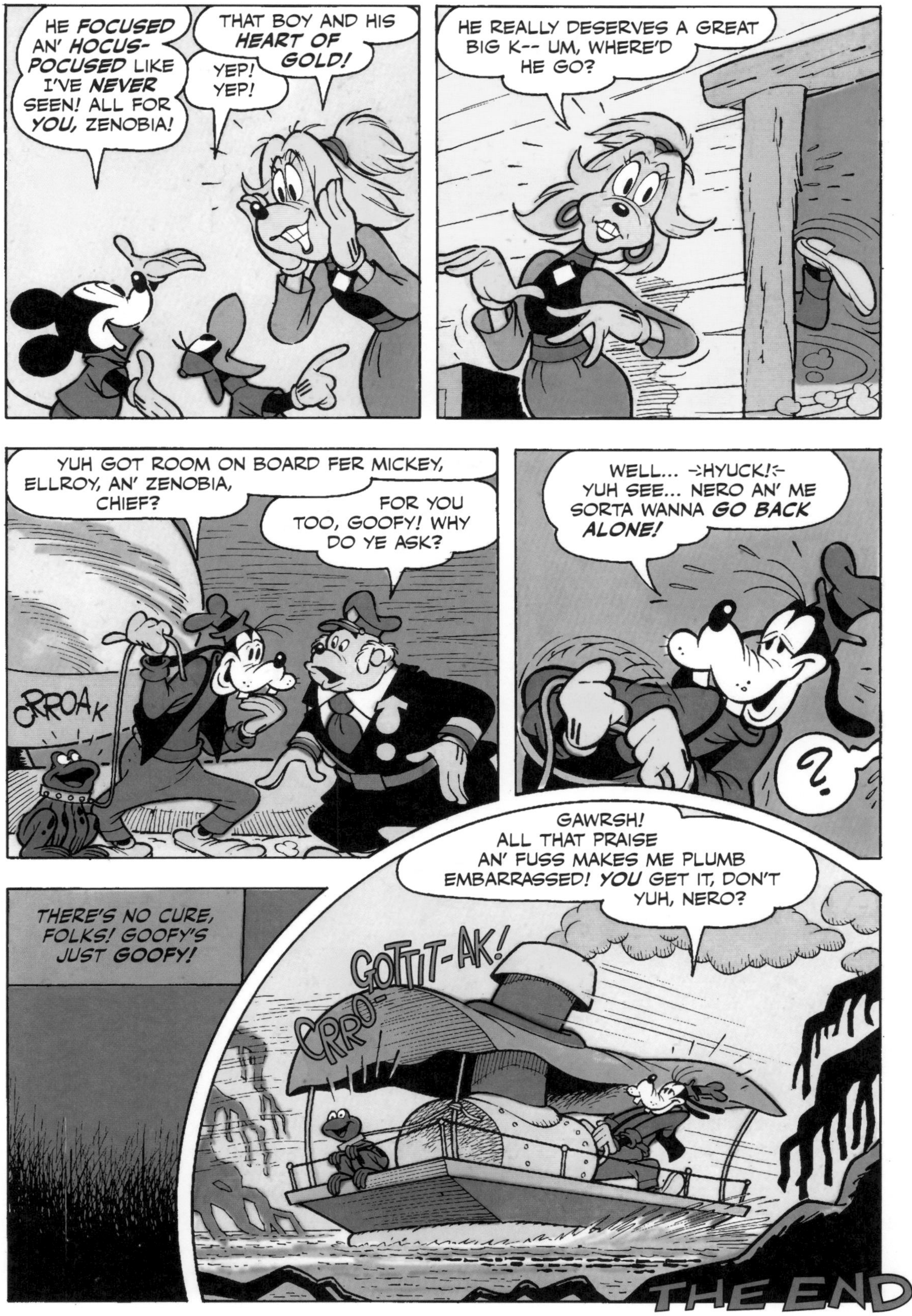
HE FOCUSED AN' HOCUS-POCUSED LIKE I'VE NEVER SEEN! ALL FOR YOU, ZENOBIA!
THAT BOY AND HIS HEART OF GOLD!
YEP! YEP!
HE REALLY DESERVES A GREAT BIG K-- UM, WHERE'D HE GO?
YUH GOT ROOM ON BOARD FER MICKEY, ELLROY, AN' ZENOBIA, CHIEF?
FOR YOU TOO, GOOFY! WHY DO YE ASK?
CRROAK
WELL... HYUCK! YUH SEE... NERO AN' ME SORTA WANNA GO BACK ALONE!
?
THERE'S NO CURE, FOLKS! GOOFY'S JUST GOOFY!
GAWRSH! ALL THAT PRAISE AN' FUSS MAKES ME PLUMB EMBARRASSED! YOU GET IT, DON'T YUH, NERO?
CRRO-GOTTIT-AK!
THE END

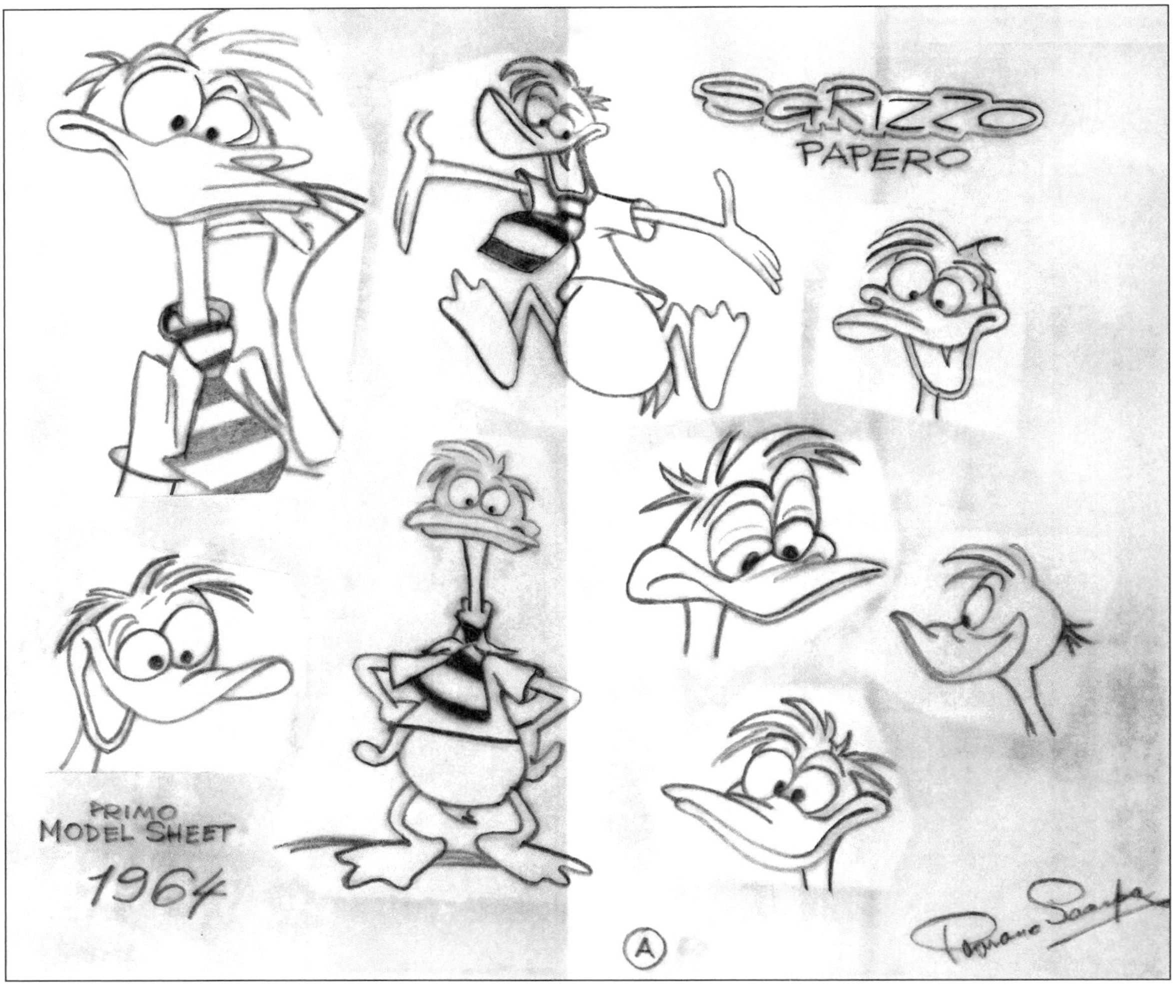
SGRIZZO
PAPERO
PRIMO
MODEL SHEET
1964
Romano Scarpa

The first model sheet for "Sgrizzo Papero," created by Romano Scarpa in 1964; his English name of Kildare Coot was greenlit by Scarpa and Italian Disney comics colleagues in 1998. Image courtesy Disney Publishing Worldwide.

Family Ties

GREAT MINDS think alike. In mid-1964, Romano Scarpa created a new character: Kildare Coot, Donald Duck's screwball cousin, who would debut in October in the Italian Disney comic book *Topolino*. At the start of the year, however, California-based Disney comics writer Dick Kinney had already developed an eccentric cousin for Donald — the beatnik-inspired Fethry Duck. In print, Fethry beat Kildare to the punch, making his *Topolino* debut in August. In effect, two Disney masters, an ocean apart and unbeknownst to each other, simultaneously conceived nerdy, obsessive, slightly unhinged relatives for Donald, both even related to him the same way.

Kildare is the loonier of the two — first seen being discharged from a hospital after a medical team judges him "perfectly clear-headed," perhaps a bit too hastily. Entering Donald's house like a whirlwind, the wacky duck at first causes chaos, but redeems himself by battling a counterfeiter — whom Scarpa designed as a relative of the pig-faced villain whom Carl Barks had been portraying, under various aliases, since 1957. •

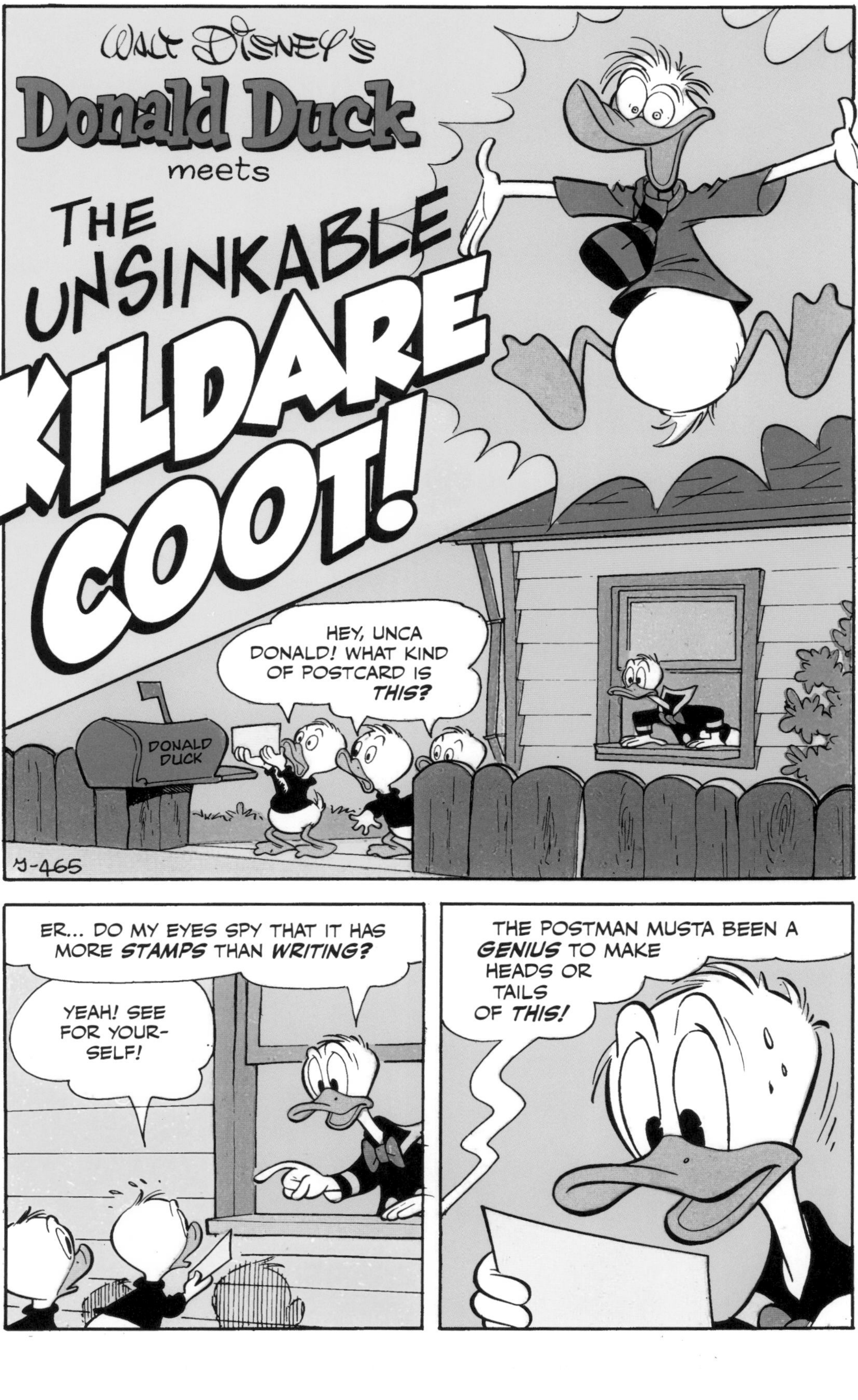
WALT DISNEY'S
Donald Duck
meets
THE UNSINKABLE KILDARE COOT!
HEY, UNCA DONALD! WHAT KIND OF POSTCARD IS THIS?
DONALD DUCK
G-465
ER... DO MY EYES SPY THAT IT HAS MORE STAMPS THAN WRITING?
YEAH! SEE FOR YOUR-SELF!
THE POSTMAN MUSTA BEEN A GENIUS TO MAKE HEADS OR TAILS OF THIS!

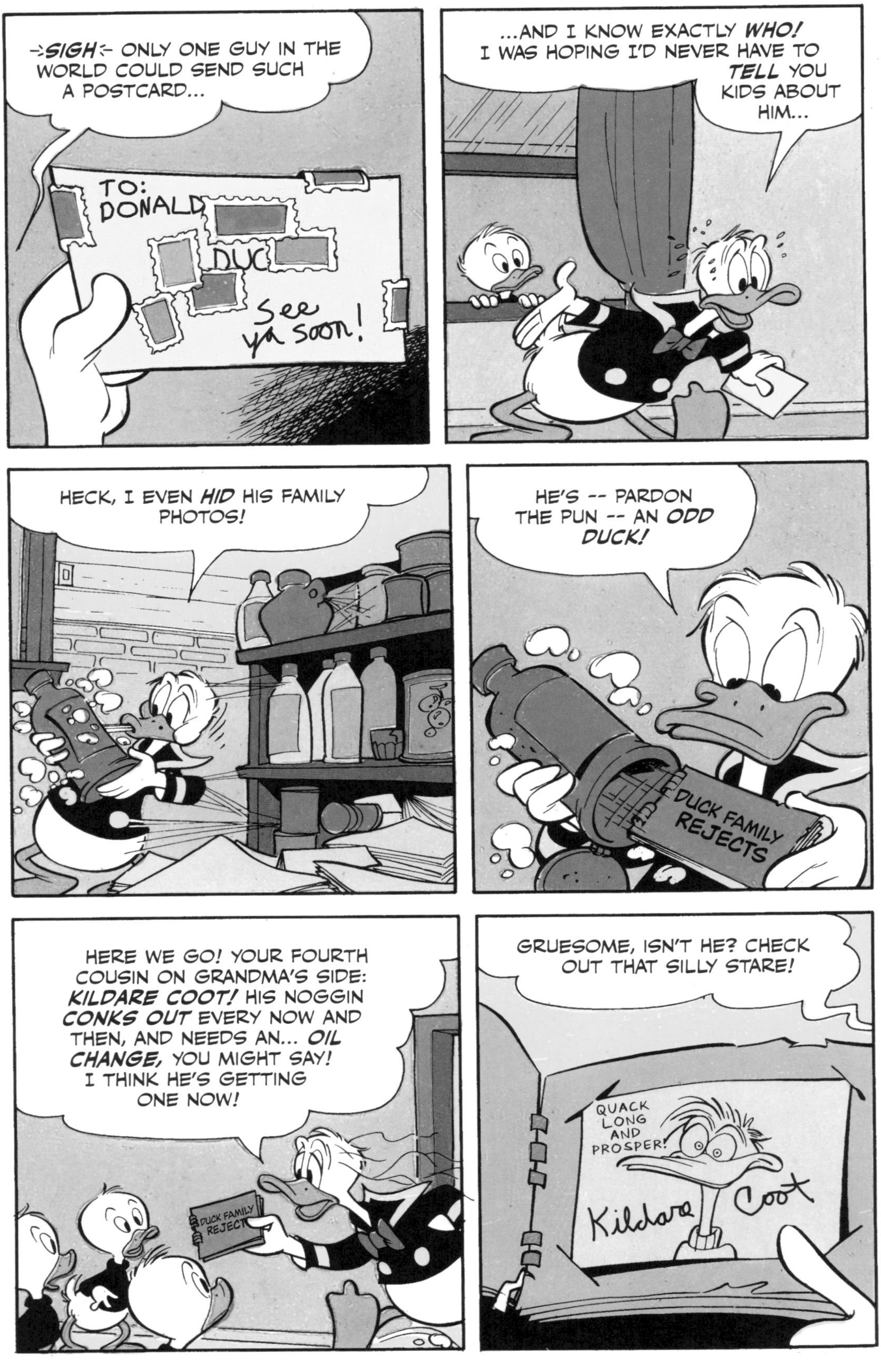

-SIGH- ONLY ONE GUY IN THE WORLD COULD SEND SUCH A POSTCARD...
TO: DONALD DUC
See ya soon!
...AND I KNOW EXACTLY WHO! I WAS HOPING I'D NEVER HAVE TO TELL YOU KIDS ABOUT HIM...
HECK, I EVEN HID HIS FAMILY PHOTOS!
HE'S -- PARDON THE PUN -- AN ODD DUCK!
DUCK FAMILY REJECTS
HERE WE GO! YOUR FOURTH COUSIN ON GRANDMA'S SIDE: KILDARE COOT! HIS NOGGIN CONKS OUT EVERY NOW AND THEN, AND NEEDS AN... OIL CHANGE, YOU MIGHT SAY! I THINK HE'S GETTING ONE NOW!
DUCK FAMILY REJECT
GRUESOME, ISN'T HE? CHECK OUT THAT SILLY STARE!
QUACK LONG AND PROSPER!
Kildare Coot

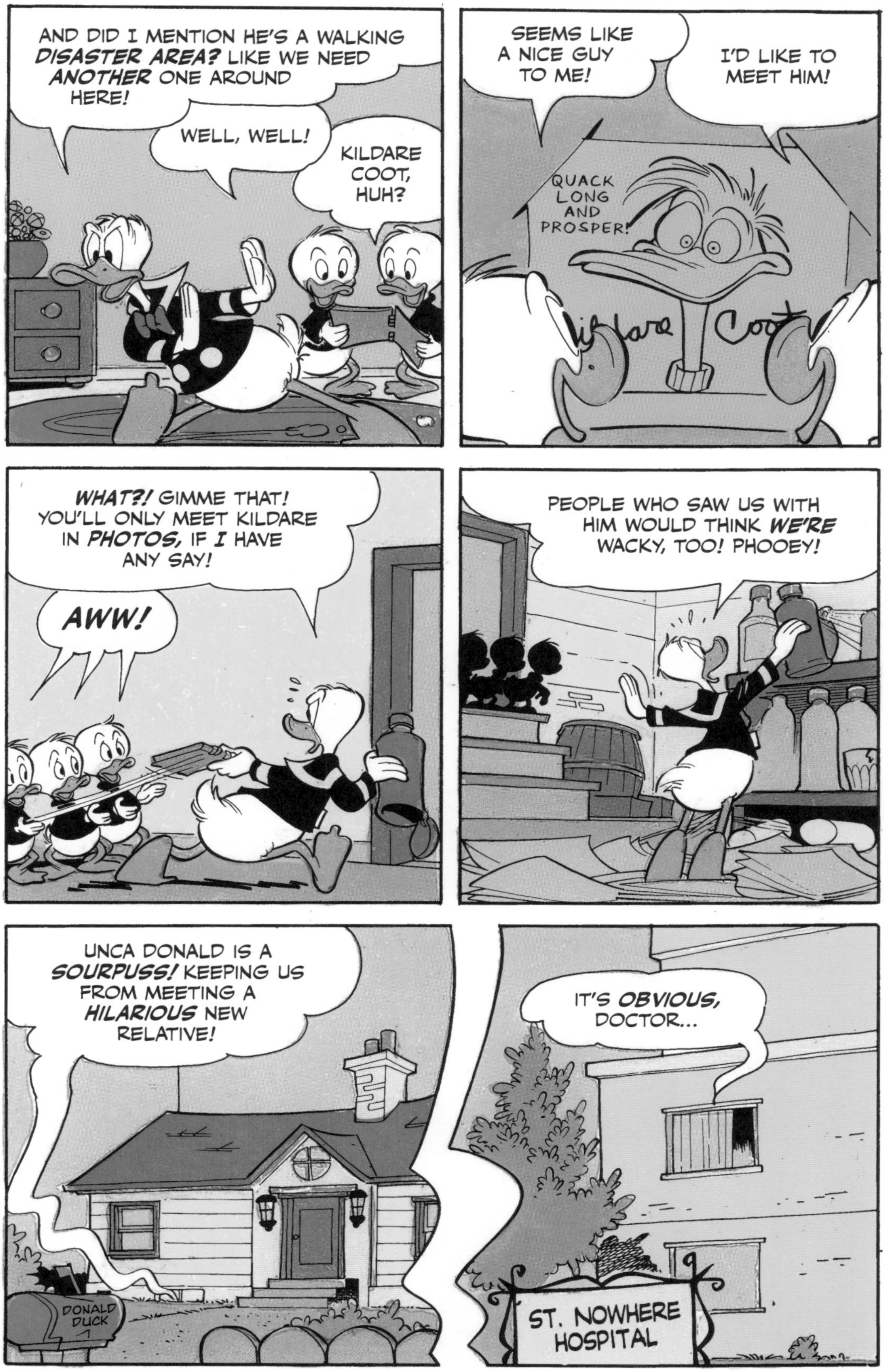
AND DID I MENTION HE'S A WALKING *DISASTER AREA?* LIKE WE NEED *ANOTHER* ONE AROUND HERE!
WELL, WELL!
KILDARE COOT, HUH?
SEEMS LIKE A NICE GUY TO ME!
I'D LIKE TO MEET HIM!
QUACK LONG AND PROSPER!
WHAT?! GIMME THAT! YOU'LL ONLY MEET KILDARE IN *PHOTOS,* IF *I* HAVE ANY SAY!
AWW!
PEOPLE WHO SAW US WITH HIM WOULD THINK *WE'RE* WACKY, TOO! PHOOEY!
UNCA DONALD IS A *SOURPUSS!* KEEPING US FROM MEETING A *HILARIOUS* NEW RELATIVE!
DONALD DUCK
IT'S *OBVIOUS,* DOCTOR...
ST. NOWHERE HOSPITAL

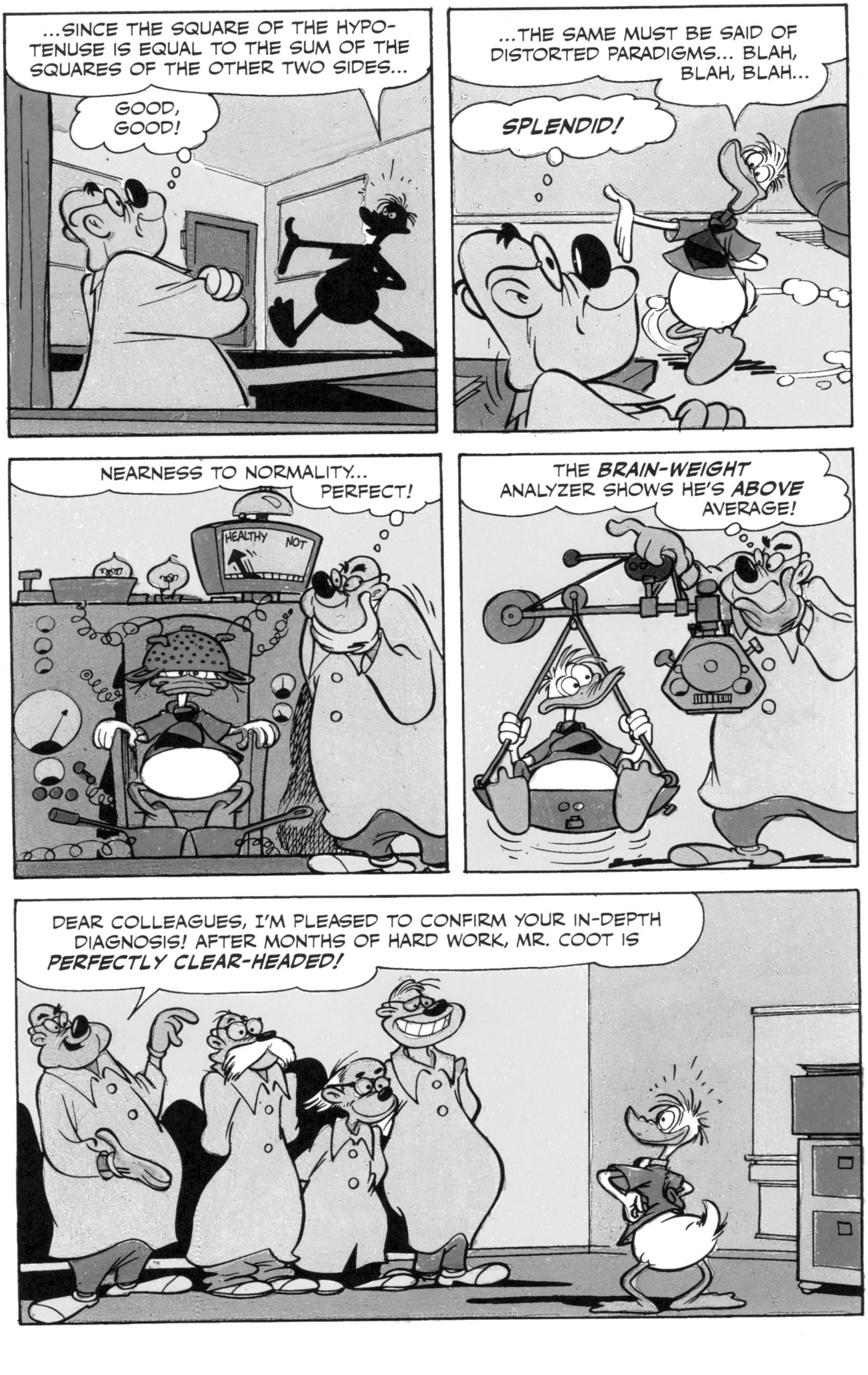

...SINCE THE SQUARE OF THE HYPO-TENUSE IS EQUAL TO THE SUM OF THE SQUARES OF THE OTHER TWO SIDES...
GOOD, GOOD!
...THE SAME MUST BE SAID OF DISTORTED PARADIGMS... BLAH, BLAH, BLAH...
SPLENDID!
NEARNESS TO NORMALITY... PERFECT!
HEALTHY
NOT
THE BRAIN-WEIGHT ANALYZER SHOWS HE'S ABOVE AVERAGE!
DEAR COLLEAGUES, I'M PLEASED TO CONFIRM YOUR IN-DEPTH DIAGNOSIS! AFTER MONTHS OF HARD WORK, MR. COOT IS PERFECTLY CLEAR-HEADED!

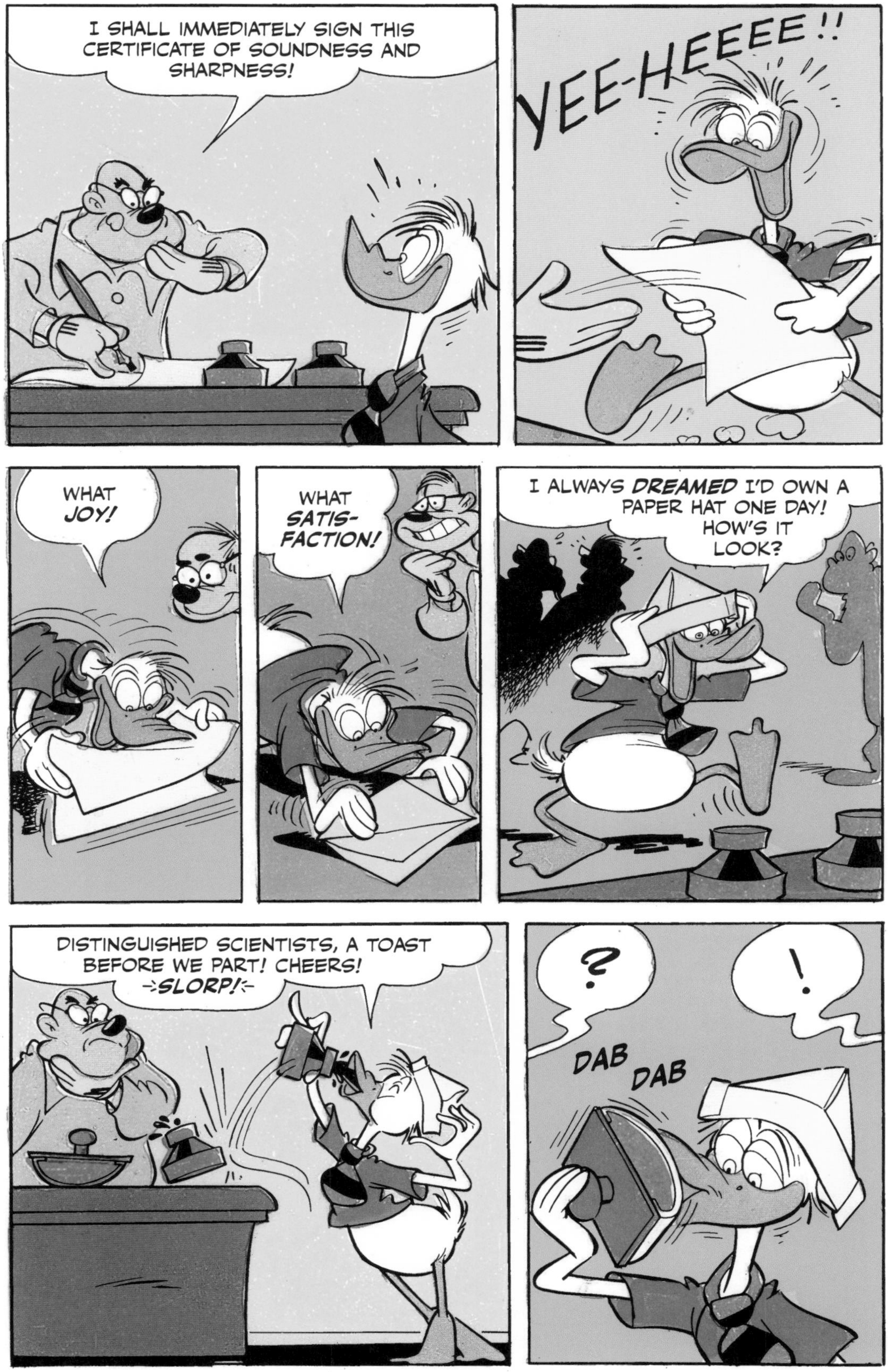
I SHALL IMMEDIATELY SIGN THIS CERTIFICATE OF SOUNDNESS AND SHARPNESS!
YEE-HEEEEE!!
WHAT JOY!
WHAT SATIS-FACTION!
I ALWAYS DREAMED I'D OWN A PAPER HAT ONE DAY! HOW'S IT LOOK?
DISTINGUISHED SCIENTISTS, A TOAST BEFORE WE PART! CHEERS! -SLORP!-
?
!
DAB DAB

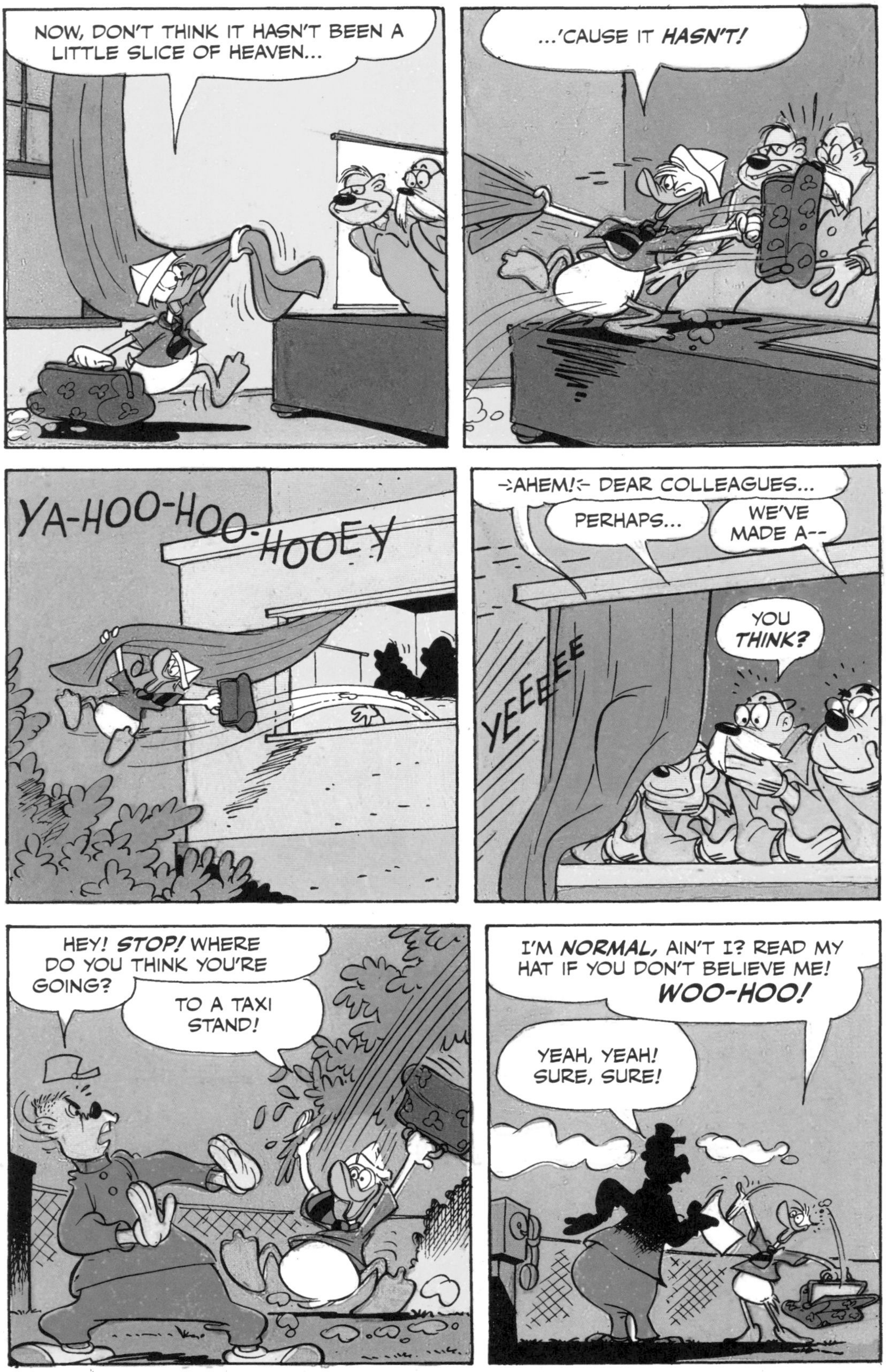
NOW, DON'T THINK IT HASN'T BEEN A LITTLE SLICE OF HEAVEN...
...'CAUSE IT **HASN'T!**
YA-HOO-HOO-HOOEY
AHEM! DEAR COLLEAGUES...
PERHAPS...
WE'VE MADE A--
YOU **THINK?**
YEEEEEE
HEY! **STOP!** WHERE DO YOU THINK YOU'RE GOING?
TO A TAXI STAND!
I'M **NORMAL,** AIN'T I? READ MY HAT IF YOU DON'T BELIEVE ME! **WOO-HOO!**
YEAH, YEAH! SURE, SURE!

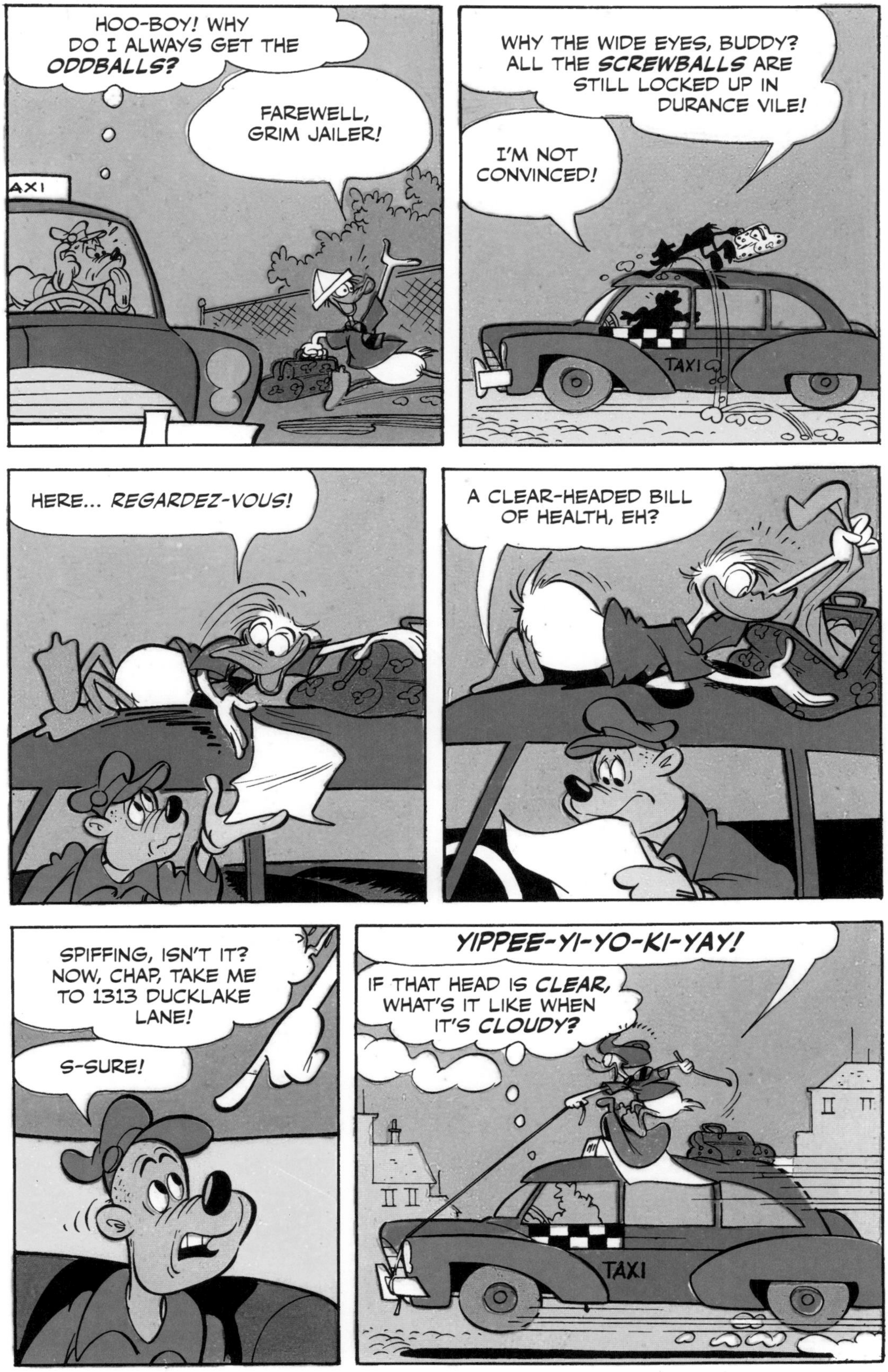
HOO-BOY! WHY DO I ALWAYS GET THE ODDBALLS?
FAREWELL, GRIM JAILER!
AXI
WHY THE WIDE EYES, BUDDY? ALL THE SCREWBALLS ARE STILL LOCKED UP IN DURANCE VILE!
I'M NOT CONVINCED!
TAXI
HERE... REGARDEZ-VOUS!
A CLEAR-HEADED BILL OF HEALTH, EH?
SPIFFING, ISN'T IT? NOW, CHAP, TAKE ME TO 1313 DUCKLAKE LANE!
S-SURE!
YIPPEE-YI-YO-KI-YAY!
IF THAT HEAD IS CLEAR, WHAT'S IT LIKE WHEN IT'S CLOUDY?
TAXI

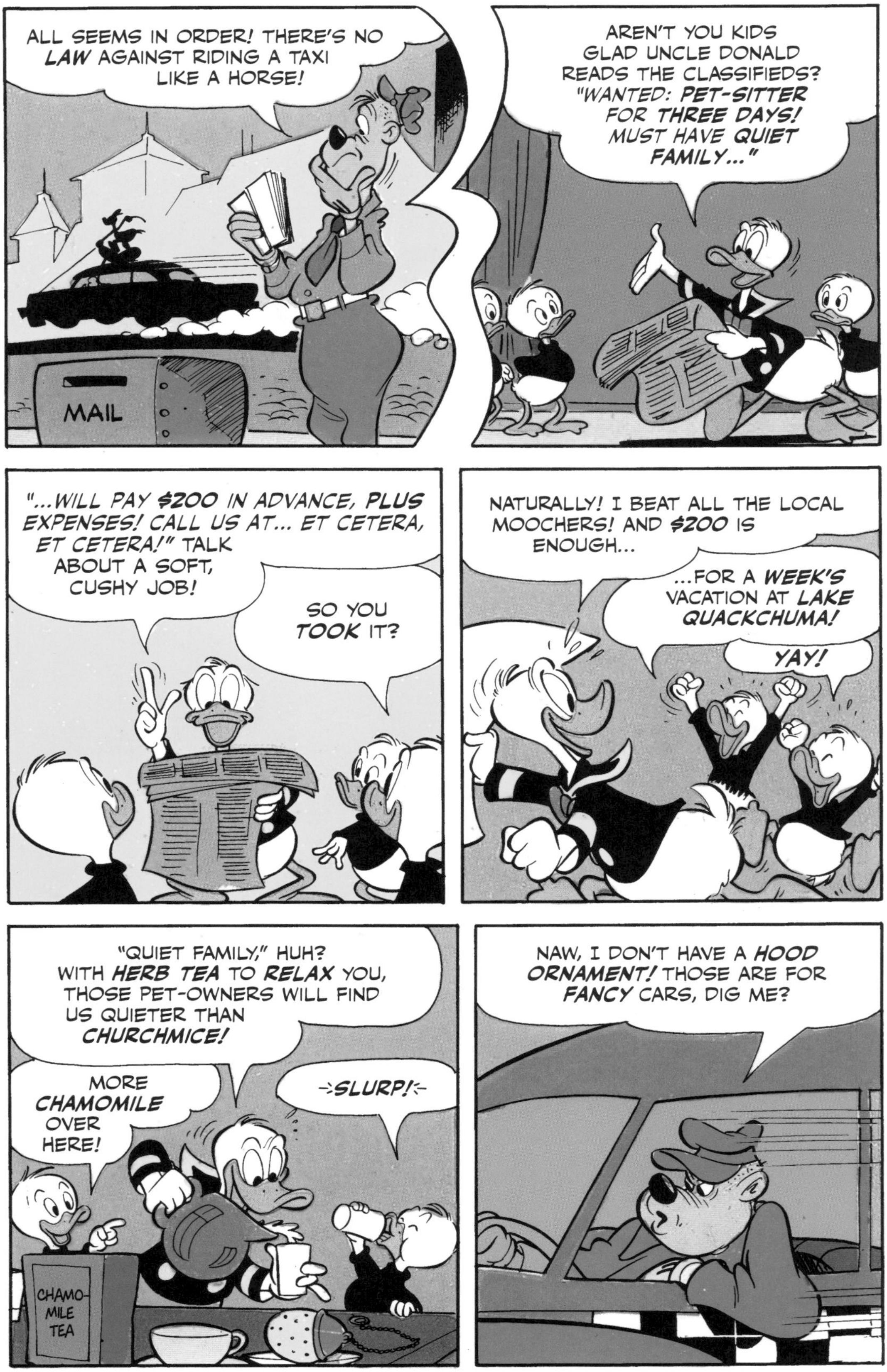
ALL SEEMS IN ORDER! THERE'S NO LAW AGAINST RIDING A TAXI LIKE A HORSE!
MAIL
AREN'T YOU KIDS GLAD UNCLE DONALD READS THE CLASSIFIEDS? "WANTED: PET-SITTER FOR THREE DAYS! MUST HAVE QUIET FAMILY..."
"...WILL PAY $200 IN ADVANCE, PLUS EXPENSES! CALL US AT... ET CETERA, ET CETERA!" TALK ABOUT A SOFT, CUSHY JOB!
SO YOU TOOK IT?
NATURALLY! I BEAT ALL THE LOCAL MOOCHERS! AND $200 IS ENOUGH...
...FOR A WEEK'S VACATION AT LAKE QUACKCHUMA!
YAY!
"QUIET FAMILY," HUH? WITH HERB TEA TO RELAX YOU, THOSE PET-OWNERS WILL FIND US QUIETER THAN CHURCHMICE!
MORE CHAMOMILE OVER HERE!
SLURP!
CHAMO-MILE TEA
NAW, I DON'T HAVE A HOOD ORNAMENT! THOSE ARE FOR FANCY CARS, DIG ME?

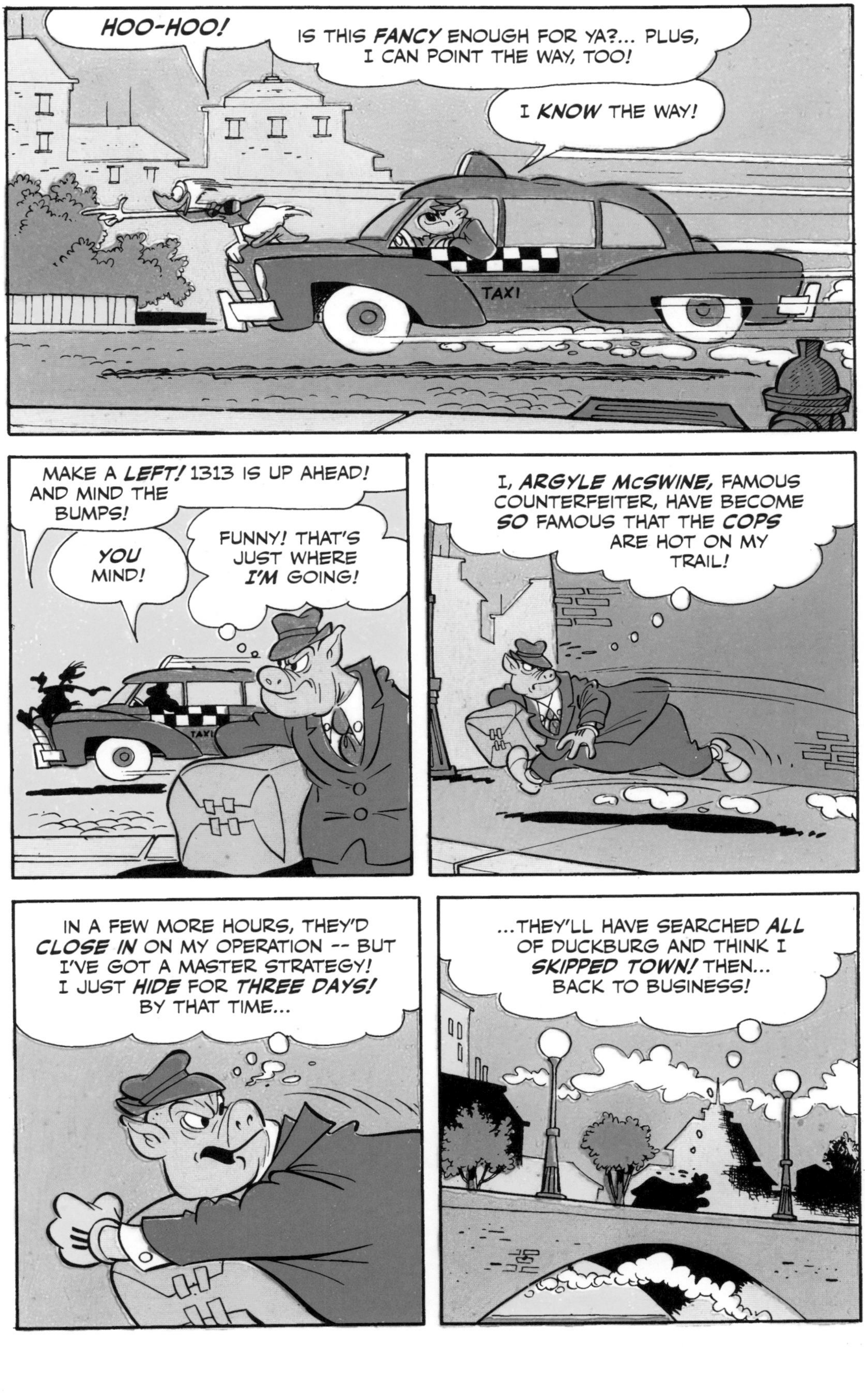
HOO-HOO!
IS THIS FANCY ENOUGH FOR YA?... PLUS, I CAN POINT THE WAY, TOO!
I KNOW THE WAY!
TAXI
MAKE A LEFT! 1313 IS UP AHEAD! AND MIND THE BUMPS!
YOU MIND!
FUNNY! THAT'S JUST WHERE I'M GOING!
I, ARGYLE McSWINE, FAMOUS COUNTERFEITER, HAVE BECOME SO FAMOUS THAT THE COPS ARE HOT ON MY TRAIL!
IN A FEW MORE HOURS, THEY'D CLOSE IN ON MY OPERATION -- BUT I'VE GOT A MASTER STRATEGY! I JUST HIDE FOR THREE DAYS! BY THAT TIME...
...THEY'LL HAVE SEARCHED ALL OF DUCKBURG AND THINK I SKIPPED TOWN! THEN... BACK TO BUSINESS!

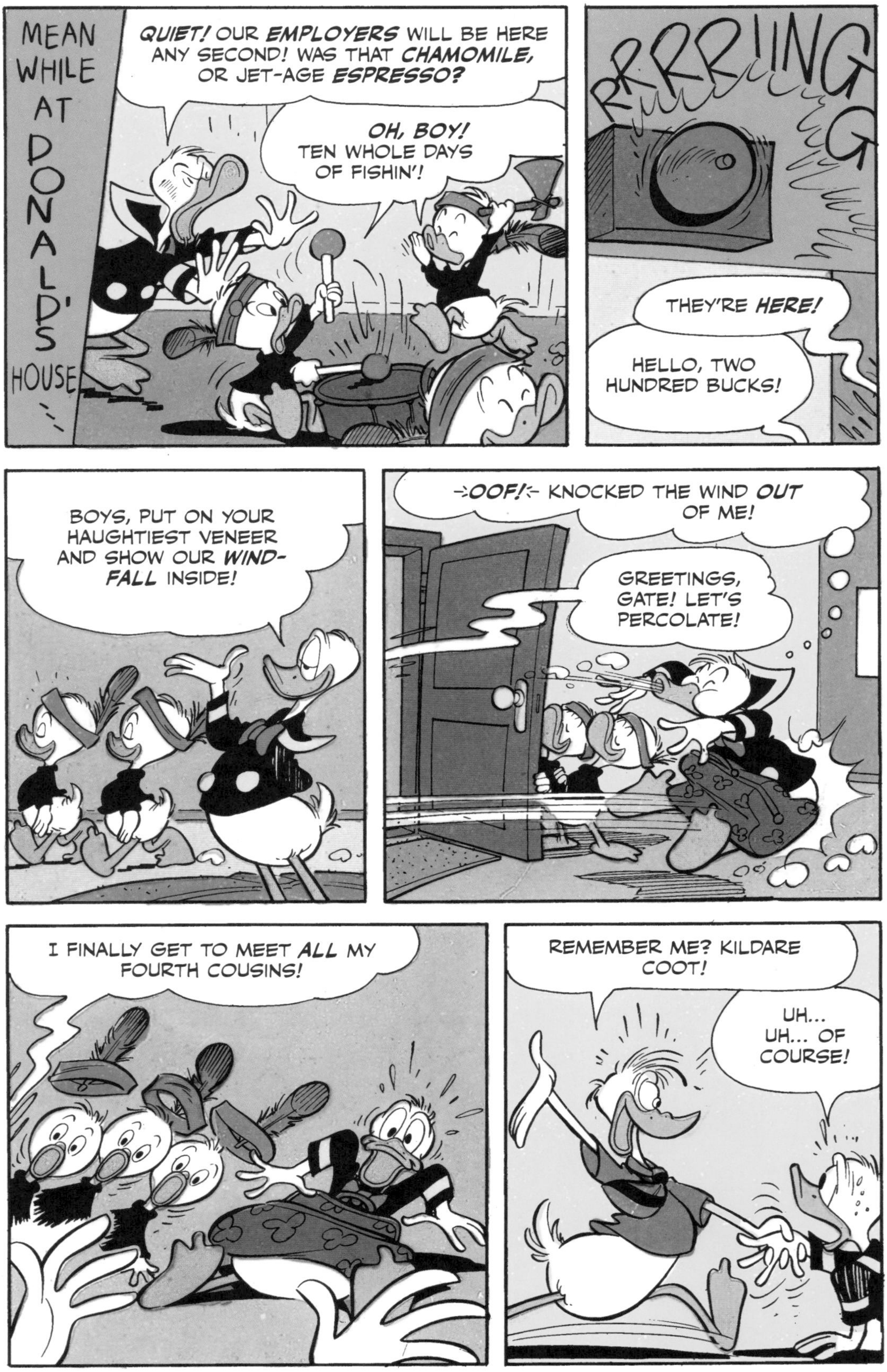
MEAN WHILE AT DONALD'S HOUSE
QUIET! OUR EMPLOYERS WILL BE HERE ANY SECOND! WAS THAT CHAMOMILE, OR JET-AGE ESPRESSO?
OH, BOY! TEN WHOLE DAYS OF FISHIN'!
RRRRIIING
THEY'RE HERE!
HELLO, TWO HUNDRED BUCKS!
BOYS, PUT ON YOUR HAUGHTIEST VENEER AND SHOW OUR WINDFALL INSIDE!
OOF! KNOCKED THE WIND OUT OF ME!
GREETINGS, GATE! LET'S PERCOLATE!
I FINALLY GET TO MEET ALL MY FOURTH COUSINS!
REMEMBER ME? KILDARE COOT!
UH... UH... OF COURSE!

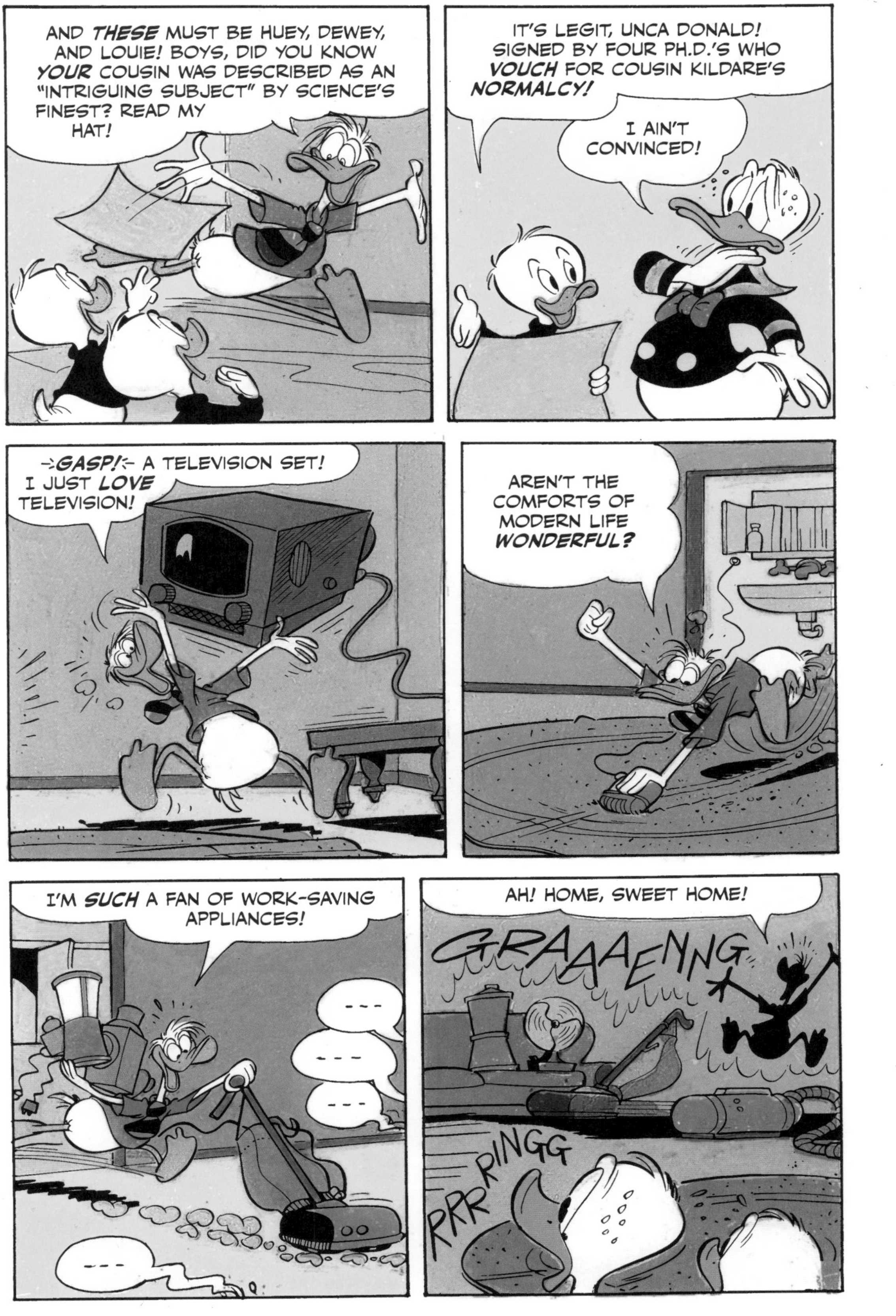

AND THESE MUST BE HUEY, DEWEY, AND LOUIE! BOYS, DID YOU KNOW YOUR COUSIN WAS DESCRIBED AS AN "INTRIGUING SUBJECT" BY SCIENCE'S FINEST? READ MY HAT!
IT'S LEGIT, UNCA DONALD! SIGNED BY FOUR PH.D.'S WHO VOUCH FOR COUSIN KILDARE'S NORMALCY!
I AIN'T CONVINCED!
-GASP!- A TELEVISION SET! I JUST LOVE TELEVISION!
AREN'T THE COMFORTS OF MODERN LIFE WONDERFUL?
I'M SUCH A FAN OF WORK-SAVING APPLIANCES!
- - -
- - -
- - -
- - -
AH! HOME, SWEET HOME!
GRAAAAENNG
RRRRINGG

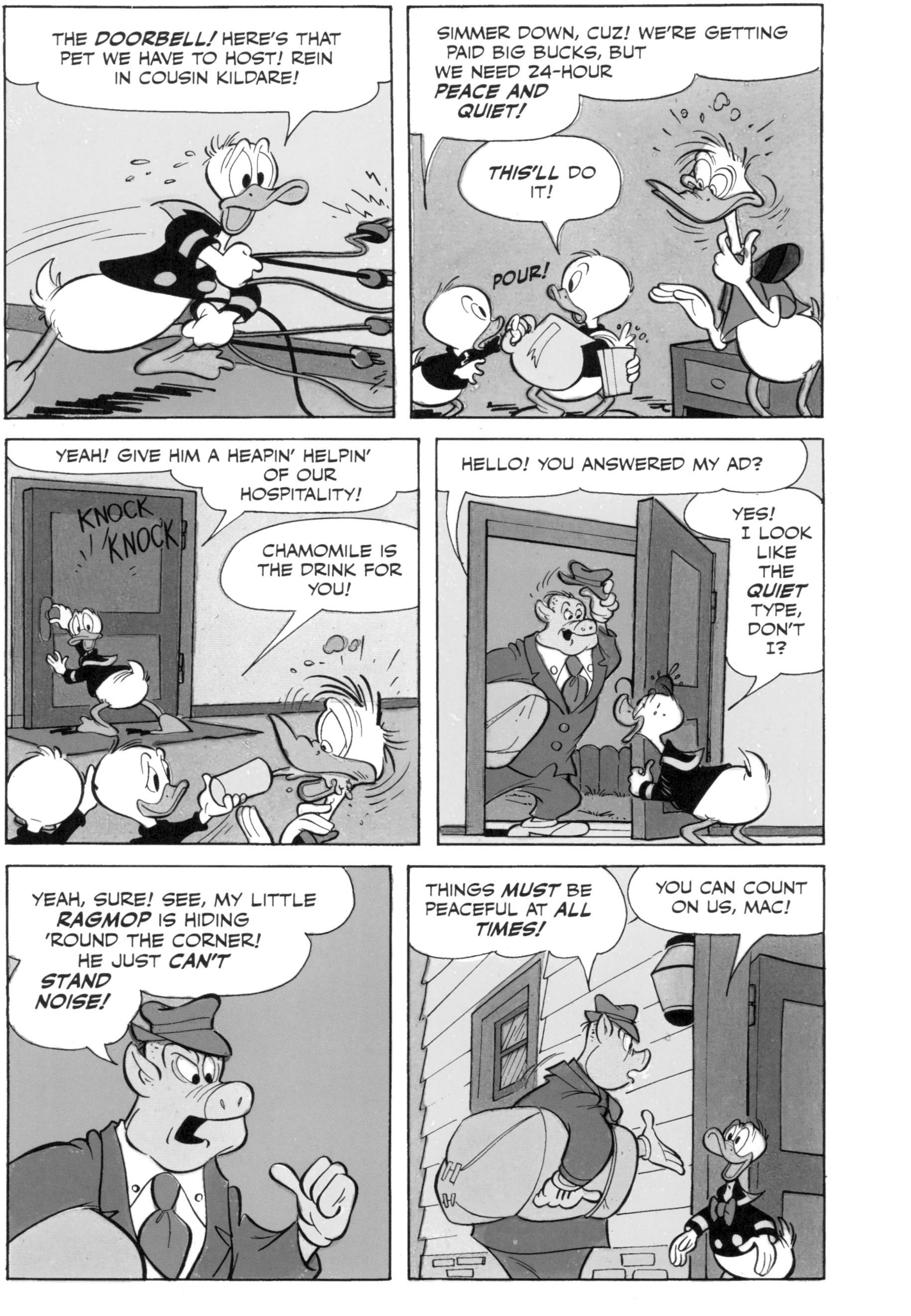
THE DOORBELL! HERE'S THAT PET WE HAVE TO HOST! REIN IN COUSIN KILDARE!
SIMMER DOWN, CUZ! WE'RE GETTING PAID BIG BUCKS, BUT WE NEED 24-HOUR PEACE AND QUIET!
THIS'LL DO IT!
POUR!
YEAH! GIVE HIM A HEAPIN' HELPIN' OF OUR HOSPITALITY!
KNOCK KNOCK
CHAMOMILE IS THE DRINK FOR YOU!
HELLO! YOU ANSWERED MY AD?
YES! I LOOK LIKE THE QUIET TYPE, DON'T I?
YEAH, SURE! SEE, MY LITTLE RAGMOP IS HIDING 'ROUND THE CORNER! HE JUST CAN'T STAND NOISE!
THINGS MUST BE PEACEFUL AT ALL TIMES!
YOU CAN COUNT ON US, MAC!

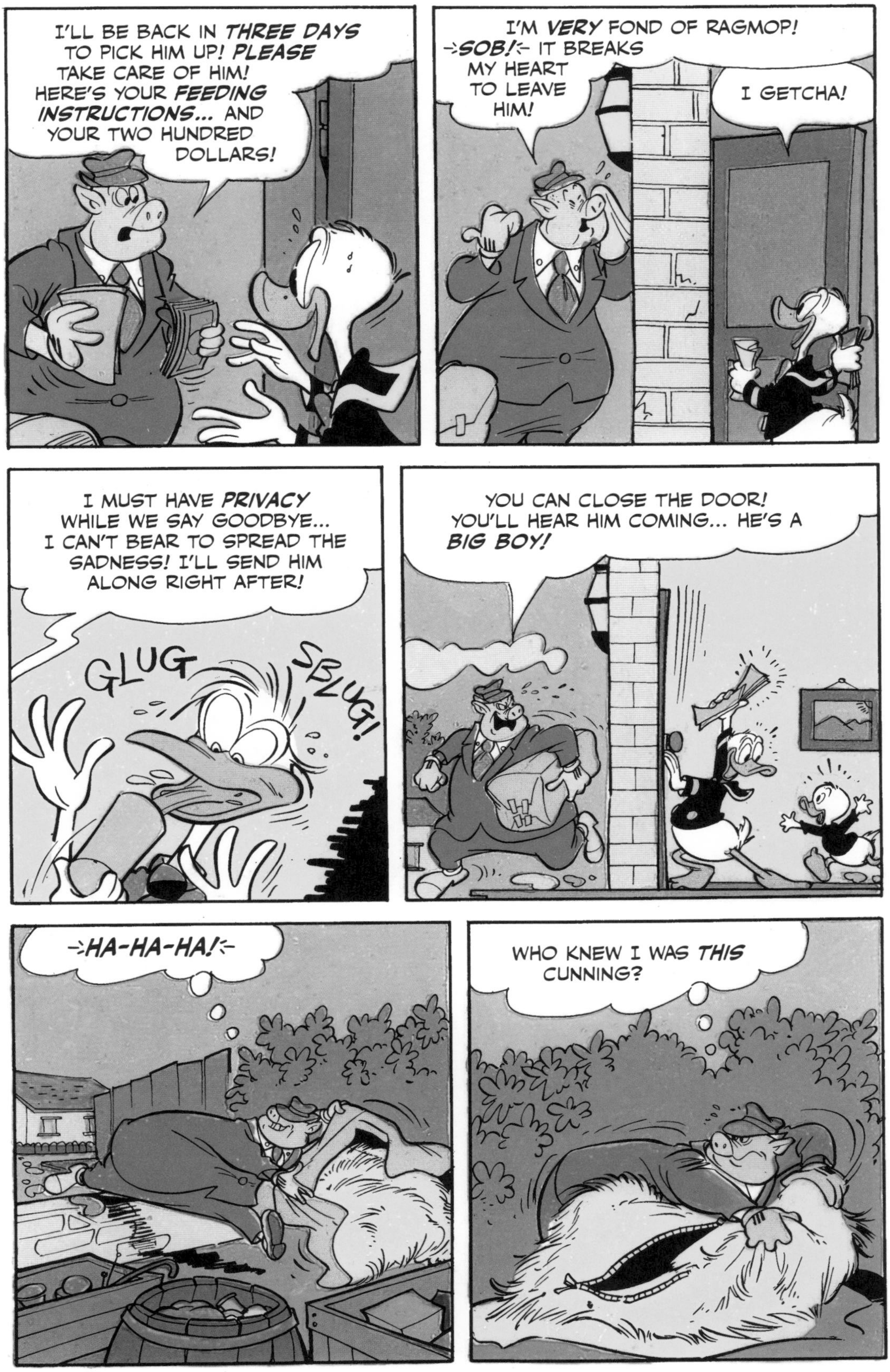

I'LL BE BACK IN THREE DAYS TO PICK HIM UP! PLEASE TAKE CARE OF HIM! HERE'S YOUR FEEDING INSTRUCTIONS... AND YOUR TWO HUNDRED DOLLARS!
I'M VERY FOND OF RAGMOP! -SOB!- IT BREAKS MY HEART TO LEAVE HIM!
I GETCHA!
I MUST HAVE PRIVACY WHILE WE SAY GOODBYE... I CAN'T BEAR TO SPREAD THE SADNESS! I'LL SEND HIM ALONG RIGHT AFTER!
GLUG
SBLUG!
YOU CAN CLOSE THE DOOR! YOU'LL HEAR HIM COMING... HE'S A BIG BOY!
-HA-HA-HA!-
WHO KNEW I WAS THIS CUNNING?

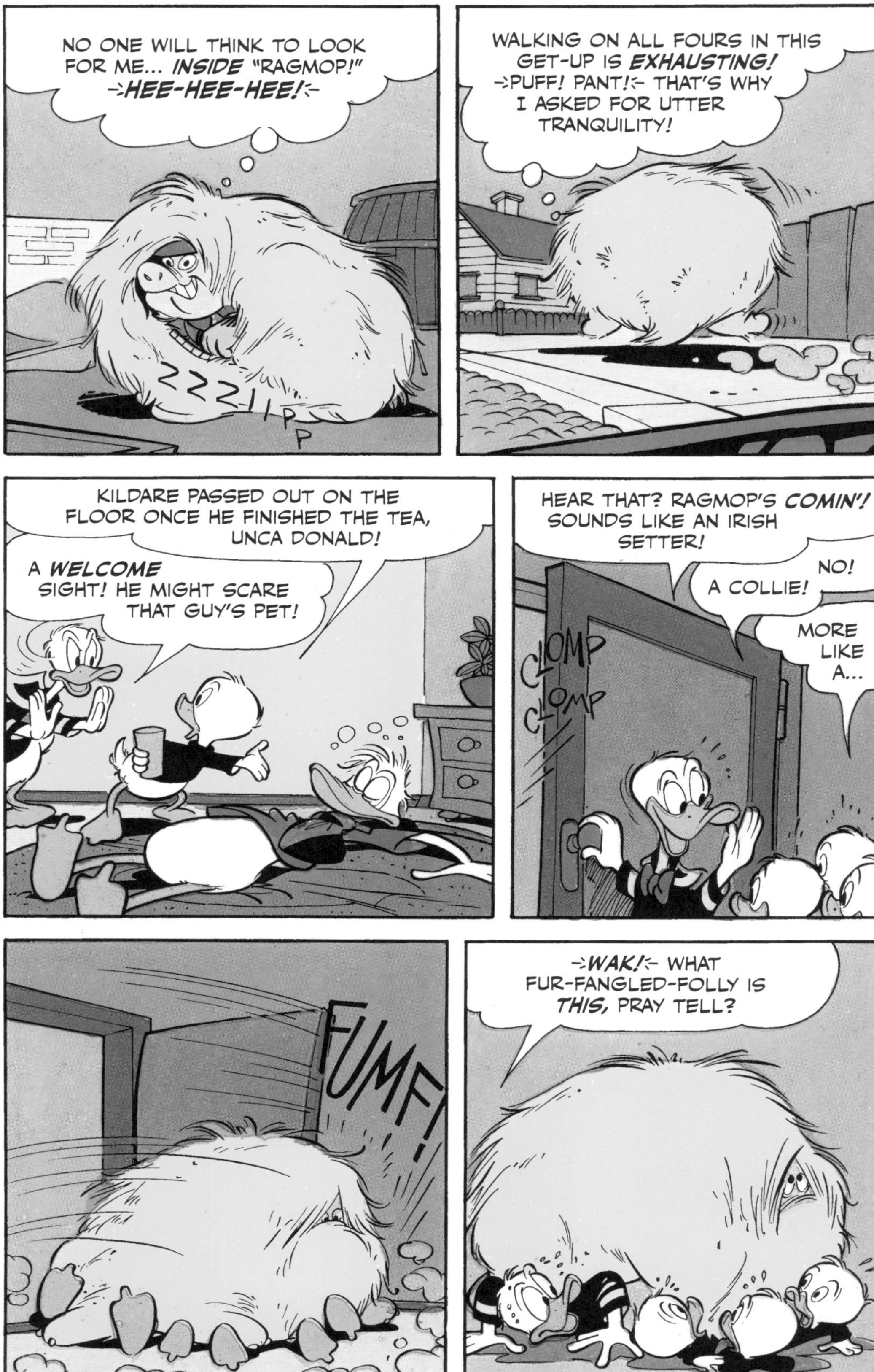
NO ONE WILL THINK TO LOOK FOR ME... INSIDE "RAGMOP!" -HEE-HEE-HEE!-
ZZZZIIPP
WALKING ON ALL FOURS IN THIS GET-UP IS EXHAUSTING! -PUFF! PANT!- THAT'S WHY I ASKED FOR UTTER TRANQUILITY!
KILDARE PASSED OUT ON THE FLOOR ONCE HE FINISHED THE TEA, UNCA DONALD!
A WELCOME SIGHT! HE MIGHT SCARE THAT GUY'S PET!
HEAR THAT? RAGMOP'S COMIN'! SOUNDS LIKE AN IRISH SETTER!
NO! A COLLIE!
MORE LIKE A...
CLOMP CLOMP
FUMF!
-WAK!- WHAT FUR-FANGLED-FOLLY IS THIS, PRAY TELL?

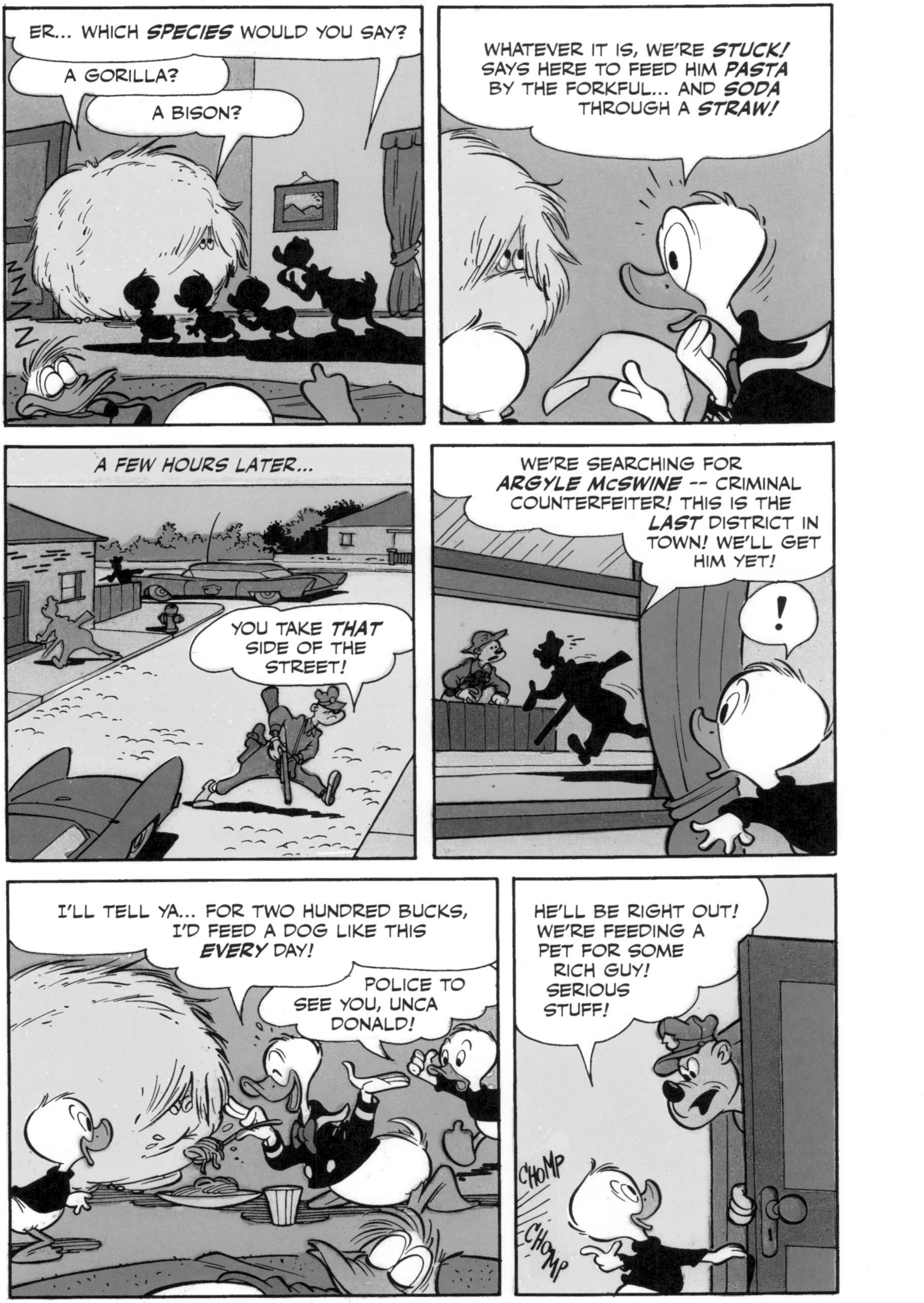
ER... WHICH SPECIES WOULD YOU SAY?
A GORILLA?
A BISON?
Z Z Z
WHATEVER IT IS, WE'RE STUCK! SAYS HERE TO FEED HIM PASTA BY THE FORKFUL... AND SODA THROUGH A STRAW!
A FEW HOURS LATER...
YOU TAKE THAT SIDE OF THE STREET!
WE'RE SEARCHING FOR ARGYLE McSWINE -- CRIMINAL COUNTERFEITER! THIS IS THE LAST DISTRICT IN TOWN! WE'LL GET HIM YET!
!
I'LL TELL YA... FOR TWO HUNDRED BUCKS, I'D FEED A DOG LIKE THIS EVERY DAY!
POLICE TO SEE YOU, UNCA DONALD!
HE'LL BE RIGHT OUT! WE'RE FEEDING A PET FOR SOME RICH GUY! SERIOUS STUFF!
CHOMP
CHOMP

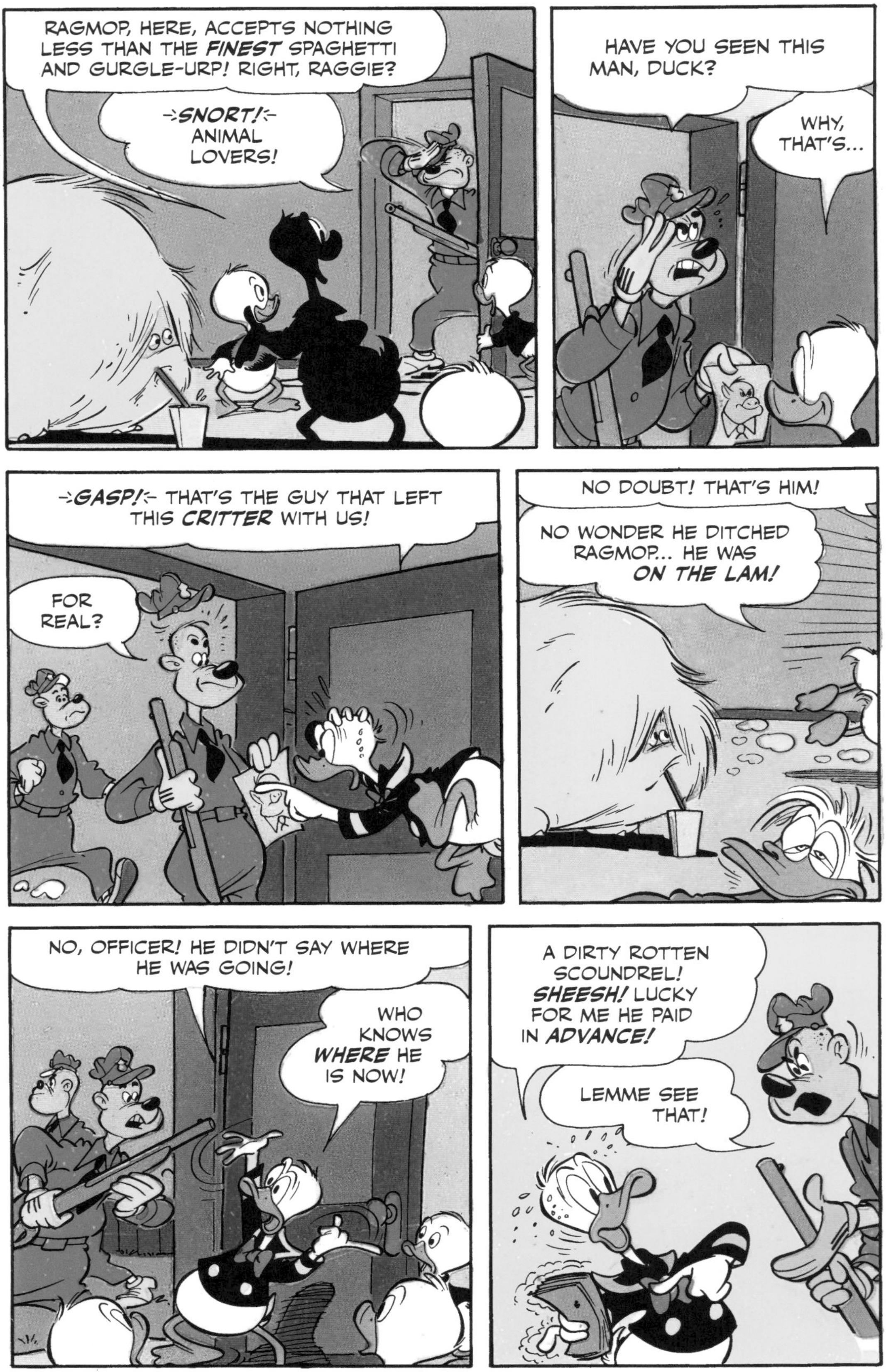
RAGMOP, HERE, ACCEPTS NOTHING LESS THAN THE *FINEST* SPAGHETTI AND GURGLE-URP! RIGHT, RAGGIE?
SNORT! ANIMAL LOVERS!
HAVE YOU SEEN THIS MAN, DUCK?
WHY, THAT'S...
GASP! THAT'S THE GUY THAT LEFT THIS *CRITTER* WITH US!
FOR REAL?
NO DOUBT! THAT'S HIM!
NO WONDER HE DITCHED RAGMOP... HE WAS *ON THE LAM!*
NO, OFFICER! HE DIDN'T SAY WHERE HE WAS GOING!
WHO KNOWS *WHERE* HE IS NOW!
A DIRTY ROTTEN SCOUNDREL! *SHEESH!* LUCKY FOR ME HE PAID IN *ADVANCE!*
LEMME SEE THAT!

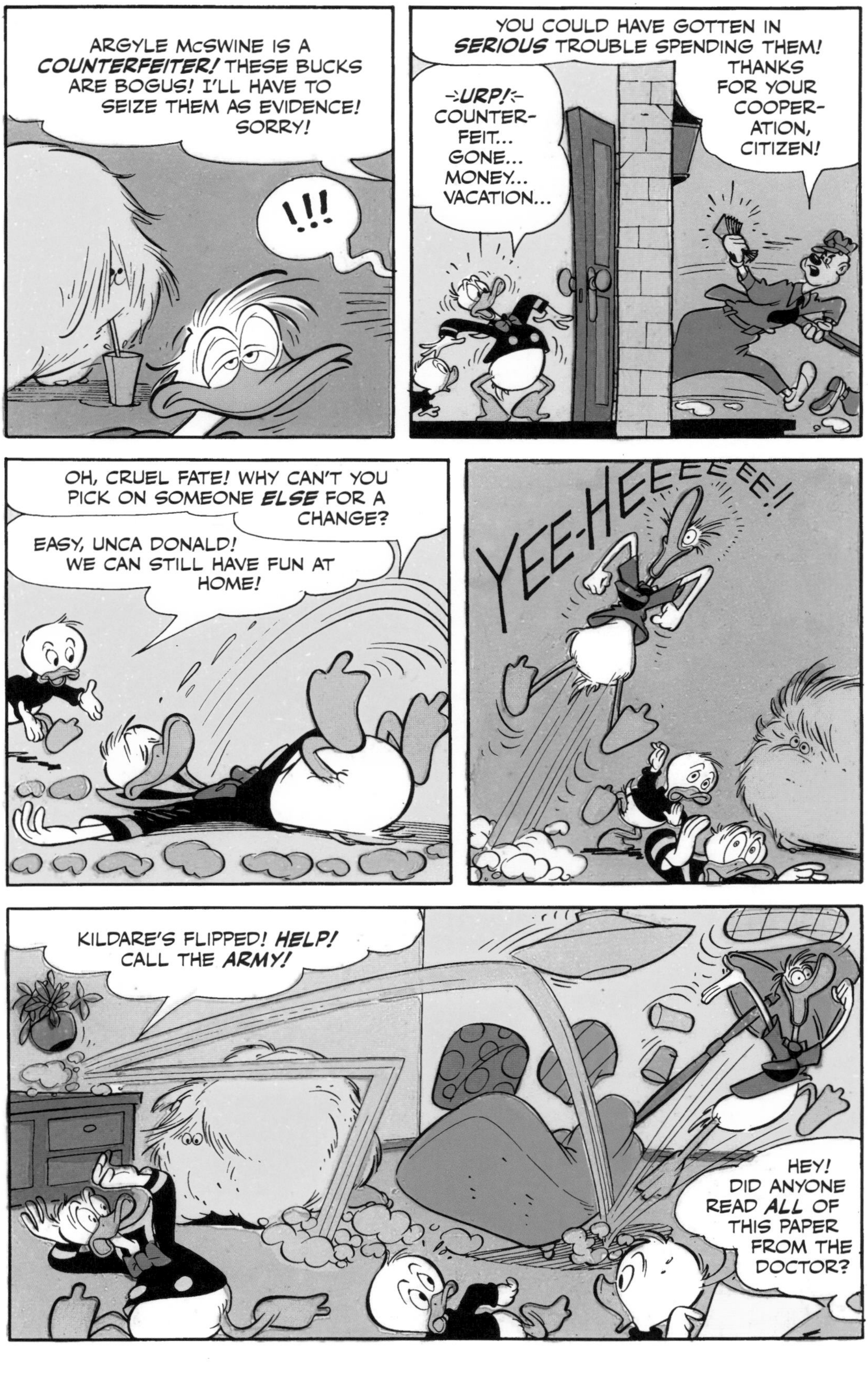
ARGYLE McSWINE IS A COUNTERFEITER! THESE BUCKS ARE BOGUS! I'LL HAVE TO SEIZE THEM AS EVIDENCE! SORRY!
!!!
YOU COULD HAVE GOTTEN IN SERIOUS TROUBLE SPENDING THEM!
-URP!- COUNTERFEIT... GONE... MONEY... VACATION...
THANKS FOR YOUR COOPERATION, CITIZEN!
OH, CRUEL FATE! WHY CAN'T YOU PICK ON SOMEONE ELSE FOR A CHANGE?
EASY, UNCA DONALD! WE CAN STILL HAVE FUN AT HOME!
YEE-HEEEEEEE!!
KILDARE'S FLIPPED! HELP! CALL THE ARMY!
HEY! DID ANYONE READ ALL OF THIS PAPER FROM THE DOCTOR?

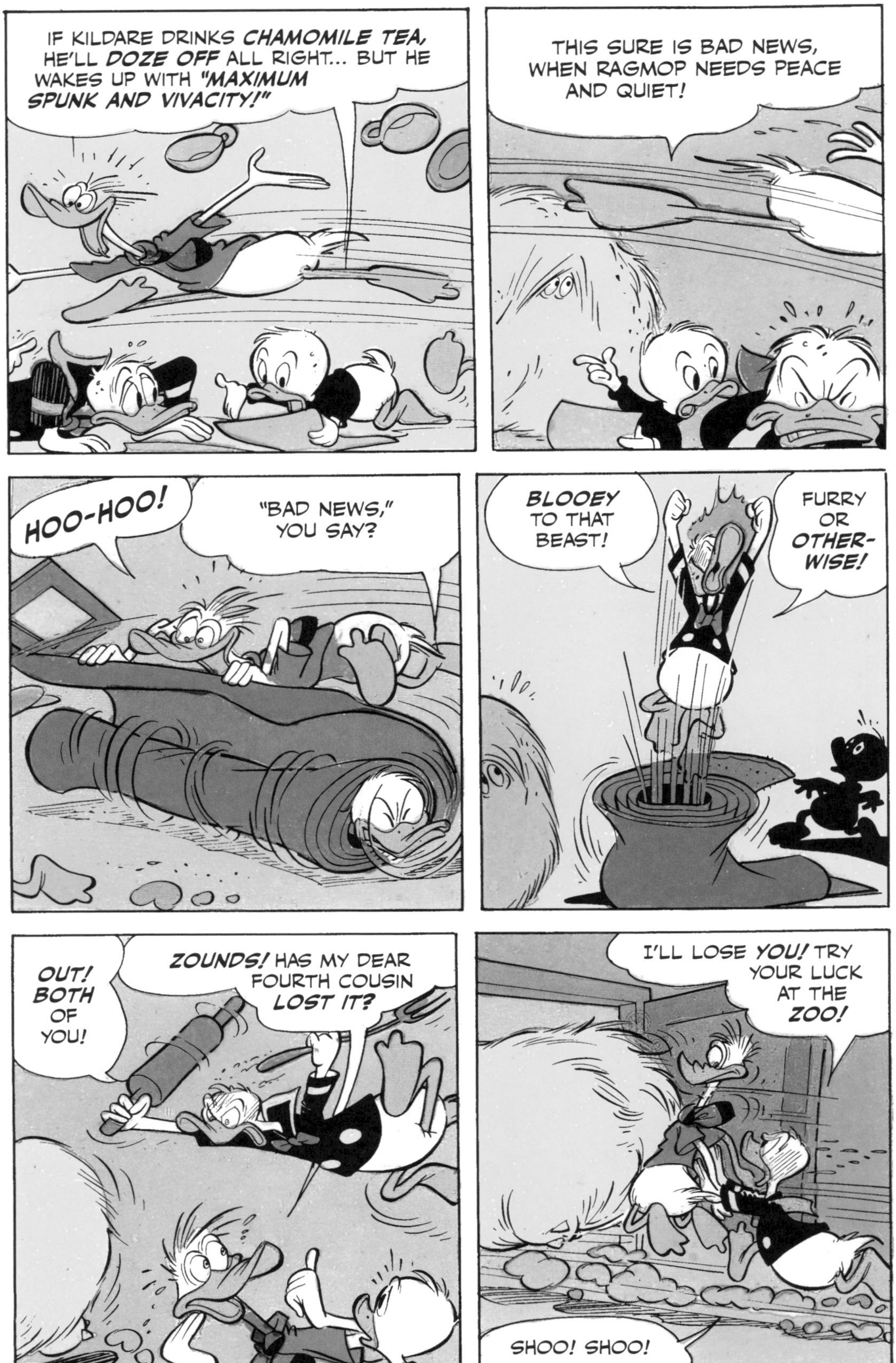
IF KILDARE DRINKS CHAMOMILE TEA, HE'LL DOZE OFF ALL RIGHT... BUT HE WAKES UP WITH "MAXIMUM SPUNK AND VIVACITY!"
THIS SURE IS BAD NEWS, WHEN RAGMOP NEEDS PEACE AND QUIET!
HOO-HOO!
"BAD NEWS," YOU SAY?
BLOOEY TO THAT BEAST!
FURRY OR OTHER-WISE!
OUT! BOTH OF YOU!
ZOUNDS! HAS MY DEAR FOURTH COUSIN LOST IT?
I'LL LOSE YOU! TRY YOUR LUCK AT THE ZOO!
SHOO! SHOO!

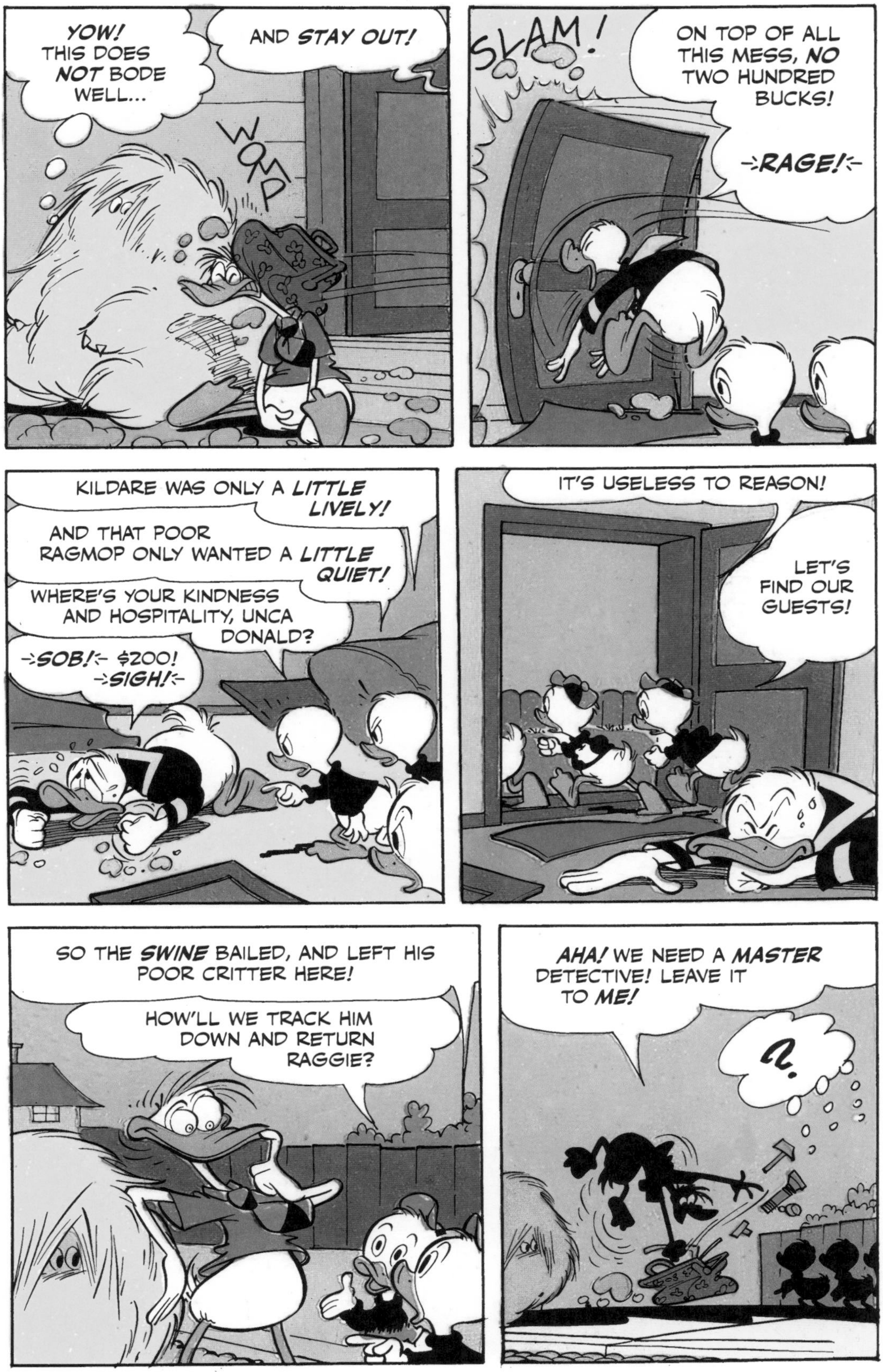
YOW! THIS DOES NOT BODE WELL...
AND STAY OUT!
WOMP
SLAM!
ON TOP OF ALL THIS MESS, NO TWO HUNDRED BUCKS!
RAGE!
KILDARE WAS ONLY A LITTLE LIVELY!
AND THAT POOR RAGMOP ONLY WANTED A LITTLE QUIET!
WHERE'S YOUR KINDNESS AND HOSPITALITY, UNCA DONALD?
SOB! $200! SIGH!
IT'S USELESS TO REASON!
LET'S FIND OUR GUESTS!
SO THE SWINE BAILED, AND LEFT HIS POOR CRITTER HERE!
HOW'LL WE TRACK HIM DOWN AND RETURN RAGGIE?
AHA! WE NEED A MASTER DETECTIVE! LEAVE IT TO ME!
?

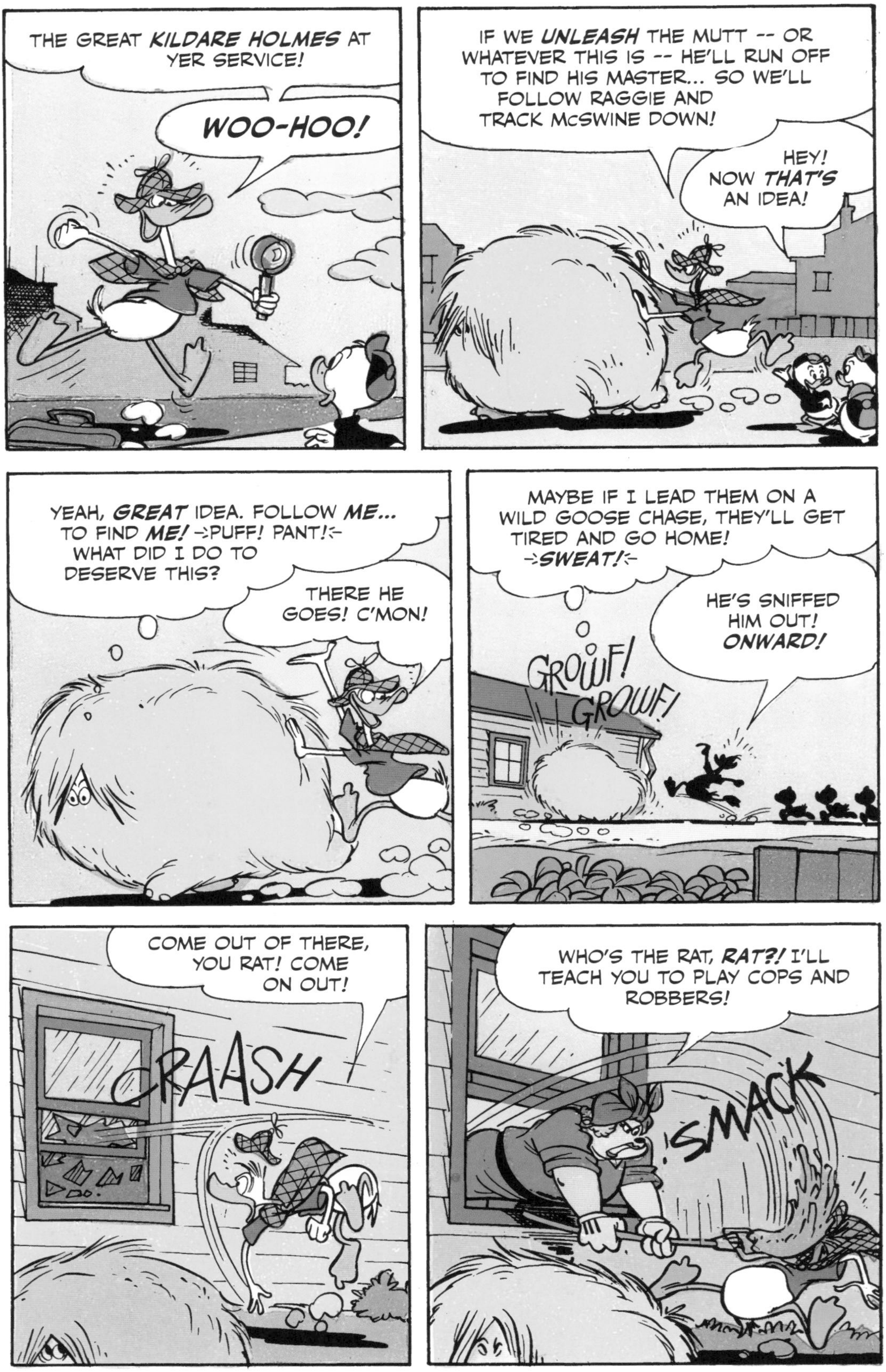
THE GREAT KILDARE HOLMES AT YER SERVICE!
WOO-HOO!
IF WE UNLEASH THE MUTT -- OR WHATEVER THIS IS -- HE'LL RUN OFF TO FIND HIS MASTER... SO WE'LL FOLLOW RAGGIE AND TRACK McSWINE DOWN!
HEY! NOW THAT'S AN IDEA!
YEAH, GREAT IDEA. FOLLOW ME... TO FIND ME! ->PUFF! PANT!<- WHAT DID I DO TO DESERVE THIS?
THERE HE GOES! C'MON!
MAYBE IF I LEAD THEM ON A WILD GOOSE CHASE, THEY'LL GET TIRED AND GO HOME! ->SWEAT!<-
HE'S SNIFFED HIM OUT! ONWARD!
GROWF! GROWF!
COME OUT OF THERE, YOU RAT! COME ON OUT!
CRAASH
WHO'S THE RAT, RAT?! I'LL TEACH YOU TO PLAY COPS AND ROBBERS!
SMACK

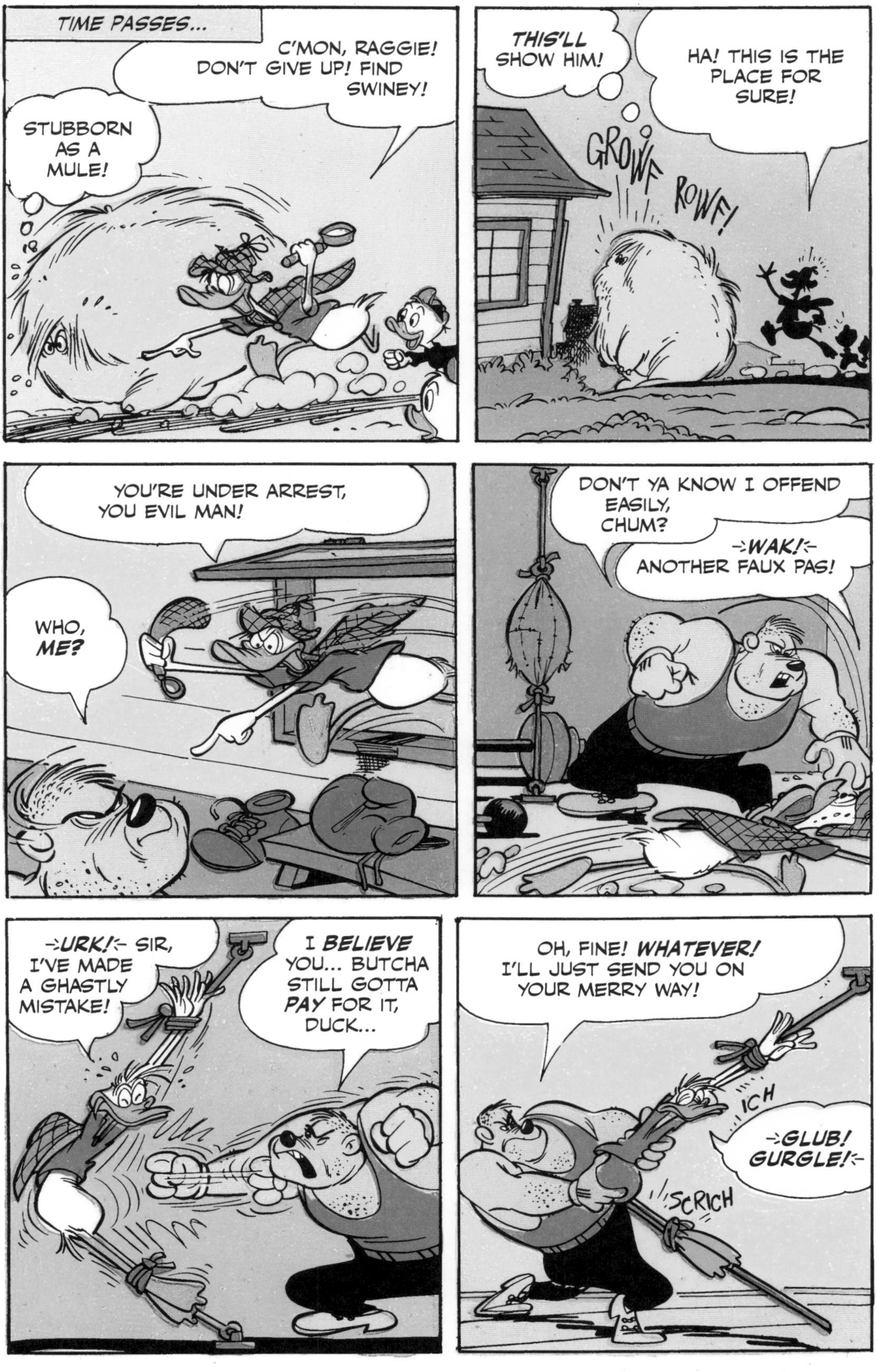
TIME PASSES...
C'MON, RAGGIE! DON'T GIVE UP! FIND SWINEY!
STUBBORN AS A MULE!
THIS'LL SHOW HIM!
HA! THIS IS THE PLACE FOR SURE!
GROWF ROWF!
YOU'RE UNDER ARREST, YOU EVIL MAN!
WHO, ME?
DON'T YA KNOW I OFFEND EASILY, CHUM?
-WAK!- ANOTHER FAUX PAS!
-URK!- SIR, I'VE MADE A GHASTLY MISTAKE!
I BELIEVE YOU... BUTCHA STILL GOTTA PAY FOR IT, DUCK...
OH, FINE! WHATEVER! I'LL JUST SEND YOU ON YOUR MERRY WAY!
ICH
-GLUB! GURGLE!-
SCRICH

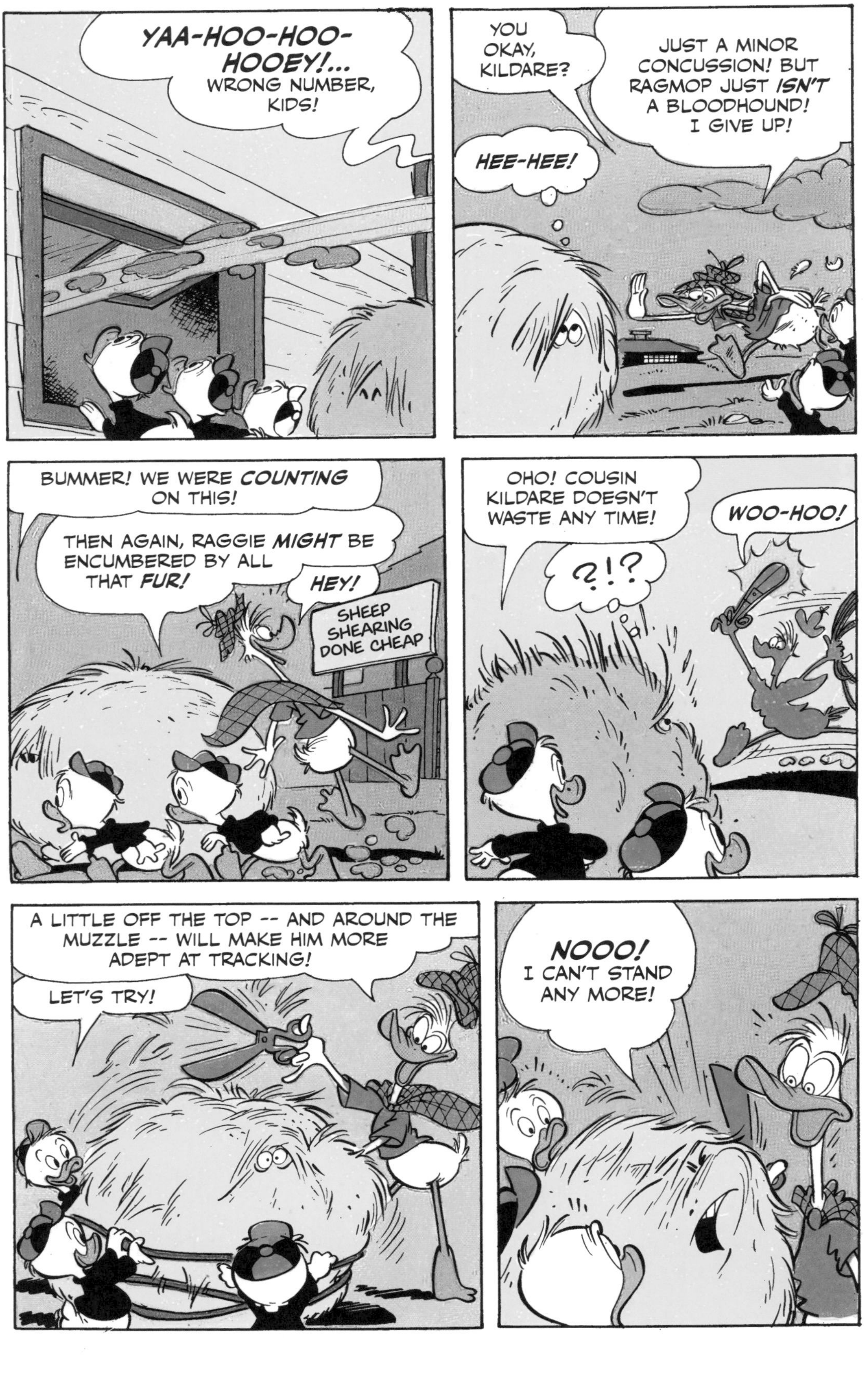
YAA-HOO-HOO-HOOEY!... WRONG NUMBER, KIDS!
YOU OKAY, KILDARE?
JUST A MINOR CONCUSSION! BUT RAGMOP JUST ISN'T A BLOODHOUND! I GIVE UP!
HEE-HEE!
BUMMER! WE WERE COUNTING ON THIS!
THEN AGAIN, RAGGIE MIGHT BE ENCUMBERED BY ALL THAT FUR!
HEY!
SHEEP SHEARING DONE CHEAP
OHO! COUSIN KILDARE DOESN'T WASTE ANY TIME!
?!?
WOO-HOO!
A LITTLE OFF THE TOP -- AND AROUND THE MUZZLE -- WILL MAKE HIM MORE ADEPT AT TRACKING!
LET'S TRY!
NOOO! I CAN'T STAND ANY MORE!

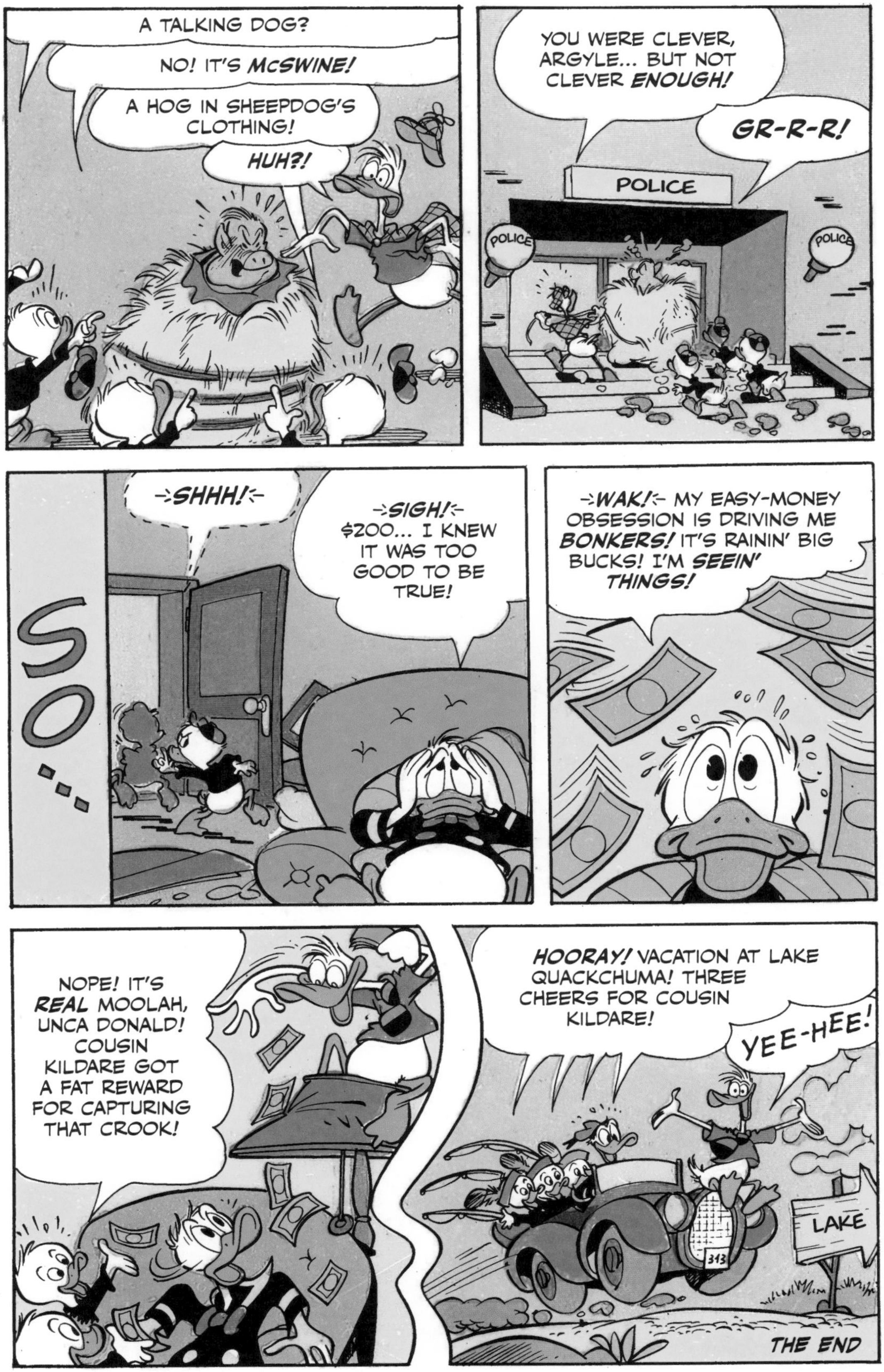

A TALKING DOG?
NO! IT'S McSWINE!
A HOG IN SHEEPDOG'S CLOTHING!
HUH?!
YOU WERE CLEVER, ARGYLE... BUT NOT CLEVER ENOUGH!
GR-R-R!
POLICE
POLICE
POLICE
-SHHH!-
SO...
-SIGH!- $200... I KNEW IT WAS TOO GOOD TO BE TRUE!
-WAK!- MY EASY-MONEY OBSESSION IS DRIVING ME BONKERS! IT'S RAININ' BIG BUCKS! I'M SEEIN' THINGS!
NOPE! IT'S REAL MOOLAH, UNCA DONALD! COUSIN KILDARE GOT A FAT REWARD FOR CAPTURING THAT CROOK!
HOORAY! VACATION AT LAKE QUACKCHUMA! THREE CHEERS FOR COUSIN KILDARE!
YEE-HEE!
313
LAKE
THE END

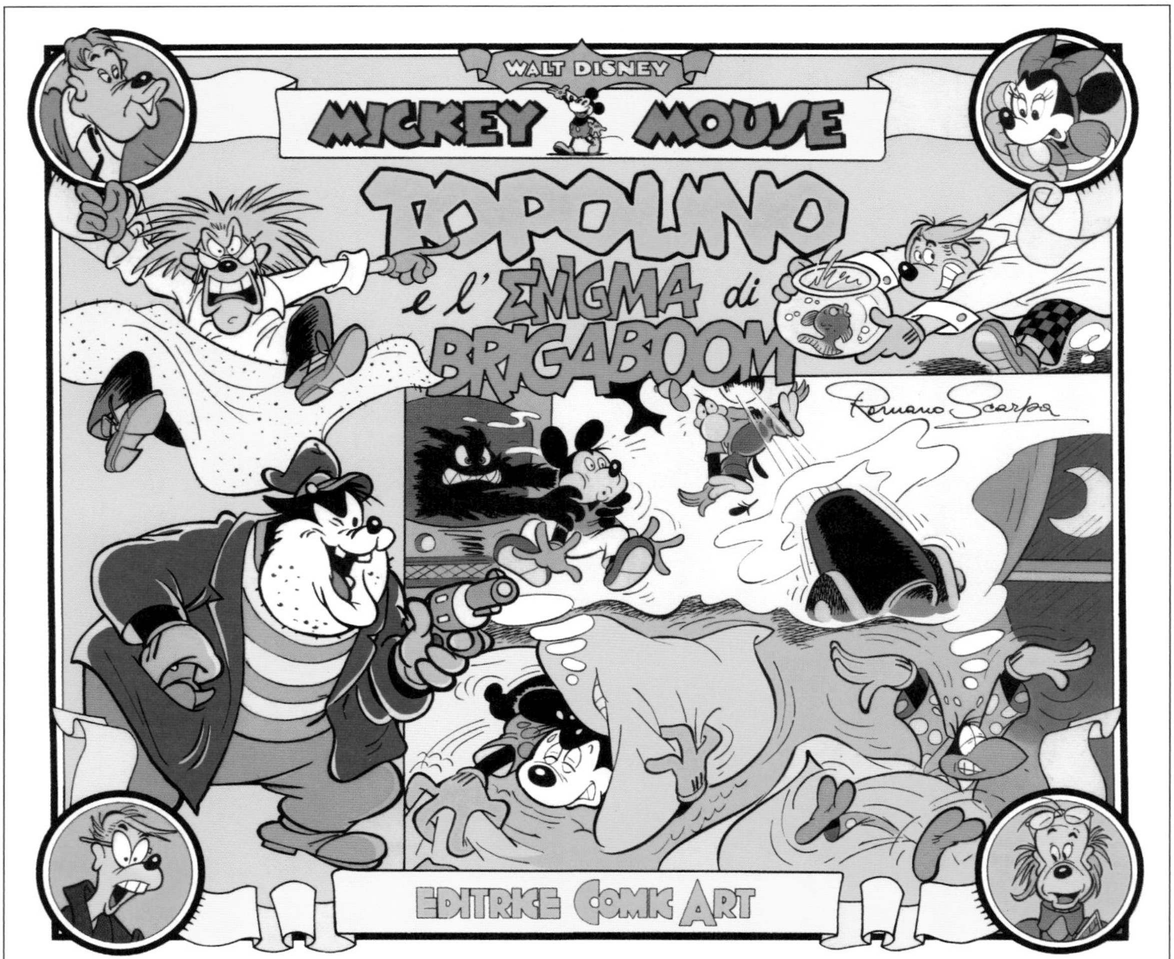
WALT DISNEY
MICKEY MOUSE
TOPOLINO
e l'ENIGMA di
BRIGABOOM
Romano Scarpa
EDITRICE COMIC ART

As an homage to American *Mickey Mouse* newspaper strip master Floyd Gottfredson, Romano Scarpa created four Mickey "strip stories" in the style of Gottfredson's daily serials. "The Riddle of Brigaboom," starting on the next page, was the longest of these adventures. Look for faux Walt Disney signatures — lettered by Scarpa in the Gottfredson style — in panels meant to simulate the finish of individual daily strips.

In 1992, for an oversized Italian album reprinting "Brigaboom" in strip-style landscape format, Scarpa created the title-panel art opposite and the new cover above, lettering the title afresh and adapting art from panels of the story. For the present volume, "Brigaboom" has been remounted in traditional comic book layout, as when The Walt Disney Company Italia reprinted it again in 2000.

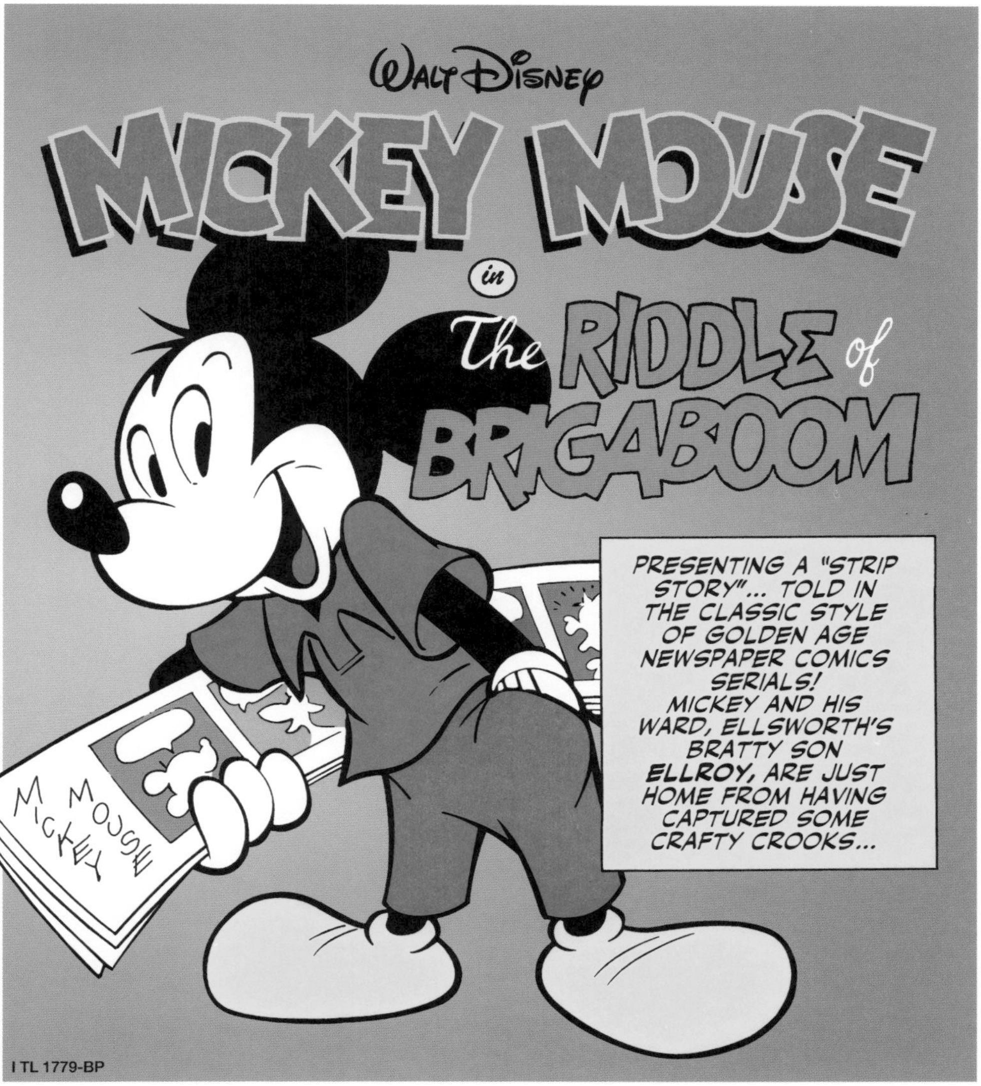
WALT DISNEY
MICKEY MOUSE
in
The RIDDLE of BRIGABOOM
PRESENTING A "STRIP STORY"... TOLD IN THE CLASSIC STYLE OF GOLDEN AGE NEWSPAPER COMICS SERIALS! MICKEY AND HIS WARD, ELLSWORTH'S BRATTY SON ELLROY, ARE JUST HOME FROM HAVING CAPTURED SOME CRAFTY CROOKS...
MICKEY MOUSE
I TL 1779-BP

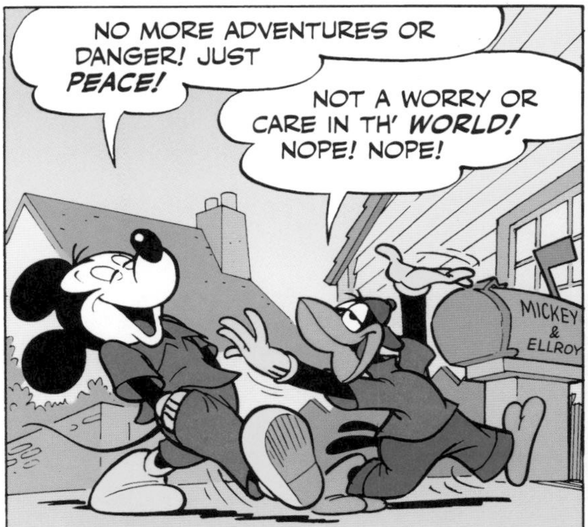
NO MORE ADVENTURES OR DANGER! JUST PEACE!
NOT A WORRY OR CARE IN TH' WORLD! NOPE! NOPE!
MICKEY & ELLROY

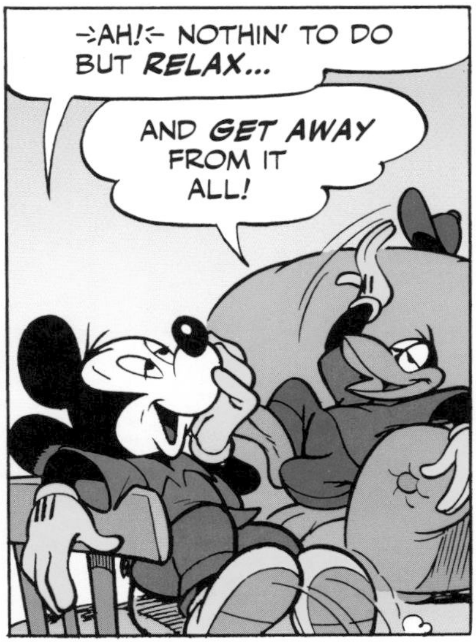
AH! NOTHIN' TO DO BUT RELAX...
AND GET AWAY FROM IT ALL!

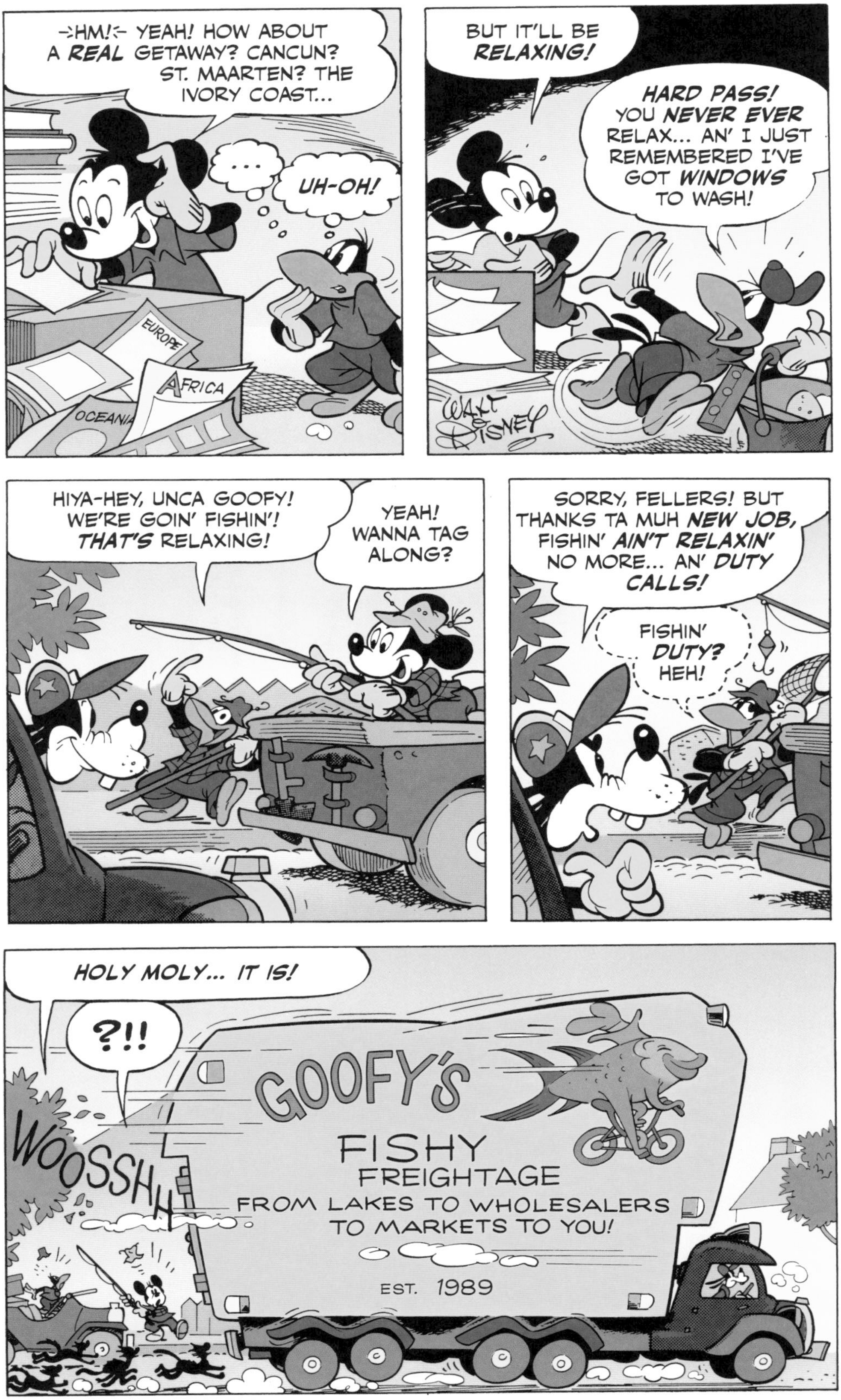
-HM!- YEAH! HOW ABOUT A REAL GETAWAY? CANCUN? ST. MAARTEN? THE IVORY COAST...
...
UH-OH!
EUROPE
AFRICA
OCEANIA
BUT IT'LL BE RELAXING!
HARD PASS! YOU NEVER EVER RELAX... AN' I JUST REMEMBERED I'VE GOT WINDOWS TO WASH!
HIYA-HEY, UNCA GOOFY! WE'RE GOIN' FISHIN'! THAT'S RELAXING!
YEAH! WANNA TAG ALONG?
SORRY, FELLERS! BUT THANKS TA MUH NEW JOB, FISHIN' AIN'T RELAXIN' NO MORE... AN' DUTY CALLS!
FISHIN' DUTY? HEH!
HOLY MOLY... IT IS!
?!!
WOOSSHH
GOOFY'S
FISHY
FREIGHTAGE
FROM LAKES TO WHOLESALERS TO MARKETS TO YOU!
EST. 1989

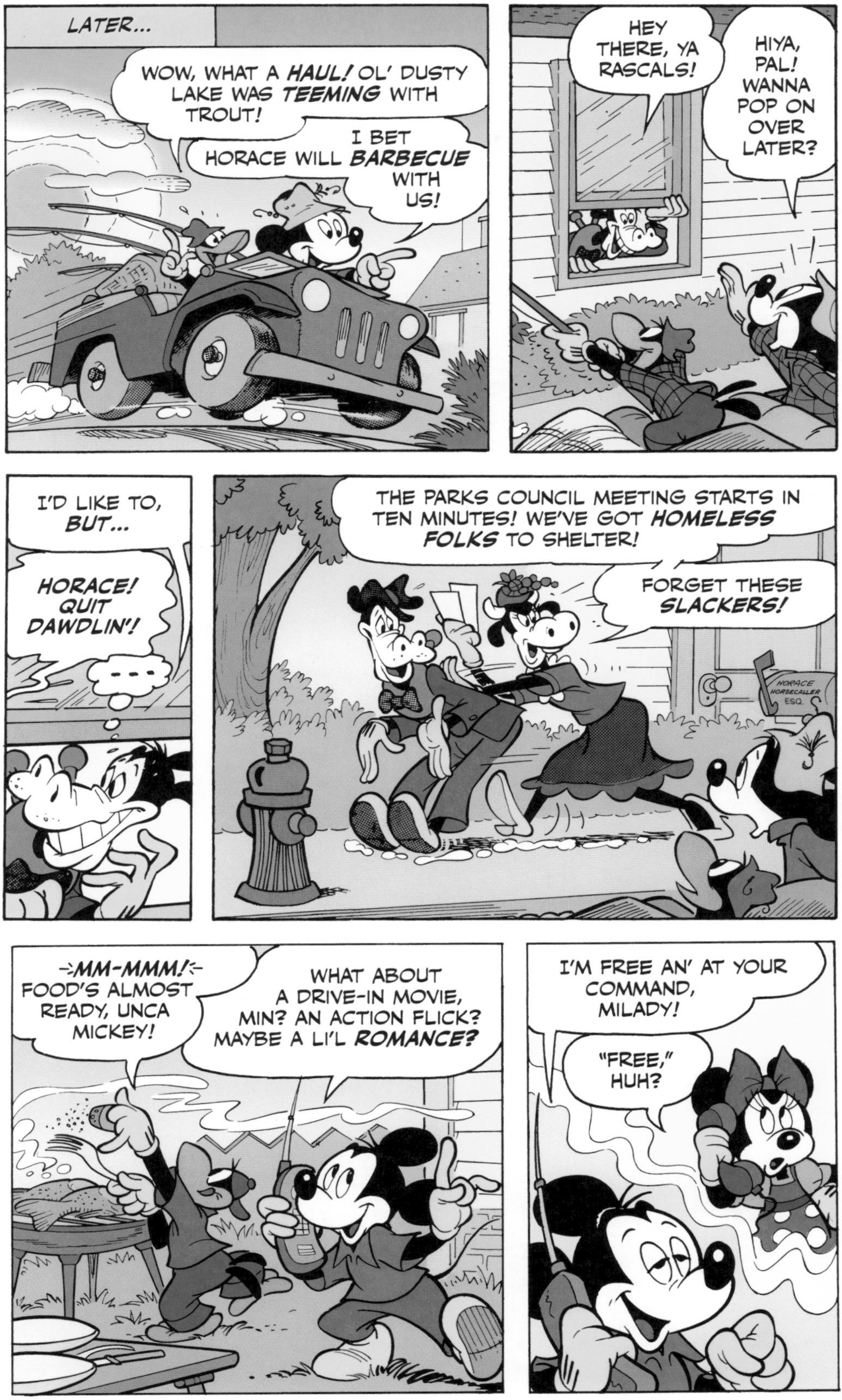
LATER...
WOW, WHAT A HAUL! OL' DUSTY LAKE WAS TEEMING WITH TROUT!
I BET HORACE WILL BARBECUE WITH US!
HEY THERE, YA RASCALS!
HIYA, PAL! WANNA POP ON OVER LATER?
I'D LIKE TO, BUT...
HORACE! QUIT DAWDLIN'!

THE PARKS COUNCIL MEETING STARTS IN TEN MINUTES! WE'VE GOT HOMELESS FOLKS TO SHELTER!
FORGET THESE SLACKERS!
HORACE HORSECOLLAR ESQ.
MM-MMM! FOOD'S ALMOST READY, UNCA MICKEY!
WHAT ABOUT A DRIVE-IN MOVIE, MIN? AN ACTION FLICK? MAYBE A LI'L ROMANCE?
I'M FREE AN' AT YOUR COMMAND, MILADY!
"FREE," HUH?

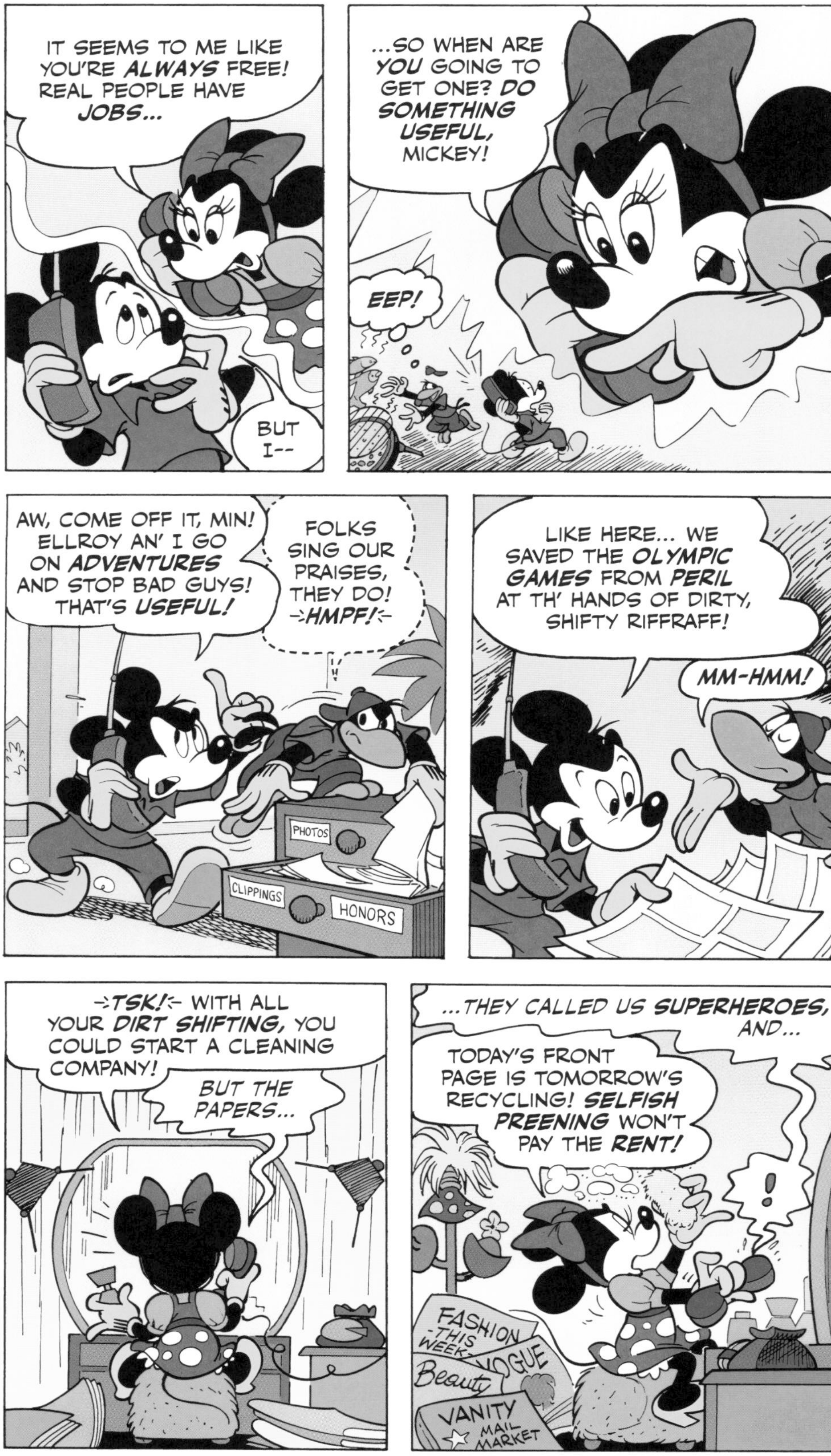
IT SEEMS TO ME LIKE YOU'RE ALWAYS FREE! REAL PEOPLE HAVE JOBS...
BUT I--
...SO WHEN ARE YOU GOING TO GET ONE? DO SOMETHING USEFUL, MICKEY!
EEP!
AW, COME OFF IT, MIN! ELLROY AN' I GO ON ADVENTURES AND STOP BAD GUYS! THAT'S USEFUL!
FOLKS SING OUR PRAISES, THEY DO! -HMPF!-
PHOTOS
CLIPPINGS
HONORS
LIKE HERE... WE SAVED THE OLYMPIC GAMES FROM PERIL AT TH' HANDS OF DIRTY, SHIFTY RIFFRAFF!
MM-HMM!
-TSK!- WITH ALL YOUR DIRT SHIFTING, YOU COULD START A CLEANING COMPANY!
BUT THE PAPERS...
...THEY CALLED US SUPERHEROES, AND...
TODAY'S FRONT PAGE IS TOMORROW'S RECYCLING! SELFISH PREENING WON'T PAY THE RENT!
!
FASHION THIS WEEK
VOGUE
Beauty
VANITY
MAIL MARKET

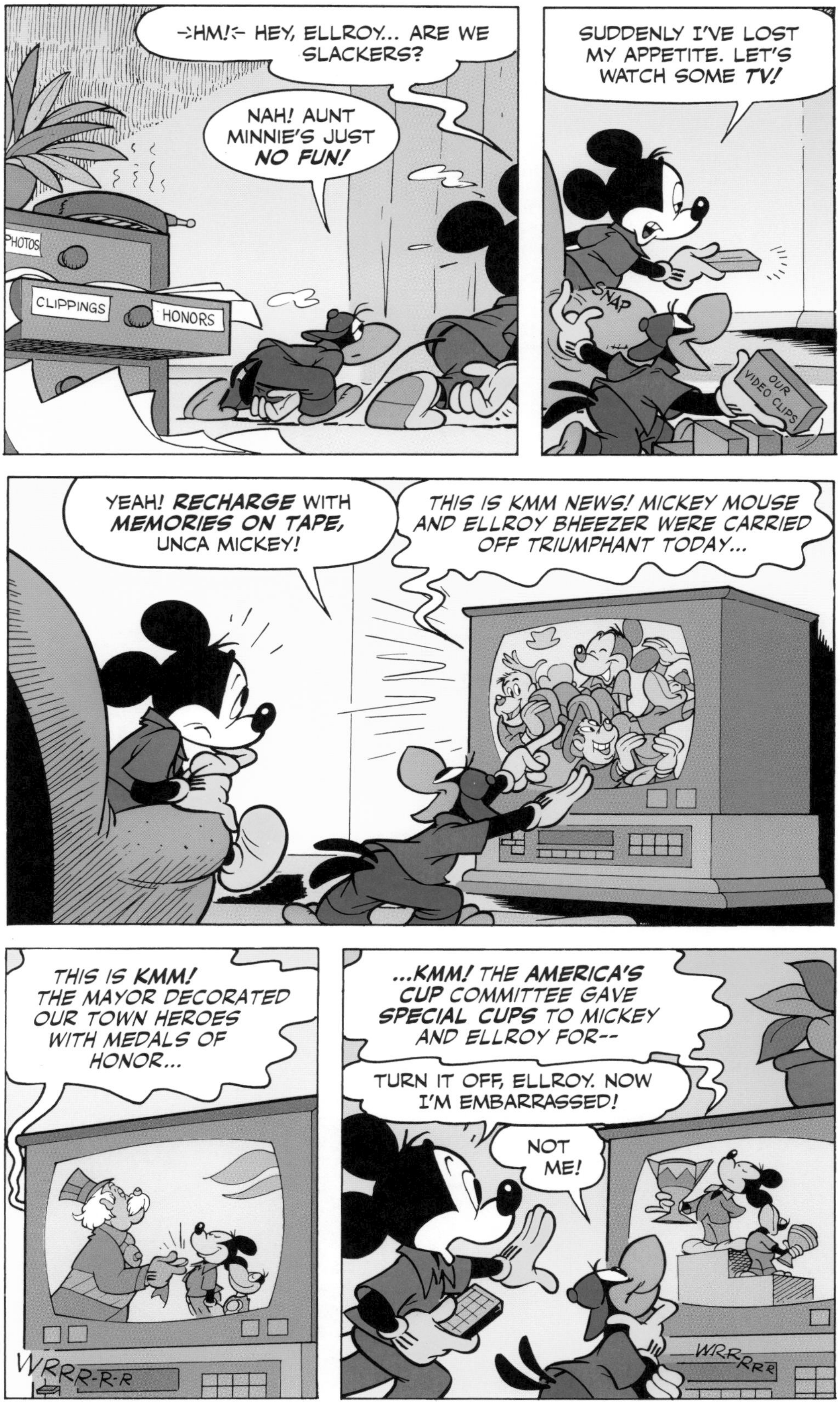

→HM!← HEY, ELLROY... ARE WE SLACKERS?
NAH! AUNT MINNIE'S JUST NO FUN!
PHOTOS
CLIPPINGS
HONORS
SUDDENLY I'VE LOST MY APPETITE. LET'S WATCH SOME TV!
SNAP
OUR VIDEO CLIPS
YEAH! RECHARGE WITH MEMORIES ON TAPE, UNCA MICKEY!
THIS IS KMM NEWS! MICKEY MOUSE AND ELLROY BHEEZER WERE CARRIED OFF TRIUMPHANT TODAY...
THIS IS KMM! THE MAYOR DECORATED OUR TOWN HEROES WITH MEDALS OF HONOR...
WRRR-R-R
...KMM! THE AMERICA'S CUP COMMITTEE GAVE SPECIAL CUPS TO MICKEY AND ELLROY FOR--
TURN IT OFF, ELLROY. NOW I'M EMBARRASSED!
NOT ME!
WRRRRR

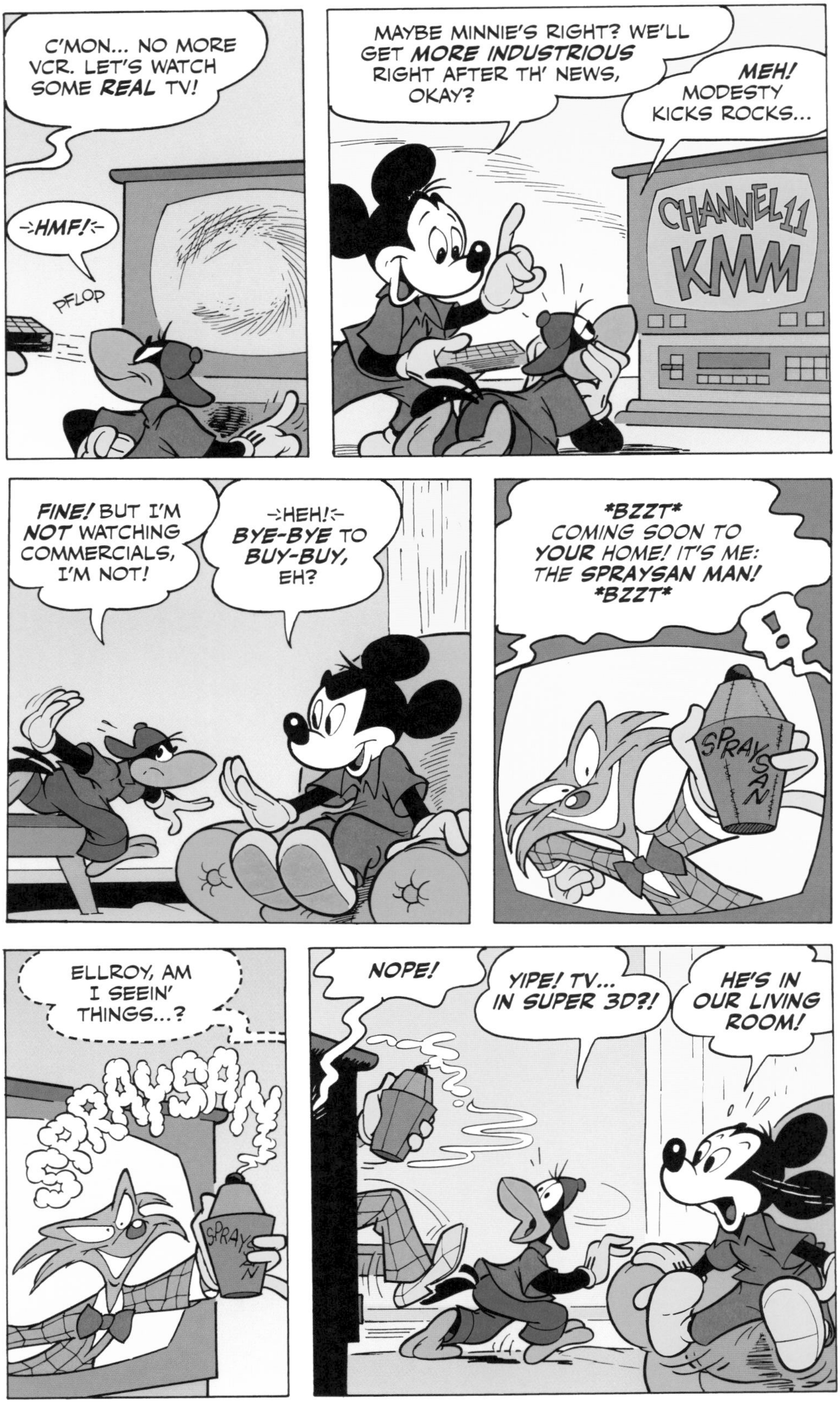
C'MON... NO MORE VCR. LET'S WATCH SOME REAL TV!
HMF!
PFLOP
MAYBE MINNIE'S RIGHT? WE'LL GET MORE INDUSTRIOUS RIGHT AFTER TH' NEWS, OKAY?
MEH! MODESTY KICKS ROCKS...
CHANNEL 11 KMM
FINE! BUT I'M NOT WATCHING COMMERCIALS, I'M NOT!
HEH! BYE-BYE TO BUY-BUY, EH?
BZZT COMING SOON TO YOUR HOME! IT'S ME: THE SPRAYSAN MAN! *BZZT*
!
SPRAYSAN
ELLROY, AM I SEEIN' THINGS...?
SPRAYSAN
SPRAYSAN
NOPE!
YIPE! TV... IN SUPER 3D?!
HE'S IN OUR LIVING ROOM!

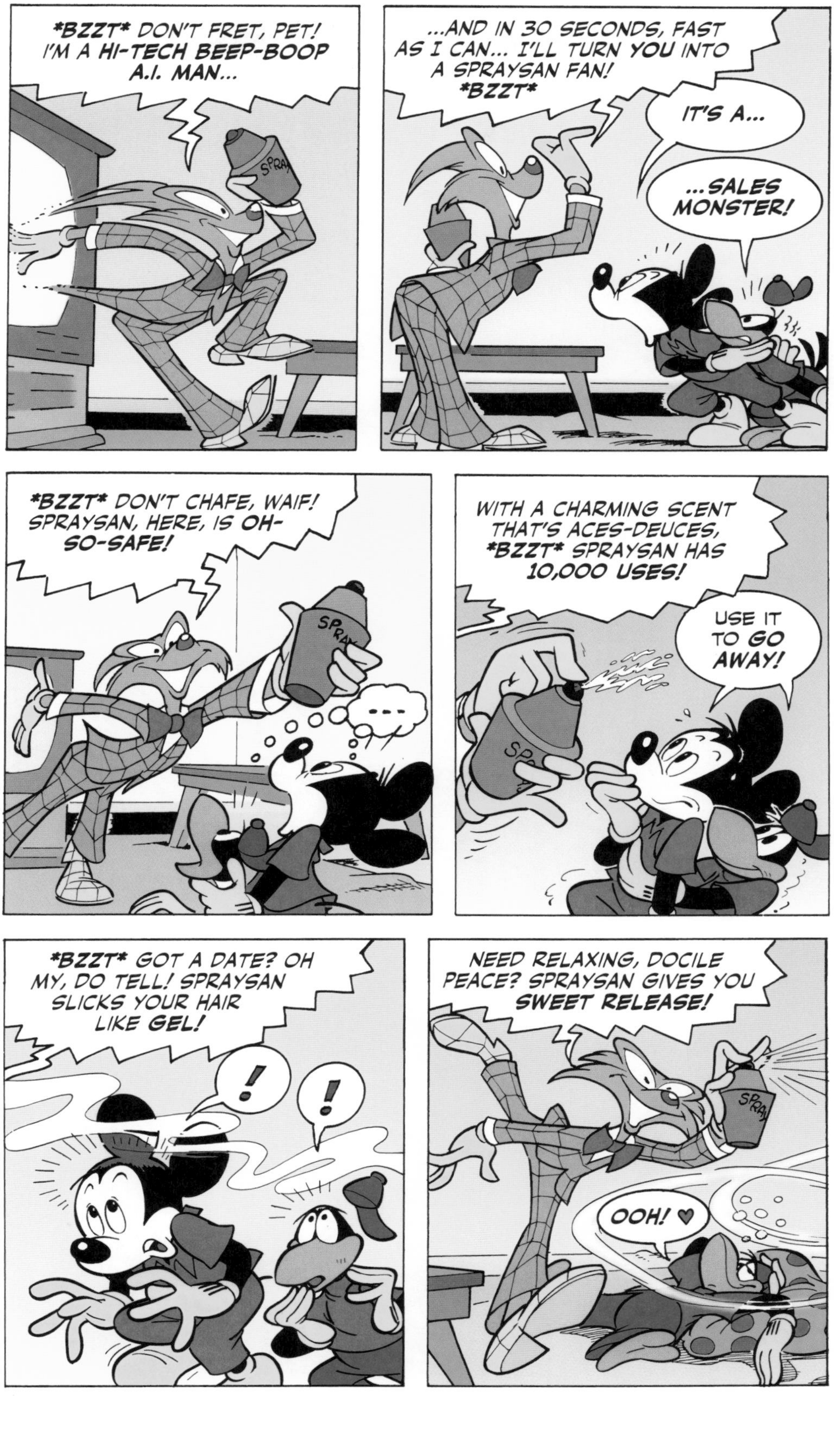
BZZT DON'T FRET, PET! I'M A HI-TECH BEEP-BOOP A.I. MAN...
SPRAY
...AND IN 30 SECONDS, FAST AS I CAN... I'LL TURN YOU INTO A SPRAYSAN FAN! *BZZT*
IT'S A...
...SALES MONSTER!
BZZT DON'T CHAFE, WAIF! SPRAYSAN, HERE, IS OH-SO-SAFE!
SPRAY
...
WITH A CHARMING SCENT THAT'S ACES-DEUCES, *BZZT* SPRAYSAN HAS 10,000 USES!
USE IT TO GO AWAY!
BZZT GOT A DATE? OH MY, DO TELL! SPRAYSAN SLICKS YOUR HAIR LIKE GEL!
!
!
NEED RELAXING, DOCILE PEACE? SPRAYSAN GIVES YOU SWEET RELEASE!
SPRAY
OOH! ♥

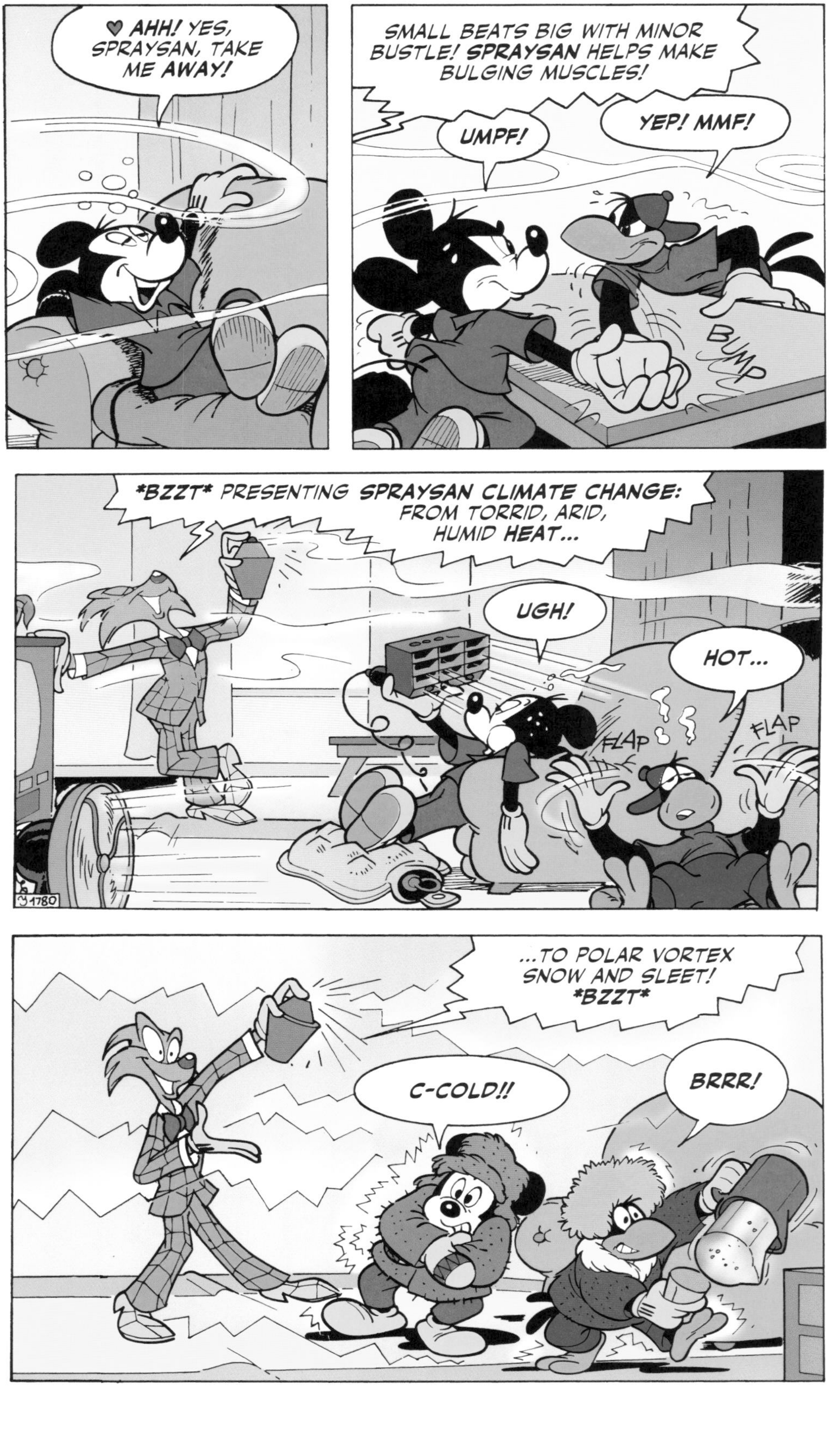
♥ AHH! YES, SPRAYSAN, TAKE ME AWAY!
SMALL BEATS BIG WITH MINOR BUSTLE! SPRAYSAN HELPS MAKE BULGING MUSCLES!
UMPF!
YEP! MMF!
BUMP
BZZT PRESENTING SPRAYSAN CLIMATE CHANGE: FROM TORRID, ARID, HUMID HEAT...
UGH!
HOT...
FLAP
FLAP
...TO POLAR VORTEX SNOW AND SLEET! *BZZT*
C-COLD!!
BRRR!

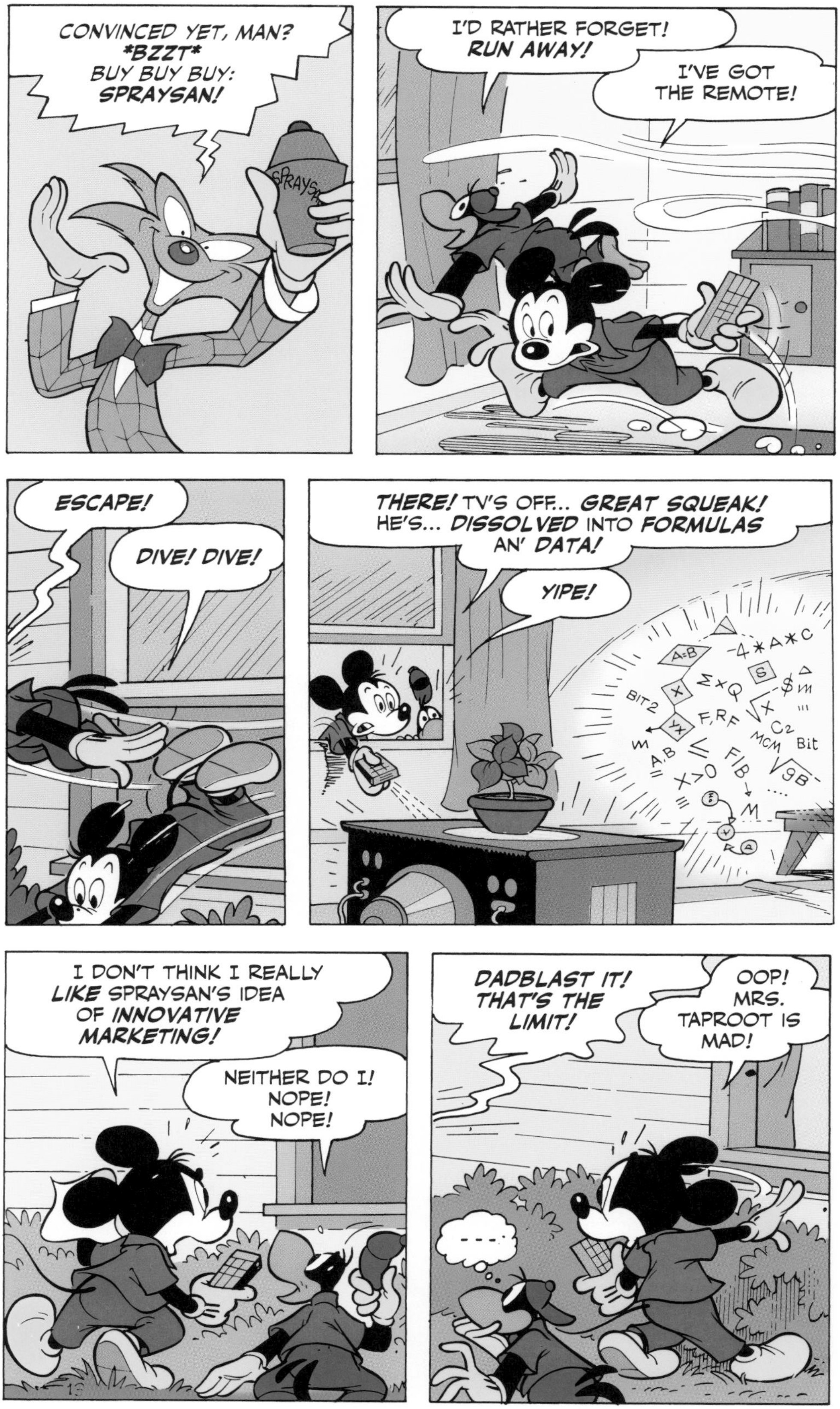
CONVINCED YET, MAN? *BZZT* BUY BUY BUY: SPRAYSAN!
SPRAYSAN
I'D RATHER FORGET! RUN AWAY!
I'VE GOT THE REMOTE!
ESCAPE!
DIVE! DIVE!
THERE! TV'S OFF... GREAT SQUEAK! HE'S... DISSOLVED INTO FORMULAS AN' DATA!
YIPE!
I DON'T THINK I REALLY LIKE SPRAYSAN'S IDEA OF INNOVATIVE MARKETING!
NEITHER DO I! NOPE! NOPE!
DADBLAST IT! THAT'S THE LIMIT!
OOP! MRS. TAPROOT IS MAD!

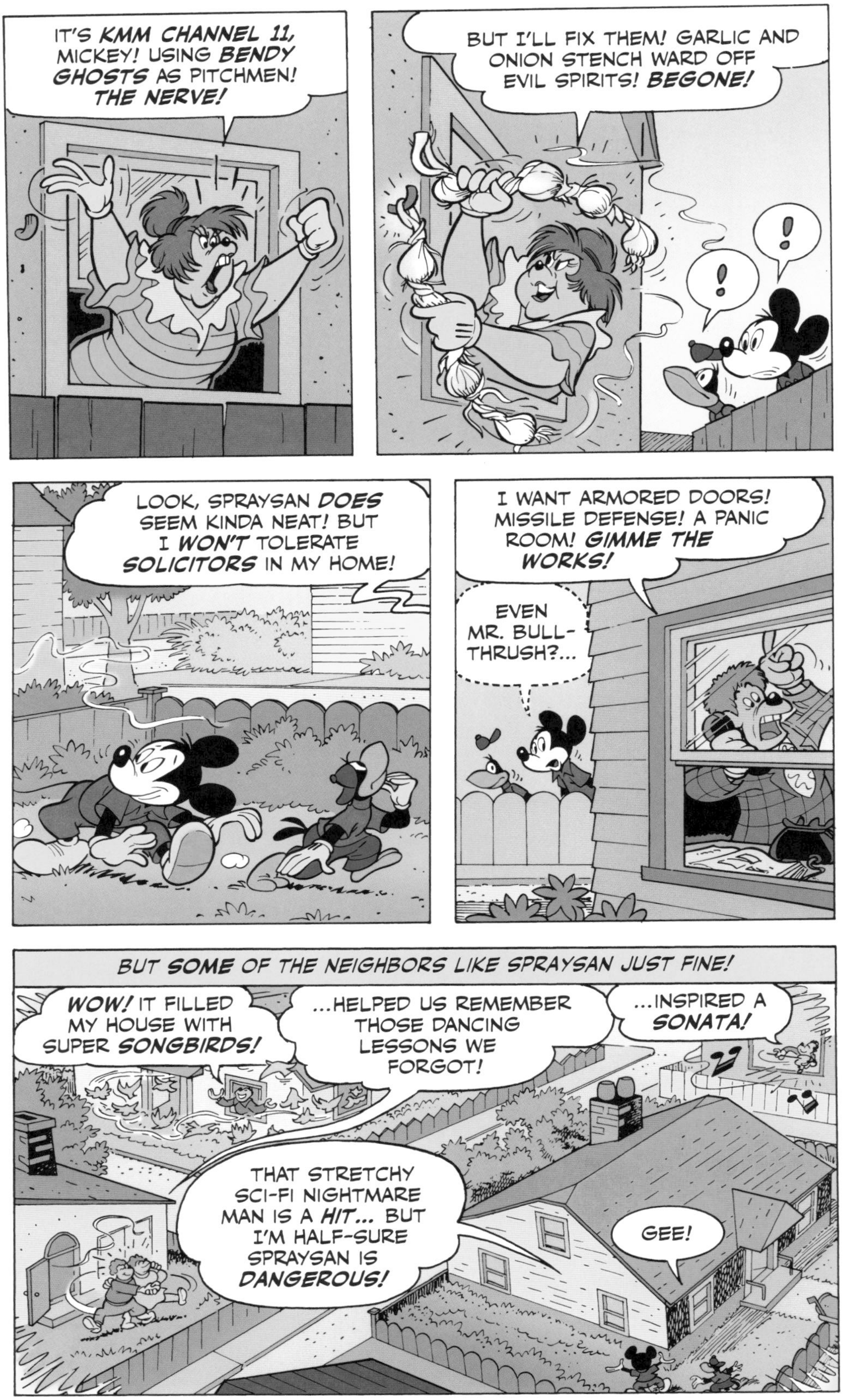
IT'S KMM CHANNEL 11, MICKEY! USING BENDY GHOSTS AS PITCHMEN! THE NERVE!
BUT I'LL FIX THEM! GARLIC AND ONION STENCH WARD OFF EVIL SPIRITS! BEGONE!
!
!
LOOK, SPRAYSAN DOES SEEM KINDA NEAT! BUT I WON'T TOLERATE SOLICITORS IN MY HOME!
I WANT ARMORED DOORS! MISSILE DEFENSE! A PANIC ROOM! GIMME THE WORKS!
EVEN MR. BULL-THRUSH?...
BUT SOME OF THE NEIGHBORS LIKE SPRAYSAN JUST FINE!
WOW! IT FILLED MY HOUSE WITH SUPER SONGBIRDS!
...HELPED US REMEMBER THOSE DANCING LESSONS WE FORGOT!
...INSPIRED A SONATA!
THAT STRETCHY SCI-FI NIGHTMARE MAN IS A HIT... BUT I'M HALF-SURE SPRAYSAN IS DANGEROUS!
GEE!

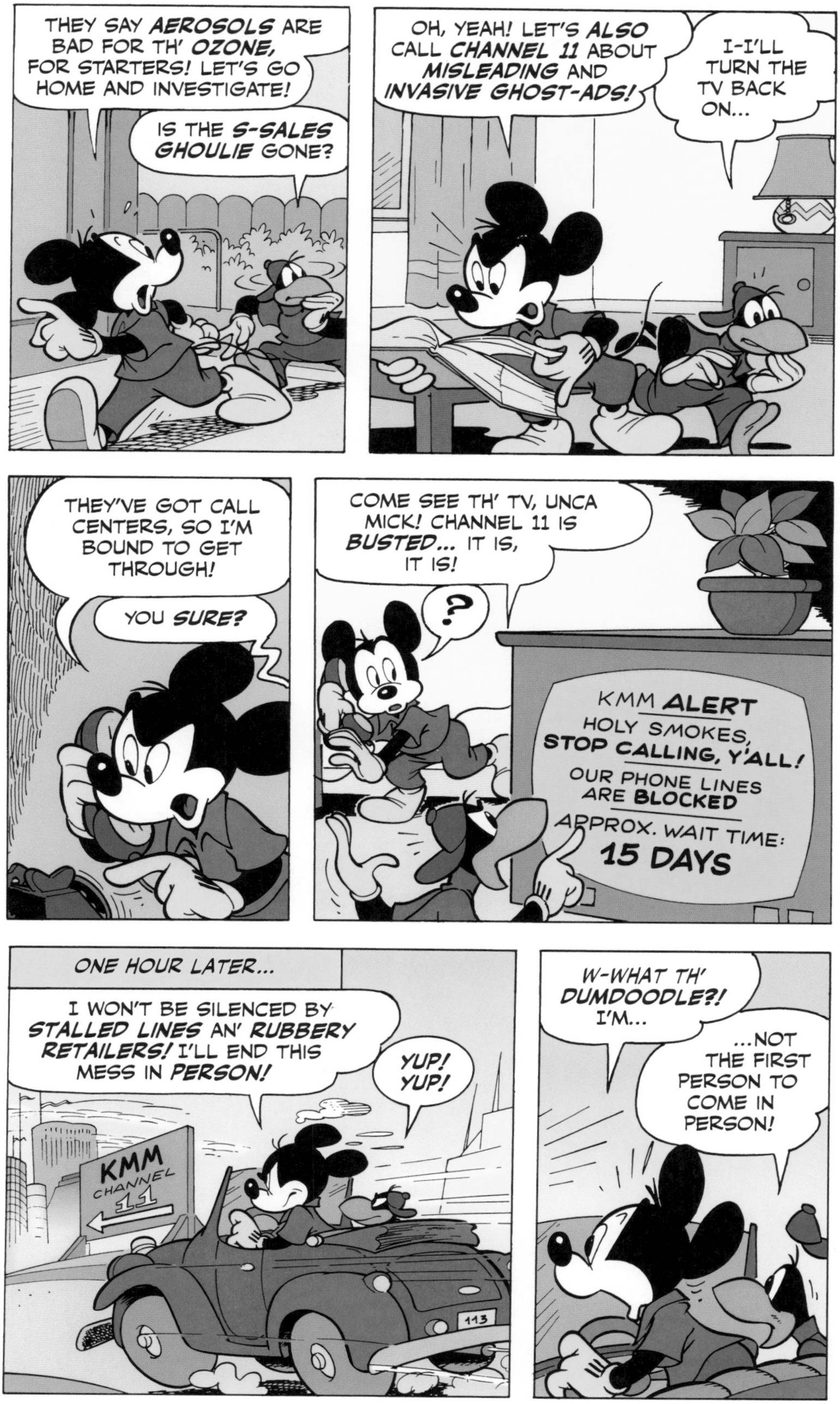
THEY SAY AEROSOLS ARE BAD FOR TH' OZONE, FOR STARTERS! LET'S GO HOME AND INVESTIGATE!
IS THE S-SALES GHOULIE GONE?
OH, YEAH! LET'S ALSO CALL CHANNEL 11 ABOUT MISLEADING AND INVASIVE GHOST-ADS!
I-I'LL TURN THE TV BACK ON...
THEY'VE GOT CALL CENTERS, SO I'M BOUND TO GET THROUGH!
YOU SURE?
COME SEE TH' TV, UNCA MICK! CHANNEL 11 IS BUSTED... IT IS, IT IS!
?
KMM ALERT
HOLY SMOKES, STOP CALLING, Y'ALL!
OUR PHONE LINES ARE BLOCKED
APPROX. WAIT TIME: 15 DAYS
ONE HOUR LATER...
I WON'T BE SILENCED BY STALLED LINES AN' RUBBERY RETAILERS! I'LL END THIS MESS IN PERSON!
YUP! YUP!
KMM CHANNEL 11
113
W-WHAT TH' DUMDOODLE?! I'M...
...NOT THE FIRST PERSON TO COME IN PERSON!

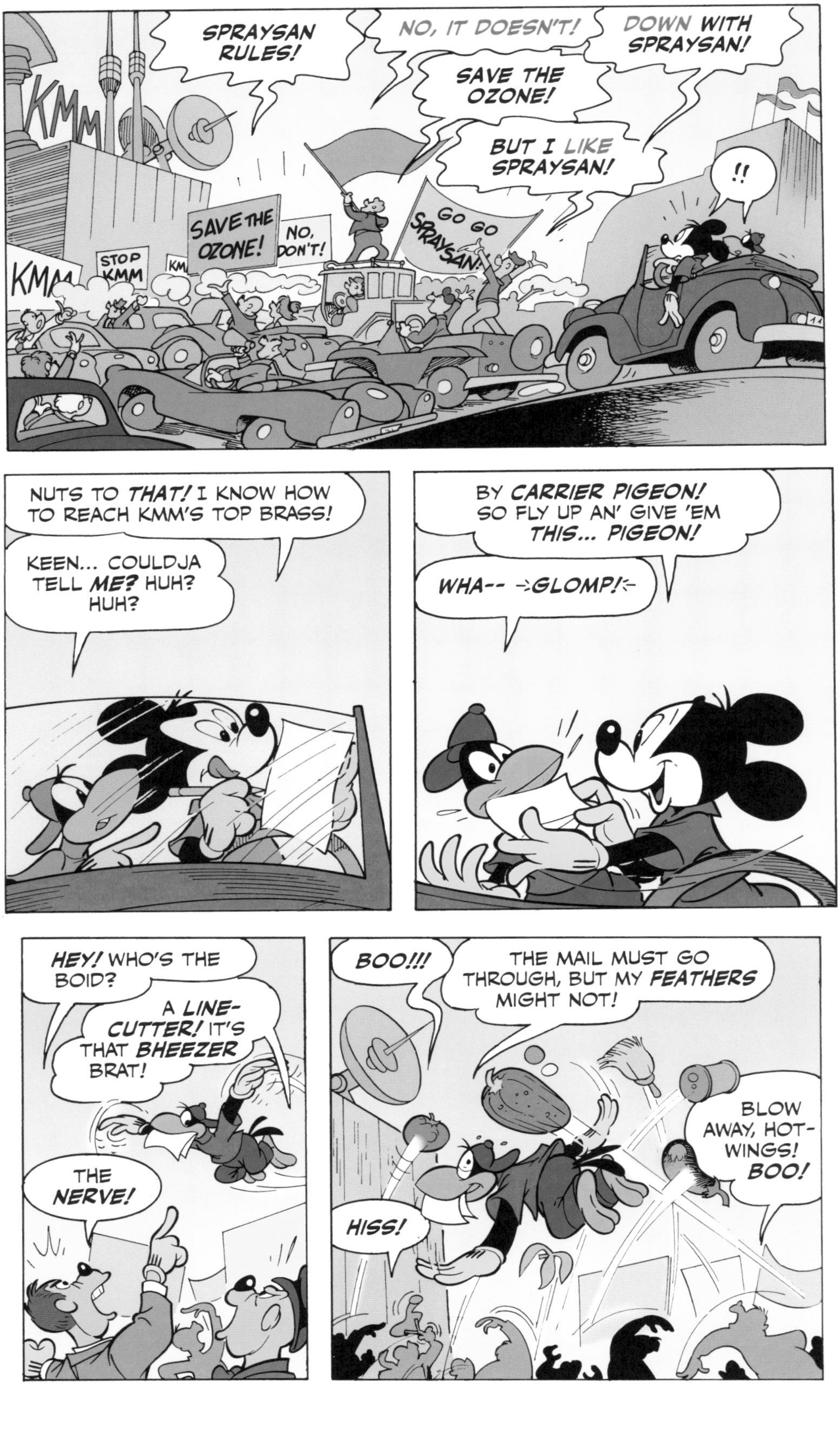

SPRAYSAN RULES!
NO, IT DOESN'T!
DOWN WITH SPRAYSAN!
SAVE THE OZONE!
BUT I LIKE SPRAYSAN!
!!
KMM
SAVE THE OZONE!
NO, DON'T!
GO GO SPRAYSAN!
STOP KMM
NUTS TO THAT! I KNOW HOW TO REACH KMM'S TOP BRASS!
KEEN... COULDJA TELL ME? HUH? HUH?
BY CARRIER PIGEON! SO FLY UP AN' GIVE 'EM THIS... PIGEON!
WHA-- GLOMP!
HEY! WHO'S THE BOID?
A LINE-CUTTER! IT'S THAT BHEEZER BRAT!
THE NERVE!
BOO!!!
THE MAIL MUST GO THROUGH, BUT MY FEATHERS MIGHT NOT!
BLOW AWAY, HOT-WINGS! BOO!
HISS!

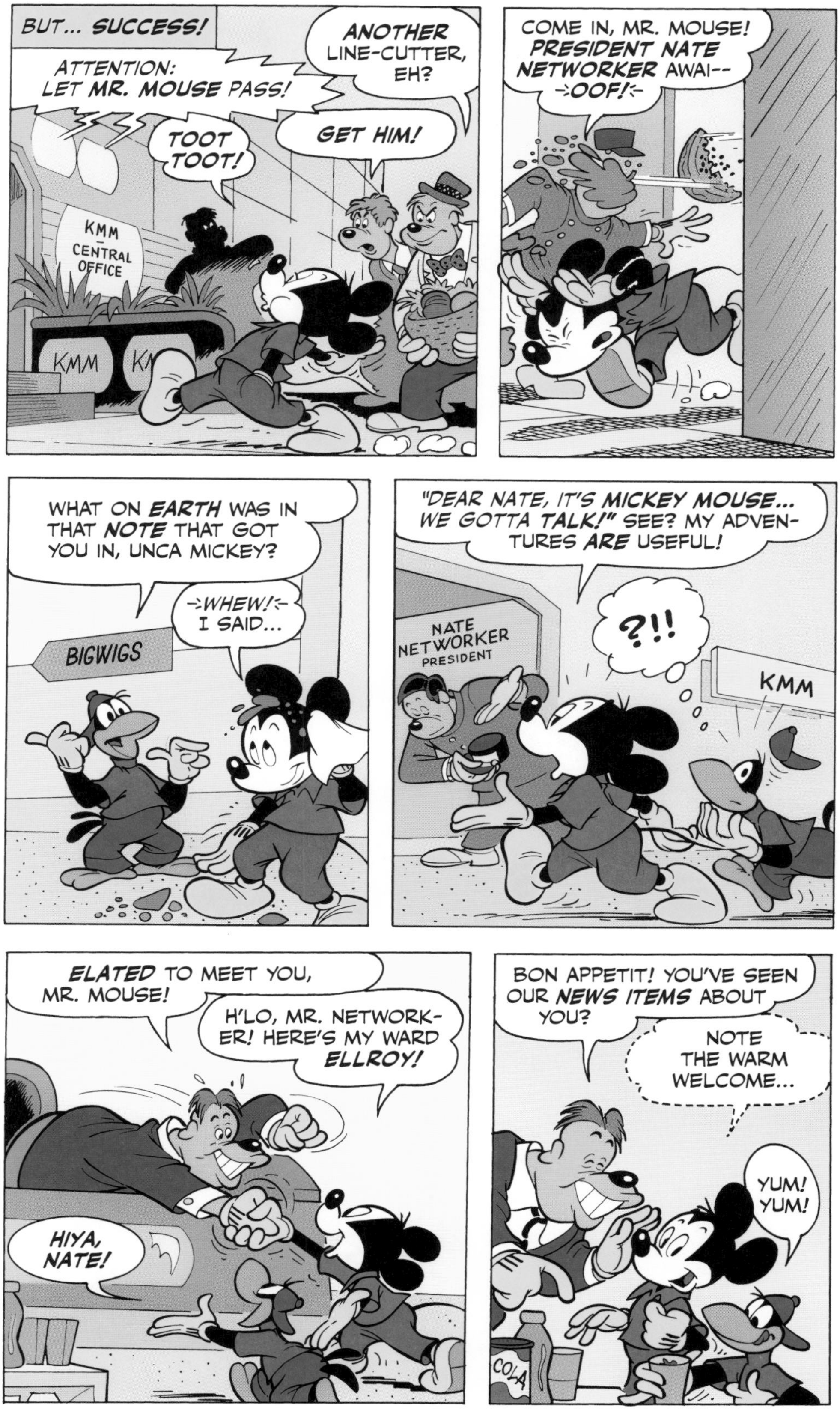
BUT... SUCCESS!
ATTENTION: LET MR. MOUSE PASS!
TOOT TOOT!
ANOTHER LINE-CUTTER, EH?
GET HIM!
KMM — CENTRAL OFFICE
KMM
COME IN, MR. MOUSE! PRESIDENT NATE NETWORKER AWAI-- OOF!
WHAT ON EARTH WAS IN THAT NOTE THAT GOT YOU IN, UNCA MICKEY?
WHEW! I SAID...
BIGWIGS
"DEAR NATE, IT'S MICKEY MOUSE... WE GOTTA TALK!" SEE? MY ADVENTURES ARE USEFUL!
NATE NETWORKER PRESIDENT
?!!
KMM
ELATED TO MEET YOU, MR. MOUSE!
H'LO, MR. NETWORKER! HERE'S MY WARD ELLROY!
HIYA, NATE!
BON APPETIT! YOU'VE SEEN OUR NEWS ITEMS ABOUT YOU?
NOTE THE WARM WELCOME...
YUM! YUM!
COLA

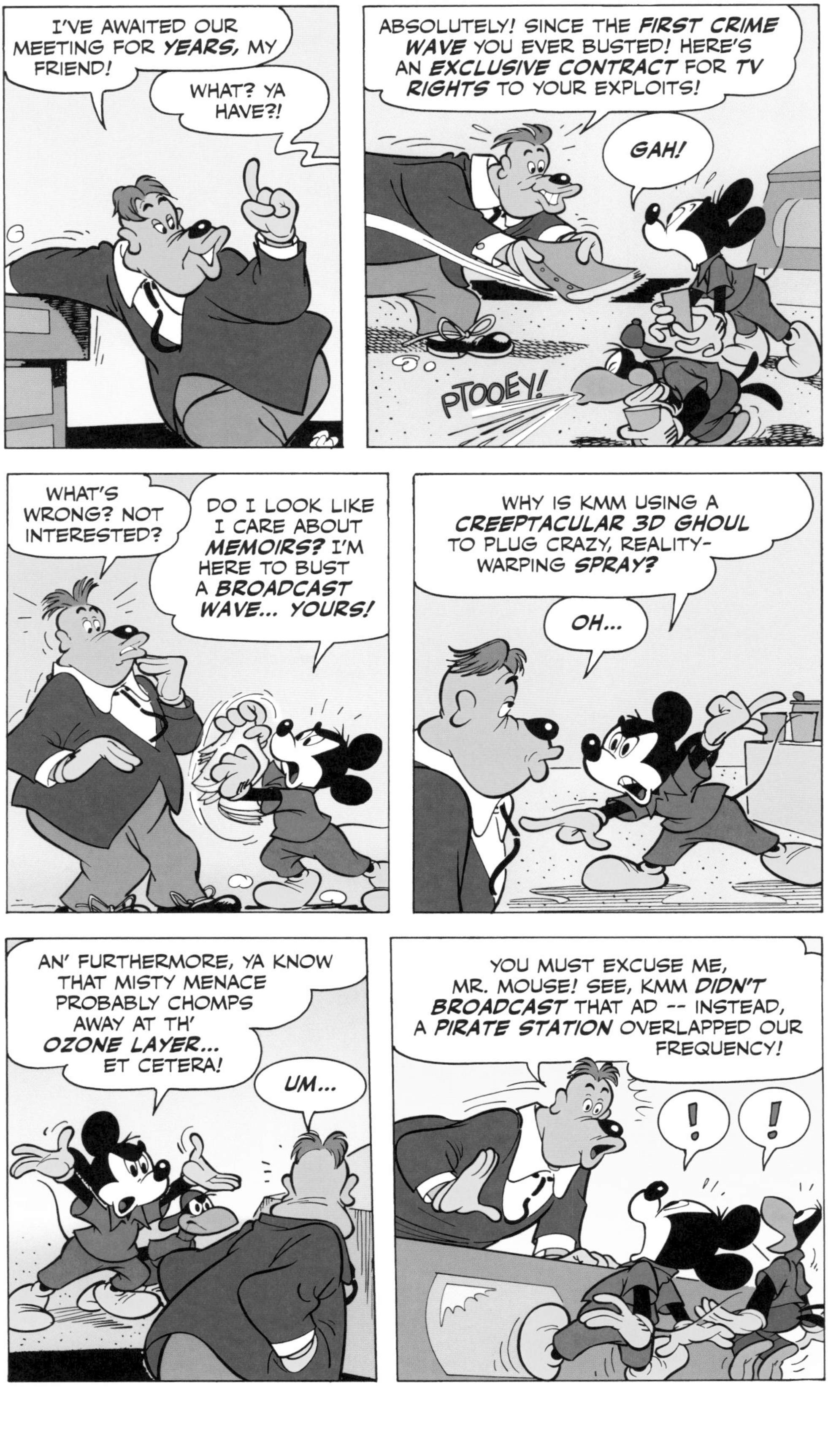
I'VE AWAITED OUR MEETING FOR YEARS, MY FRIEND!
WHAT? YA HAVE?!
ABSOLUTELY! SINCE THE FIRST CRIME WAVE YOU EVER BUSTED! HERE'S AN EXCLUSIVE CONTRACT FOR TV RIGHTS TO YOUR EXPLOITS!
GAH!
PTOOEY!
WHAT'S WRONG? NOT INTERESTED?
DO I LOOK LIKE I CARE ABOUT MEMOIRS? I'M HERE TO BUST A BROADCAST WAVE... YOURS!
WHY IS KMM USING A CREEPTACULAR 3D GHOUL TO PLUG CRAZY, REALITY-WARPING SPRAY?
OH...
AN' FURTHERMORE, YA KNOW THAT MISTY MENACE PROBABLY CHOMPS AWAY AT TH' OZONE LAYER... ET CETERA!
UM...
YOU MUST EXCUSE ME, MR. MOUSE! SEE, KMM DIDN'T BROADCAST THAT AD -- INSTEAD, A PIRATE STATION OVERLAPPED OUR FREQUENCY!
!
!

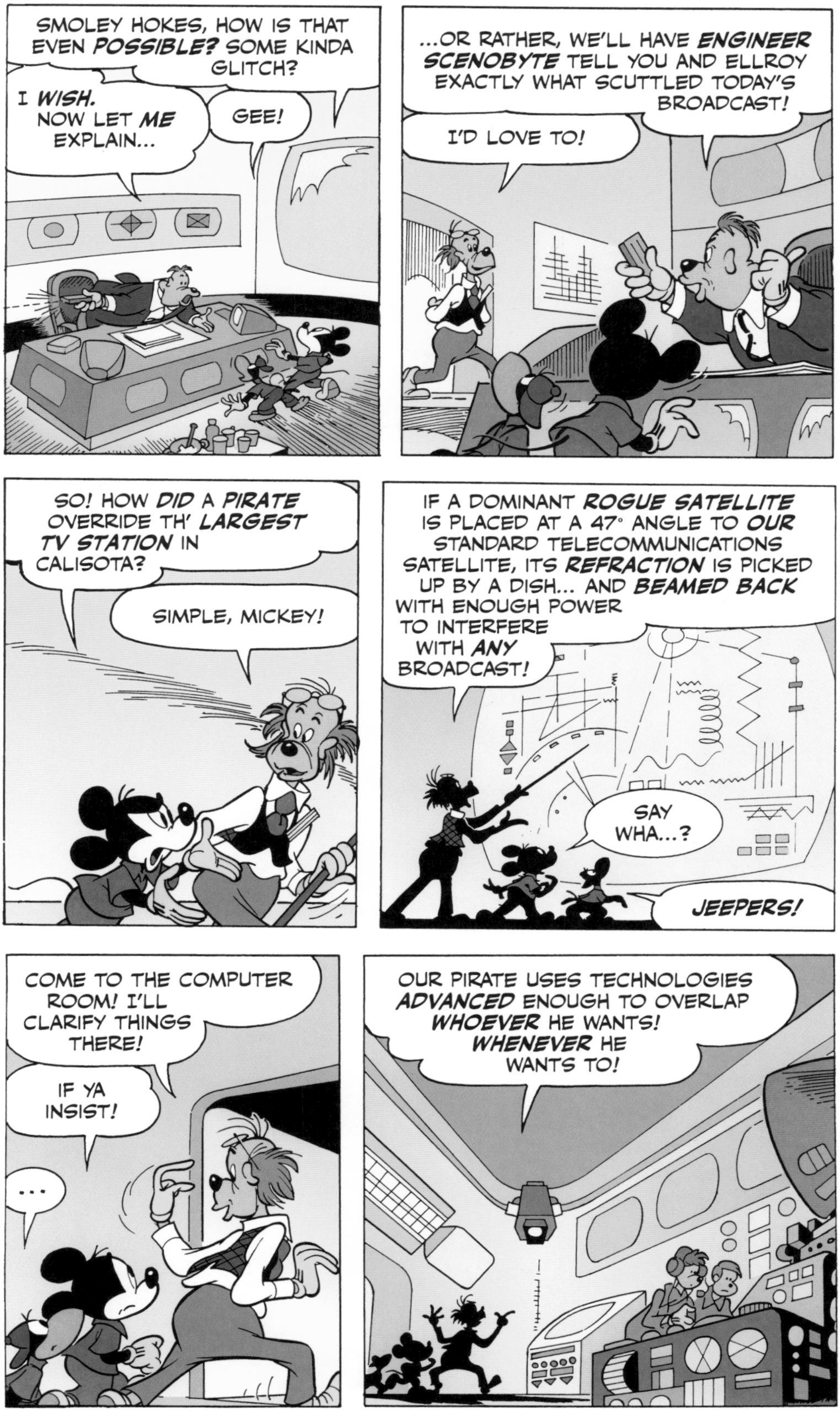
SMOLEY HOKES, HOW IS THAT EVEN POSSIBLE? SOME KINDA GLITCH?
I WISH. NOW LET ME EXPLAIN...
GEE!
...OR RATHER, WE'LL HAVE ENGINEER SCENOBYTE TELL YOU AND ELLROY EXACTLY WHAT SCUTTLED TODAY'S BROADCAST!
I'D LOVE TO!
SO! HOW DID A PIRATE OVERRIDE TH' LARGEST TV STATION IN CALISOTA?
SIMPLE, MICKEY!
IF A DOMINANT ROGUE SATELLITE IS PLACED AT A 47° ANGLE TO OUR STANDARD TELECOMMUNICATIONS SATELLITE, ITS REFRACTION IS PICKED UP BY A DISH... AND BEAMED BACK WITH ENOUGH POWER TO INTERFERE WITH ANY BROADCAST!
SAY WHA...?
JEEPERS!
COME TO THE COMPUTER ROOM! I'LL CLARIFY THINGS THERE!
IF YA INSIST!
...
OUR PIRATE USES TECHNOLOGIES ADVANCED ENOUGH TO OVERLAP WHOEVER HE WANTS! WHENEVER HE WANTS TO!

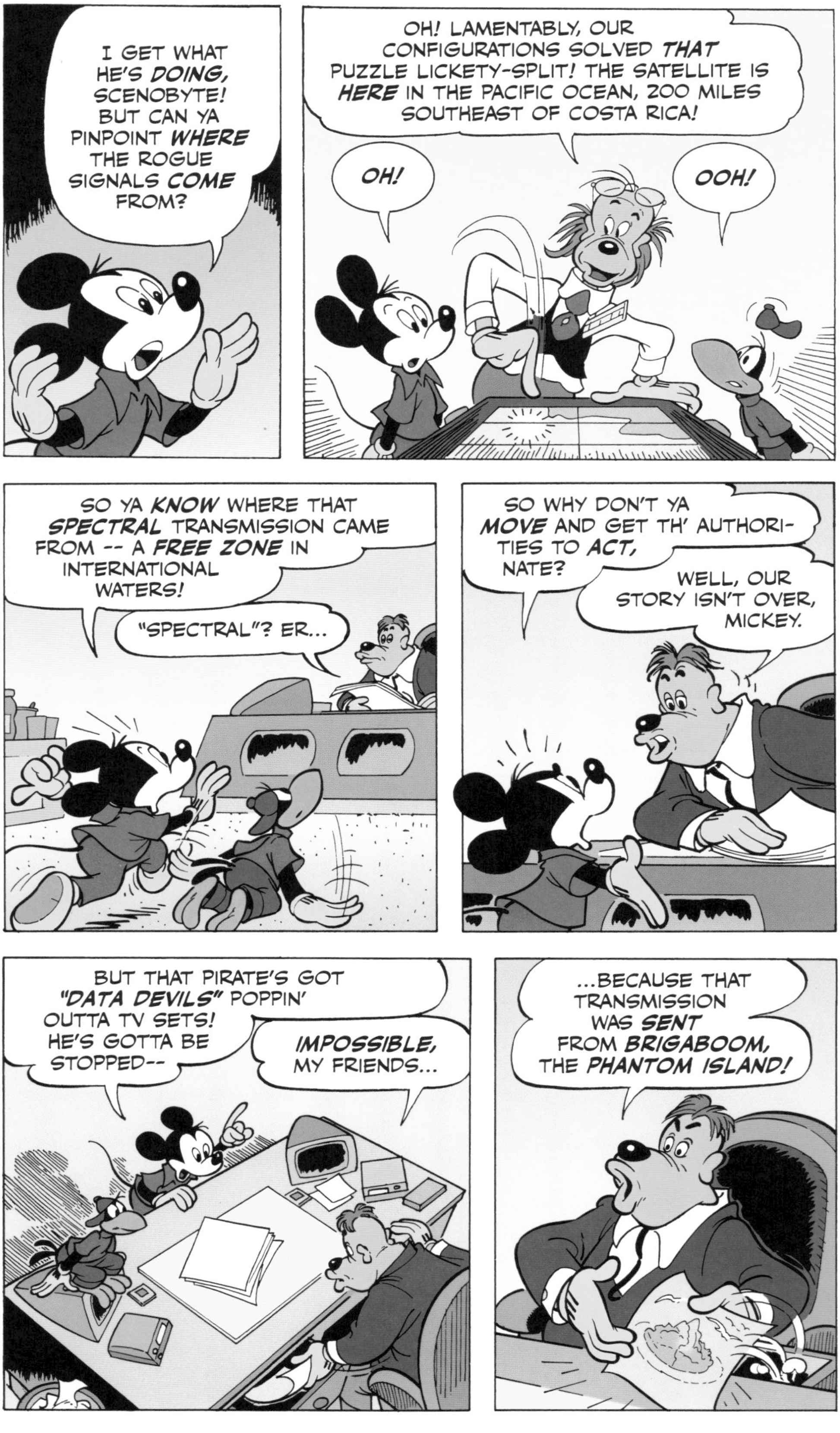
I GET WHAT HE'S DOING, SCENOBYTE! BUT CAN YA PINPOINT WHERE THE ROGUE SIGNALS COME FROM?
OH! LAMENTABLY, OUR CONFIGURATIONS SOLVED THAT PUZZLE LICKETY-SPLIT! THE SATELLITE IS HERE IN THE PACIFIC OCEAN, 200 MILES SOUTHEAST OF COSTA RICA!
OH!
OOH!
SO YA KNOW WHERE THAT SPECTRAL TRANSMISSION CAME FROM -- A FREE ZONE IN INTERNATIONAL WATERS!
"SPECTRAL"? ER...
SO WHY DON'T YA MOVE AND GET TH' AUTHORI-TIES TO ACT, NATE?
WELL, OUR STORY ISN'T OVER, MICKEY.
BUT THAT PIRATE'S GOT "DATA DEVILS" POPPIN' OUTTA TV SETS! HE'S GOTTA BE STOPPED--
IMPOSSIBLE, MY FRIENDS...
...BECAUSE THAT TRANSMISSION WAS SENT FROM BRIGABOOM, THE PHANTOM ISLAND!

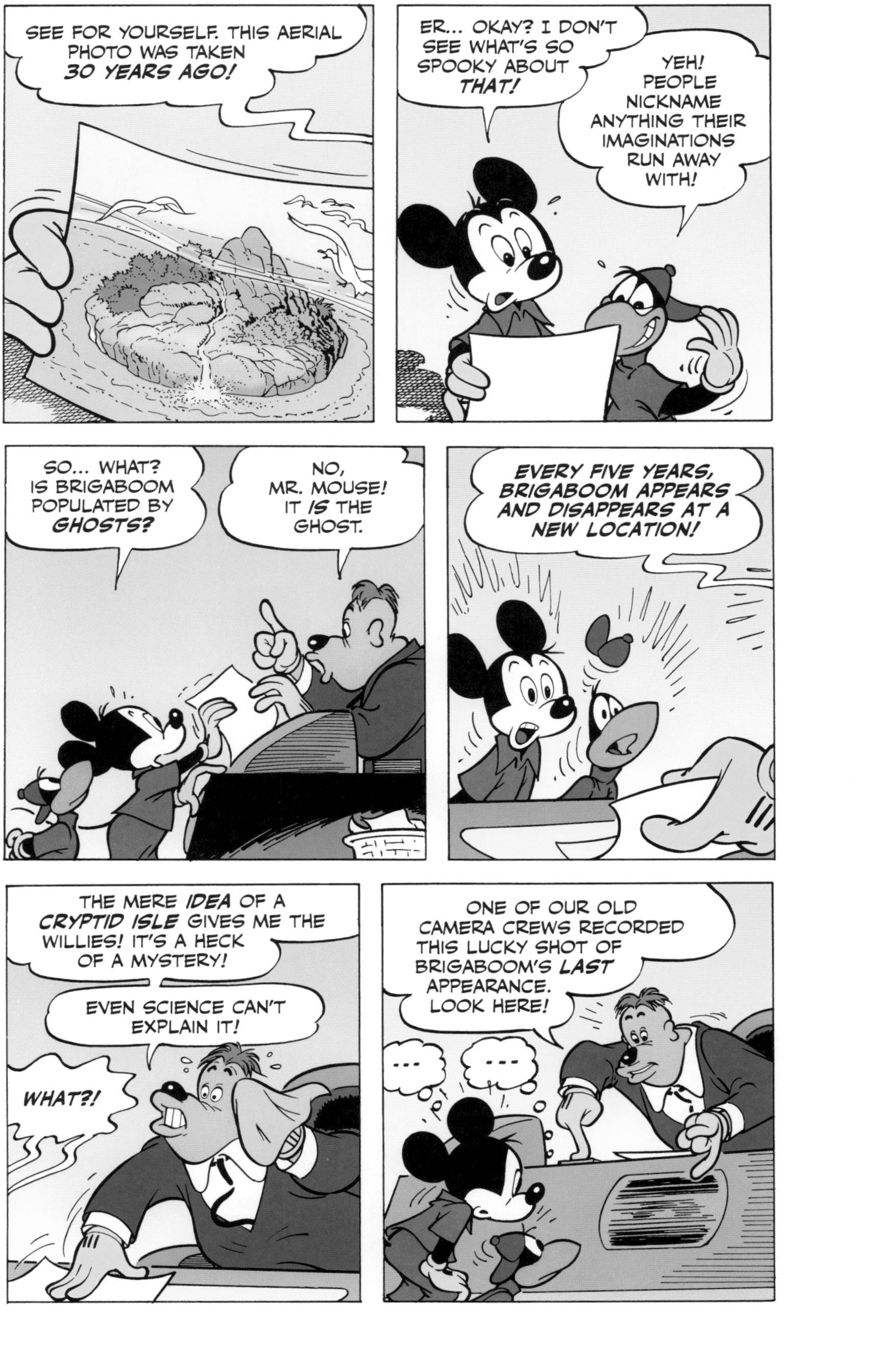

SEE FOR YOURSELF. THIS AERIAL PHOTO WAS TAKEN 30 YEARS AGO!
ER... OKAY? I DON'T SEE WHAT'S SO SPOOKY ABOUT THAT!
YEH! PEOPLE NICKNAME ANYTHING THEIR IMAGINATIONS RUN AWAY WITH!
SO... WHAT? IS BRIGABOOM POPULATED BY GHOSTS?
NO, MR. MOUSE! IT IS THE GHOST.
EVERY FIVE YEARS, BRIGABOOM APPEARS AND DISAPPEARS AT A NEW LOCATION!
THE MERE IDEA OF A CRYPTID ISLE GIVES ME THE WILLIES! IT'S A HECK OF A MYSTERY!
EVEN SCIENCE CAN'T EXPLAIN IT!
WHAT?!
ONE OF OUR OLD CAMERA CREWS RECORDED THIS LUCKY SHOT OF BRIGABOOM'S LAST APPEARANCE. LOOK HERE!
...
...

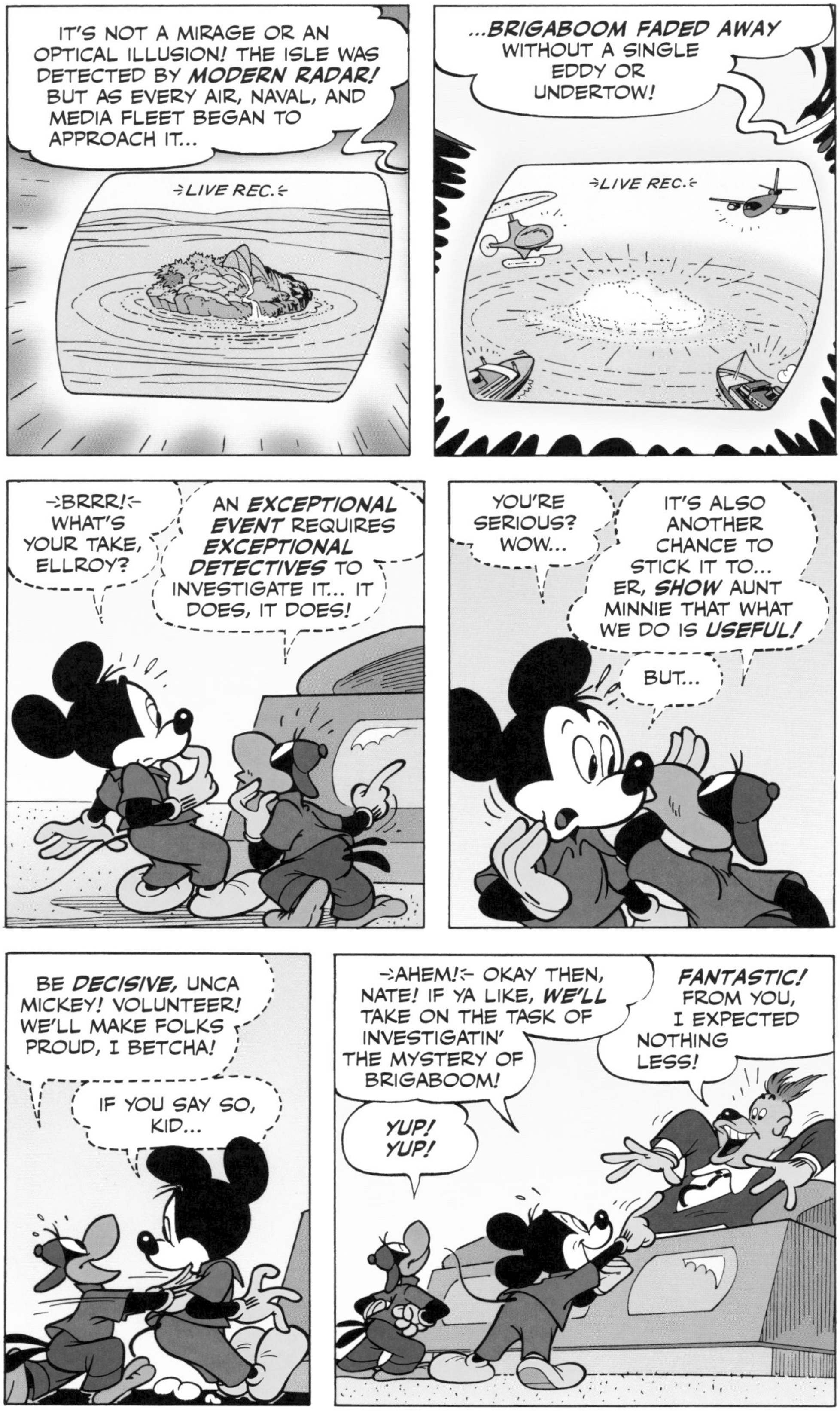

IT'S NOT A MIRAGE OR AN OPTICAL ILLUSION! THE ISLE WAS DETECTED BY MODERN RADAR! BUT AS EVERY AIR, NAVAL, AND MEDIA FLEET BEGAN TO APPROACH IT...
LIVE REC.
...BRIGABOOM FADED AWAY WITHOUT A SINGLE EDDY OR UNDERTOW!
LIVE REC.
BRRR! WHAT'S YOUR TAKE, ELLROY?
AN EXCEPTIONAL EVENT REQUIRES EXCEPTIONAL DETECTIVES TO INVESTIGATE IT... IT DOES, IT DOES!
YOU'RE SERIOUS? WOW...
IT'S ALSO ANOTHER CHANCE TO STICK IT TO... ER, SHOW AUNT MINNIE THAT WHAT WE DO IS USEFUL!
BUT...
BE DECISIVE, UNCA MICKEY! VOLUNTEER! WE'LL MAKE FOLKS PROUD, I BETCHA!
IF YOU SAY SO, KID...
AHEM! OKAY THEN, NATE! IF YA LIKE, WE'LL TAKE ON THE TASK OF INVESTIGATIN' THE MYSTERY OF BRIGABOOM!
YUP! YUP!
FANTASTIC! FROM YOU, I EXPECTED NOTHING LESS!

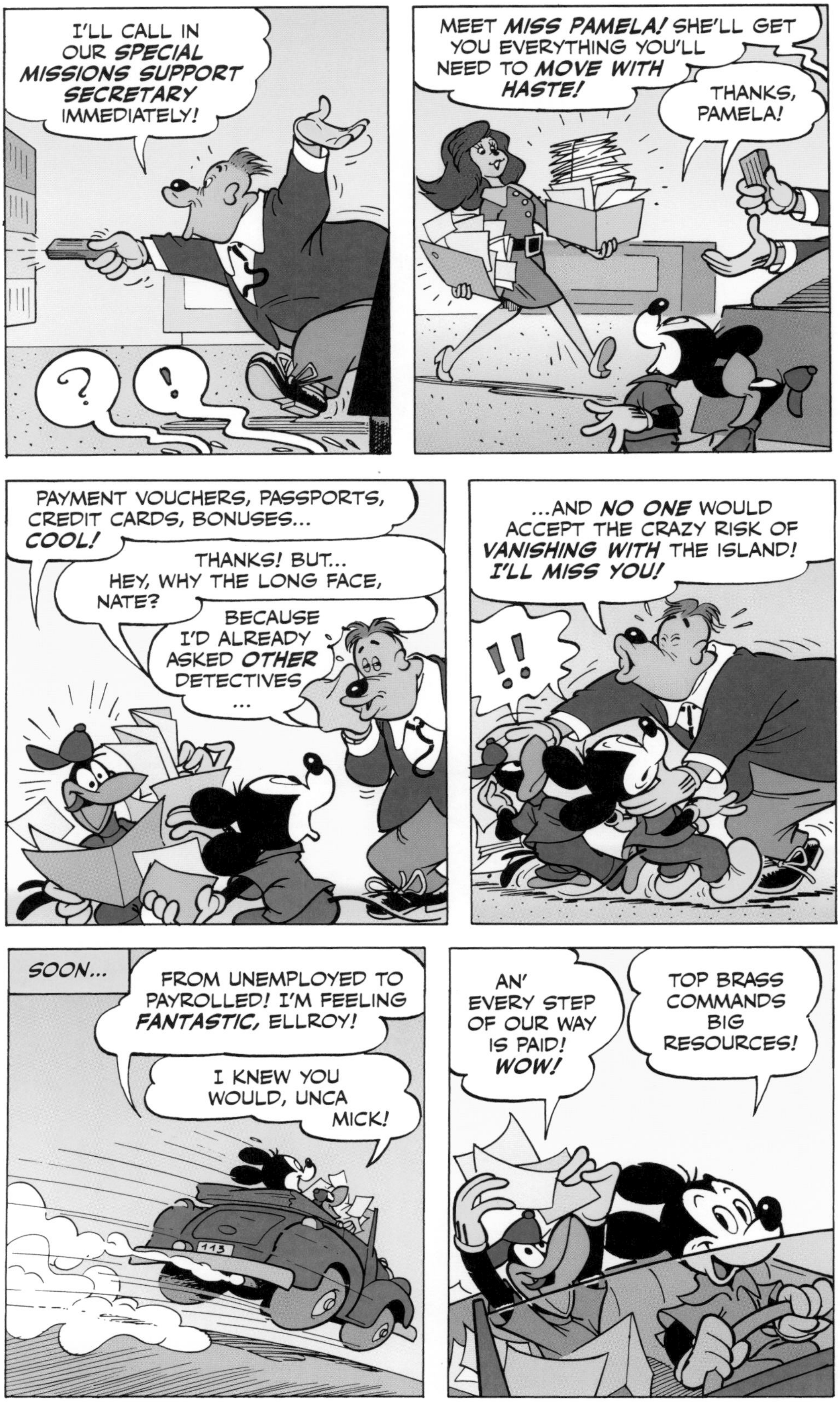

I'LL CALL IN OUR SPECIAL MISSIONS SUPPORT SECRETARY IMMEDIATELY!
?
!
MEET MISS PAMELA! SHE'LL GET YOU EVERYTHING YOU'LL NEED TO MOVE WITH HASTE!
THANKS, PAMELA!
PAYMENT VOUCHERS, PASSPORTS, CREDIT CARDS, BONUSES... COOL!
THANKS! BUT... HEY, WHY THE LONG FACE, NATE?
BECAUSE I'D ALREADY ASKED OTHER DETECTIVES ...
...AND NO ONE WOULD ACCEPT THE CRAZY RISK OF VANISHING WITH THE ISLAND! I'LL MISS YOU!
!!
SOON...
FROM UNEMPLOYED TO PAYROLLED! I'M FEELING FANTASTIC, ELLROY!
I KNEW YOU WOULD, UNCA MICK!
113
AN' EVERY STEP OF OUR WAY IS PAID! WOW!
TOP BRASS COMMANDS BIG RESOURCES!

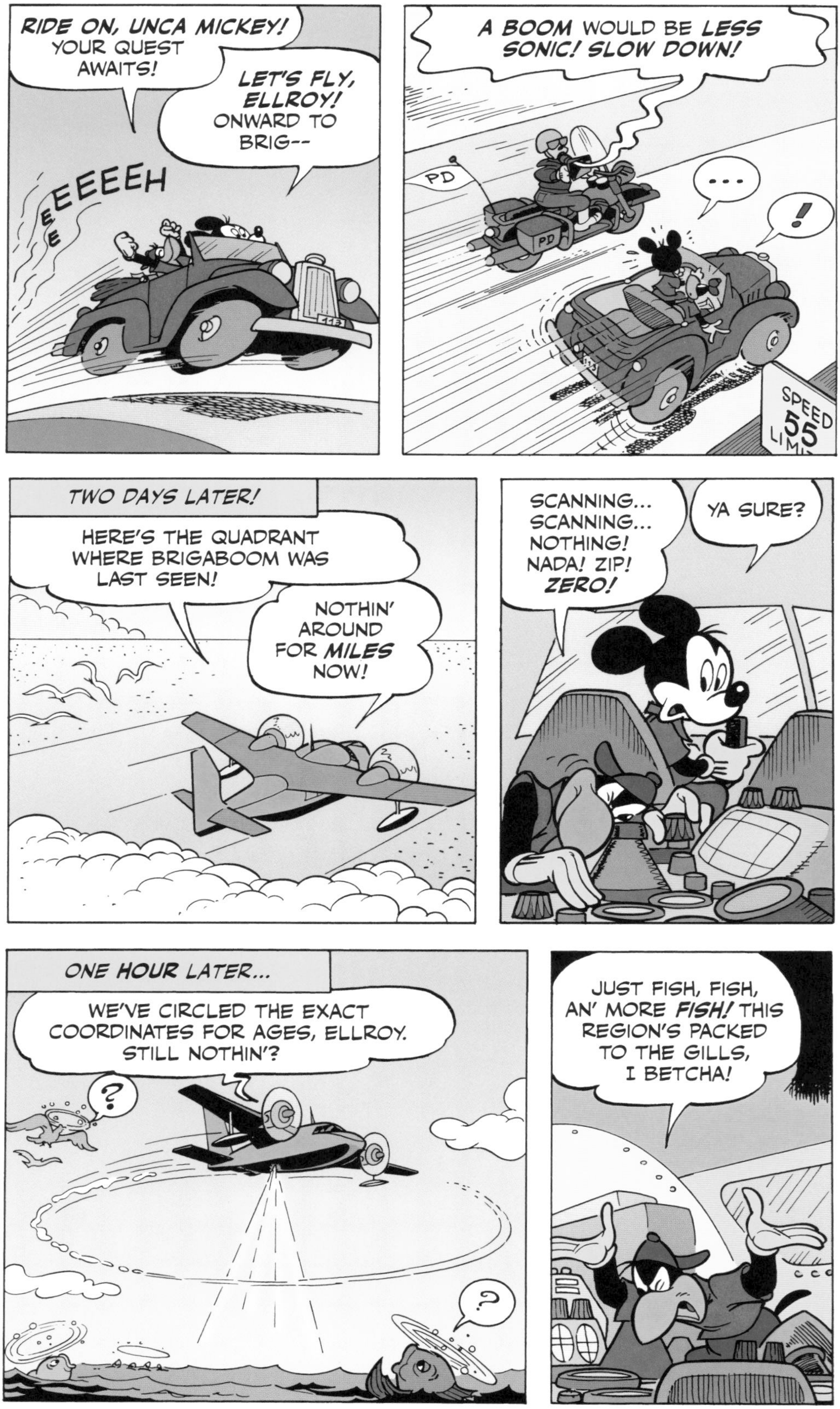
RIDE ON, UNCA MICKEY! YOUR QUEST AWAITS!
LET'S FLY, ELLROY! ONWARD TO BRIG--
EEEEEEH
A BOOM WOULD BE LESS SONIC! SLOW DOWN!
PD
PD
...
!
SPEED 55
TWO DAYS LATER!
HERE'S THE QUADRANT WHERE BRIGABOOM WAS LAST SEEN!
NOTHIN' AROUND FOR MILES NOW!
SCANNING... SCANNING... NOTHING! NADA! ZIP! ZERO!
YA SURE?
ONE HOUR LATER...
WE'VE CIRCLED THE EXACT COORDINATES FOR AGES, ELLROY. STILL NOTHIN'?
?
?
JUST FISH, FISH, AN' MORE FISH! THIS REGION'S PACKED TO THE GILLS, I BETCHA!

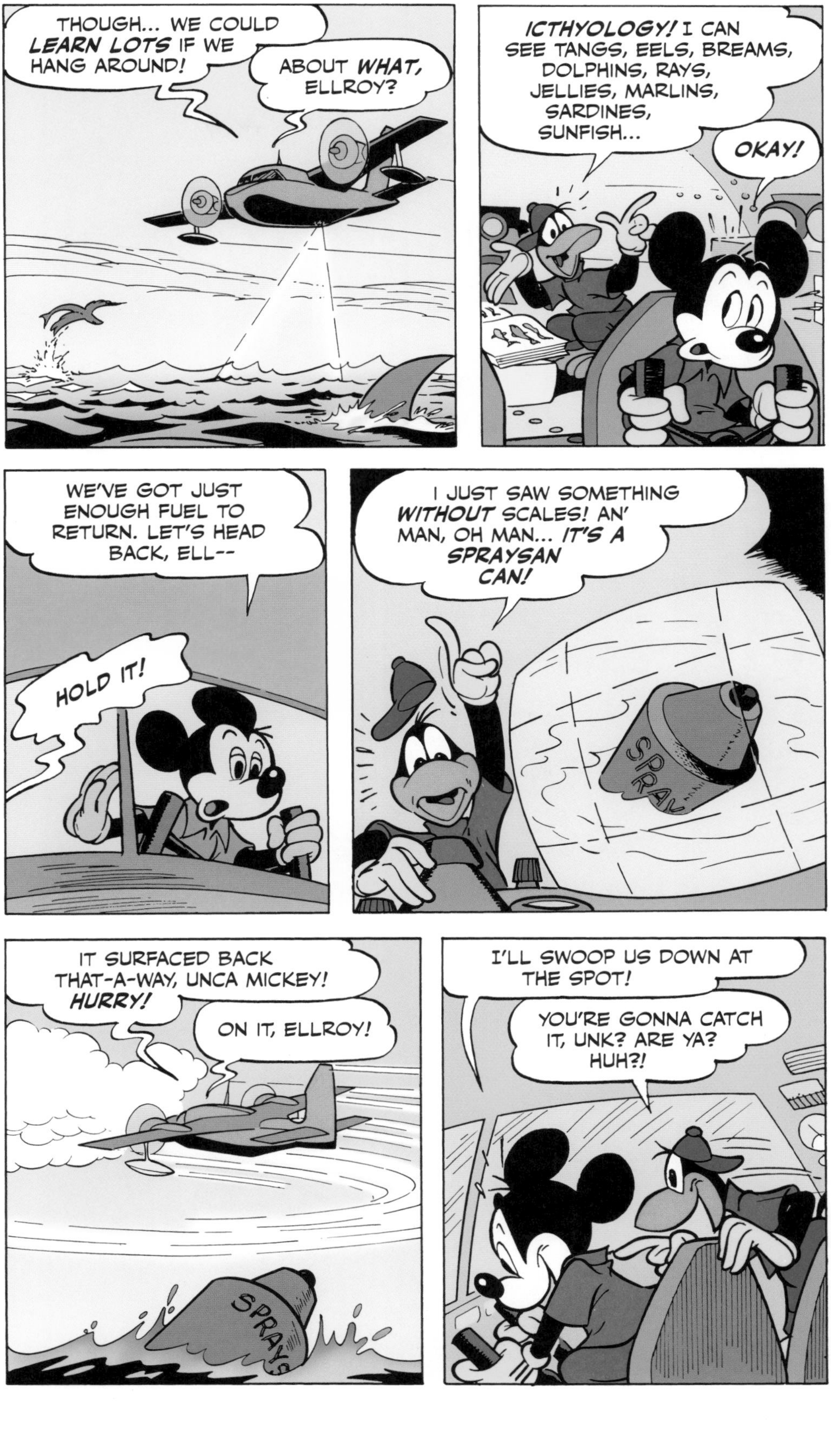
THOUGH... WE COULD LEARN LOTS IF WE HANG AROUND!
ABOUT WHAT, ELLROY?
ICTHYOLOGY! I CAN SEE TANGS, EELS, BREAMS, DOLPHINS, RAYS, JELLIES, MARLINS, SARDINES, SUNFISH...
OKAY!
WE'VE GOT JUST ENOUGH FUEL TO RETURN. LET'S HEAD BACK, ELL--
HOLD IT!
I JUST SAW SOMETHING WITHOUT SCALES! AN' MAN, OH MAN... IT'S A SPRAYSAN CAN!
SPRAY
IT SURFACED BACK THAT-A-WAY, UNCA MICKEY! HURRY!
ON IT, ELLROY!
SPRAYS
I'LL SWOOP US DOWN AT THE SPOT!
YOU'RE GONNA CATCH IT, UNK? ARE YA? HUH?!

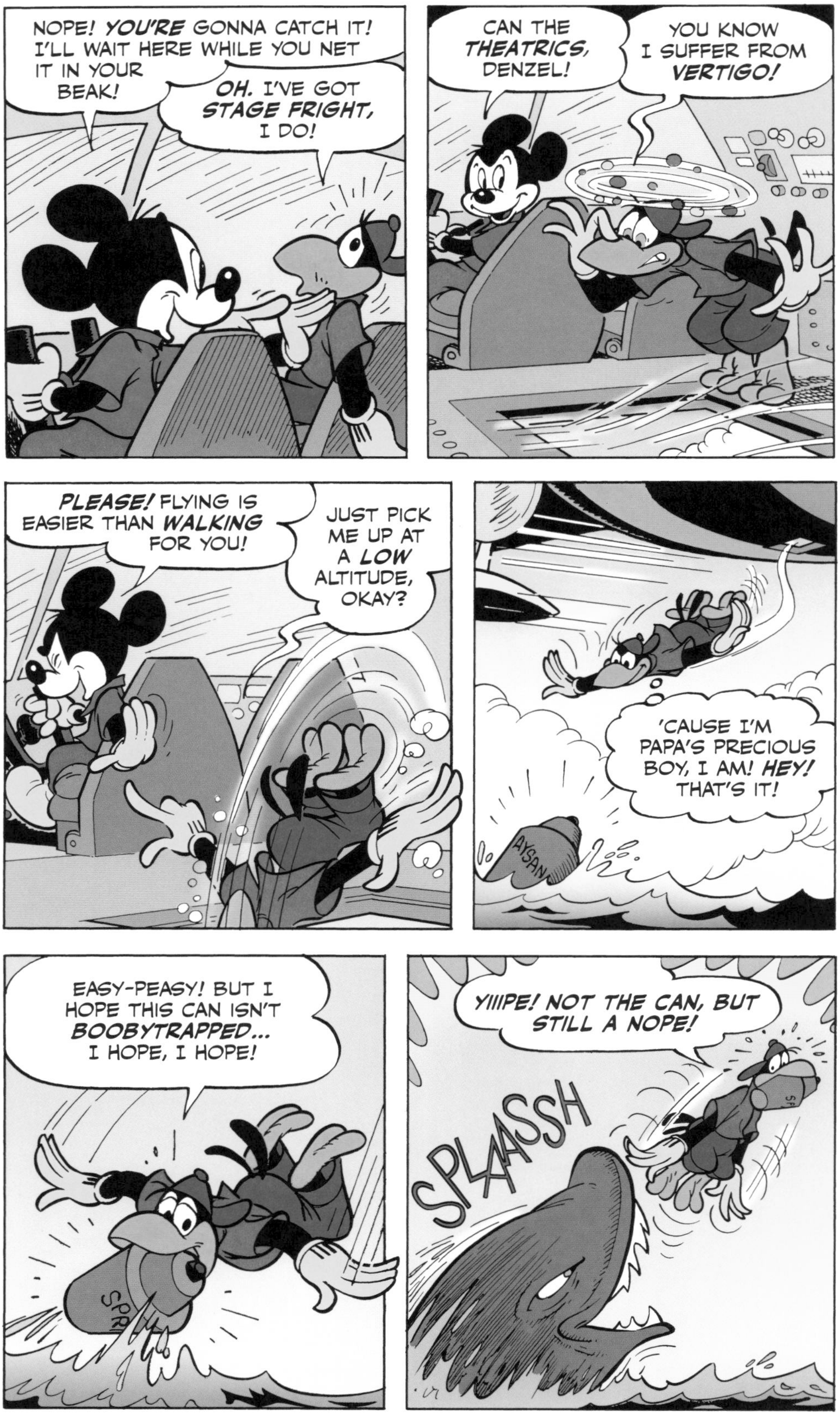
NOPE! YOU'RE GONNA CATCH IT! I'LL WAIT HERE WHILE YOU NET IT IN YOUR BEAK!
OH. I'VE GOT STAGE FRIGHT, I DO!
CAN THE THEATRICS, DENZEL!
YOU KNOW I SUFFER FROM VERTIGO!
PLEASE! FLYING IS EASIER THAN WALKING FOR YOU!
JUST PICK ME UP AT A LOW ALTITUDE, OKAY?
'CAUSE I'M PAPA'S PRECIOUS BOY, I AM! HEY! THAT'S IT!
AYSAN
EASY-PEASY! BUT I HOPE THIS CAN ISN'T BOOBYTRAPPED... I HOPE, I HOPE!
SPR
YIIIPE! NOT THE CAN, BUT STILL A NOPE!
SPLAASSH

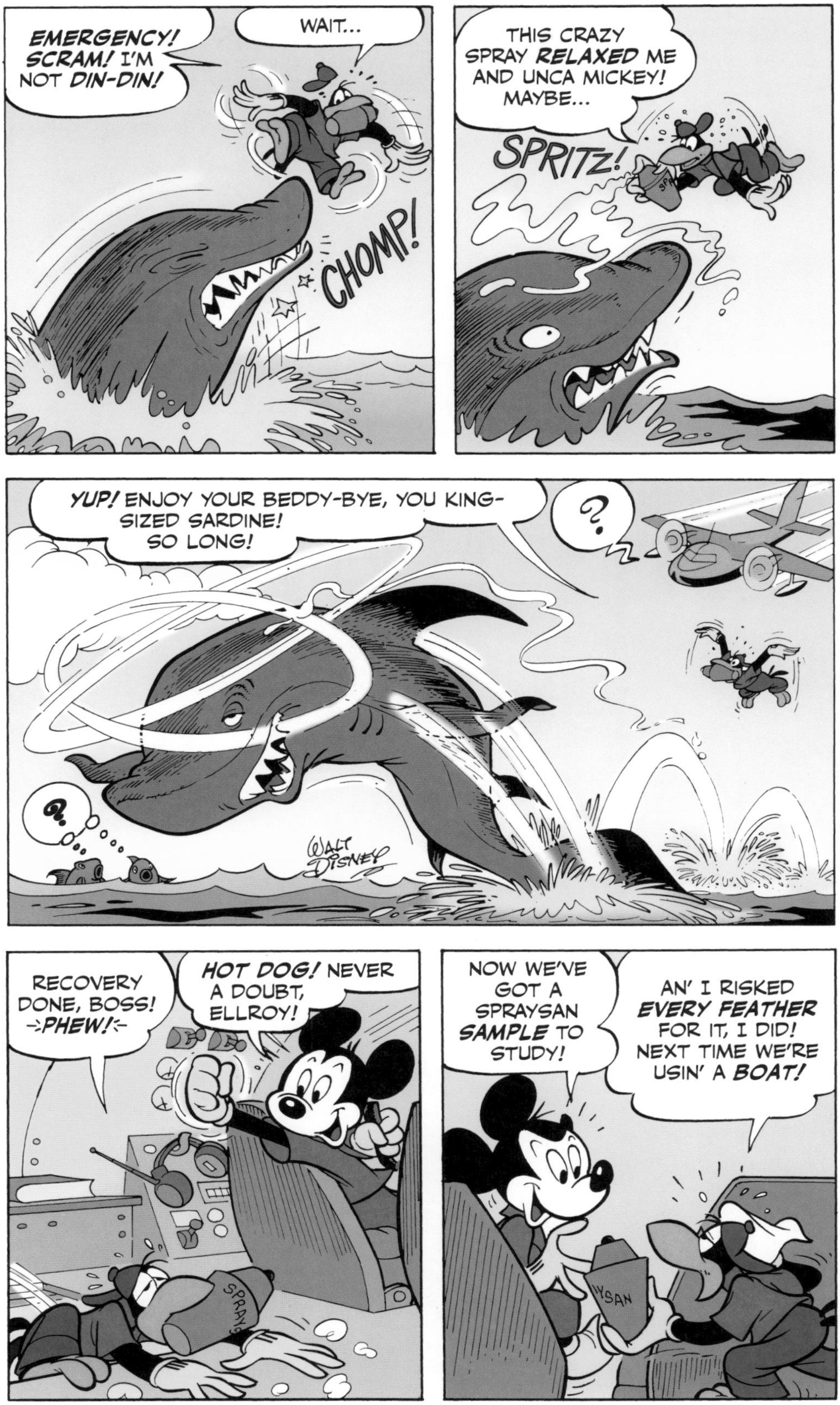
EMERGENCY! SCRAM! I'M NOT DIN-DIN!
WAIT...
CHOMP!
THIS CRAZY SPRAY RELAXED ME AND UNCA MICKEY! MAYBE...
SPRITZ!
YUP! ENJOY YOUR BEDDY-BYE, YOU KING-SIZED SARDINE! SO LONG!
?
?
WALT DISNEY
RECOVERY DONE, BOSS! -PHEW!-
HOT DOG! NEVER A DOUBT, ELLROY!
SPRAYS
NOW WE'VE GOT A SPRAYSAN SAMPLE TO STUDY!
AN' I RISKED EVERY FEATHER FOR IT, I DID! NEXT TIME WE'RE USIN' A BOAT!
YSAN

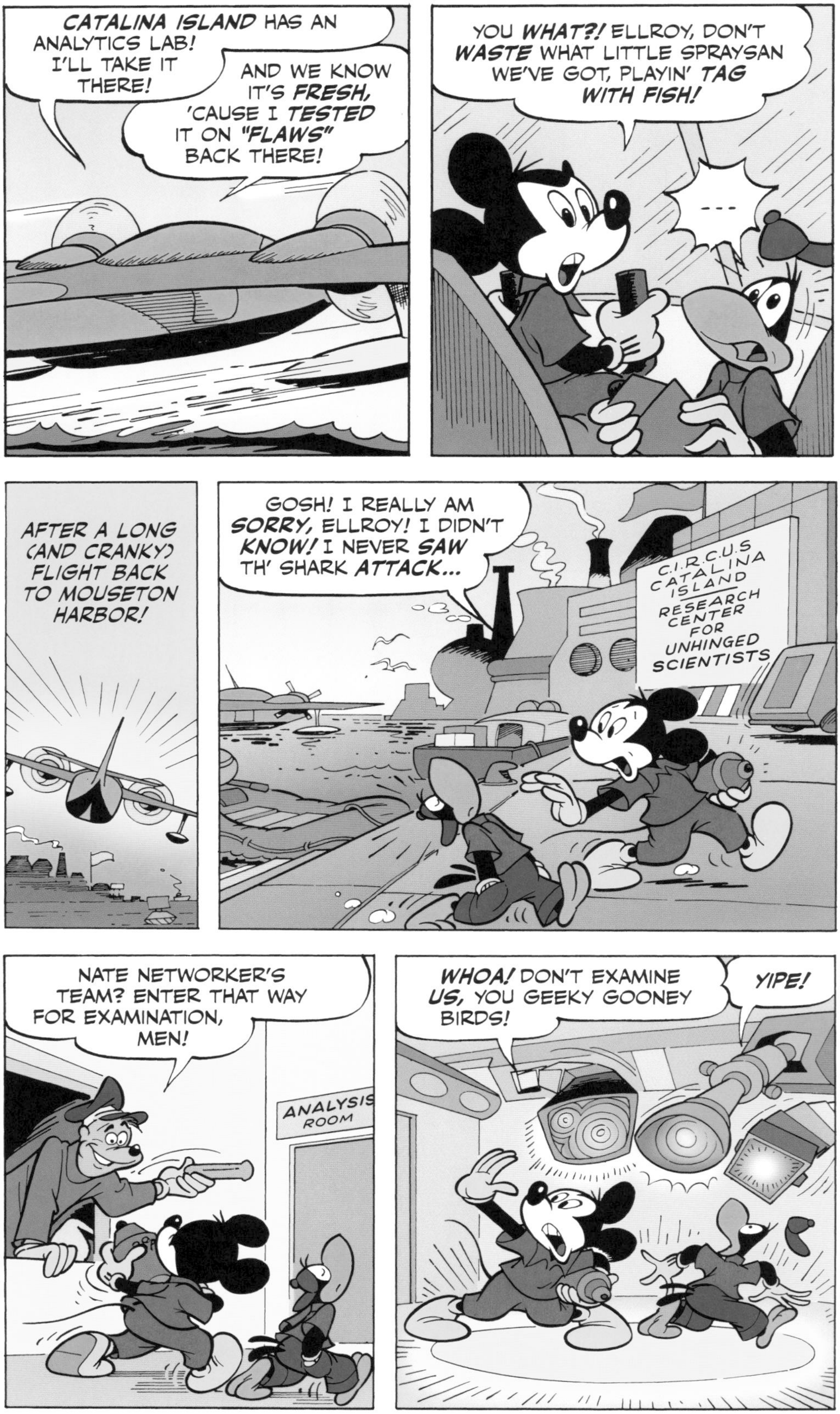
CATALINA ISLAND HAS AN ANALYTICS LAB! I'LL TAKE IT THERE!
AND WE KNOW IT'S FRESH, 'CAUSE I TESTED IT ON "FLAWS" BACK THERE!
YOU WHAT?! ELLROY, DON'T WASTE WHAT LITTLE SPRAYSAN WE'VE GOT, PLAYIN' TAG WITH FISH!
- - -
AFTER A LONG (AND CRANKY) FLIGHT BACK TO MOUSETON HARBOR!
GOSH! I REALLY AM SORRY, ELLROY! I DIDN'T KNOW! I NEVER SAW TH' SHARK ATTACK...
C.I.R.C.U.S CATALINA ISLAND RESEARCH CENTER FOR UNHINGED SCIENTISTS
NATE NETWORKER'S TEAM? ENTER THAT WAY FOR EXAMINATION, MEN!
ANALYSIS ROOM
WHOA! DON'T EXAMINE US, YOU GEEKY GOONEY BIRDS!
YIPE!

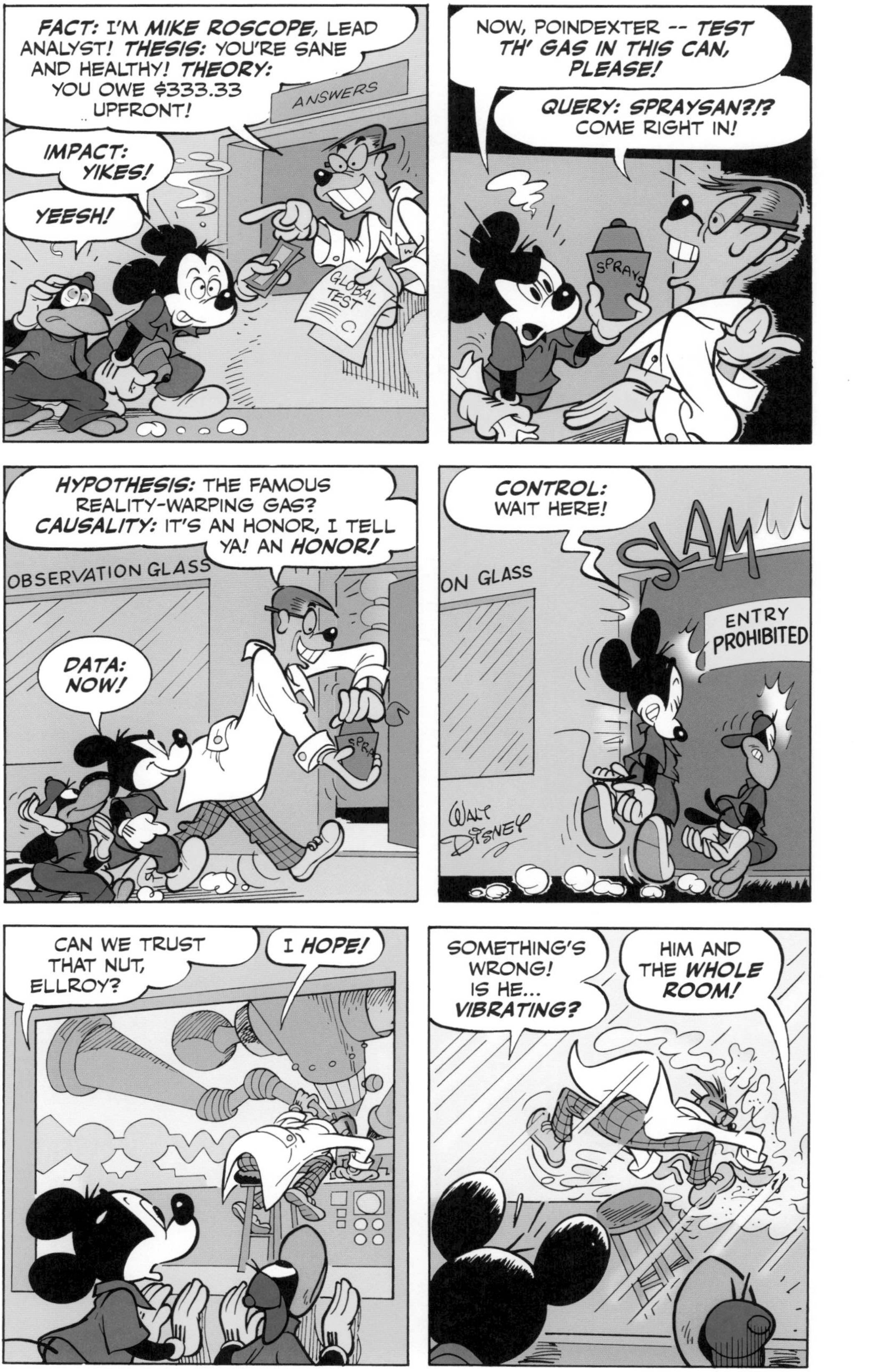
FACT: I'M MIKE ROSCOPE, LEAD ANALYST! THESIS: YOU'RE SANE AND HEALTHY! THEORY: YOU OWE $333.33 UPFRONT!
ANSWERS
IMPACT: YIKES!
YEESH!
GLOBAL TEST
NOW, POINDEXTER -- TEST TH' GAS IN THIS CAN, PLEASE!
QUERY: SPRAYSAN?!? COME RIGHT IN!
SPRAYS
HYPOTHESIS: THE FAMOUS REALITY-WARPING GAS? CAUSALITY: IT'S AN HONOR, I TELL YA! AN HONOR!
OBSERVATION GLASS
DATA: NOW!
CONTROL: WAIT HERE!
SLAM
ON GLASS
ENTRY PROHIBITED
WALT DISNEY
CAN WE TRUST THAT NUT, ELLROY?
I HOPE!
SOMETHING'S WRONG! IS HE... VIBRATING?
HIM AND THE WHOLE ROOM!

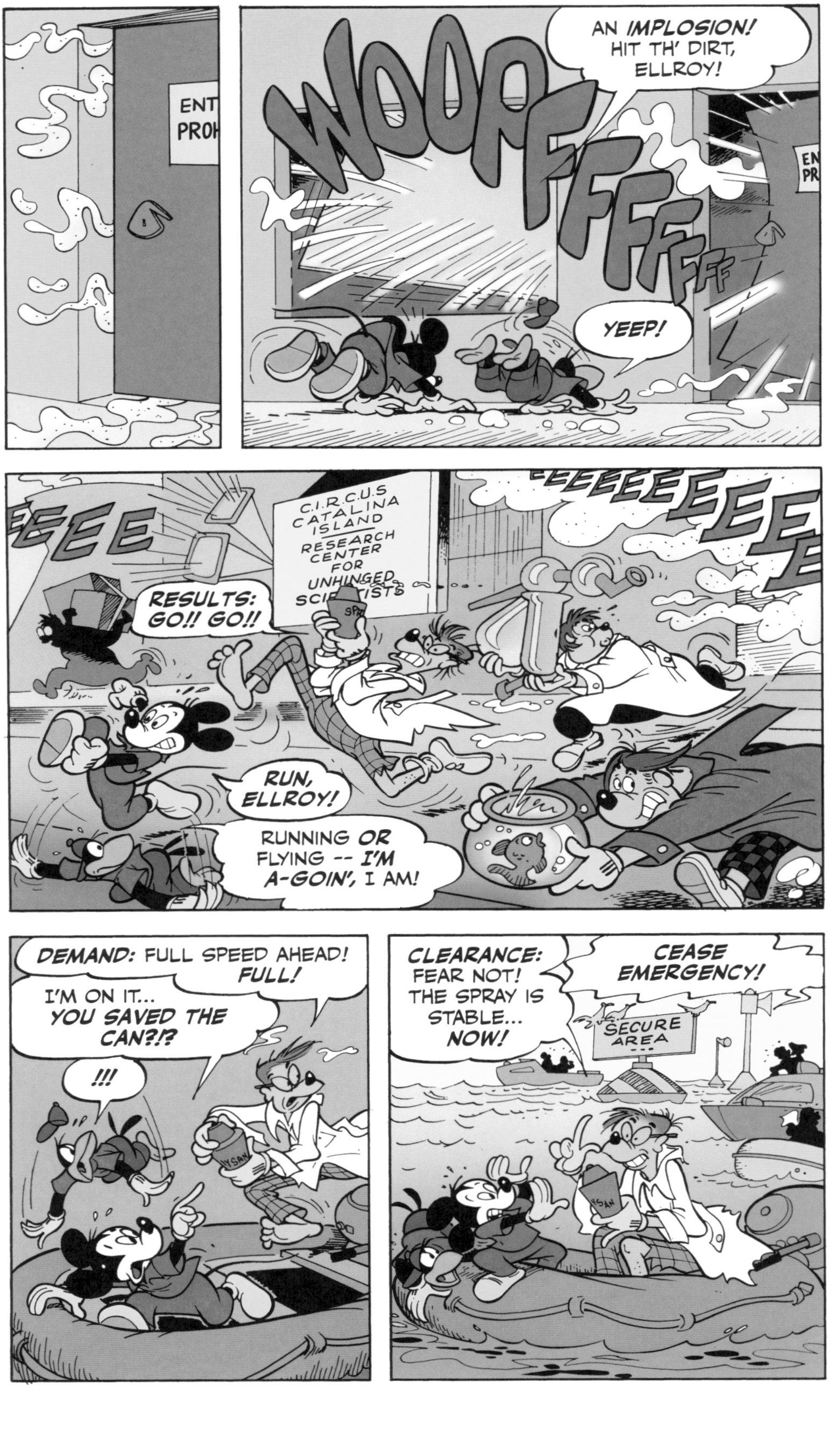

ENT
PROH
WOOPFFFFFFF
AN IMPLOSION! HIT TH' DIRT, ELLROY!
YEEP!
EEEE
C.I.R.C.U.S CATALINA ISLAND RESEARCH CENTER FOR UNHINGED SCIENTISTS
EEEEEEEEEEE
RESULTS: GO!! GO!!
RUN, ELLROY!
RUNNING OR FLYING -- I'M A-GOIN', I AM!
DEMAND: FULL SPEED AHEAD! FULL!
I'M ON IT... YOU SAVED THE CAN?!?
!!!
CLEARANCE: FEAR NOT! THE SPRAY IS STABLE... NOW!
CEASE EMERGENCY!
SECURE AREA

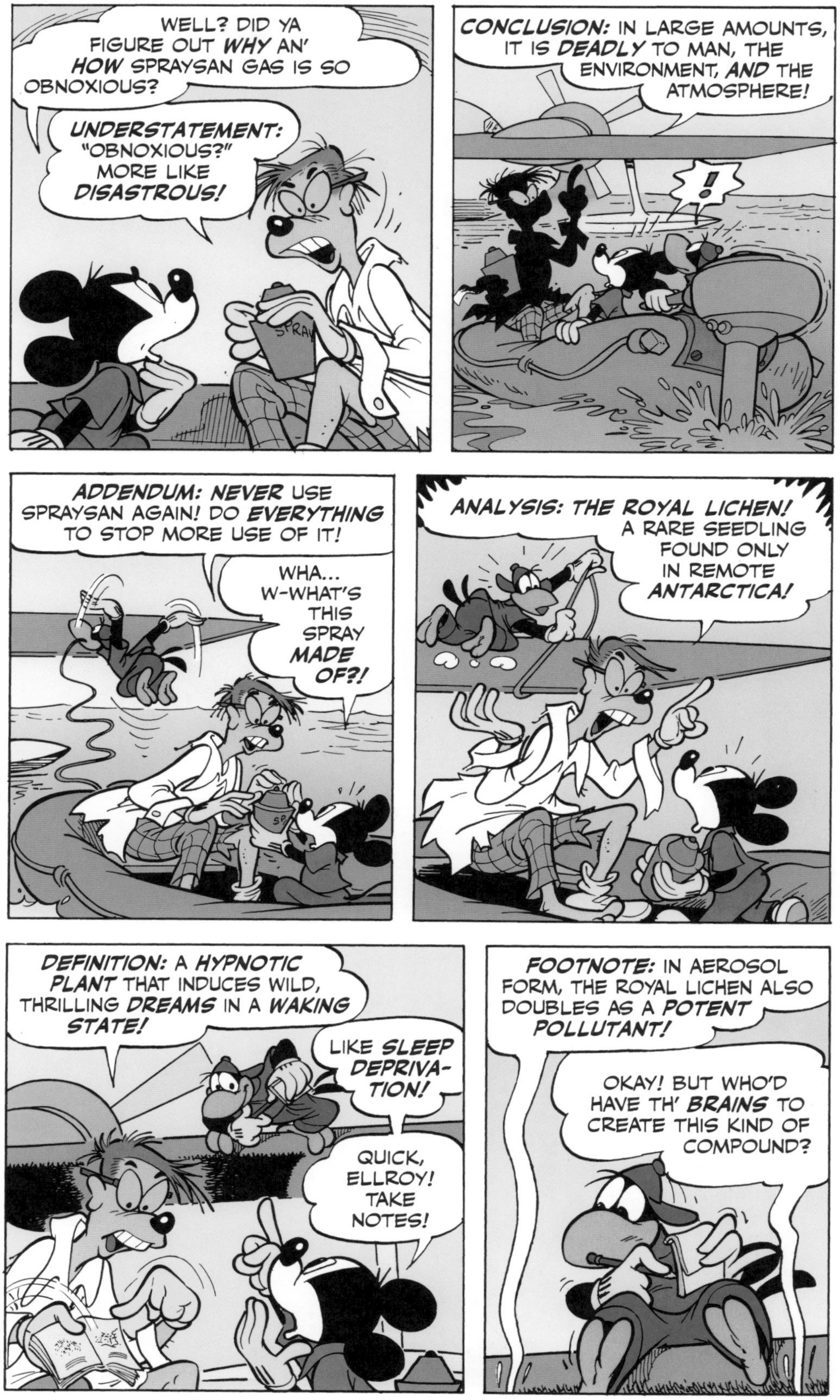
WELL? DID YA FIGURE OUT *WHY* AN' *HOW* SPRAYSAN GAS IS SO OBNOXIOUS?
UNDERSTATEMENT: "OBNOXIOUS?" MORE LIKE *DISASTROUS!*
SPRAY
CONCLUSION: IN LARGE AMOUNTS, IT IS *DEADLY* TO MAN, THE ENVIRONMENT, *AND* THE ATMOSPHERE!
!
ADDENDUM: NEVER USE SPRAYSAN AGAIN! DO *EVERYTHING* TO STOP MORE USE OF IT!
WHA... W-WHAT'S THIS SPRAY *MADE OF?!*
SP
ANALYSIS: THE ROYAL LICHEN! A RARE SEEDLING FOUND ONLY IN REMOTE *ANTARCTICA!*
DEFINITION: A *HYPNOTIC PLANT* THAT INDUCES WILD, THRILLING *DREAMS* IN A *WAKING STATE!*
LIKE *SLEEP DEPRIVATION!*
QUICK, ELLROY! TAKE NOTES!
FOOTNOTE: IN AEROSOL FORM, THE ROYAL LICHEN ALSO DOUBLES AS A *POTENT POLLUTANT!*
OKAY! BUT WHO'D HAVE TH' *BRAINS* TO CREATE THIS KIND OF COMPOUND?

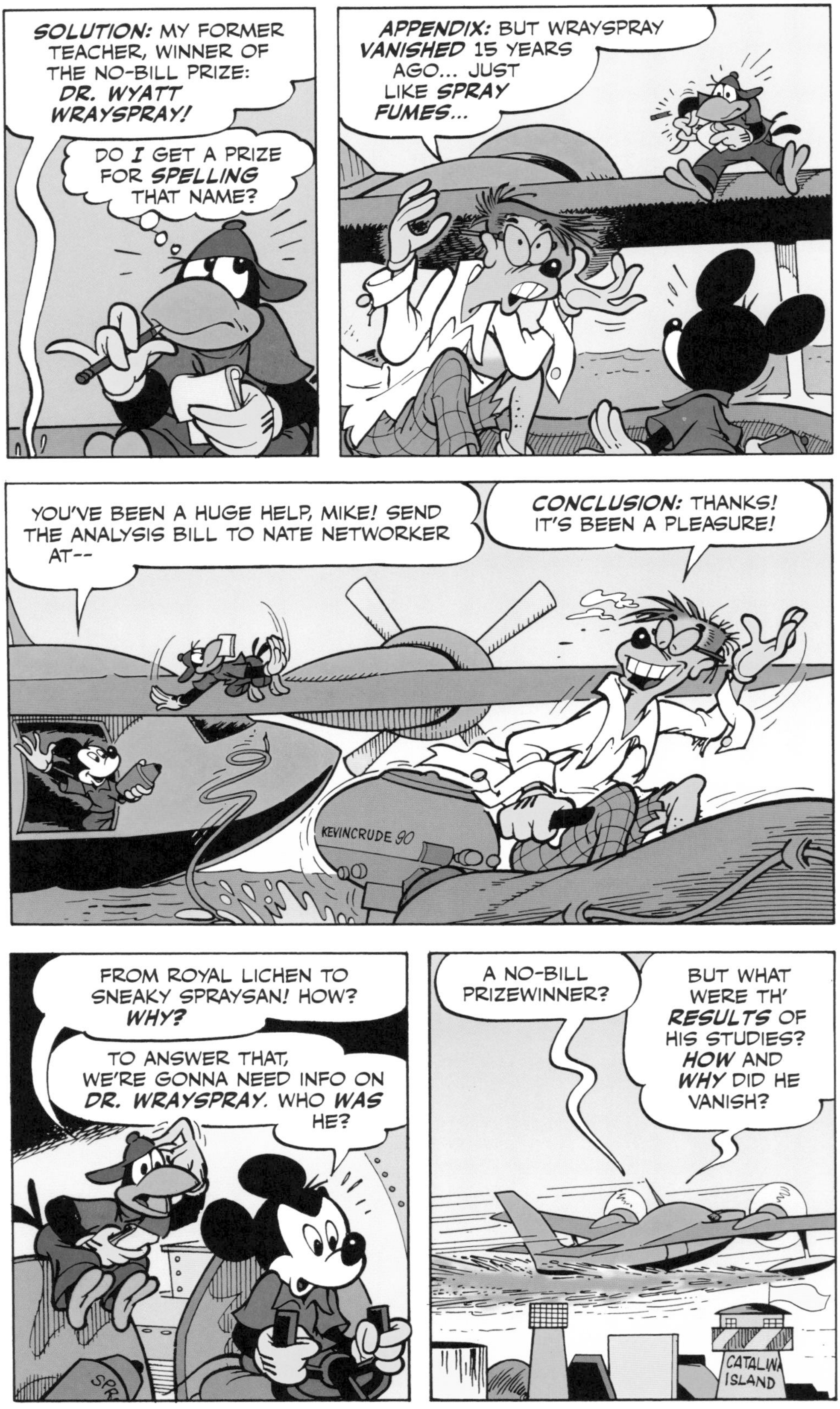
SOLUTION: MY FORMER TEACHER, WINNER OF THE NO-BILL PRIZE: DR. WYATT WRAYSPRAY!
DO I GET A PRIZE FOR SPELLING THAT NAME?
APPENDIX: BUT WRAYSPRAY VANISHED 15 YEARS AGO... JUST LIKE SPRAY FUMES...
YOU'VE BEEN A HUGE HELP, MIKE! SEND THE ANALYSIS BILL TO NATE NETWORKER AT--
CONCLUSION: THANKS! IT'S BEEN A PLEASURE!
KEVINCRUDE 90
FROM ROYAL LICHEN TO SNEAKY SPRAYSAN! HOW? WHY?
TO ANSWER THAT, WE'RE GONNA NEED INFO ON DR. WRAYSPRAY. WHO WAS HE?
A NO-BILL PRIZEWINNER?
BUT WHAT WERE TH' RESULTS OF HIS STUDIES? HOW AND WHY DID HE VANISH?
CATALINA ISLAND

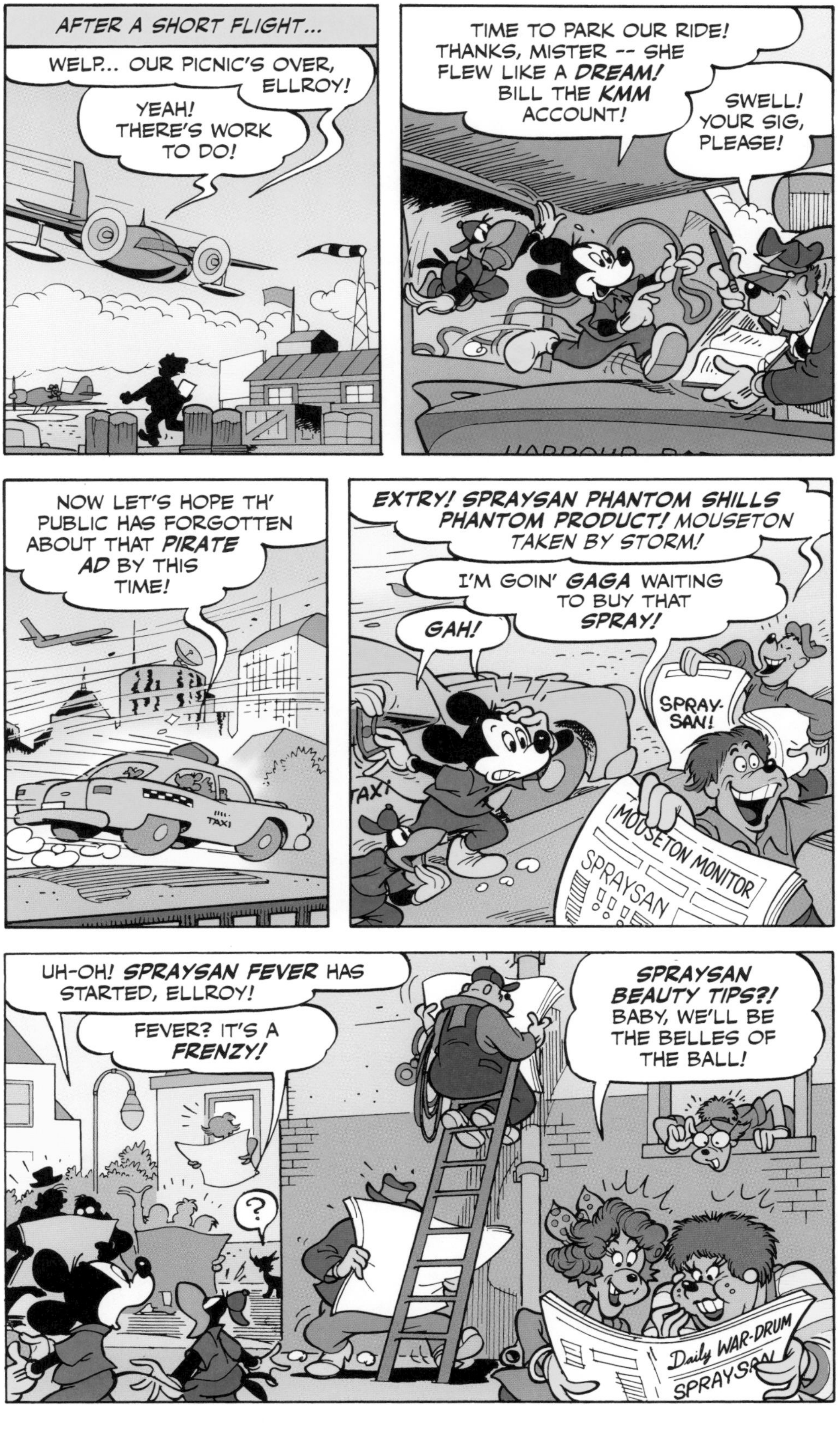

AFTER A SHORT FLIGHT...
WELP... OUR PICNIC'S OVER, ELLROY!
YEAH! THERE'S WORK TO DO!
TIME TO PARK OUR RIDE! THANKS, MISTER -- SHE FLEW LIKE A DREAM! BILL THE KMM ACCOUNT!
SWELL! YOUR SIG, PLEASE!
NOW LET'S HOPE TH' PUBLIC HAS FORGOTTEN ABOUT THAT PIRATE AD BY THIS TIME!
TAXI
EXTRY! SPRAYSAN PHANTOM SHILLS PHANTOM PRODUCT! MOUSETON TAKEN BY STORM!
I'M GOIN' GAGA WAITING TO BUY THAT SPRAY!
GAH!
SPRAY-SAN!
TAXI
MOUSETON MONITOR
SPRAYSAN
UH-OH! SPRAYSAN FEVER HAS STARTED, ELLROY!
FEVER? IT'S A FRENZY!
SPRAYSAN BEAUTY TIPS?! BABY, WE'LL BE THE BELLES OF THE BALL!
?
Daily WAR-DRUM

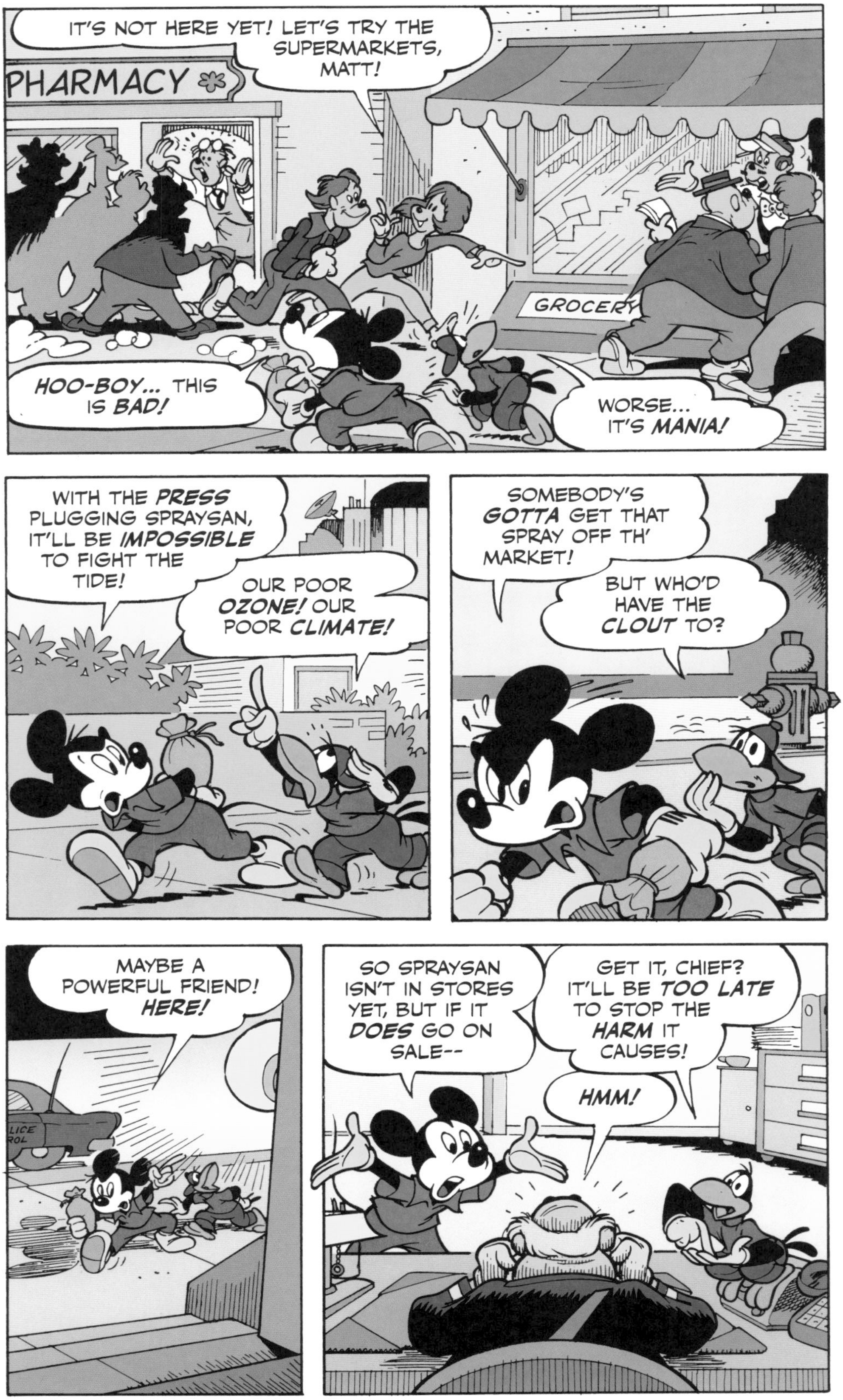
PHARMACY
IT'S NOT HERE YET! LET'S TRY THE SUPERMARKETS, MATT!
GROCERY
HOO-BOY... THIS IS BAD!
WORSE... IT'S MANIA!
WITH THE PRESS PLUGGING SPRAYSAN, IT'LL BE IMPOSSIBLE TO FIGHT THE TIDE!
OUR POOR OZONE! OUR POOR CLIMATE!
SOMEBODY'S GOTTA GET THAT SPRAY OFF TH' MARKET!
BUT WHO'D HAVE THE CLOUT TO?
MAYBE A POWERFUL FRIEND! HERE!
SO SPRAYSAN ISN'T IN STORES YET, BUT IF IT DOES GO ON SALE--
GET IT, CHIEF? IT'LL BE TOO LATE TO STOP THE HARM IT CAUSES!
HMM!

MESSY SITUATION HERE, LADS... WITHOUT CONCRETE EVIDENCE, WE CAN'T *SUE* THE SPRAY'S MANUFACTURER *OR* STOP THE PRODUCT.

I KNOW. BUT I'VE GOT A LEAD...

I NEED *COLD CASEFILES* ON A GUY WHO VANISHED INTO THIN AIR: *DR. WYATT WRAYSPRAY!*

WAIT... I *KNOW* THAT NAME.

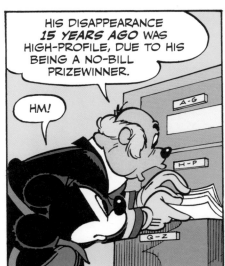

HIS DISAPPEARANCE *15 YEARS AGO* WAS HIGH-PROFILE, DUE TO HIS BEING A NO-BILL PRIZEWINNER.

HM!

MULTIFACETED LAD. PROFESSOR OF ELECTRONICS AND HYDRODYNAMICS AT DRYUPP UNIVERSITY. LATER, HE DEVOTED HIMSELF TO THE *COSMETICS* INDUSTRY.

?!

DR. WYATT WRAYSPRAY

1960 NO-BILL PRIZEWINNER IN SCIENCE

CASEY! GO TO CABINET 6⅜ AND BRING ME THE FILES ON *WYATT WRAYSPRAY!*

SURE, CHIEF!

LOOK WHO'S HERE! SHERLOCK MICKEY AND HIS CUTE LITTLE DR. *BIRDSON!*

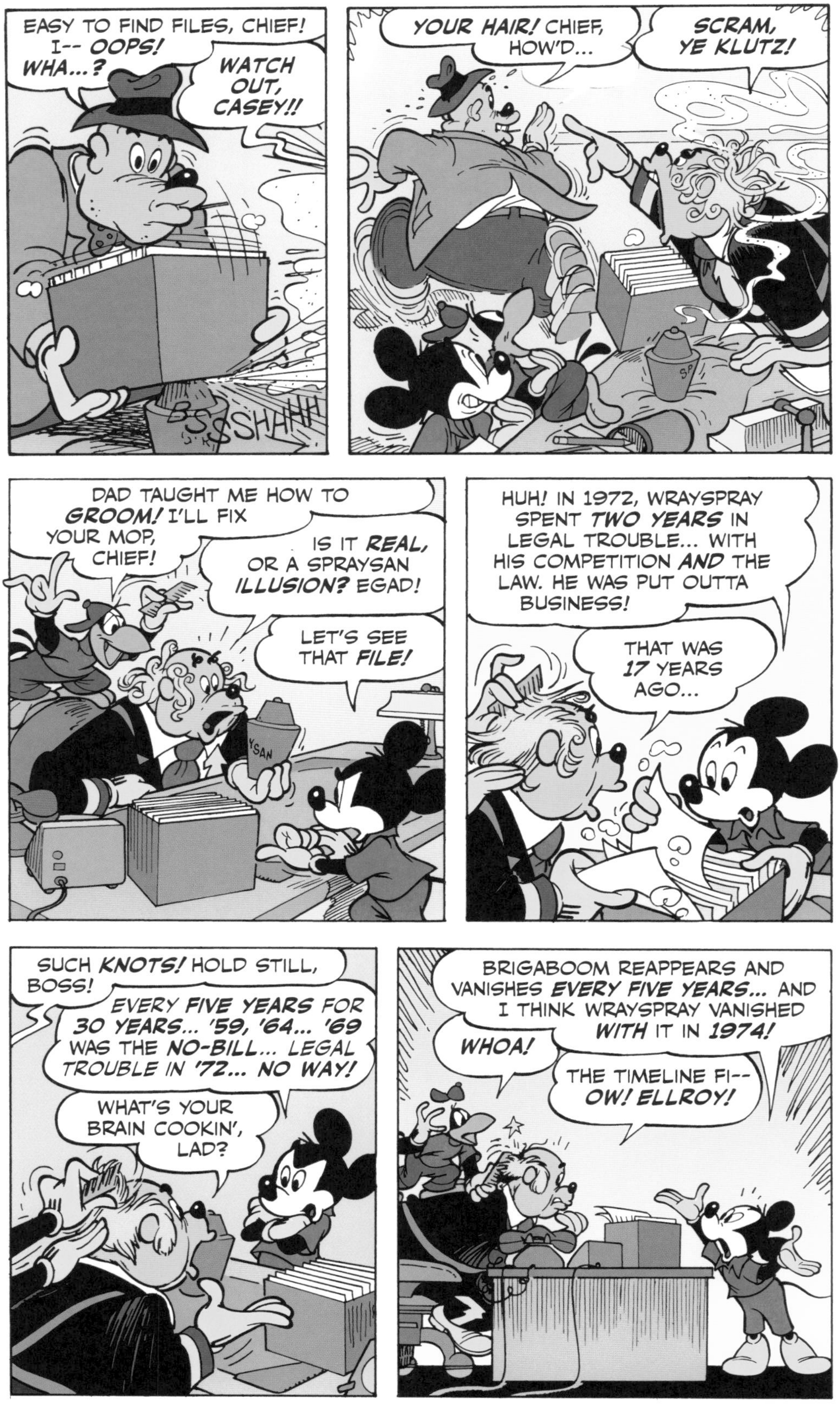
EASY TO FIND FILES, CHIEF! I-- OOPS! WHA...?
WATCH OUT, CASEY!!
BSSSHHH!
YOUR HAIR! CHIEF, HOW'D...
SCRAM, YE KLUTZ!
DAD TAUGHT ME HOW TO GROOM! I'LL FIX YOUR MOP, CHIEF!
IS IT REAL, OR A SPRAYSAN ILLUSION? EGAD!
LET'S SEE THAT FILE!
HUH! IN 1972, WRAYSPRAY SPENT TWO YEARS IN LEGAL TROUBLE... WITH HIS COMPETITION AND THE LAW. HE WAS PUT OUTTA BUSINESS!
THAT WAS 17 YEARS AGO...
SUCH KNOTS! HOLD STILL, BOSS!
EVERY FIVE YEARS FOR 30 YEARS... '59, '64... '69 WAS THE NO-BILL... LEGAL TROUBLE IN '72... NO WAY!
WHAT'S YOUR BRAIN COOKIN', LAD?
BRIGABOOM REAPPEARS AND VANISHES EVERY FIVE YEARS... AND I THINK WRAYSPRAY VANISHED WITH IT IN 1974!
WHOA!
THE TIMELINE FI-- OW! ELLROY!

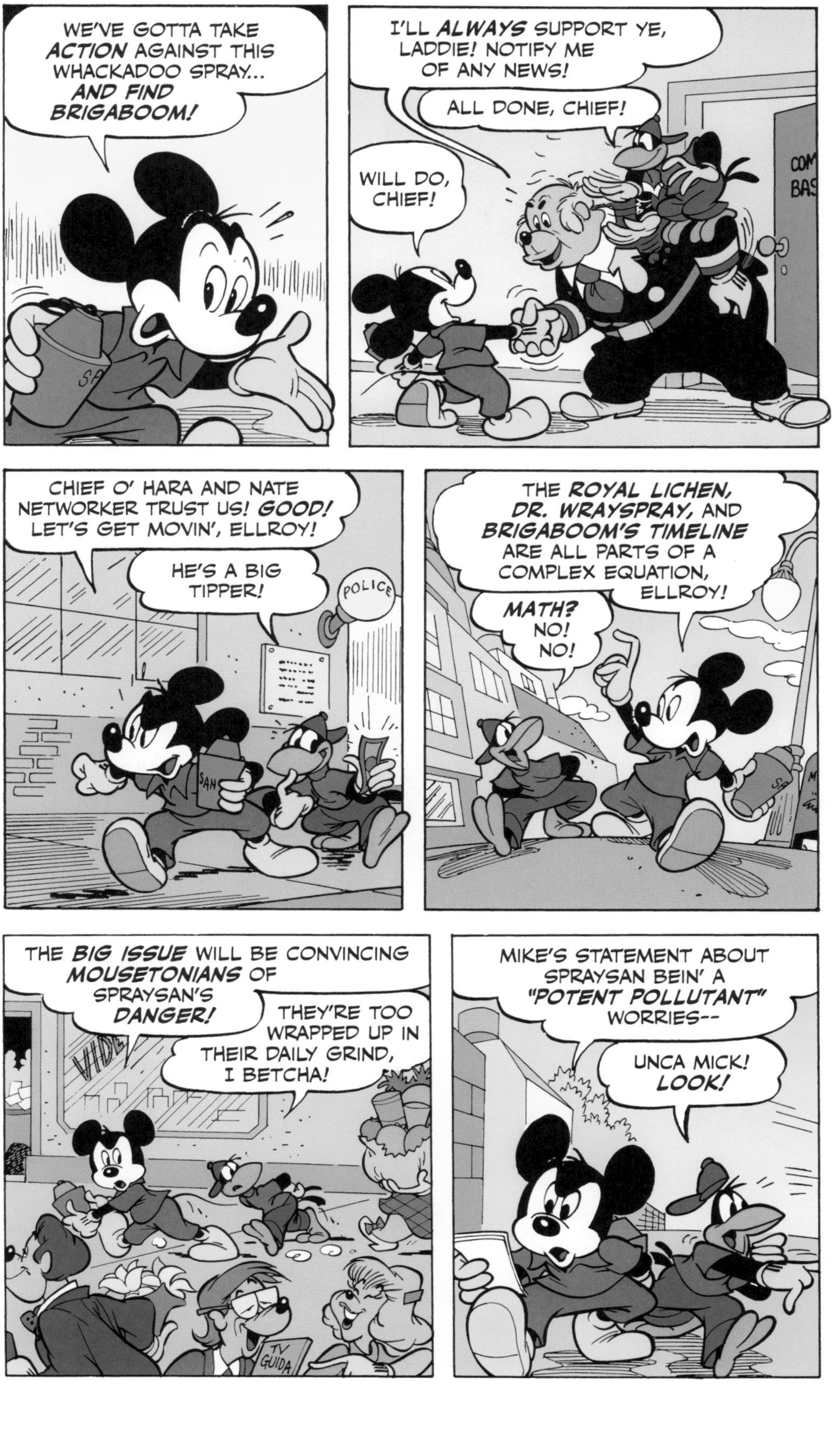
WE'VE GOTTA TAKE ACTION AGAINST THIS WHACKADOO SPRAY... AND FIND BRIGABOOM!
I'LL ALWAYS SUPPORT YE, LADDIE! NOTIFY ME OF ANY NEWS!
WILL DO, CHIEF!
ALL DONE, CHIEF!
CHIEF O' HARA AND NATE NETWORKER TRUST US! GOOD! LET'S GET MOVIN', ELLROY!
HE'S A BIG TIPPER!
POLICE
THE ROYAL LICHEN, DR. WRAYSPRAY, AND BRIGABOOM'S TIMELINE ARE ALL PARTS OF A COMPLEX EQUATION, ELLROY!
MATH? NO! NO!
THE BIG ISSUE WILL BE CONVINCING MOUSETONIANS OF SPRAYSAN'S DANGER!
THEY'RE TOO WRAPPED UP IN THEIR DAILY GRIND, I BETCHA!
TV GUIDA
MIKE'S STATEMENT ABOUT SPRAYSAN BEIN' A "POTENT POLLUTANT" WORRIES--
UNCA MICK! LOOK!

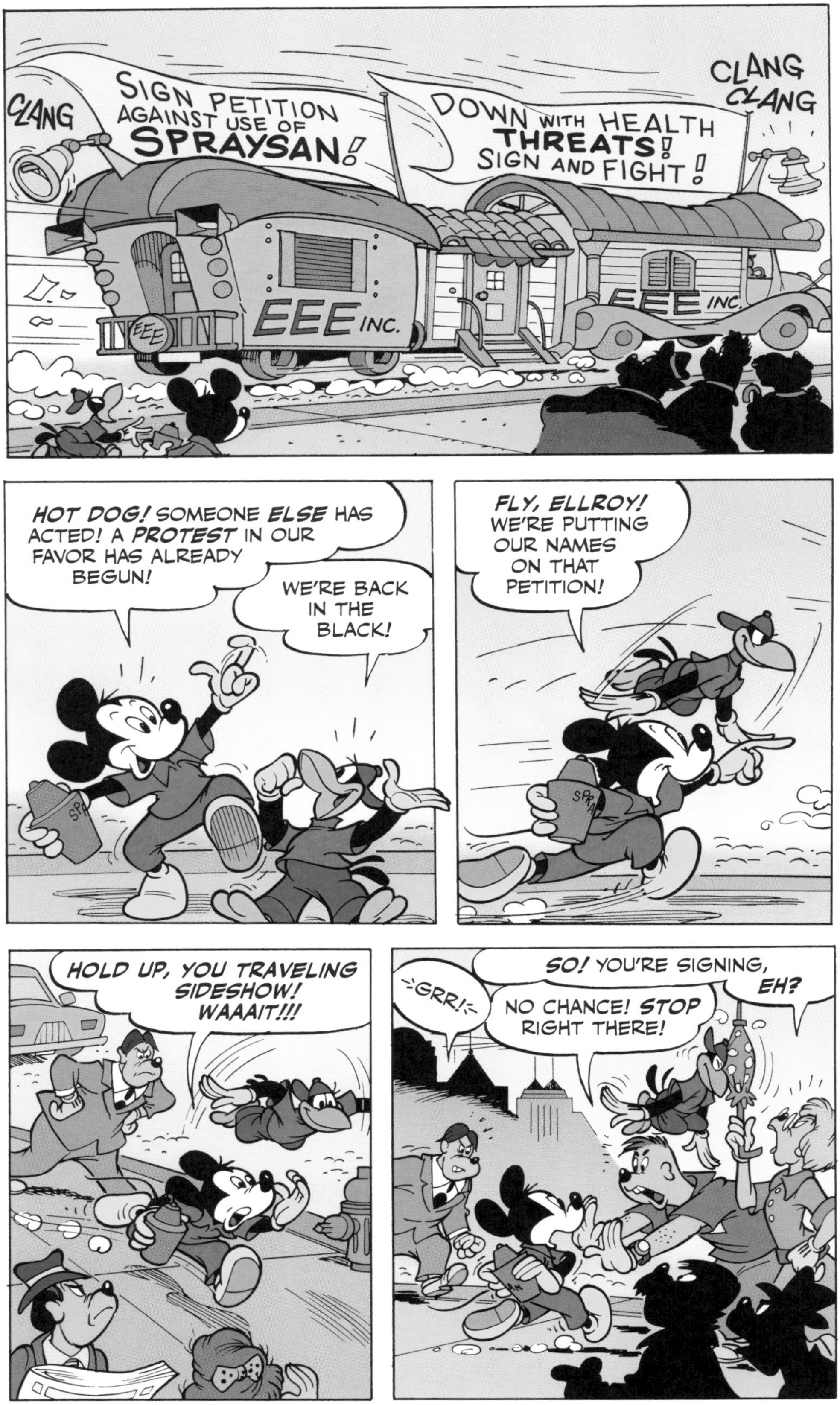
CLANG
SIGN PETITION AGAINST USE OF SPRAYSAN!
DOWN WITH HEALTH THREATS! SIGN AND FIGHT!
CLANG CLANG
EEE INC.
EEE INC.
HOT DOG! SOMEONE ELSE HAS ACTED! A PROTEST IN OUR FAVOR HAS ALREADY BEGUN!
WE'RE BACK IN THE BLACK!
FLY, ELLROY! WE'RE PUTTING OUR NAMES ON THAT PETITION!
HOLD UP, YOU TRAVELING SIDESHOW! WAAAIT!!!
SO! YOU'RE SIGNING, EH?
GRR!
NO CHANCE! STOP RIGHT THERE!

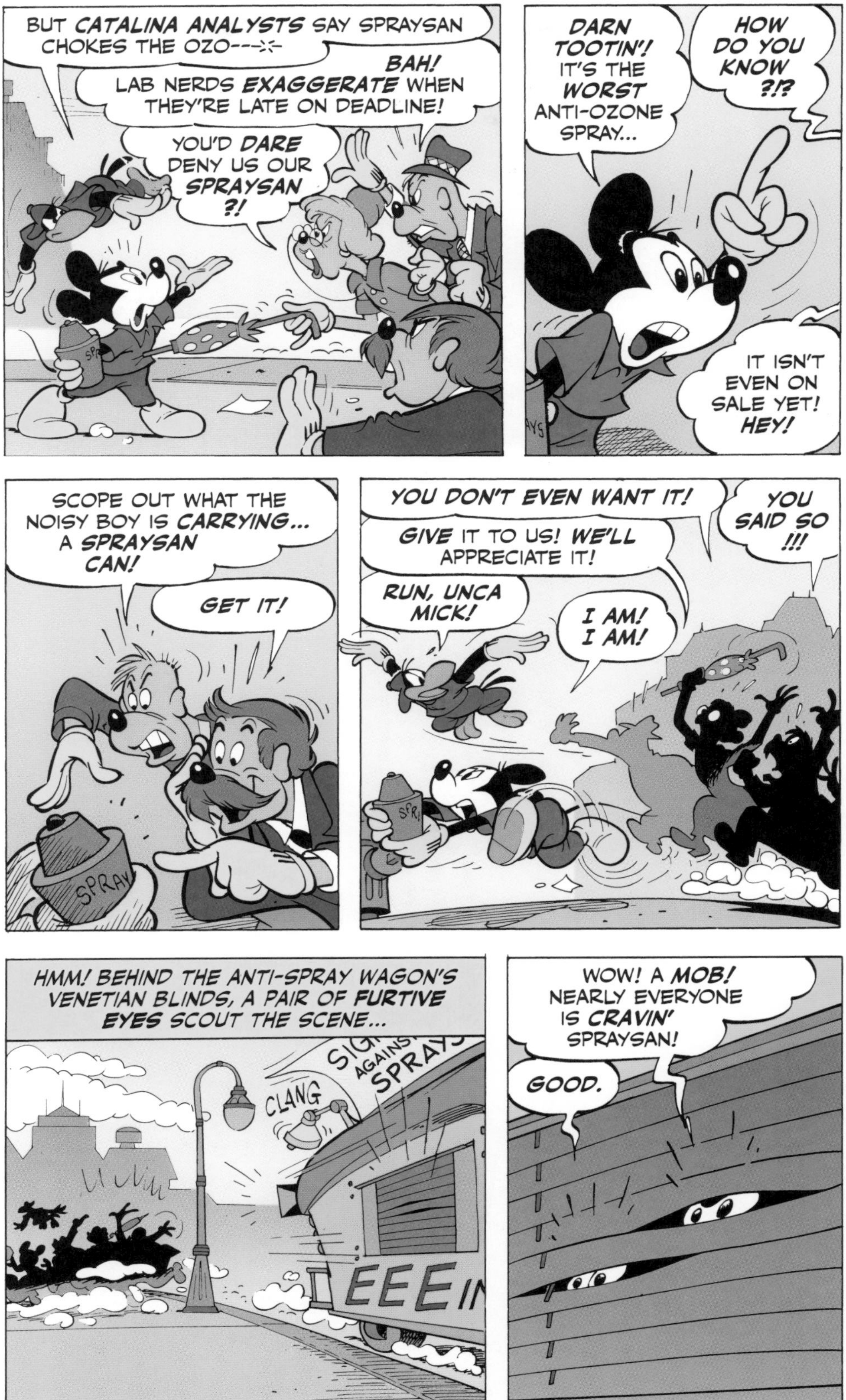

BUT CATALINA ANALYSTS SAY SPRAYSAN CHOKES THE OZO---
BAH! LAB NERDS EXAGGERATE WHEN THEY'RE LATE ON DEADLINE!
YOU'D DARE DENY US OUR SPRAYSAN ?!
DARN TOOTIN'! IT'S THE WORST ANTI-OZONE SPRAY...
HOW DO YOU KNOW ?!?
IT ISN'T EVEN ON SALE YET! HEY!
SCOPE OUT WHAT THE NOISY BOY IS CARRYING... A SPRAYSAN CAN!
GET IT!
SPRAY
YOU DON'T EVEN WANT IT!
GIVE IT TO US! WE'LL APPRECIATE IT!
YOU SAID SO !!!
RUN, UNCA MICK!
I AM! I AM!
HMM! BEHIND THE ANTI-SPRAY WAGON'S VENETIAN BLINDS, A PAIR OF FURTIVE EYES SCOUT THE SCENE...
CLANG
EEEIN
WOW! A MOB! NEARLY EVERYONE IS CRAVIN' SPRAYSAN!
GOOD.

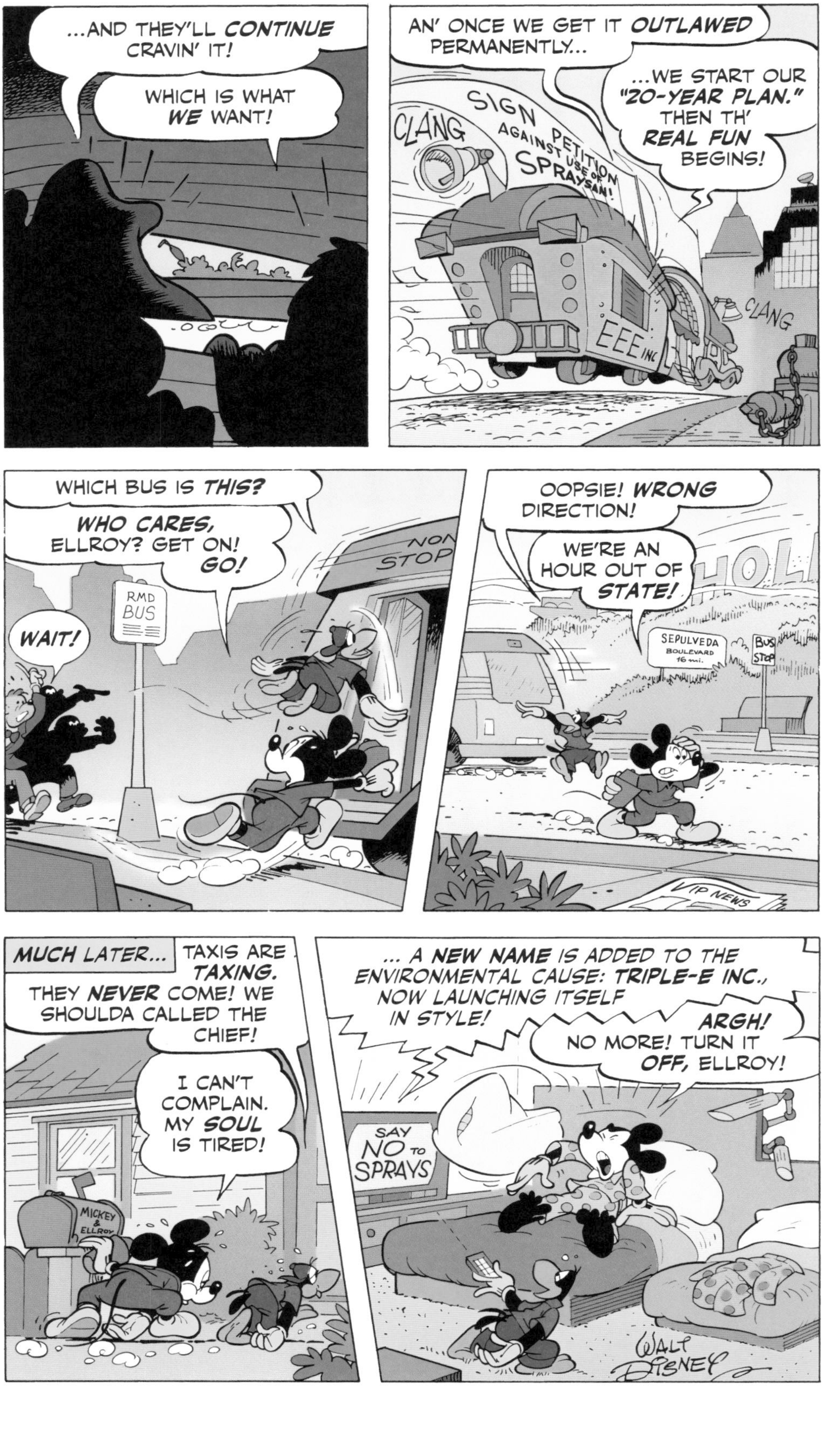
...AND THEY'LL CONTINUE CRAVIN' IT!
WHICH IS WHAT WE WANT!
AN' ONCE WE GET IT OUTLAWED PERMANENTLY...
...WE START OUR "20-YEAR PLAN." THEN TH' REAL FUN BEGINS!
CLANG
SIGN PETITION AGAINST USE OF SPRAYSAN!
EEE INC
CLANG
WHICH BUS IS THIS?
WHO CARES, ELLROY? GET ON! GO!
NON STOP
RMD BUS
WAIT!
OOPSIE! WRONG DIRECTION!
WE'RE AN HOUR OUT OF STATE!
SEPULVEDA BOULEVARD 16 mi.
BUS STOP
VIP NEWS
MUCH LATER...
TAXIS ARE TAXING. THEY NEVER COME! WE SHOULDA CALLED THE CHIEF!
I CAN'T COMPLAIN. MY SOUL IS TIRED!
MICKEY & ELLROY
... A NEW NAME IS ADDED TO THE ENVIRONMENTAL CAUSE: TRIPLE-E INC., NOW LAUNCHING ITSELF IN STYLE!
ARGH! NO MORE! TURN IT OFF, ELLROY!
SAY NO TO SPRAYS
WALT DISNEY

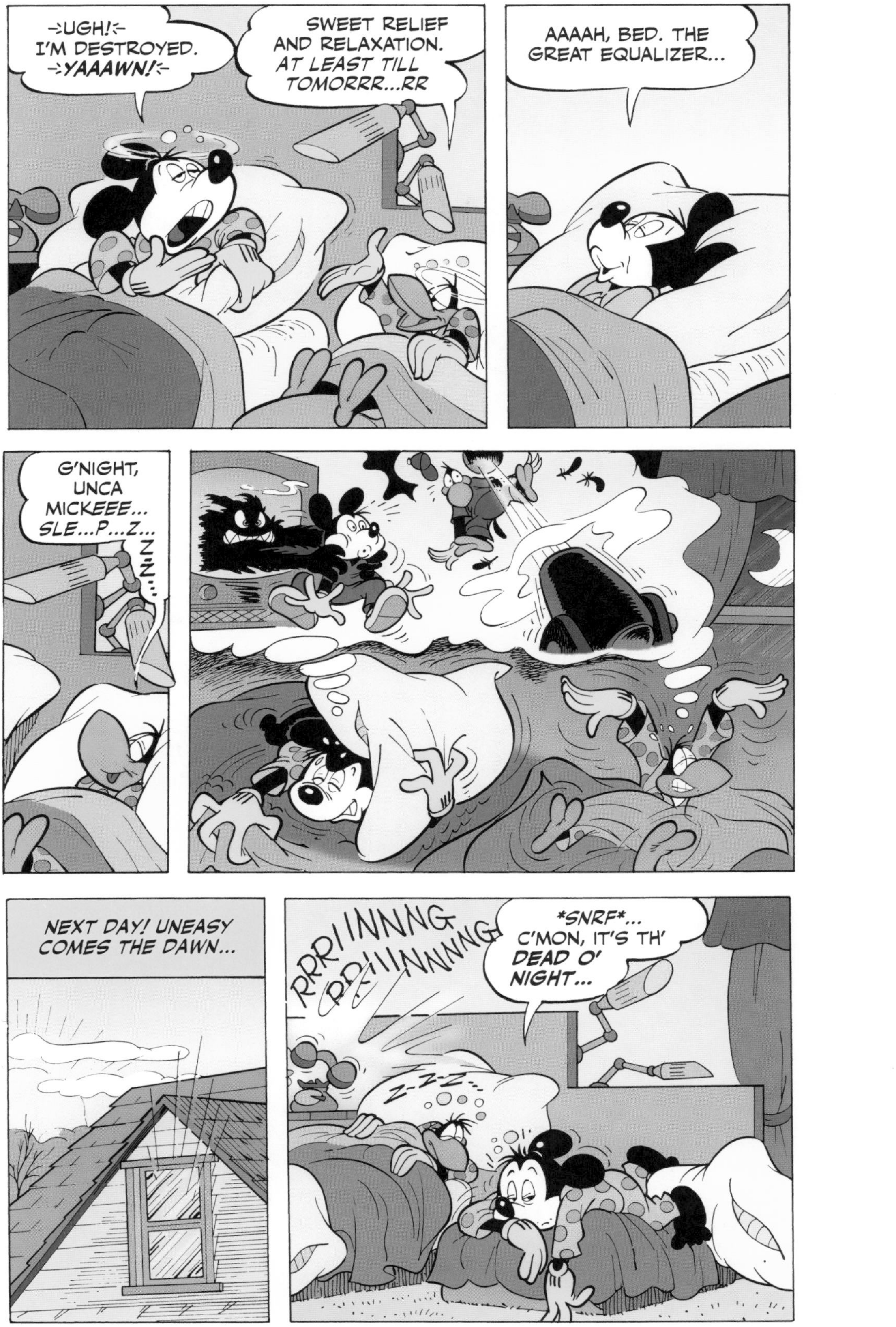

UGH!
I'M DESTROYED.
YAAAWN!
SWEET RELIEF AND RELAXATION. AT LEAST TILL TOMORRR...RR
AAAAH, BED. THE GREAT EQUALIZER...
G'NIGHT, UNCA MICKEEE... SLE...P...Z...
Z-Z...
NEXT DAY! UNEASY COMES THE DAWN...
RRRIINNNG
RRIIINNNNG
SNRF... C'MON, IT'S TH' DEAD O' NIGHT...
Z-Z-Z...

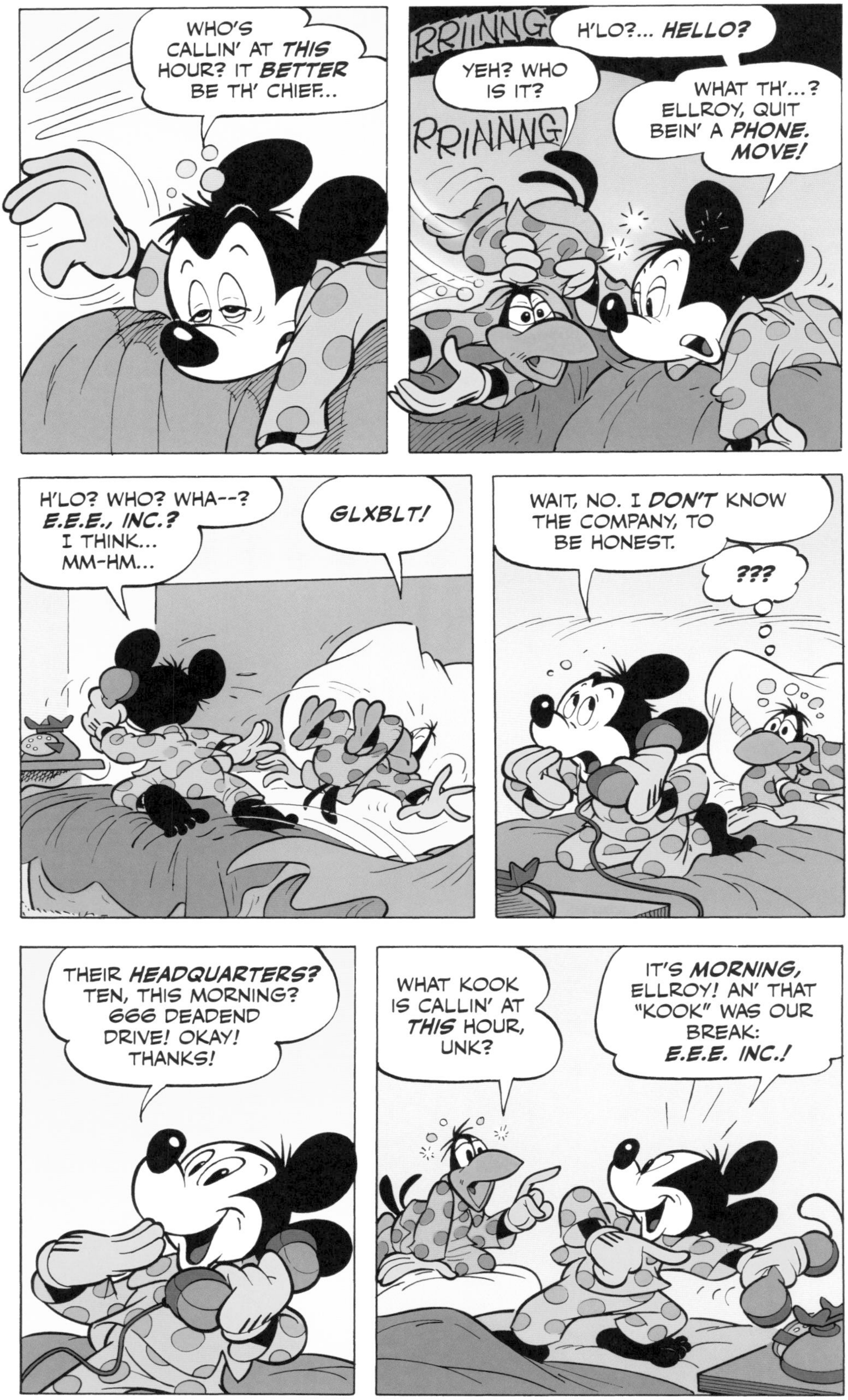
WHO'S CALLIN' AT THIS HOUR? IT BETTER BE TH' CHIEF...
RRIINNG
H'LO?... HELLO?
YEH? WHO IS IT?
RRIINNG
WHAT TH'...? ELLROY, QUIT BEIN' A PHONE. MOVE!
H'LO? WHO? WHA--? E.E.E., INC.? I THINK... MM-HM...
GLXBLT!
WAIT, NO. I DON'T KNOW THE COMPANY, TO BE HONEST.
???
THEIR HEADQUARTERS? TEN, THIS MORNING? 666 DEADEND DRIVE! OKAY! THANKS!
WHAT KOOK IS CALLIN' AT THIS HOUR, UNK?
IT'S MORNING, ELLROY! AN' THAT "KOOK" WAS OUR BREAK: E.E.E. INC.!

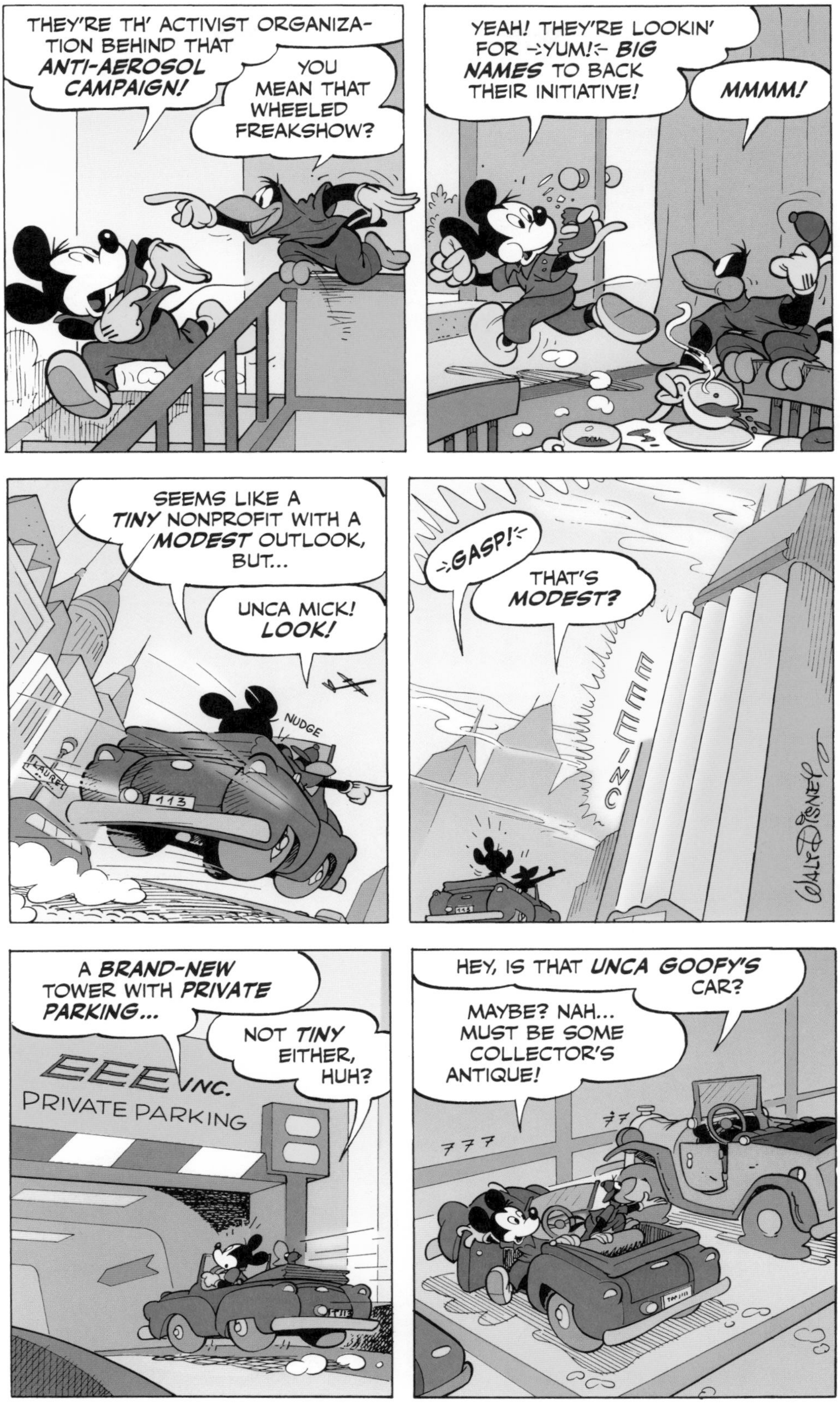
THEY'RE TH' ACTIVIST ORGANIZATION BEHIND THAT ANTI-AEROSOL CAMPAIGN!
YOU MEAN THAT WHEELED FREAKSHOW?
YEAH! THEY'RE LOOKIN' FOR -YUM!- BIG NAMES TO BACK THEIR INITIATIVE!
MMMM!
SEEMS LIKE A TINY NONPROFIT WITH A MODEST OUTLOOK, BUT...
UNCA MICK! LOOK!
NUDGE
LAUREL
113
GASP!
THAT'S MODEST?
EEE INC
A BRAND-NEW TOWER WITH PRIVATE PARKING...
NOT TINY EITHER, HUH?
EEE INC.
PRIVATE PARKING
HEY, IS THAT UNCA GOOFY'S CAR?
MAYBE? NAH... MUST BE SOME COLLECTOR'S ANTIQUE!

WAIT! THAT'S *HORACE'S* CAR! I KNOW HIS PLATES!

LIFT

CONFERENCE HALL AHEAD

HUH!

HOLY MOLY! THE GANG'S ALL HERE!

MINNIE, CLARABELLE, GOOFY, ZENOBIA...

GAWRSH! LOOK WHO MADE IT!

MICKEY AN' ELLROY! YOU *TOO?* EXCLUDING THE ODDBALLS, THAT'S *EVERY-BODY!*

HIYA, GANG! DIDN'T EXPECT TO SEE SO MANY!

AND I *NEVER* EXPECTED TO SEE *YOU* AT A *BUSINESS VENTURE!*

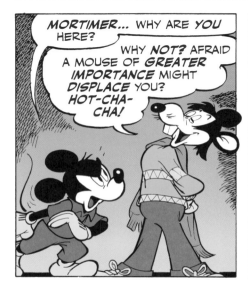

MORTIMER... WHY ARE *YOU* HERE?

WHY *NOT?* AFRAID A MOUSE OF *GREATER IMPORTANCE* MIGHT *DISPLACE* YOU? HOT-CHA-CHA!

ISN'T MORTIMER A *RICH JETSETTER*, MINNIE? MICKEY CAN'T HELP BUT BE A LITTLE *JEALOUS!*

PATRICIA...

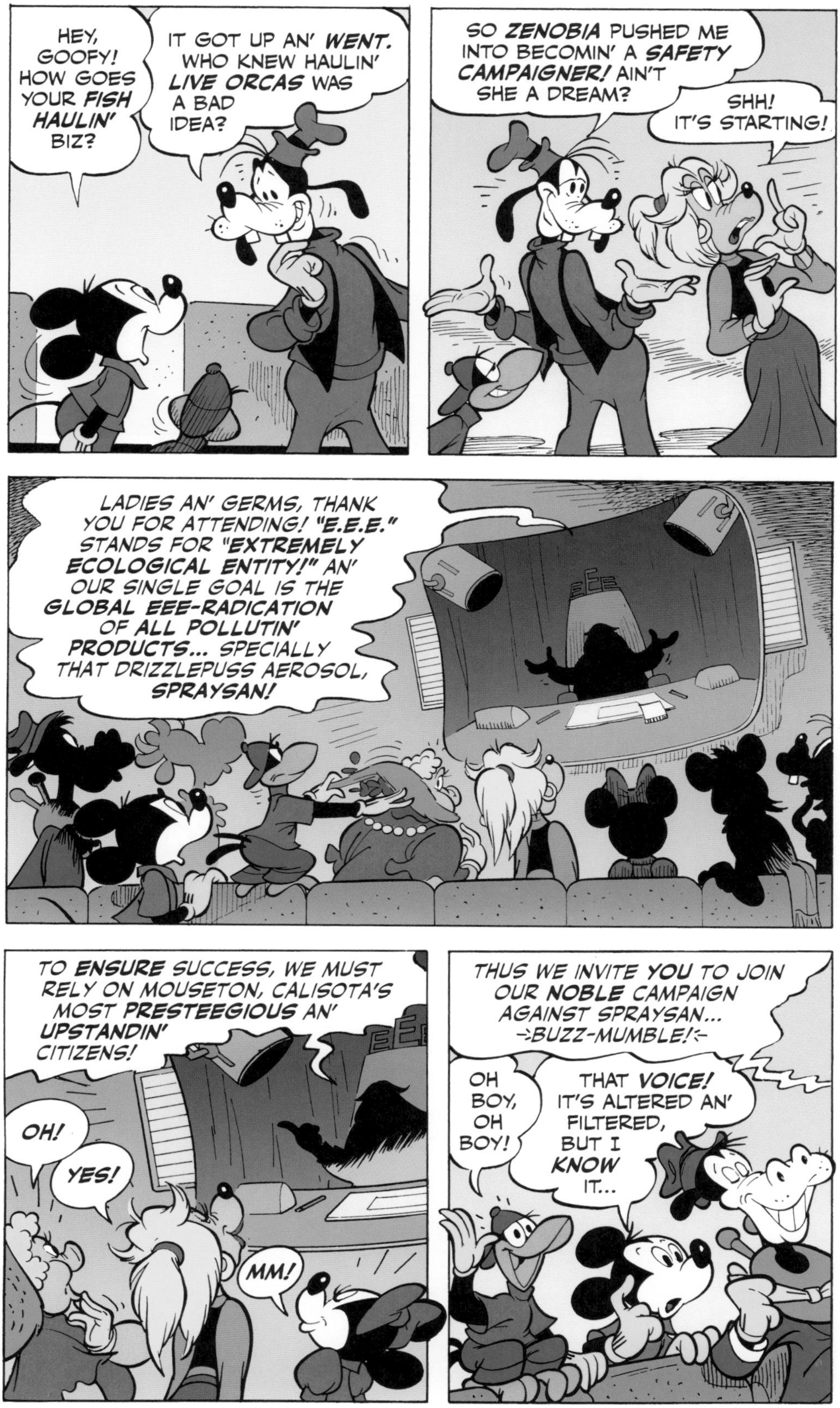
HEY, GOOFY! HOW GOES YOUR FISH HAULIN' BIZ?
IT GOT UP AN' WENT. WHO KNEW HAULIN' LIVE ORCAS WAS A BAD IDEA?
SO ZENOBIA PUSHED ME INTO BECOMIN' A SAFETY CAMPAIGNER! AIN'T SHE A DREAM?
SHH! IT'S STARTING!
LADIES AN' GERMS, THANK YOU FOR ATTENDING! "E.E.E." STANDS FOR "EXTREMELY ECOLOGICAL ENTITY!" AN' OUR SINGLE GOAL IS THE GLOBAL EEE-RADICATION OF ALL POLLUTIN' PRODUCTS... SPECIALLY THAT DRIZZLEPUSS AEROSOL, SPRAYSAN!
TO ENSURE SUCCESS, WE MUST RELY ON MOUSETON, CALISOTA'S MOST PRESTEEGIOUS AN' UPSTANDIN' CITIZENS!
OH!
YES!
MM!
THUS WE INVITE YOU TO JOIN OUR NOBLE CAMPAIGN AGAINST SPRAYSAN... →BUZZ-MUMBLE!←
OH BOY, OH BOY!
THAT VOICE! IT'S ALTERED AN' FILTERED, BUT I KNOW IT...

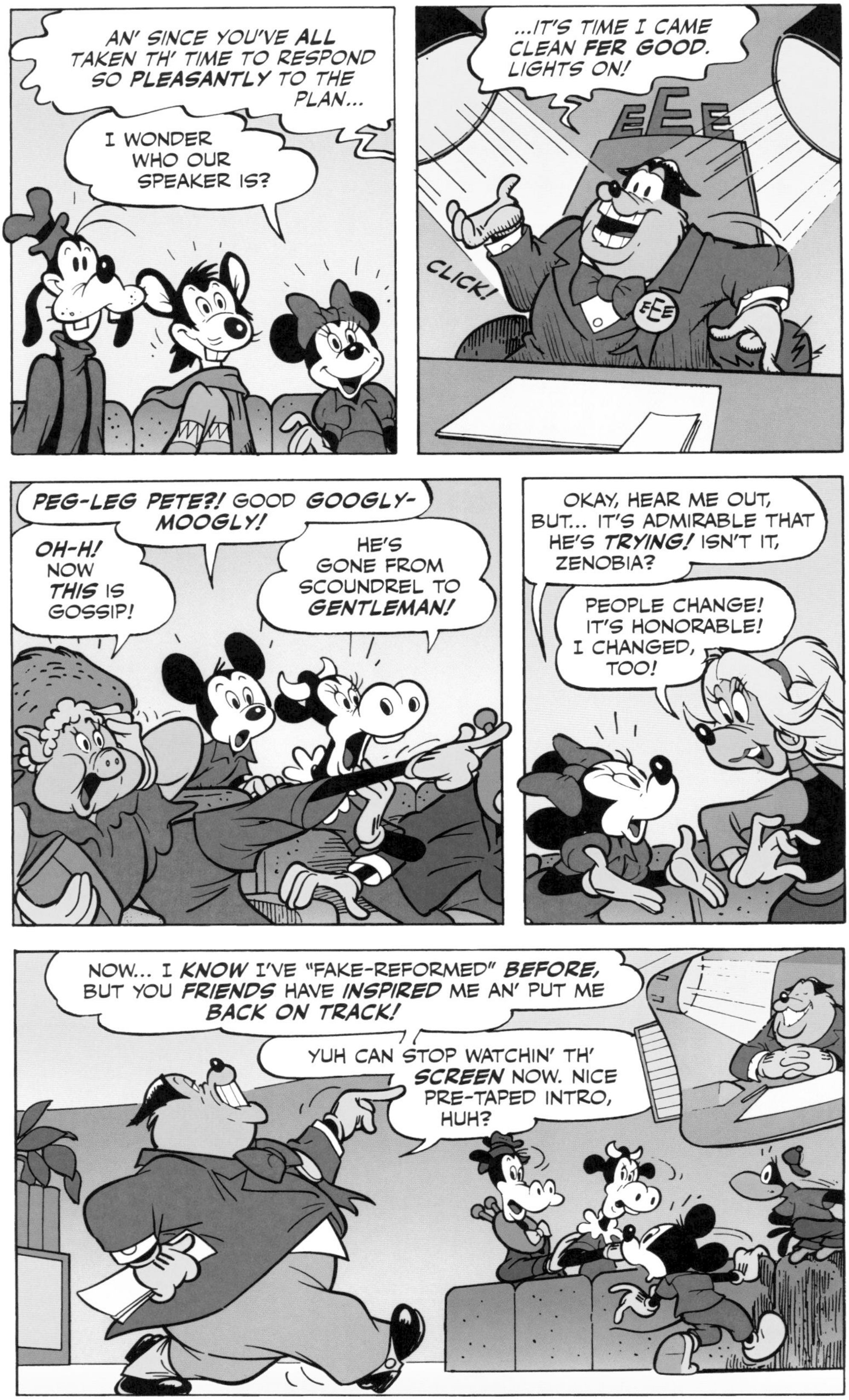
AN' SINCE YOU'VE ALL TAKEN TH' TIME TO RESPOND SO PLEASANTLY TO THE PLAN...
I WONDER WHO OUR SPEAKER IS?
...IT'S TIME I CAME CLEAN FER GOOD. LIGHTS ON!
CLICK!
PEG-LEG PETE?! GOOD GOOGLY-MOOGLY!
OH-H! NOW THIS IS GOSSIP!
HE'S GONE FROM SCOUNDREL TO GENTLEMAN!
OKAY, HEAR ME OUT, BUT... IT'S ADMIRABLE THAT HE'S TRYING! ISN'T IT, ZENOBIA?
PEOPLE CHANGE! IT'S HONORABLE! I CHANGED, TOO!
NOW... I KNOW I'VE "FAKE-REFORMED" BEFORE, BUT YOU FRIENDS HAVE INSPIRED ME AN' PUT ME BACK ON TRACK!
YUH CAN STOP WATCHIN' TH' SCREEN NOW. NICE PRE-TAPED INTRO, HUH?

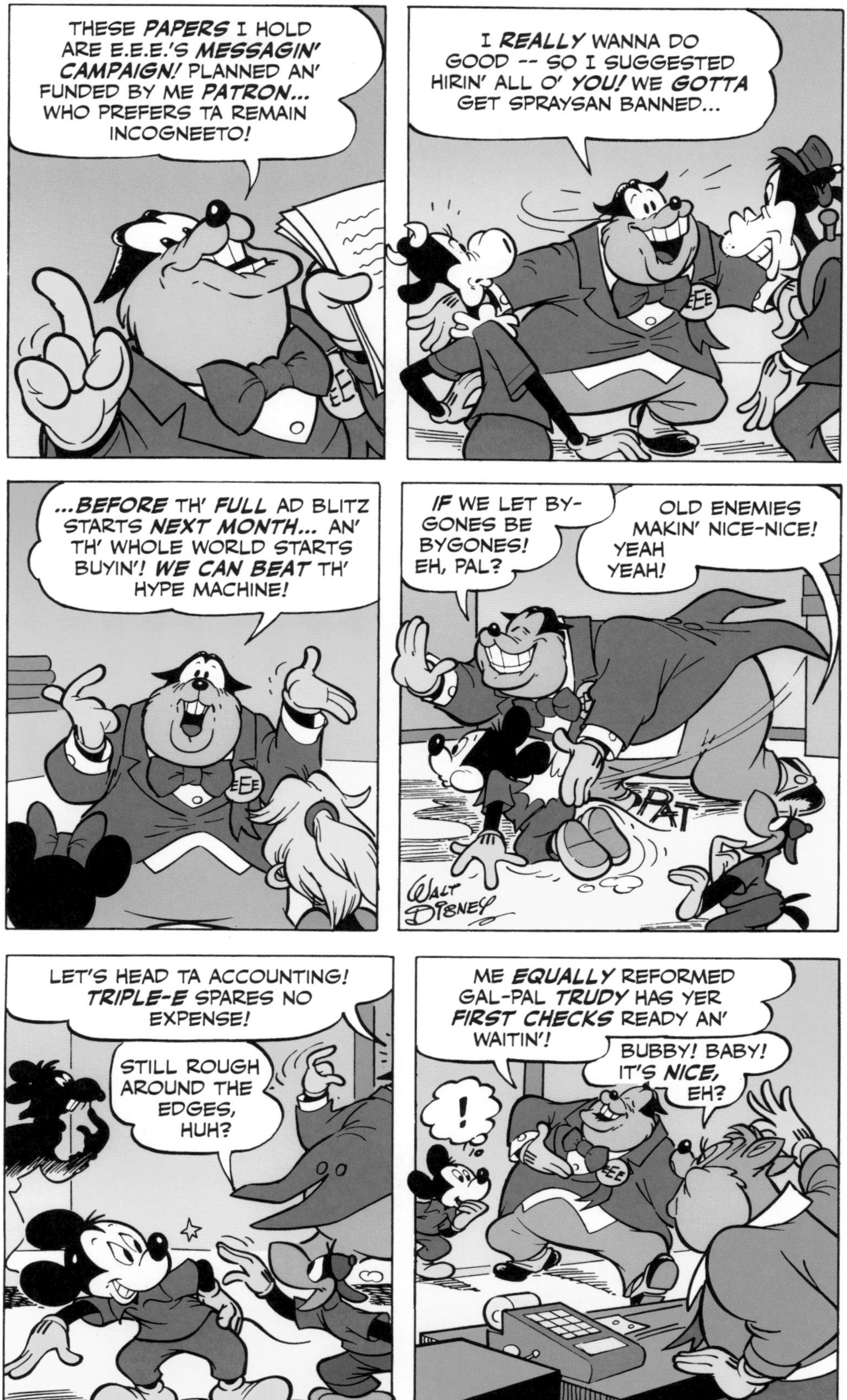
THESE PAPERS I HOLD ARE E.E.E.'S MESSAGIN' CAMPAIGN! PLANNED AN' FUNDED BY ME PATRON... WHO PREFERS TA REMAIN INCOGNEETO!
I REALLY WANNA DO GOOD -- SO I SUGGESTED HIRIN' ALL O' YOU! WE GOTTA GET SPRAYSAN BANNED...
...BEFORE TH' FULL AD BLITZ STARTS NEXT MONTH... AN' TH' WHOLE WORLD STARTS BUYIN'! WE CAN BEAT TH' HYPE MACHINE!
IF WE LET BY-GONES BE BYGONES! EH, PAL?
OLD ENEMIES MAKIN' NICE-NICE! YEAH YEAH!
SPAT
WALT DISNEY
LET'S HEAD TA ACCOUNTING! TRIPLE-E SPARES NO EXPENSE!
STILL ROUGH AROUND THE EDGES, HUH?
ME EQUALLY REFORMED GAL-PAL TRUDY HAS YER FIRST CHECKS READY AN' WAITIN'!
BUBBY! BABY! IT'S NICE, EH?
!

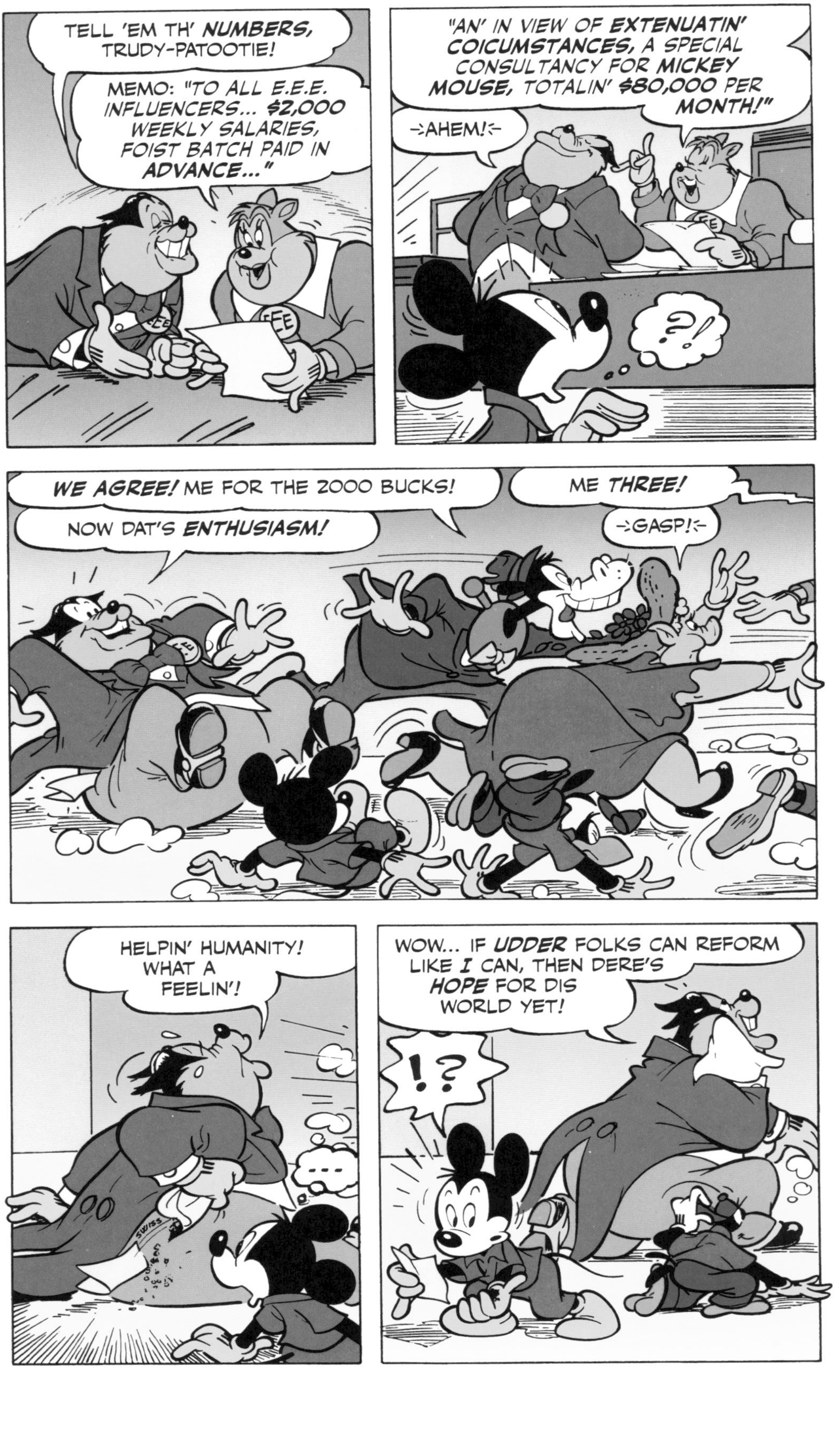
TELL 'EM TH' NUMBERS, TRUDY-PATOOTIE!
MEMO: "TO ALL E.E.E. INFLUENCERS... $2,000 WEEKLY SALARIES, FOIST BATCH PAID IN ADVANCE..."
"AN' IN VIEW OF EXTENUATIN' COICUMSTANCES, A SPECIAL CONSULTANCY FOR MICKEY MOUSE, TOTALIN' $80,000 PER MONTH!"
AHEM!
?!
WE AGREE! ME FOR THE 2000 BUCKS!
ME THREE!
NOW DAT'S ENTHUSIASM!
GASP!
HELPIN' HUMANITY! WHAT A FEELIN'!
WOW... IF UDDER FOLKS CAN REFORM LIKE I CAN, THEN DERE'S HOPE FOR DIS WORLD YET!
!?

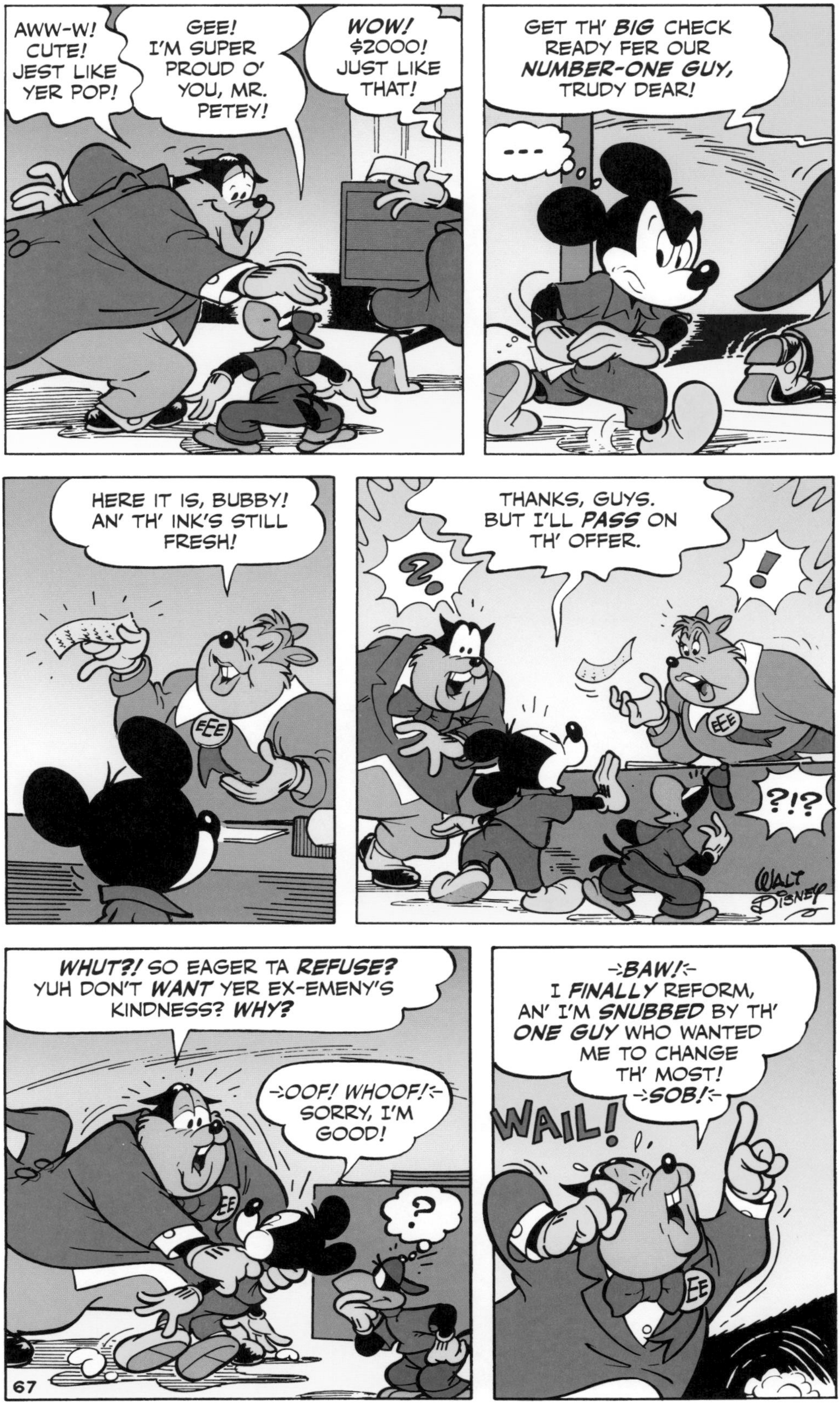
AWW-W! CUTE! JEST LIKE YER POP!
GEE! I'M SUPER PROUD O' YOU, MR. PETEY!
WOW! $2000! JUST LIKE THAT!
GET TH' BIG CHECK READY FER OUR NUMBER-ONE GUY, TRUDY DEAR!
- - -
HERE IT IS, BUBBY! AN' TH' INK'S STILL FRESH!
EEE
THANKS, GUYS. BUT I'LL PASS ON TH' OFFER.
?
!
EEE
?!?
WALT DISNEY
WHUT?! SO EAGER TA REFUSE? YUH DON'T WANT YER EX-EMENY'S KINDNESS? WHY?
-OOF! WHOOF!- SORRY, I'M GOOD!
EE
?
67
-BAW!- I FINALLY REFORM, AN' I'M SNUBBED BY TH' ONE GUY WHO WANTED ME TO CHANGE TH' MOST! -SOB!-
WAIL!
EE

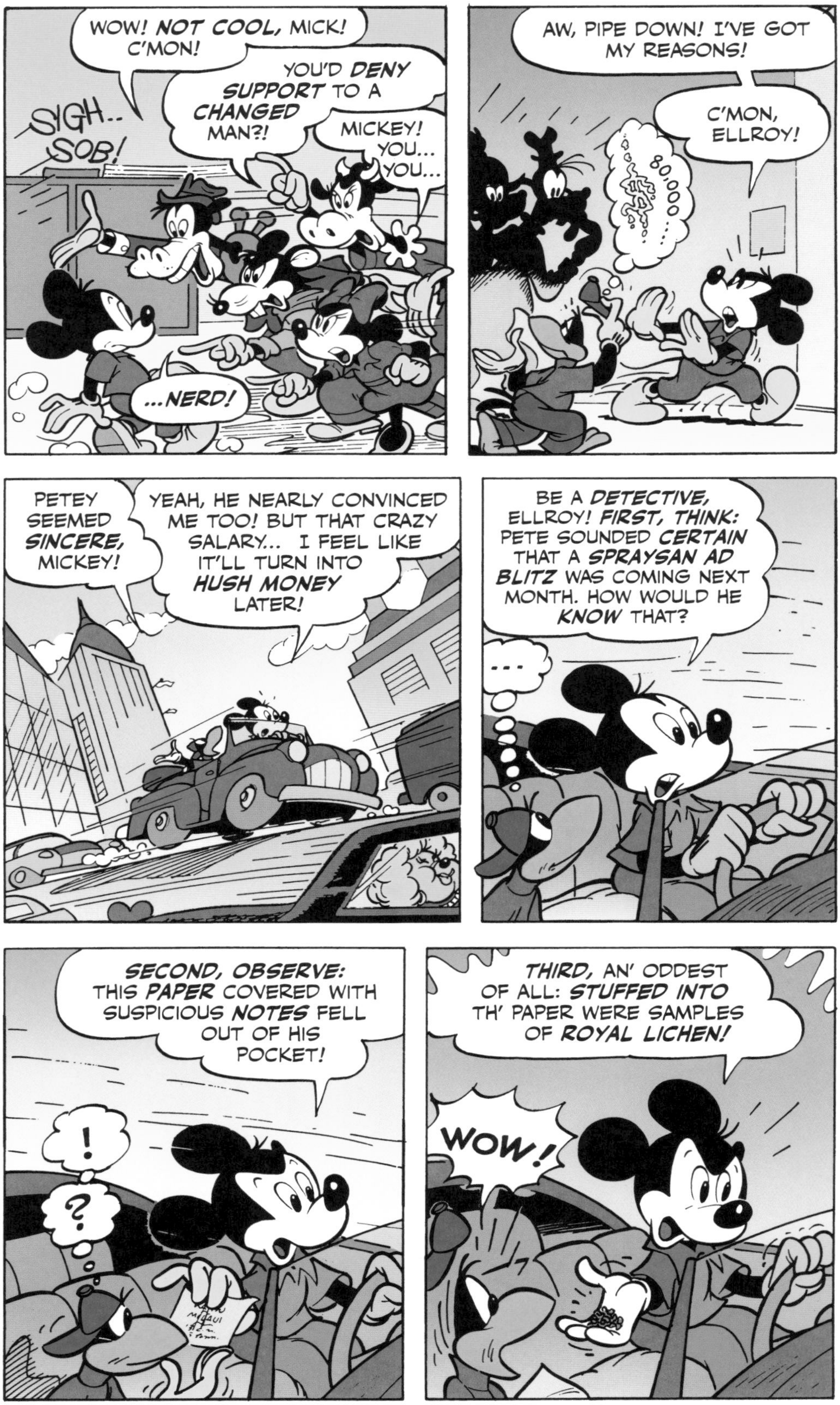
WOW! NOT COOL, MICK! C'MON!
YOU'D DENY SUPPORT TO A CHANGED MAN?!
SIGH.. SOB!
MICKEY! YOU... YOU...
...NERD!
AW, PIPE DOWN! I'VE GOT MY REASONS!
C'MON, ELLROY!
80,000...
PETEY SEEMED SINCERE, MICKEY!
YEAH, HE NEARLY CONVINCED ME TOO! BUT THAT CRAZY SALARY... I FEEL LIKE IT'LL TURN INTO HUSH MONEY LATER!
BE A DETECTIVE, ELLROY! FIRST, THINK: PETE SOUNDED CERTAIN THAT A SPRAYSAN AD BLITZ WAS COMING NEXT MONTH. HOW WOULD HE KNOW THAT?
...
SECOND, OBSERVE: THIS PAPER COVERED WITH SUSPICIOUS NOTES FELL OUT OF HIS POCKET!
!
?
THIRD, AN' ODDEST OF ALL: STUFFED INTO TH' PAPER WERE SAMPLES OF ROYAL LICHEN!
WOW!

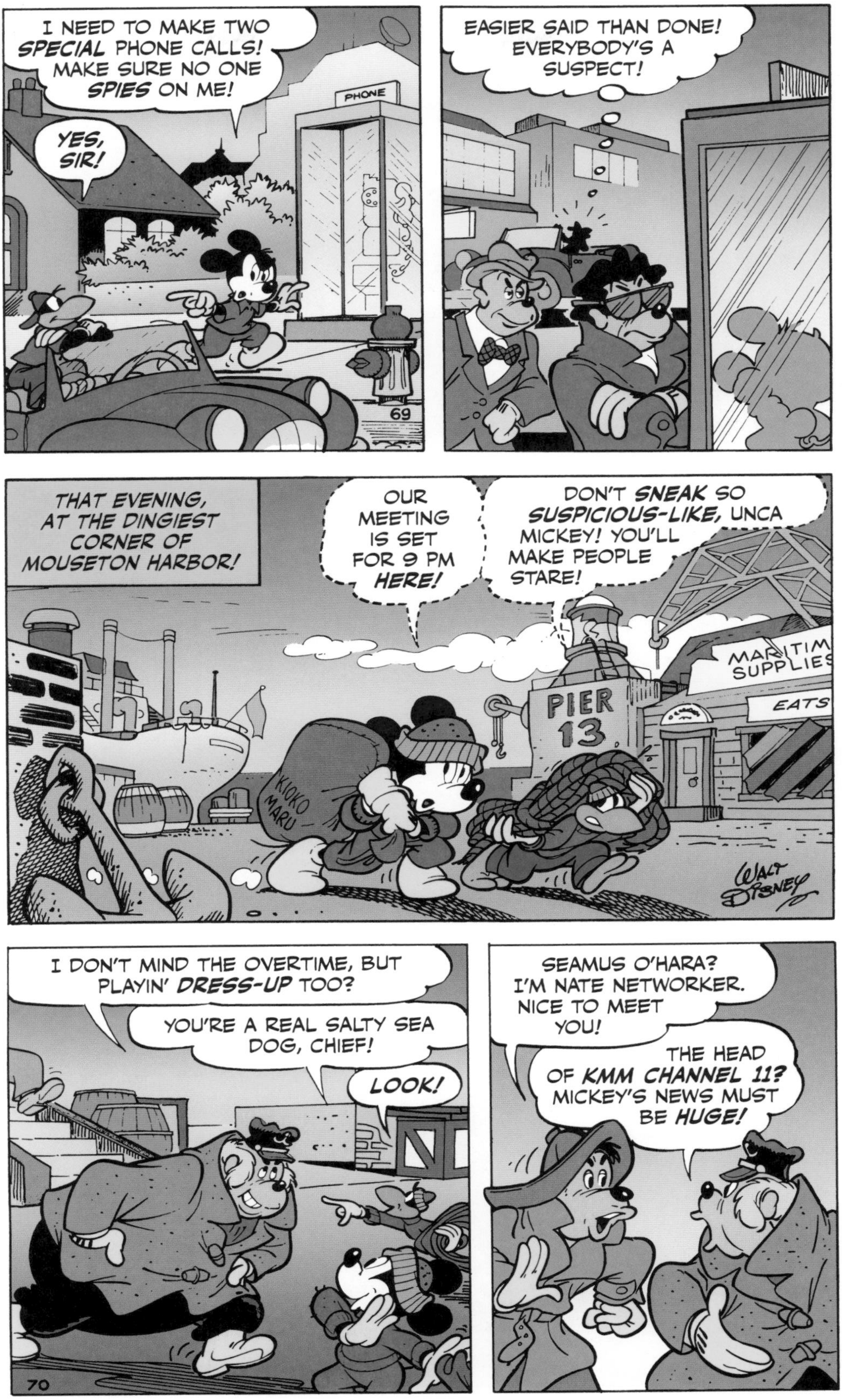
I NEED TO MAKE TWO SPECIAL PHONE CALLS! MAKE SURE NO ONE SPIES ON ME!
YES, SIR!
PHONE
69
EASIER SAID THAN DONE! EVERYBODY'S A SUSPECT!
THAT EVENING, AT THE DINGIEST CORNER OF MOUSETON HARBOR!
OUR MEETING IS SET FOR 9 PM HERE!
DON'T SNEAK SO SUSPICIOUS-LIKE, UNCA MICKEY! YOU'LL MAKE PEOPLE STARE!
MARITIM SUPPLIES
EATS
PIER 13
KIOKO MARU
WALT DISNEY
I DON'T MIND THE OVERTIME, BUT PLAYIN' DRESS-UP TOO?
YOU'RE A REAL SALTY SEA DOG, CHIEF!
LOOK!
70
SEAMUS O'HARA? I'M NATE NETWORKER. NICE TO MEET YOU!
THE HEAD OF KMM CHANNEL 11? MICKEY'S NEWS MUST BE HUGE!

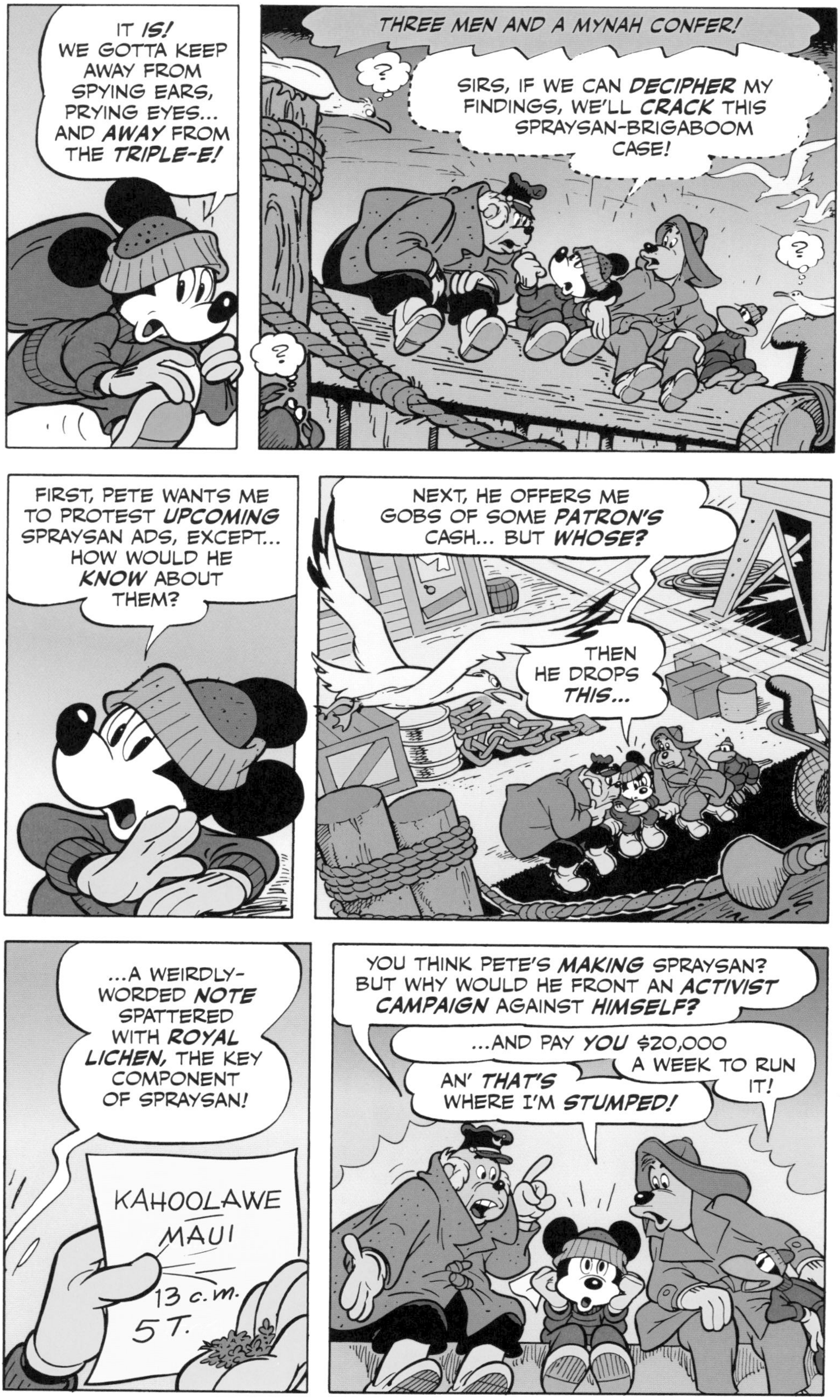
IT IS! WE GOTTA KEEP AWAY FROM SPYING EARS, PRYING EYES... AND AWAY FROM THE TRIPLE-E!
THREE MEN AND A MYNAH CONFER!
SIRS, IF WE CAN DECIPHER MY FINDINGS, WE'LL CRACK THIS SPRAYSAN-BRIGABOOM CASE!
?
?
?
FIRST, PETE WANTS ME TO PROTEST UPCOMING SPRAYSAN ADS, EXCEPT... HOW WOULD HE KNOW ABOUT THEM?
NEXT, HE OFFERS ME GOBS OF SOME PATRON'S CASH... BUT WHOSE?
THEN HE DROPS THIS...
...A WEIRDLY-WORDED NOTE SPATTERED WITH ROYAL LICHEN, THE KEY COMPONENT OF SPRAYSAN!
KAHOOLAWE
MAUI
13 c.m.
5T.
YOU THINK PETE'S MAKING SPRAYSAN? BUT WHY WOULD HE FRONT AN ACTIVIST CAMPAIGN AGAINST HIMSELF?
...AND PAY YOU $20,000 A WEEK TO RUN IT!
AN' THAT'S WHERE I'M STUMPED!

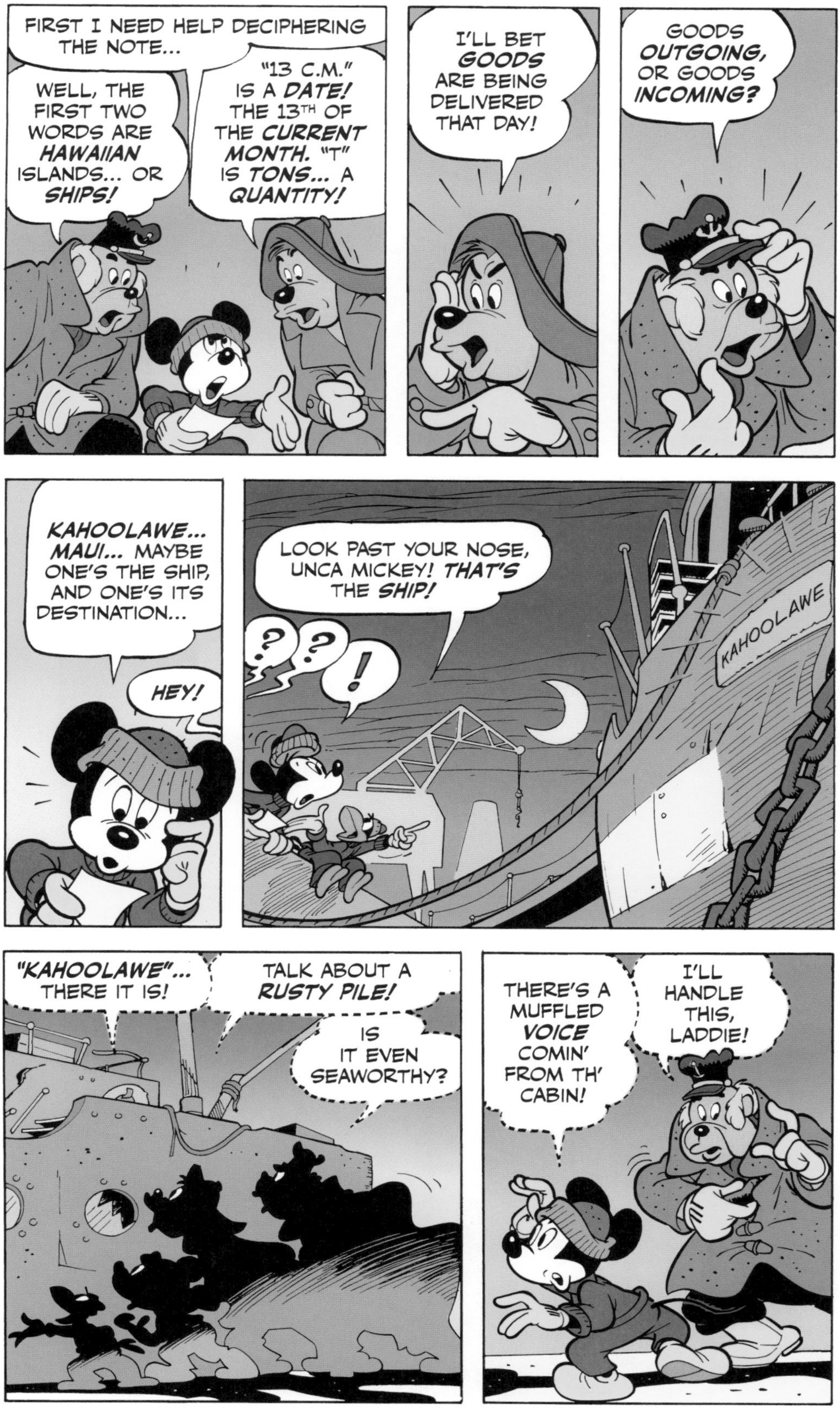

FIRST I NEED HELP DECIPHERING THE NOTE...
WELL, THE FIRST TWO WORDS ARE HAWAIIAN ISLANDS... OR SHIPS!
"13 C.M." IS A DATE! THE 13TH OF THE CURRENT MONTH. "T" IS TONS... A QUANTITY!
I'LL BET GOODS ARE BEING DELIVERED THAT DAY!
GOODS OUTGOING, OR GOODS INCOMING?
KAHOOLAWE... MAUI... MAYBE ONE'S THE SHIP, AND ONE'S ITS DESTINATION...
HEY!
LOOK PAST YOUR NOSE, UNCA MICKEY! THAT'S THE SHIP!
? ? !
KAHOOLAWE
"KAHOOLAWE"... THERE IT IS!
TALK ABOUT A RUSTY PILE!
IS IT EVEN SEAWORTHY?
THERE'S A MUFFLED VOICE COMIN' FROM TH' CABIN!
I'LL HANDLE THIS, LADDIE!

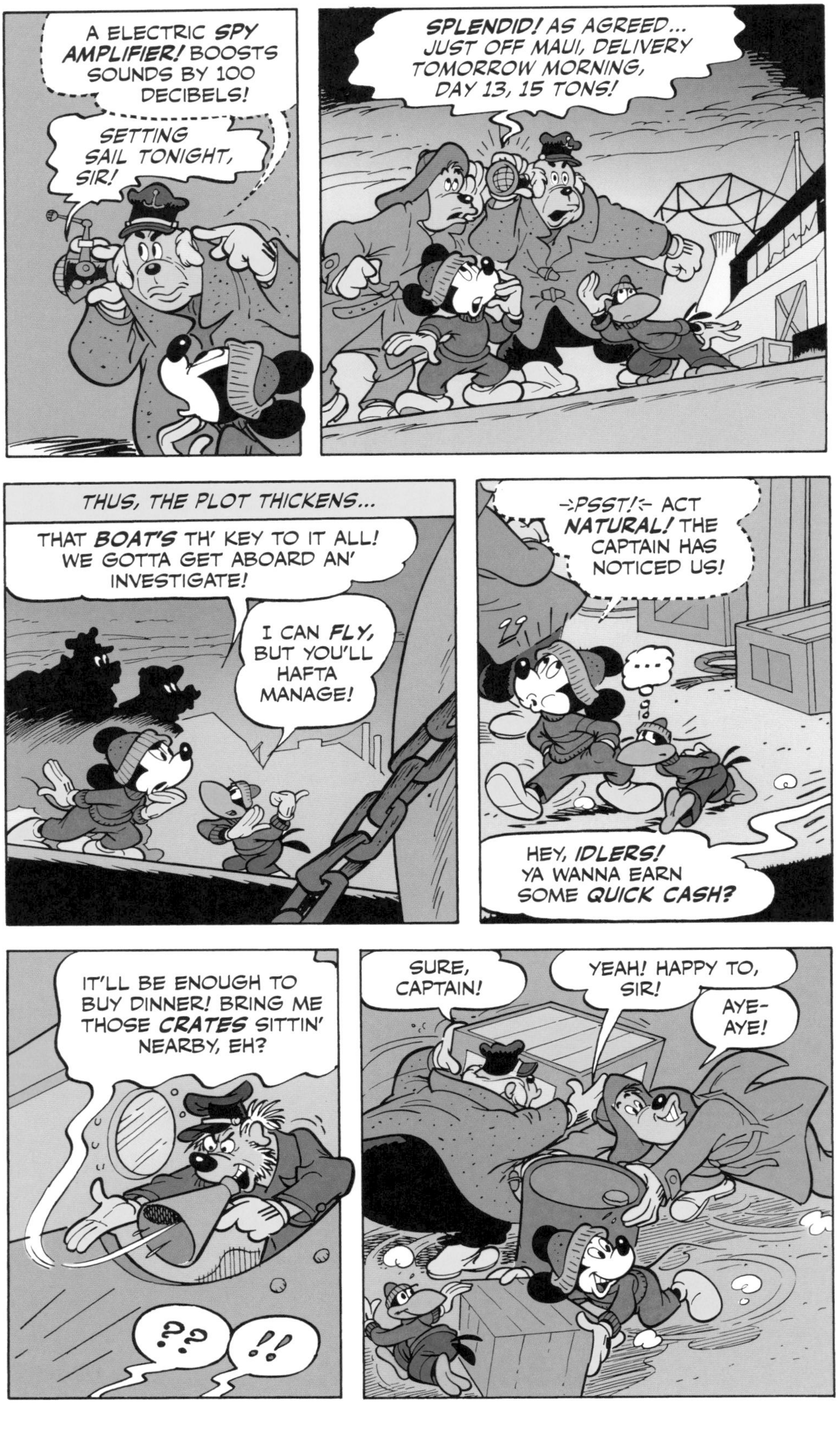

A ELECTRIC SPY AMPLIFIER! BOOSTS SOUNDS BY 100 DECIBELS!
SETTING SAIL TONIGHT, SIR!
SPLENDID! AS AGREED... JUST OFF MAUI, DELIVERY TOMORROW MORNING, DAY 13, 15 TONS!
THUS, THE PLOT THICKENS...
THAT BOAT'S TH' KEY TO IT ALL! WE GOTTA GET ABOARD AN' INVESTIGATE!
I CAN FLY, BUT YOU'LL HAFTA MANAGE!
PSST! ACT NATURAL! THE CAPTAIN HAS NOTICED US!
HEY, IDLERS! YA WANNA EARN SOME QUICK CASH?
IT'LL BE ENOUGH TO BUY DINNER! BRING ME THOSE CRATES SITTIN' NEARBY, EH?
??
!!
SURE, CAPTAIN!
YEAH! HAPPY TO, SIR!
AYE-AYE!

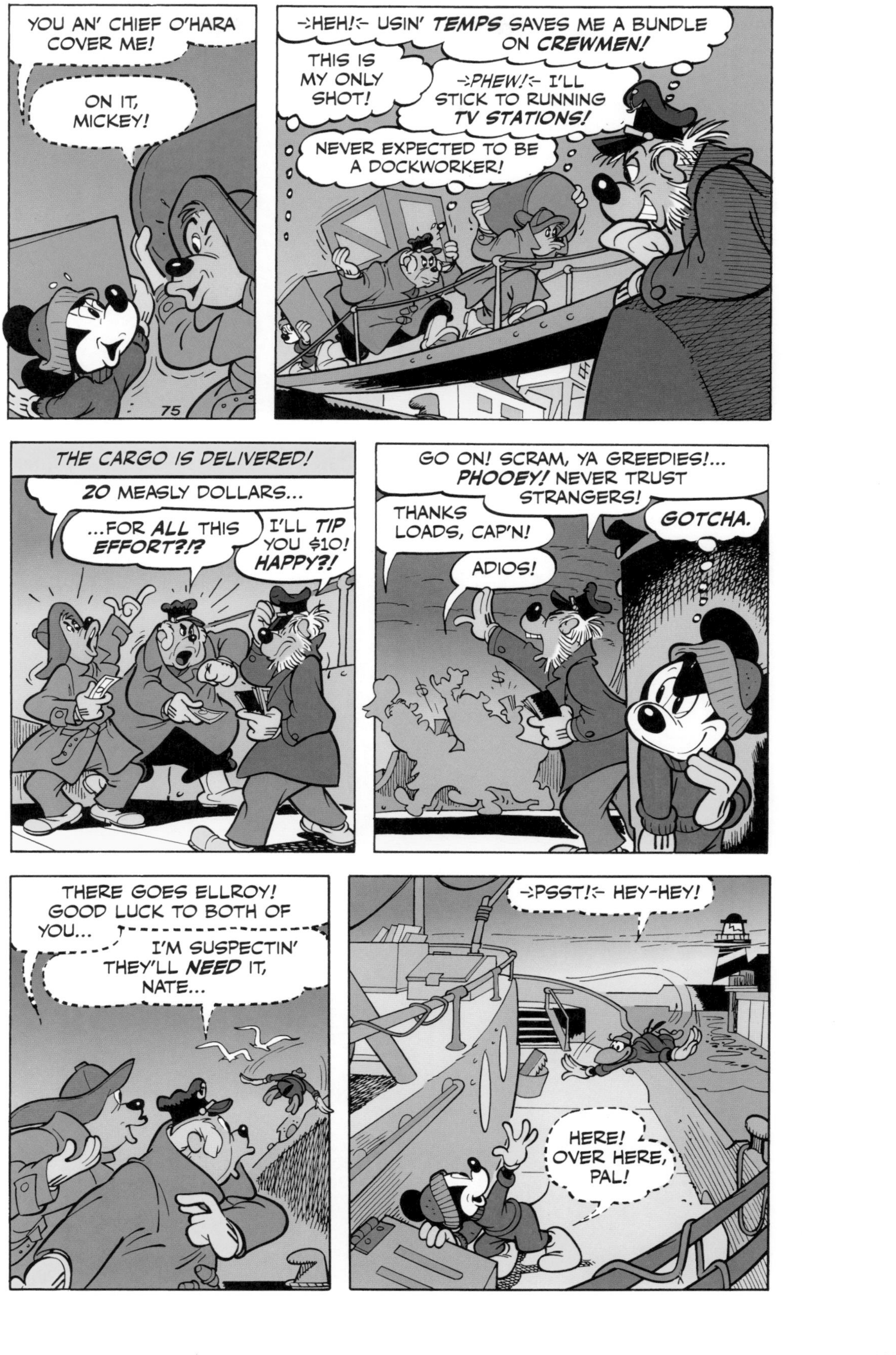
YOU AN' CHIEF O'HARA COVER ME!
ON IT, MICKEY!
75
–>HEH!<– USIN' TEMPS SAVES ME A BUNDLE ON CREWMEN!
THIS IS MY ONLY SHOT!
–>PHEW!<– I'LL STICK TO RUNNING TV STATIONS!
NEVER EXPECTED TO BE A DOCKWORKER!
THE CARGO IS DELIVERED!
20 MEASLY DOLLARS...
...FOR ALL THIS EFFORT?!?
I'LL TIP YOU $10! HAPPY?!
GO ON! SCRAM, YA GREEDIES!... PHOOEY! NEVER TRUST STRANGERS!
THANKS LOADS, CAP'N!
ADIOS!
GOTCHA.
THERE GOES ELLROY! GOOD LUCK TO BOTH OF YOU...
I'M SUSPECTIN' THEY'LL NEED IT, NATE...
–>PSST!<– HEY-HEY!
HERE! OVER HERE, PAL!

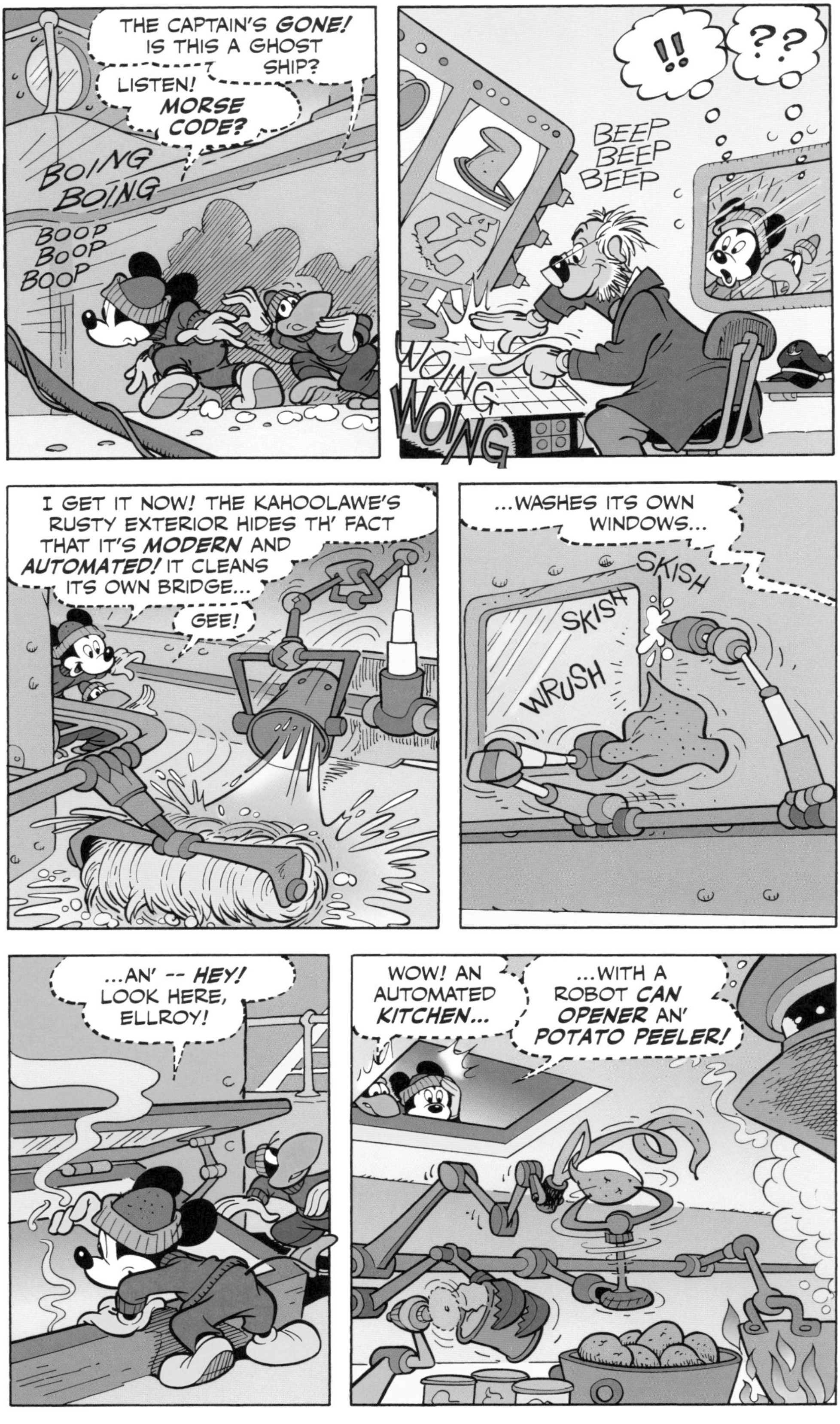
THE CAPTAIN'S GONE! IS THIS A GHOST SHIP?
LISTEN! MORSE CODE?
BOING BOING
BOOP BOOP BOOP
!!
??
BEEP BEEP BEEP
WOING WOING
I GET IT NOW! THE KAHOOLAWE'S RUSTY EXTERIOR HIDES TH' FACT THAT IT'S MODERN AND AUTOMATED! IT CLEANS ITS OWN BRIDGE...
GEE!
...WASHES ITS OWN WINDOWS...
SKISH
SKISH
WRUSH
...AN' -- HEY! LOOK HERE, ELLROY!
WOW! AN AUTOMATED KITCHEN...
...WITH A ROBOT CAN OPENER AN' POTATO PEELER!

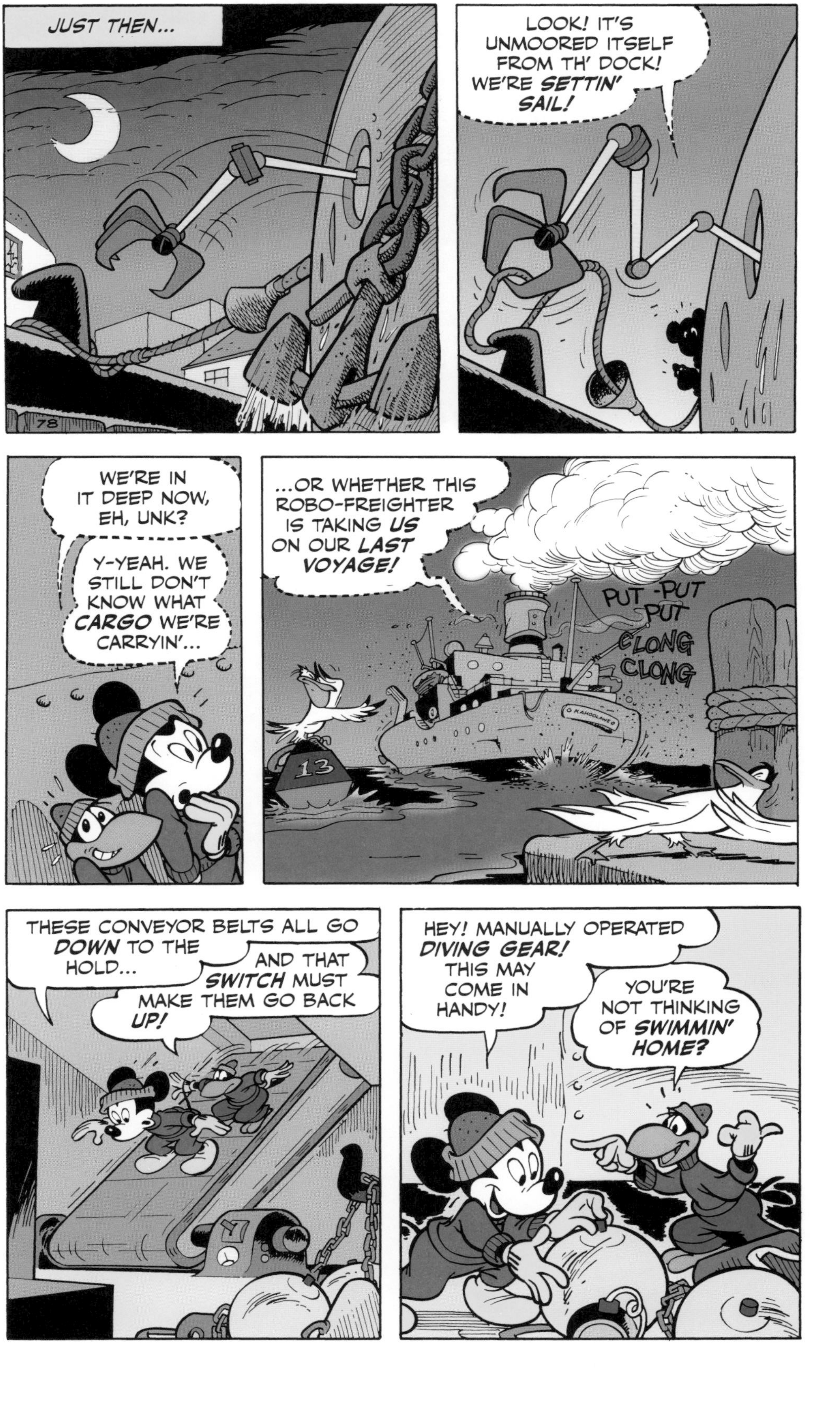
JUST THEN...
78
LOOK! IT'S UNMOORED ITSELF FROM TH' DOCK! WE'RE SETTIN' SAIL!
WE'RE IN IT DEEP NOW, EH, UNK?
Y-YEAH. WE STILL DON'T KNOW WHAT CARGO WE'RE CARRYIN'...
...OR WHETHER THIS ROBO-FREIGHTER IS TAKING US ON OUR LAST VOYAGE!
PUT-PUT PUT
CLONG CLONG
13
THESE CONVEYOR BELTS ALL GO DOWN TO THE HOLD...
AND THAT SWITCH MUST MAKE THEM GO BACK UP!
HEY! MANUALLY OPERATED DIVING GEAR! THIS MAY COME IN HANDY!
YOU'RE NOT THINKING OF SWIMMIN' HOME?

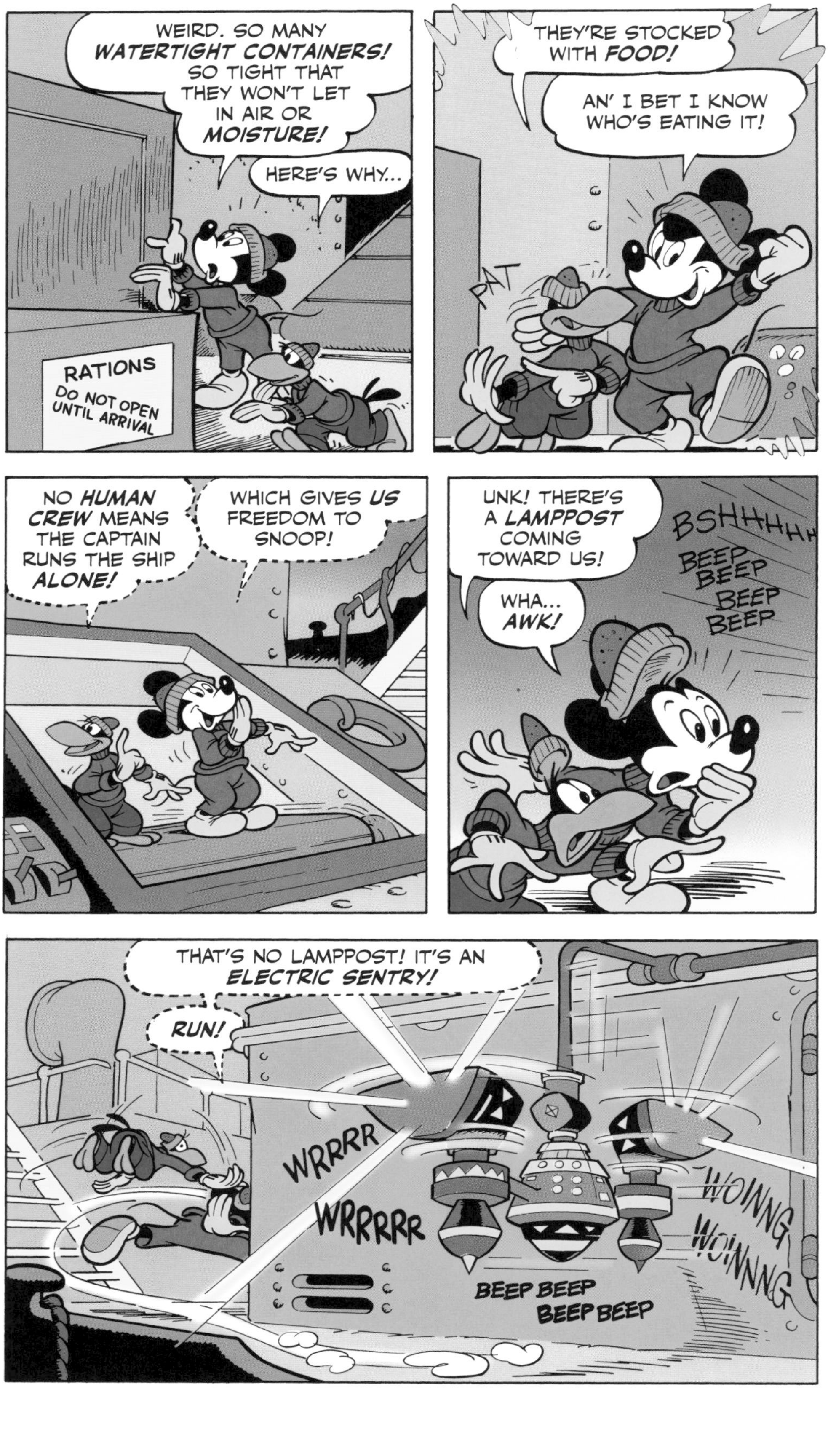
WEIRD. SO MANY WATERTIGHT CONTAINERS! SO TIGHT THAT THEY WON'T LET IN AIR OR MOISTURE!
HERE'S WHY...
RATIONS
DO NOT OPEN UNTIL ARRIVAL
THEY'RE STOCKED WITH FOOD!
AN' I BET I KNOW WHO'S EATING IT!
PAT
NO HUMAN CREW MEANS THE CAPTAIN RUNS THE SHIP ALONE!
WHICH GIVES US FREEDOM TO SNOOP!
UNK! THERE'S A LAMPPOST COMING TOWARD US!
BSHHHHHH
BEEP BEEP BEEP BEEP
WHA... AWK!
THAT'S NO LAMPPOST! IT'S AN ELECTRIC SENTRY!
RUN!
WRRRR
WRRRRR
WOINNG
WOINNNG
BEEP BEEP
BEEP BEEP

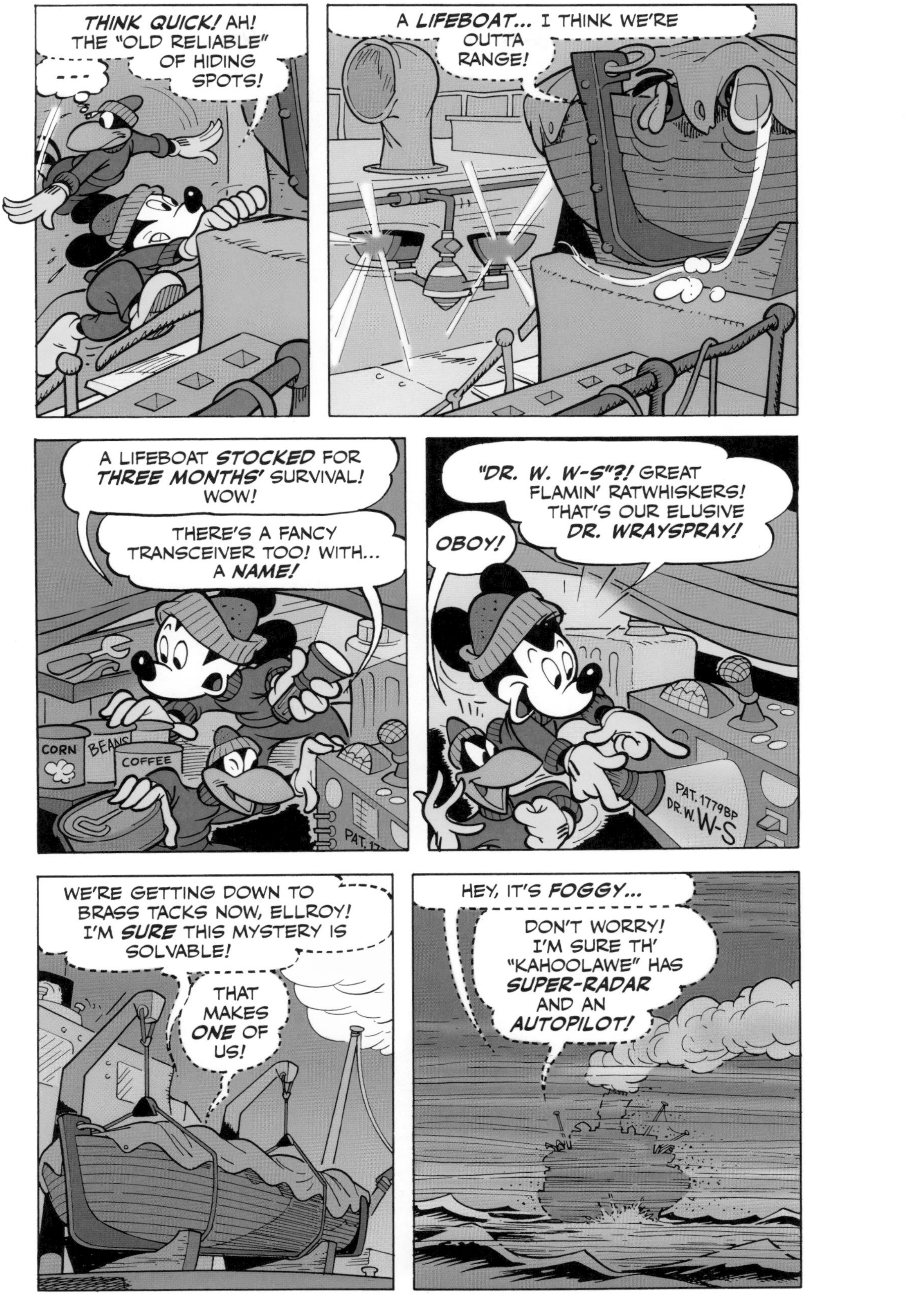
THINK QUICK! AH! THE "OLD RELIABLE" OF HIDING SPOTS!
- - -
A LIFEBOAT... I THINK WE'RE OUTTA RANGE!
A LIFEBOAT STOCKED FOR THREE MONTHS' SURVIVAL! WOW!
THERE'S A FANCY TRANSCEIVER TOO! WITH... A NAME!
CORN
BEANS
COFFEE
"DR. W. W-S"?! GREAT FLAMIN' RATWHISKERS! THAT'S OUR ELUSIVE DR. WRAYSPRAY!
OBOY!
PAT. 1779BP DR. W. W-S
WE'RE GETTING DOWN TO BRASS TACKS NOW, ELLROY! I'M SURE THIS MYSTERY IS SOLVABLE!
THAT MAKES ONE OF US!
HEY, IT'S FOGGY...
DON'T WORRY! I'M SURE TH' "KAHOOLAWE" HAS SUPER-RADAR AND AN AUTOPILOT!

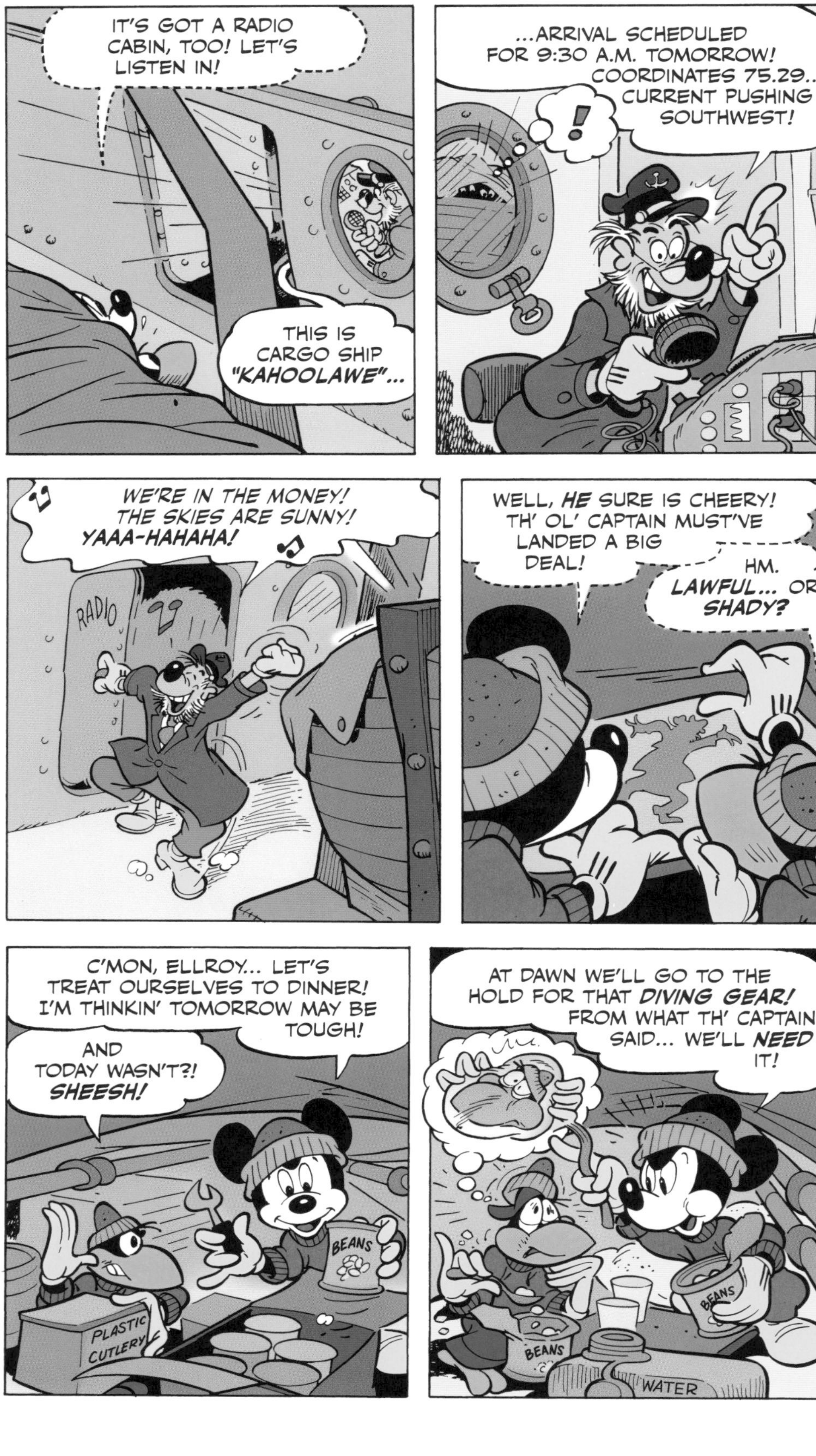
IT'S GOT A RADIO CABIN, TOO! LET'S LISTEN IN!
THIS IS CARGO SHIP "KAHOOLAWE"...
...ARRIVAL SCHEDULED FOR 9:30 A.M. TOMORROW! COORDINATES 75.29... CURRENT PUSHING SOUTHWEST!
!
WE'RE IN THE MONEY! THE SKIES ARE SUNNY! YAAA-HAHAHA!
RADIO
WELL, HE SURE IS CHEERY! TH' OL' CAPTAIN MUST'VE LANDED A BIG DEAL!
HM. LAWFUL... OR SHADY?
C'MON, ELLROY... LET'S TREAT OURSELVES TO DINNER! I'M THINKIN' TOMORROW MAY BE TOUGH!
AND TODAY WASN'T?! SHEESH!
BEANS
PLASTIC CUTLERY
AT DAWN WE'LL GO TO THE HOLD FOR THAT DIVING GEAR! FROM WHAT TH' CAPTAIN SAID... WE'LL NEED IT!
BEANS
BEANS
WATER

THE NIGHT IS LONG AND UNEASY AS THE "KAHOOLAWE" BOBS UP AND DOWN THE PACIFIC...

SPRAYSAN

ANTARCTICA

ROYAL LICHEN

BRIGABOOM

DAWN!

~EEEEP!~

PECK

WHA...?! QUIET, ELLROY! WHAT'S WRONG??

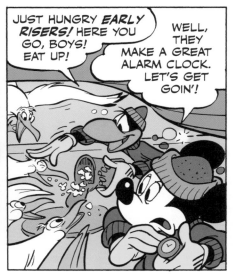

JUST HUNGRY *EARLY RISERS!* HERE YOU GO, BOYS! EAT UP!

WELL, THEY MAKE A GREAT ALARM CLOCK. LET'S GET GOIN'!

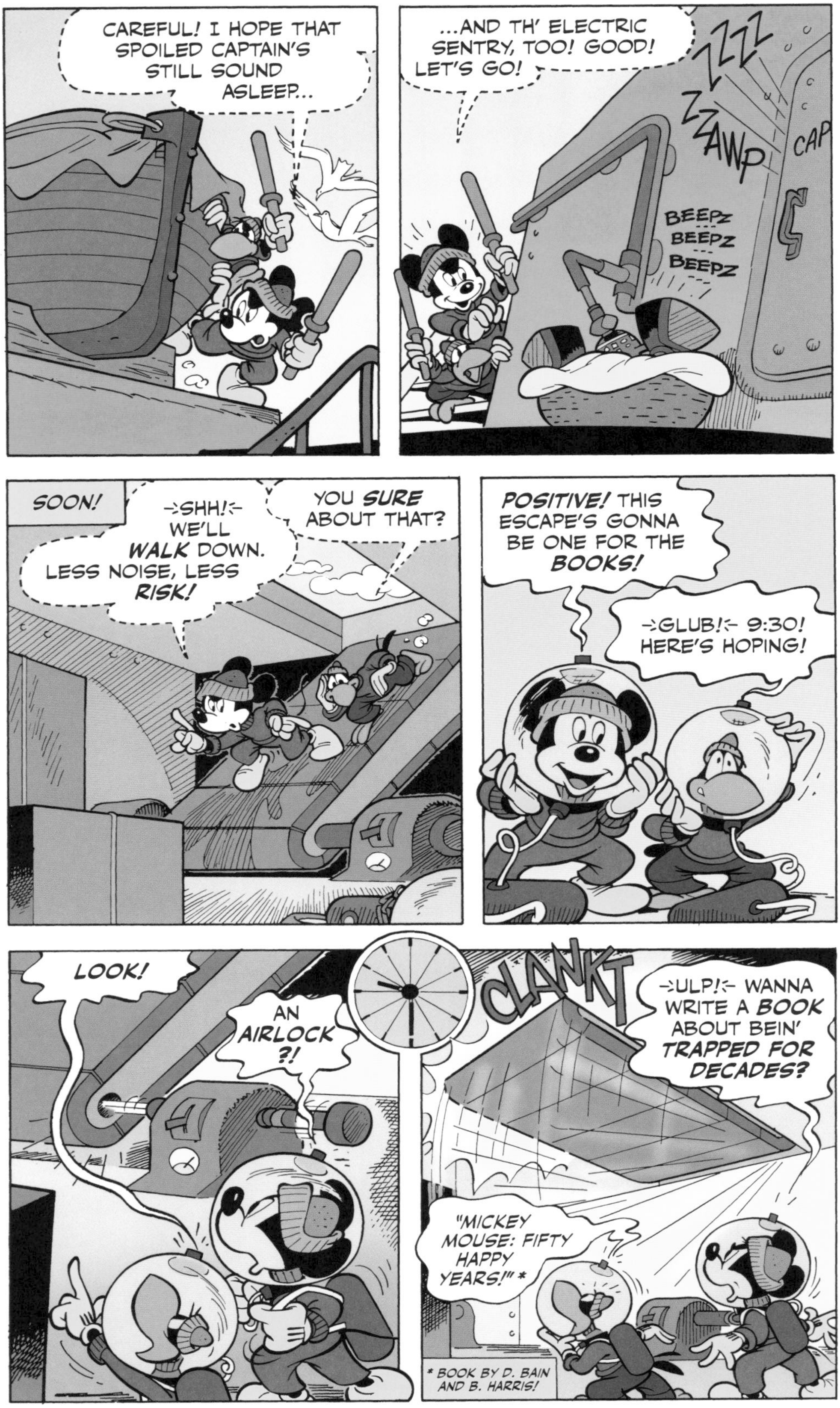
CAREFUL! I HOPE THAT SPOILED CAPTAIN'S STILL SOUND ASLEEP...
...AND TH' ELECTRIC SENTRY, TOO! GOOD! LET'S GO!
ZZZZ ZZZAWP
CAP
BEEPZ BEEPZ BEEPZ
SOON!
–SHH!– WE'LL WALK DOWN. LESS NOISE, LESS RISK!
YOU SURE ABOUT THAT?
POSITIVE! THIS ESCAPE'S GONNA BE ONE FOR THE BOOKS!
–GLUB!– 9:30! HERE'S HOPING!
LOOK!
AN AIRLOCK ?!
CLANKT
–ULP!– WANNA WRITE A BOOK ABOUT BEIN' TRAPPED FOR DECADES?
"MICKEY MOUSE: FIFTY HAPPY YEARS!" *
* BOOK BY D. BAIN AND B. HARRIS!

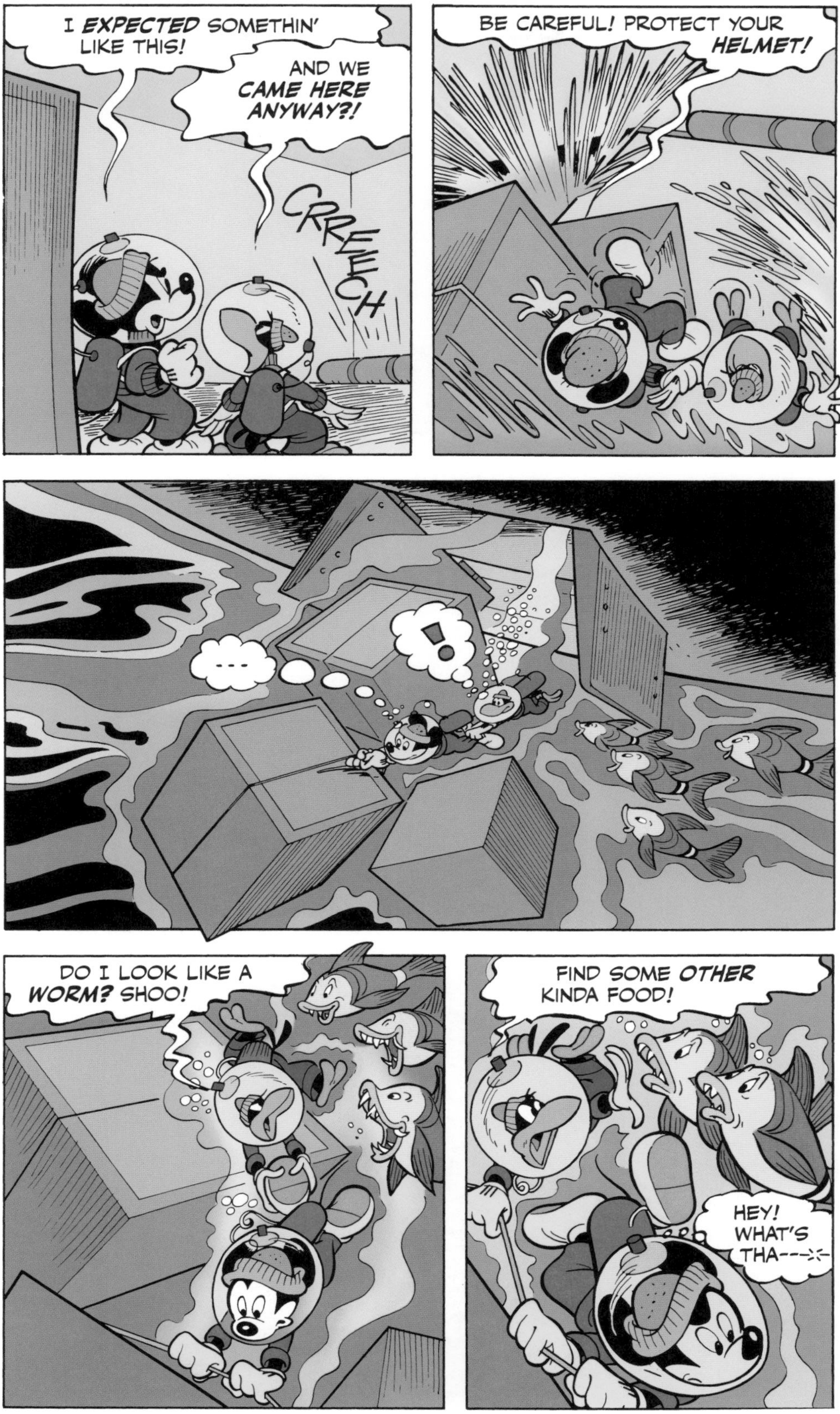
I EXPECTED SOMETHIN' LIKE THIS!
AND WE CAME HERE ANYWAY?!
CRREECH
BE CAREFUL! PROTECT YOUR HELMET!
!

DO I LOOK LIKE A WORM? SHOO!
FIND SOME OTHER KINDA FOOD!
HEY! WHAT'S THA---

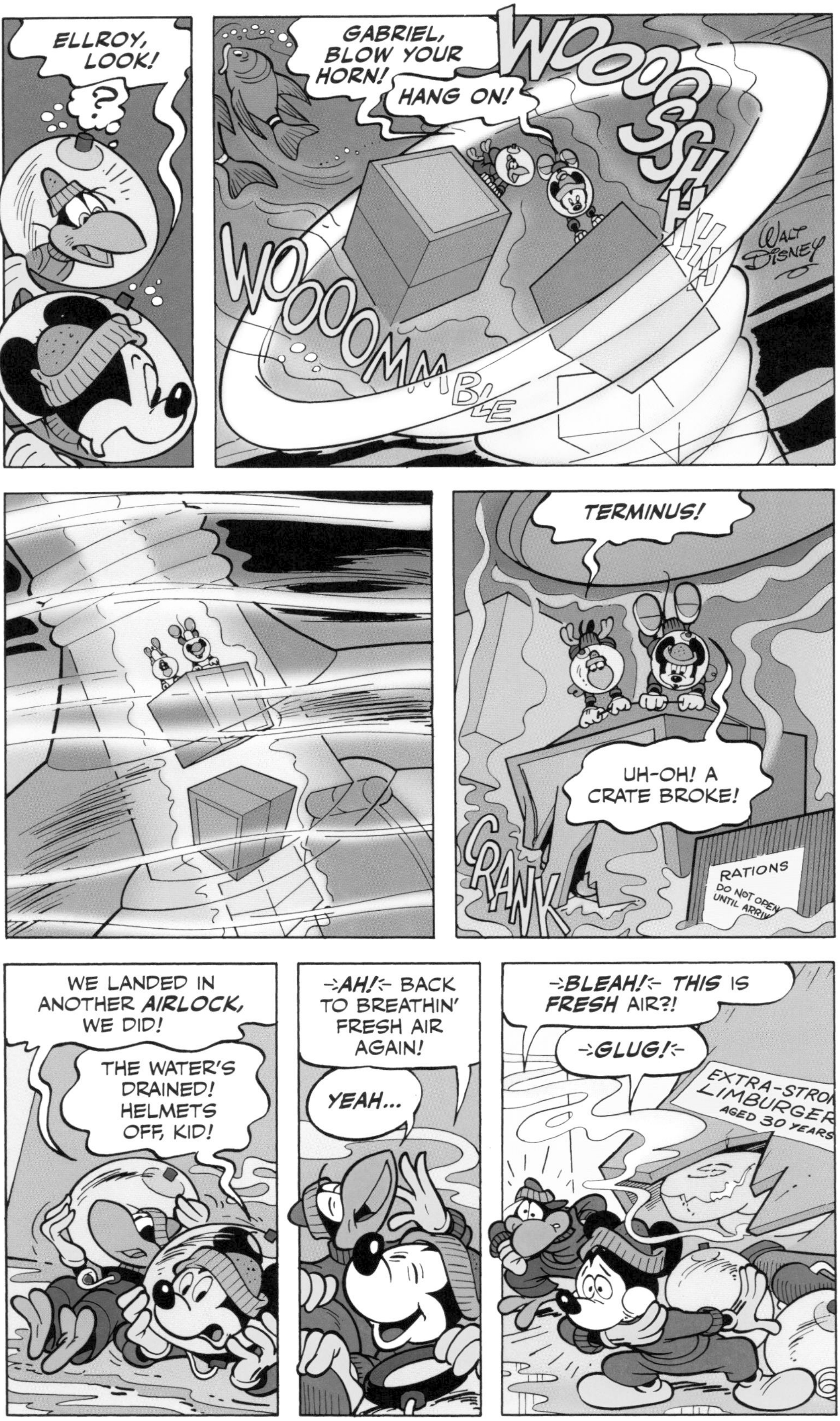
ELLROY, LOOK!
?
GABRIEL, BLOW YOUR HORN!
HANG ON!
WOOOGSSHHHH
WOOOOMMMBLE
WALT DISNEY
TERMINUS!
UH-OH! A CRATE BROKE!
CRANK
RATIONS
DO NOT OPEN UNTIL ARRIV
WE LANDED IN ANOTHER AIRLOCK, WE DID!
THE WATER'S DRAINED! HELMETS OFF, KID!
AH! BACK TO BREATHIN' FRESH AIR AGAIN!
YEAH...
BLEAH! THIS IS FRESH AIR?!
GLUG!
EXTRA-STRON LIMBURGER AGED 30 YEARS

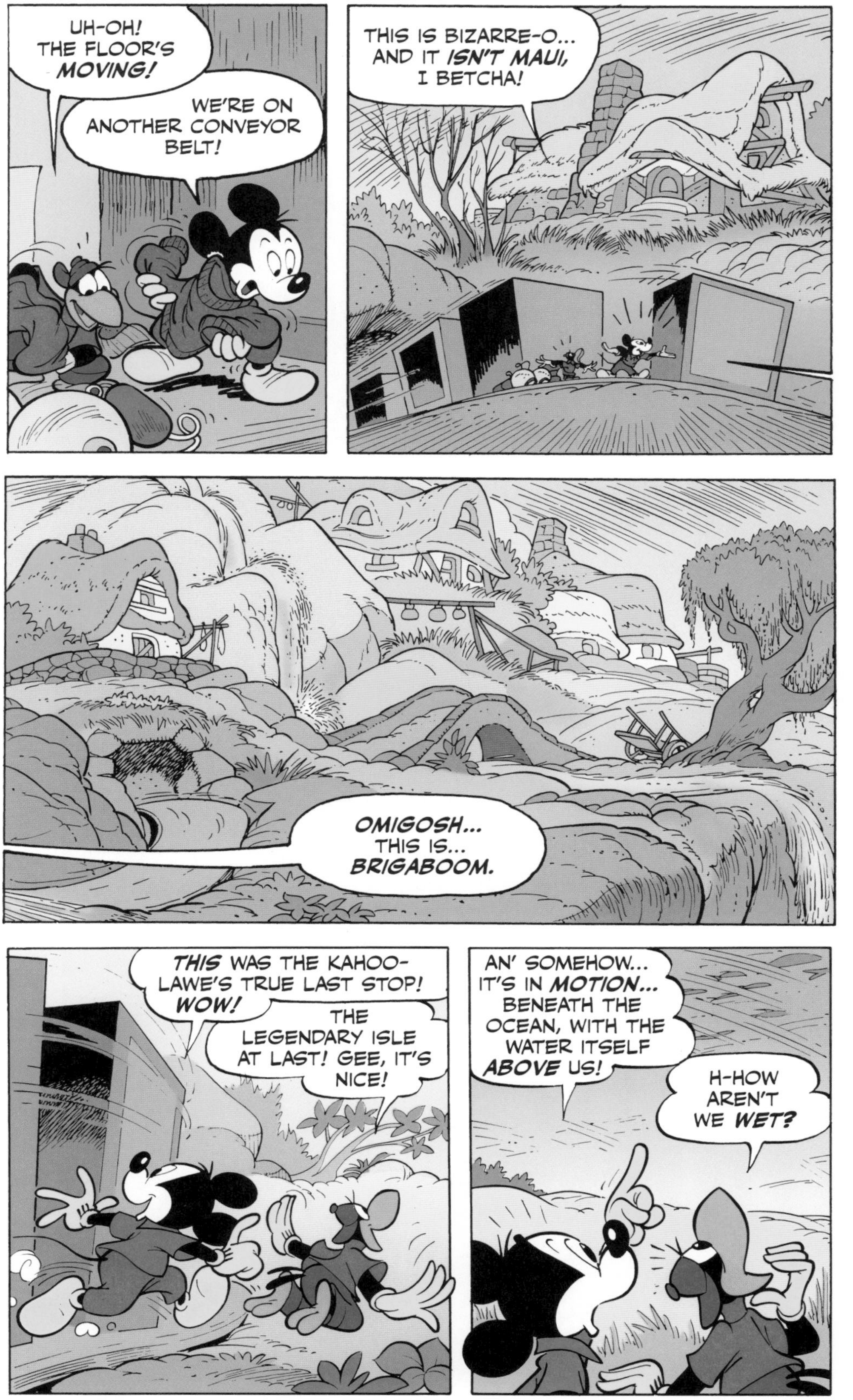
UH-OH! THE FLOOR'S MOVING!
WE'RE ON ANOTHER CONVEYOR BELT!
THIS IS BIZARRE-O... AND IT ISN'T MAUI, I BETCHA!
OMIGOSH... THIS IS... BRIGABOOM.
THIS WAS THE KAHOO-LAWE'S TRUE LAST STOP! WOW!
THE LEGENDARY ISLE AT LAST! GEE, IT'S NICE!
AN' SOMEHOW... IT'S IN MOTION... BENEATH THE OCEAN, WITH THE WATER ITSELF ABOVE US!
H-HOW AREN'T WE WET?

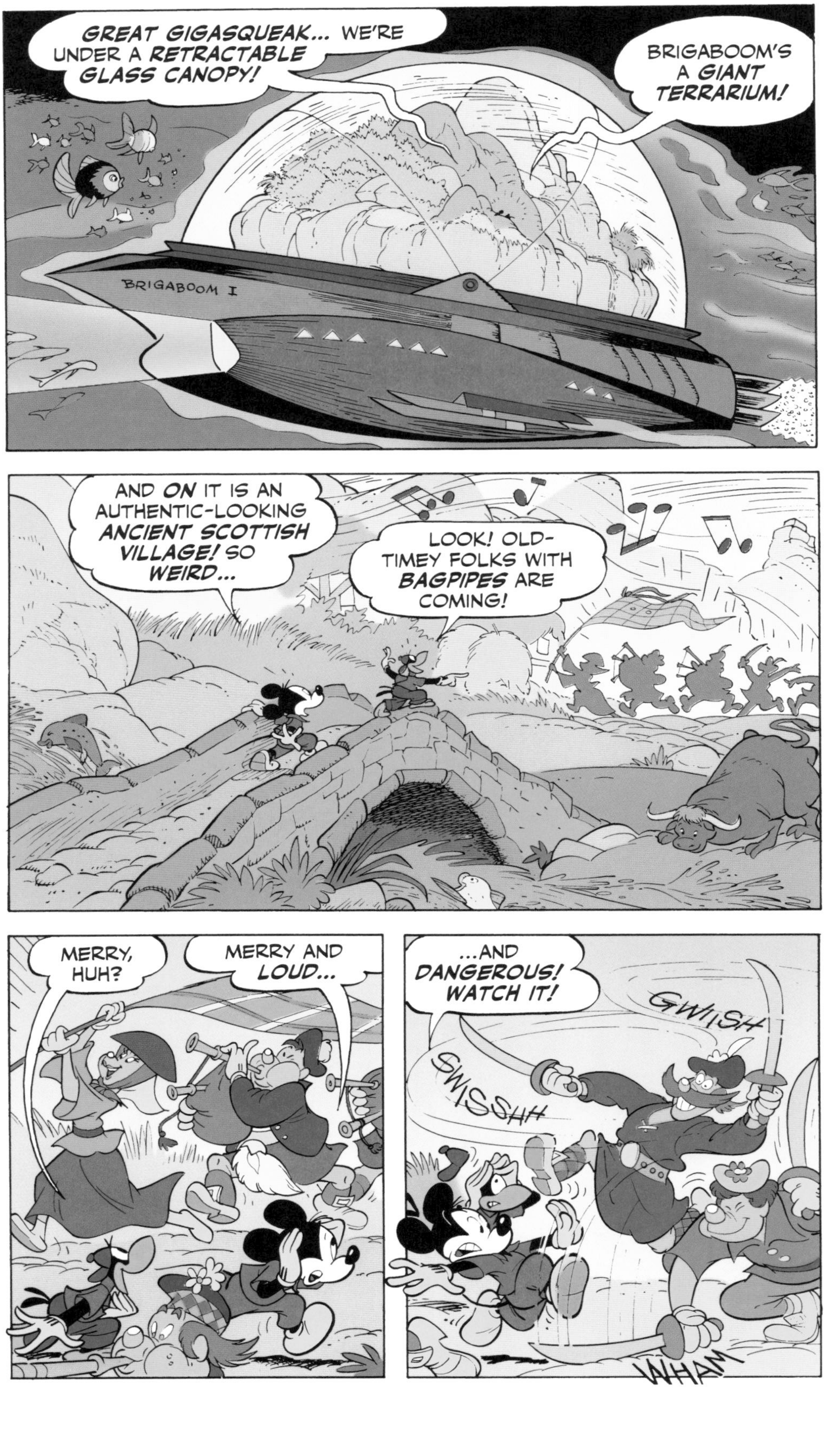
GREAT GIGASQUEAK... WE'RE UNDER A RETRACTABLE GLASS CANOPY!
BRIGABOOM'S A GIANT TERRARIUM!
BRIGABOOM I
AND ON IT IS AN AUTHENTIC-LOOKING ANCIENT SCOTTISH VILLAGE! SO WEIRD...
LOOK! OLD-TIMEY FOLKS WITH BAGPIPES ARE COMING!
MERRY, HUH?
MERRY AND LOUD...
...AND DANGEROUS! WATCH IT!
GWIISH
SWISSHH
WHAM

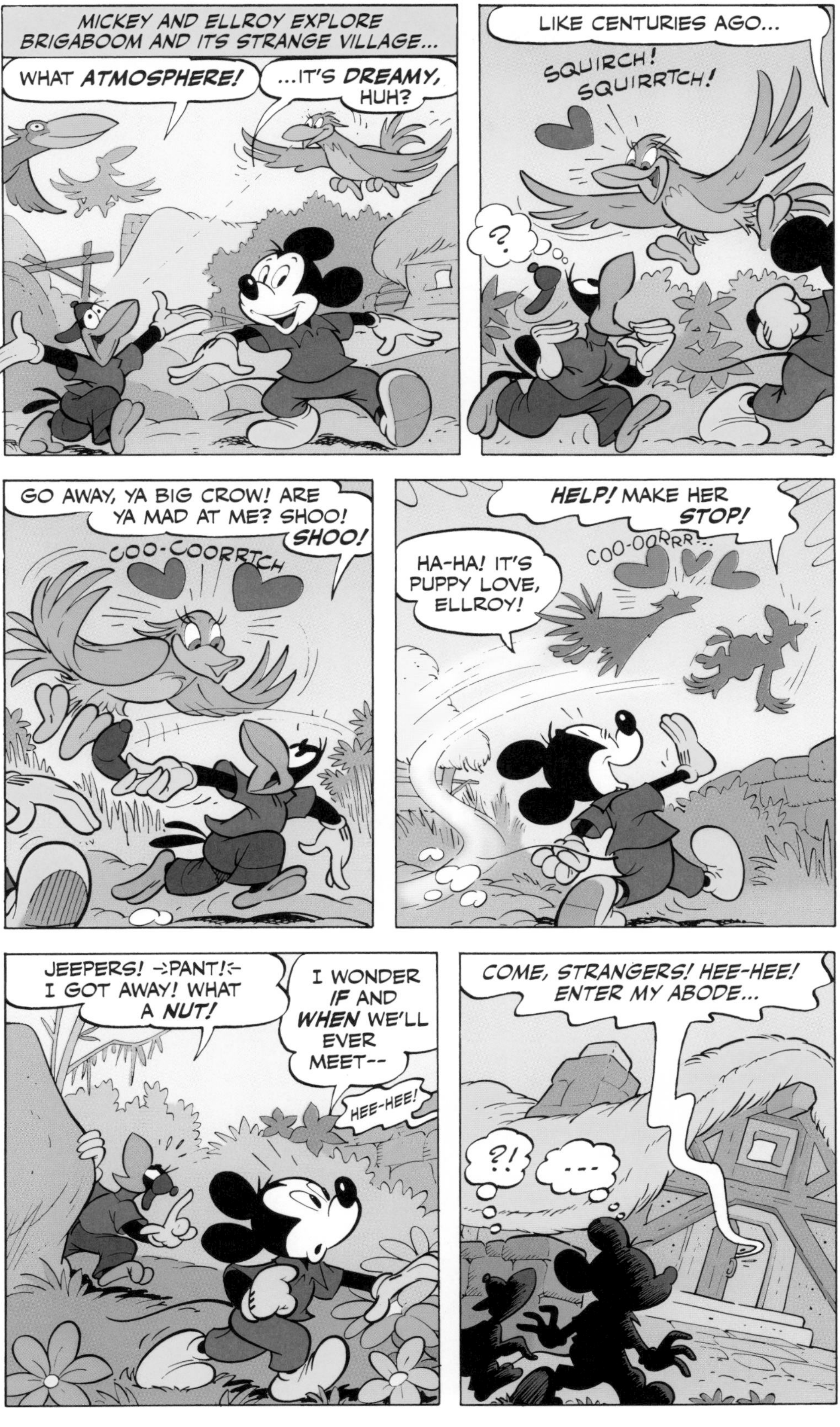
MICKEY AND ELLROY EXPLORE BRIGABOOM AND ITS STRANGE VILLAGE...
WHAT ATMOSPHERE!
...IT'S DREAMY, HUH?
LIKE CENTURIES AGO...
SQUIRCH! SQUIRRTCH!
?
GO AWAY, YA BIG CROW! ARE YA MAD AT ME? SHOO! SHOO!
COO-COORRTCH
HELP! MAKE HER STOP!
HA-HA! IT'S PUPPY LOVE, ELLROY!
COO-OORRR...
JEEPERS! -PANT!- I GOT AWAY! WHAT A NUT!
I WONDER IF AND WHEN WE'LL EVER MEET--
HEE-HEE!
COME, STRANGERS! HEE-HEE! ENTER MY ABODE...
?!

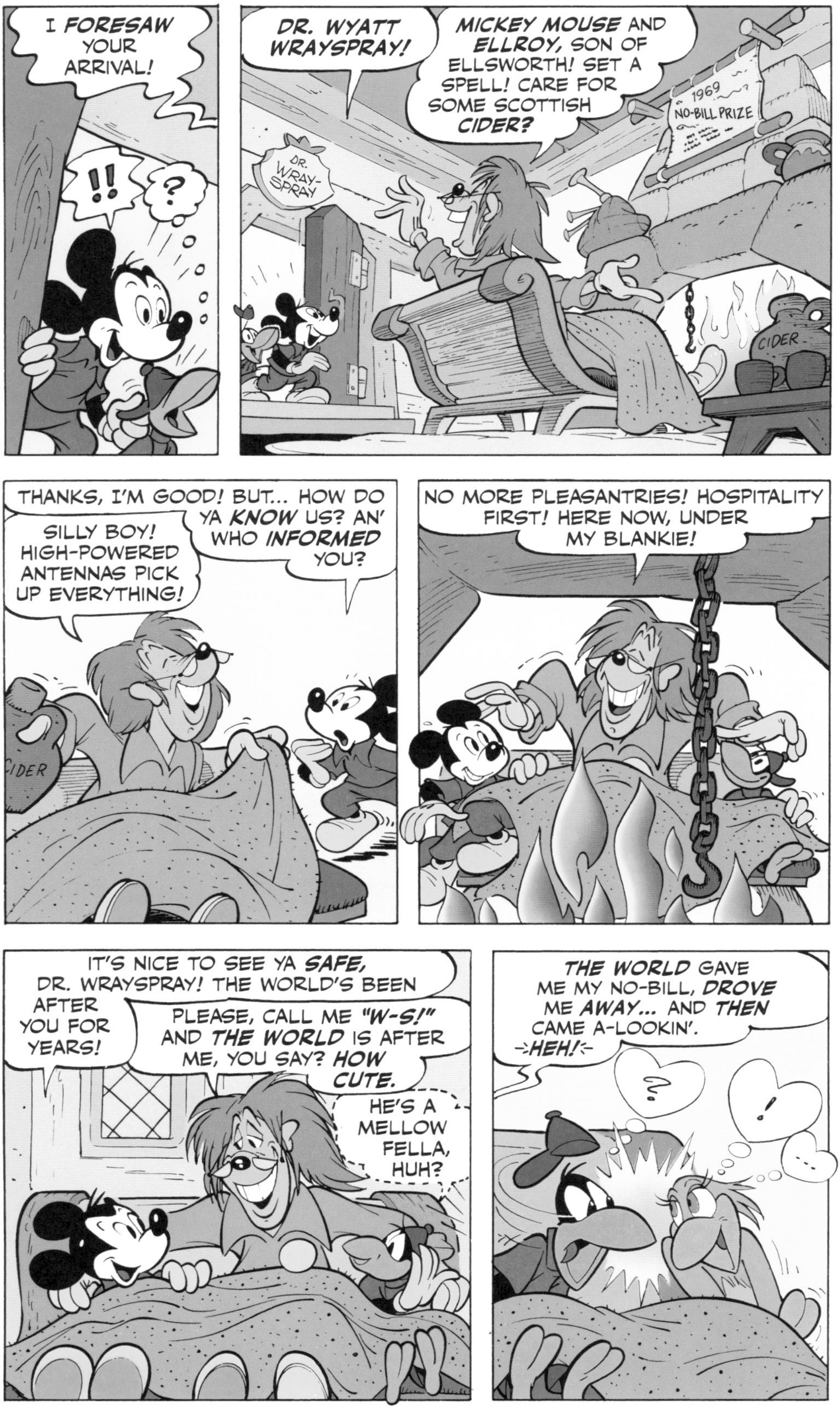
I FORESAW YOUR ARRIVAL!
!!
?
DR. WYATT WRAYSPRAY!
MICKEY MOUSE AND ELLROY, SON OF ELLSWORTH! SET A SPELL! CARE FOR SOME SCOTTISH CIDER?
DR. WRAY-SPRAY
1969 NO-BILL PRIZE
CIDER
THANKS, I'M GOOD! BUT... HOW DO YA KNOW US? AN' WHO INFORMED YOU?
SILLY BOY! HIGH-POWERED ANTENNAS PICK UP EVERYTHING!
CIDER
NO MORE PLEASANTRIES! HOSPITALITY FIRST! HERE NOW, UNDER MY BLANKIE!
IT'S NICE TO SEE YA SAFE, DR. WRAYSPRAY! THE WORLD'S BEEN AFTER YOU FOR YEARS!
PLEASE, CALL ME "W-S!" AND THE WORLD IS AFTER ME, YOU SAY? HOW CUTE.
HE'S A MELLOW FELLA, HUH?
THE WORLD GAVE ME MY NO-BILL, DROVE ME AWAY... AND THEN CAME A-LOOKIN'.
HEH!
?
!
...

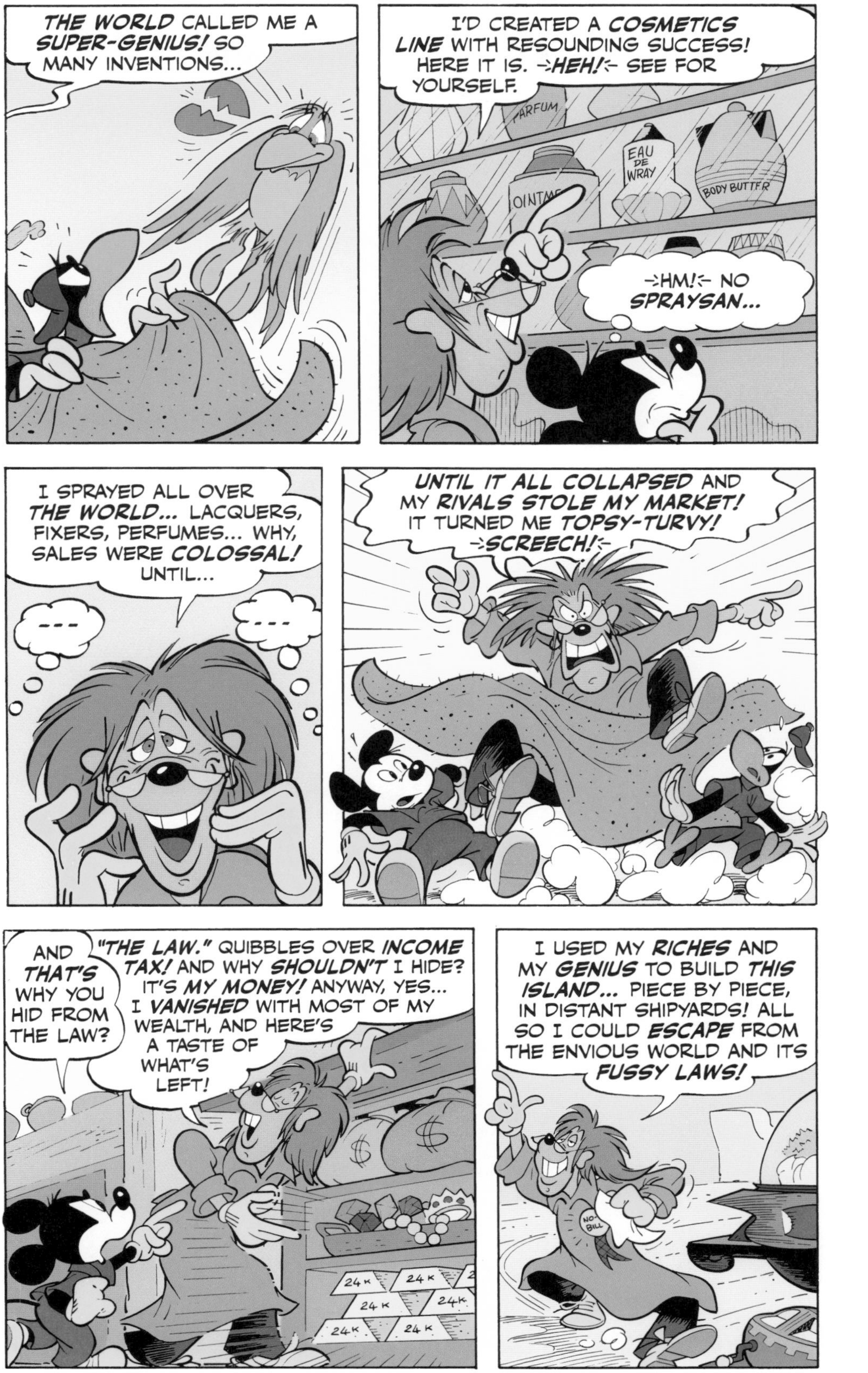
THE WORLD CALLED ME A SUPER-GENIUS! SO MANY INVENTIONS...
I'D CREATED A COSMETICS LINE WITH RESOUNDING SUCCESS! HERE IT IS. HEH! SEE FOR YOURSELF.
PARFUM
EAU DE WRAY
BODY BUTTER
HM! NO SPRAYSAN...
I SPRAYED ALL OVER THE WORLD... LACQUERS, FIXERS, PERFUMES... WHY, SALES WERE COLOSSAL! UNTIL...

UNTIL IT ALL COLLAPSED AND MY RIVALS STOLE MY MARKET! IT TURNED ME TOPSY-TURVY! SCREECH!
AND THAT'S WHY YOU HID FROM THE LAW?
"THE LAW." QUIBBLES OVER INCOME TAX! AND WHY SHOULDN'T I HIDE? IT'S MY MONEY! ANYWAY, YES... I VANISHED WITH MOST OF MY WEALTH, AND HERE'S A TASTE OF WHAT'S LEFT!
24K
I USED MY RICHES AND MY GENIUS TO BUILD THIS ISLAND... PIECE BY PIECE, IN DISTANT SHIPYARDS! ALL SO I COULD ESCAPE FROM THE ENVIOUS WORLD AND ITS FUSSY LAWS!
NO-BILL

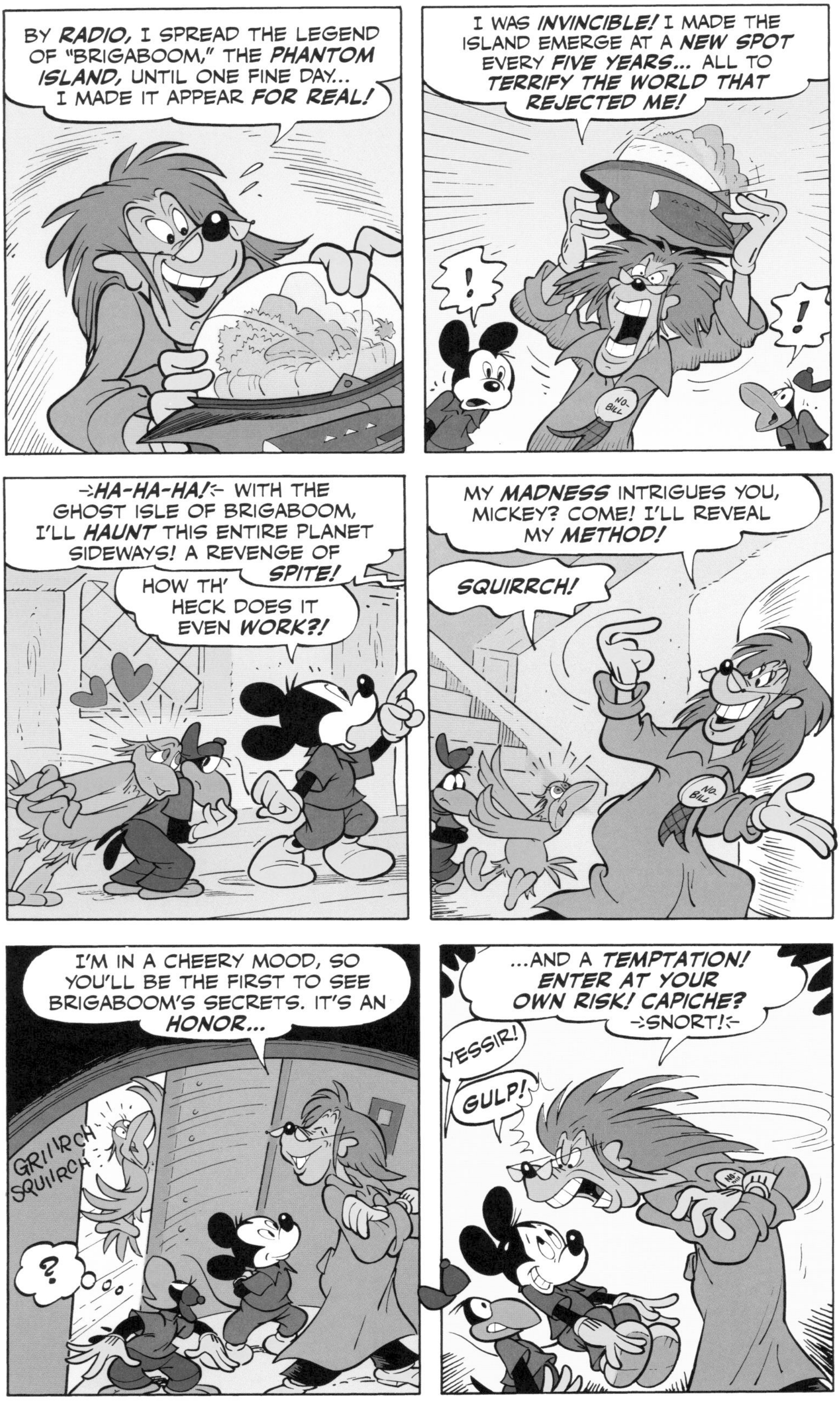
BY RADIO, I SPREAD THE LEGEND OF "BRIGABOOM," THE PHANTOM ISLAND, UNTIL ONE FINE DAY... I MADE IT APPEAR FOR REAL!
I WAS INVINCIBLE! I MADE THE ISLAND EMERGE AT A NEW SPOT EVERY FIVE YEARS... ALL TO TERRIFY THE WORLD THAT REJECTED ME!
!
!
NO-BILL
HA-HA-HA! WITH THE GHOST ISLE OF BRIGABOOM, I'LL HAUNT THIS ENTIRE PLANET SIDEWAYS! A REVENGE OF SPITE!
HOW TH' HECK DOES IT EVEN WORK?!
MY MADNESS INTRIGUES YOU, MICKEY? COME! I'LL REVEAL MY METHOD!
SQUIRRCH!
NO-BILL
I'M IN A CHEERY MOOD, SO YOU'LL BE THE FIRST TO SEE BRIGABOOM'S SECRETS. IT'S AN HONOR...
GRIIIRCH SQUIIRCH
?
...AND A TEMPTATION! ENTER AT YOUR OWN RISK! CAPICHE? SNORT!
YESSIR!
GULP!

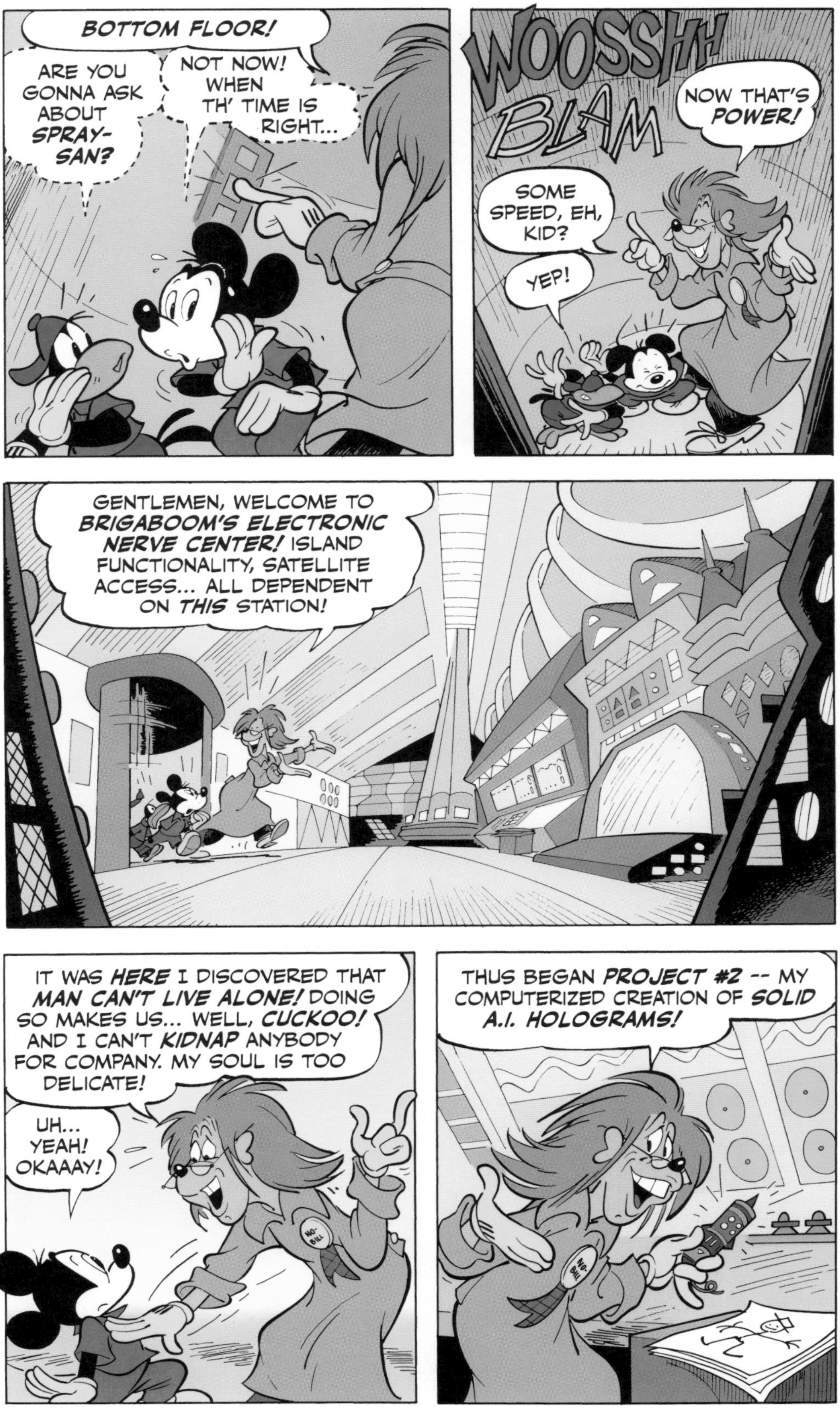
BOTTOM FLOOR!
ARE YOU GONNA ASK ABOUT SPRAY-SAN?
NOT NOW! WHEN TH' TIME IS RIGHT...
WOOSSHH
BLAM
NOW THAT'S POWER!
SOME SPEED, EH, KID?
YEP!
GENTLEMEN, WELCOME TO BRIGABOOM'S ELECTRONIC NERVE CENTER! ISLAND FUNCTIONALITY, SATELLITE ACCESS... ALL DEPENDENT ON THIS STATION!
IT WAS HERE I DISCOVERED THAT MAN CAN'T LIVE ALONE! DOING SO MAKES US... WELL, CUCKOO! AND I CAN'T KIDNAP ANYBODY FOR COMPANY. MY SOUL IS TOO DELICATE!
UH... YEAH! OKAAAY!
NO-BILL
THUS BEGAN PROJECT #2 -- MY COMPUTERIZED CREATION OF SOLID A.I. HOLOGRAMS!
NO-BILL

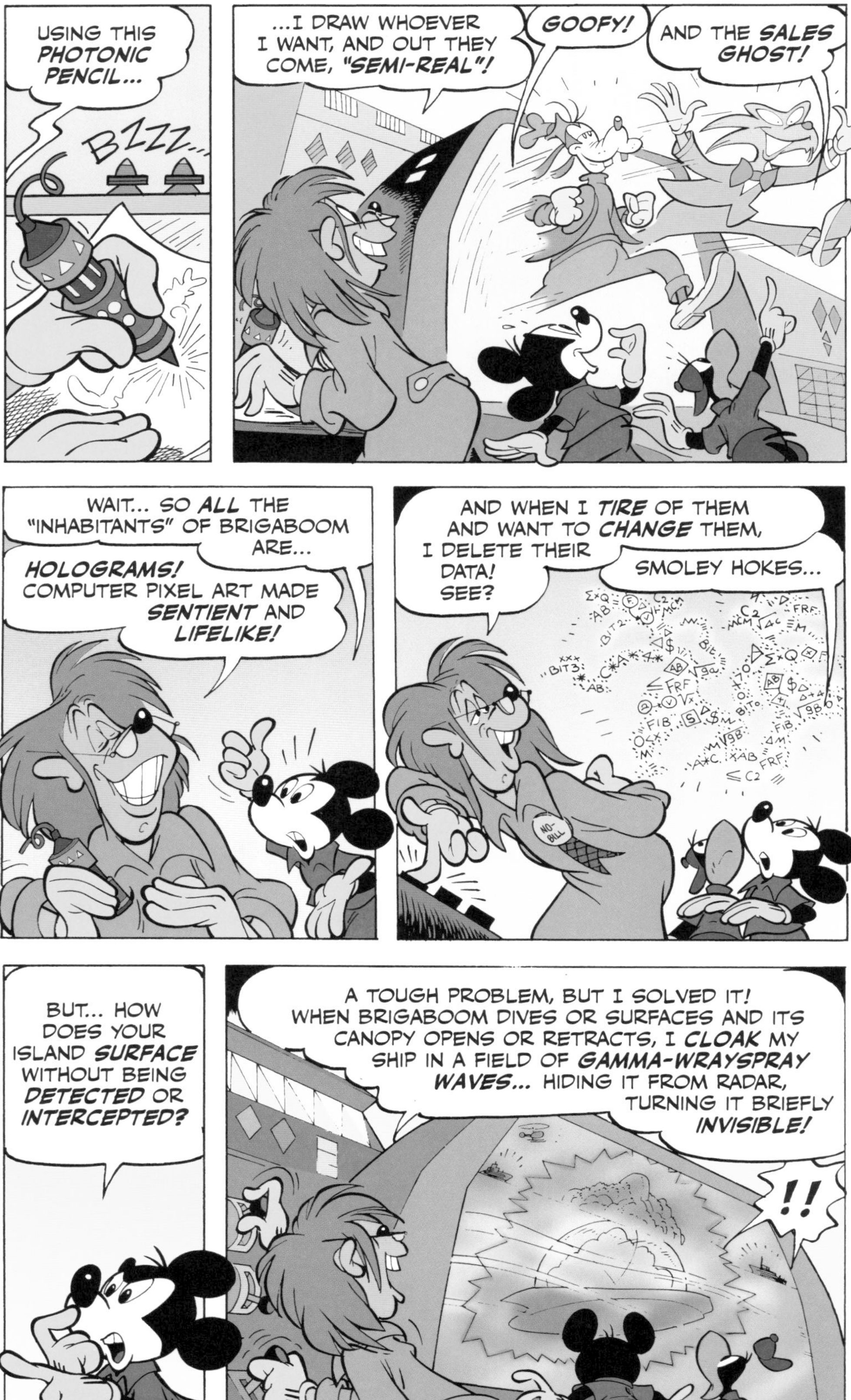
USING THIS PHOTONIC PENCIL...
BZZZ...
...I DRAW WHOEVER I WANT, AND OUT THEY COME, "SEMI-REAL"!
GOOFY!
AND THE SALES GHOST!
WAIT... SO ALL THE "INHABITANTS" OF BRIGABOOM ARE...
HOLOGRAMS! COMPUTER PIXEL ART MADE SENTIENT AND LIFELIKE!
AND WHEN I TIRE OF THEM AND WANT TO CHANGE THEM, I DELETE THEIR DATA! SEE?
SMOLEY HOKES...
NO-BILL
BUT... HOW DOES YOUR ISLAND SURFACE WITHOUT BEING DETECTED OR INTERCEPTED?
A TOUGH PROBLEM, BUT I SOLVED IT! WHEN BRIGABOOM DIVES OR SURFACES AND ITS CANOPY OPENS OR RETRACTS, I CLOAK MY SHIP IN A FIELD OF GAMMA-WRAYSPRAY WAVES... HIDING IT FROM RADAR, TURNING IT BRIEFLY INVISIBLE!
!!

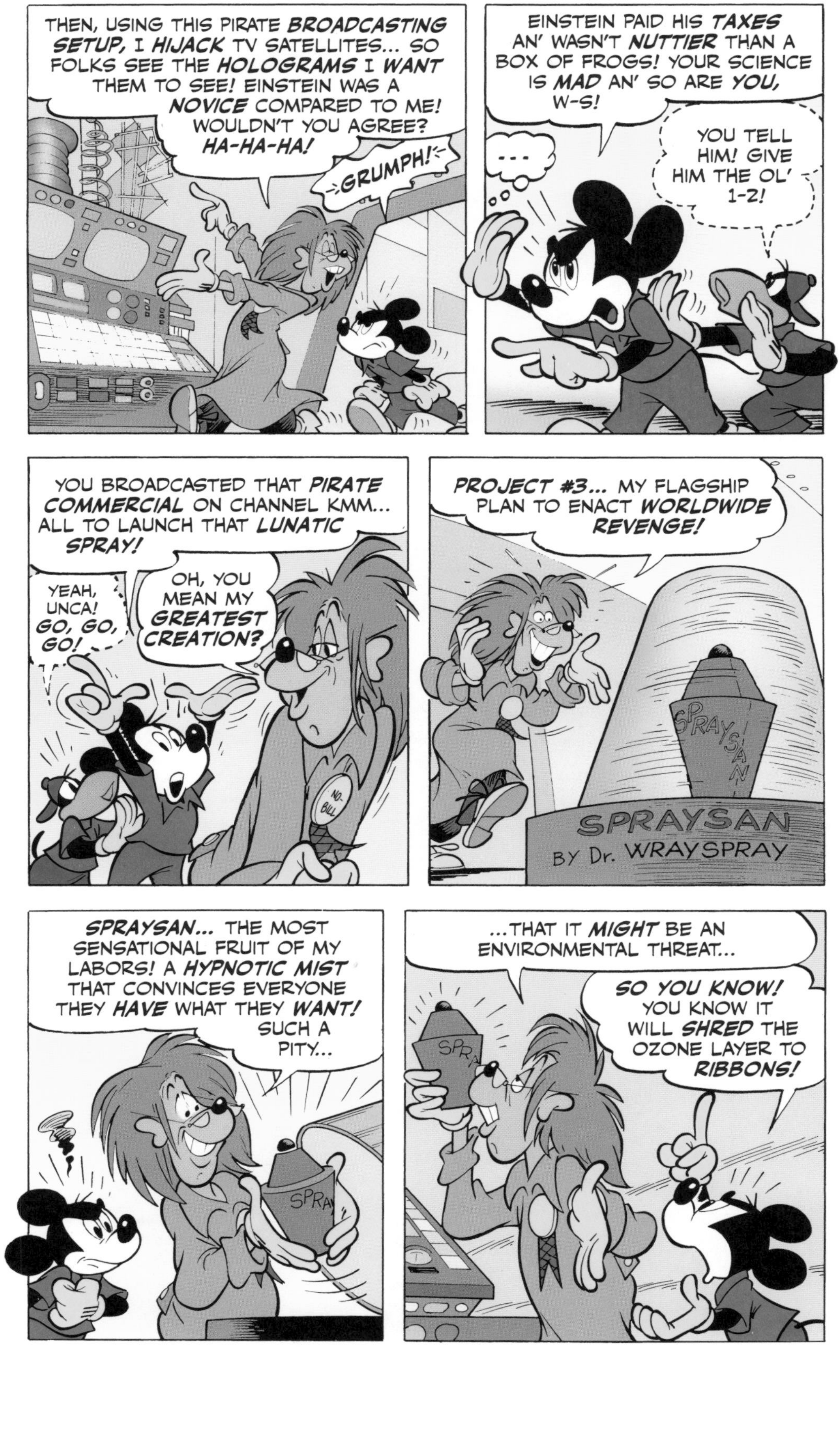

THEN, USING THIS PIRATE BROADCASTING SETUP, I HIJACK TV SATELLITES... SO FOLKS SEE THE HOLOGRAMS I WANT THEM TO SEE! EINSTEIN WAS A NOVICE COMPARED TO ME! WOULDN'T YOU AGREE? HA-HA-HA!
GRUMPH!
EINSTEIN PAID HIS TAXES AN' WASN'T NUTTIER THAN A BOX OF FROGS! YOUR SCIENCE IS MAD AN' SO ARE YOU, W-S!
...
YOU TELL HIM! GIVE HIM THE OL' 1-2!
YOU BROADCASTED THAT PIRATE COMMERCIAL ON CHANNEL KMM... ALL TO LAUNCH THAT LUNATIC SPRAY!
YEAH, UNCA! GO, GO, GO!
OH, YOU MEAN MY GREATEST CREATION?
NO-BILL
PROJECT #3... MY FLAGSHIP PLAN TO ENACT WORLDWIDE REVENGE!
SPRAYSAN
SPRAYSAN
BY Dr. WRAYSPRAY
SPRAYSAN... THE MOST SENSATIONAL FRUIT OF MY LABORS! A HYPNOTIC MIST THAT CONVINCES EVERYONE THEY HAVE WHAT THEY WANT!
SUCH A PITY...
SPRAY
...THAT IT MIGHT BE AN ENVIRONMENTAL THREAT...
SO YOU KNOW! YOU KNOW IT WILL SHRED THE OZONE LAYER TO RIBBONS!
SPRA

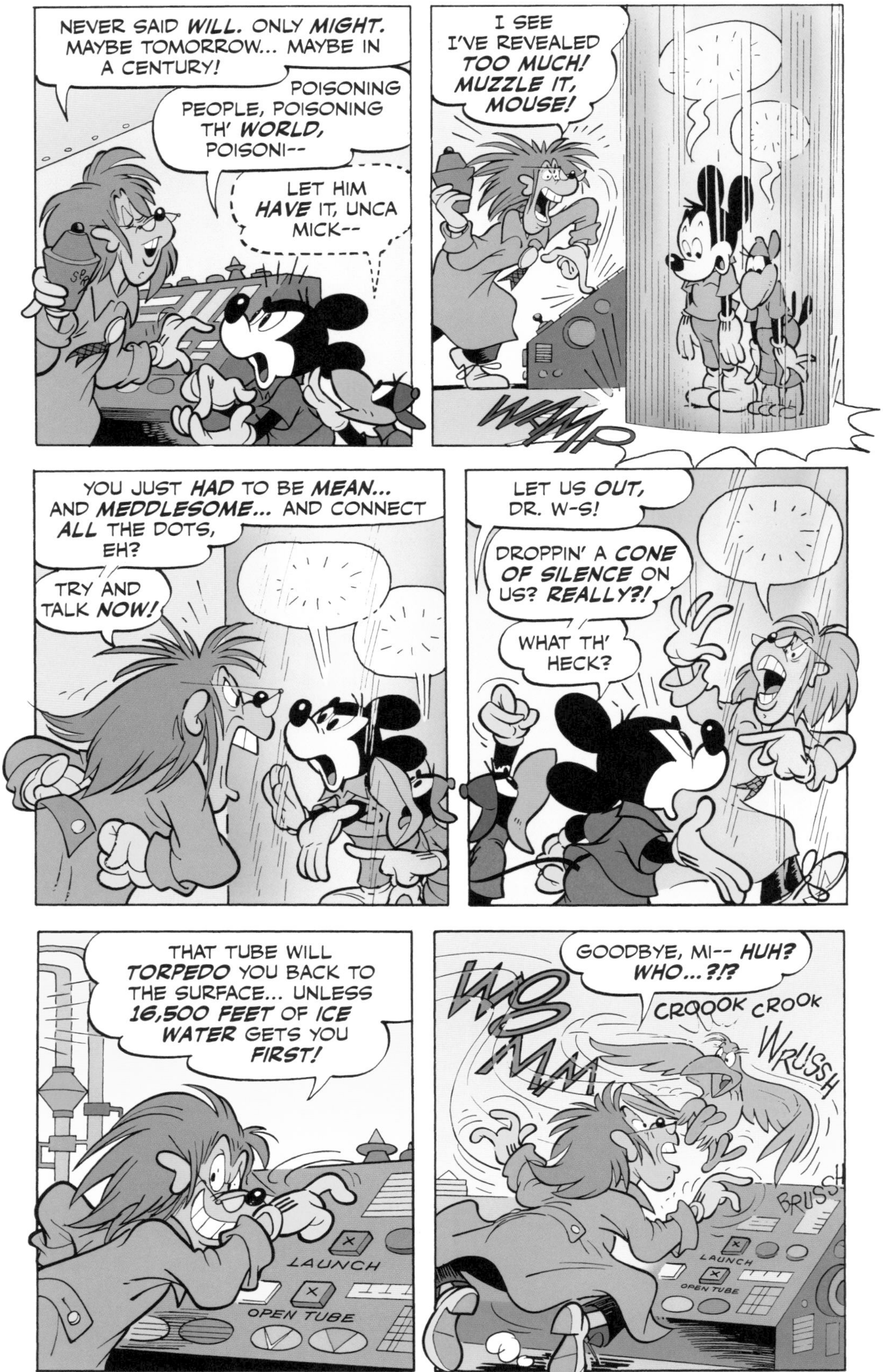
NEVER SAID WILL. ONLY MIGHT. MAYBE TOMORROW... MAYBE IN A CENTURY!
POISONING PEOPLE, POISONING TH' WORLD, POISONI--
LET HIM HAVE IT, UNCA MICK--
I SEE I'VE REVEALED TOO MUCH! MUZZLE IT, MOUSE!
WAMP
YOU JUST HAD TO BE MEAN... AND MEDDLESOME... AND CONNECT ALL THE DOTS, EH?
TRY AND TALK NOW!
LET US OUT, DR. W-S!
DROPPIN' A CONE OF SILENCE ON US? REALLY?!
WHAT TH' HECK?
THAT TUBE WILL TORPEDO YOU BACK TO THE SURFACE... UNLESS 16,500 FEET OF ICE WATER GETS YOU FIRST!
LAUNCH
OPEN TUBE
GOODBYE, MI-- HUH? WHO...?!?
WOOMM
CROOOK CROOK
WRUSSH
BRUSSH
LAUNCH
OPEN TUBE

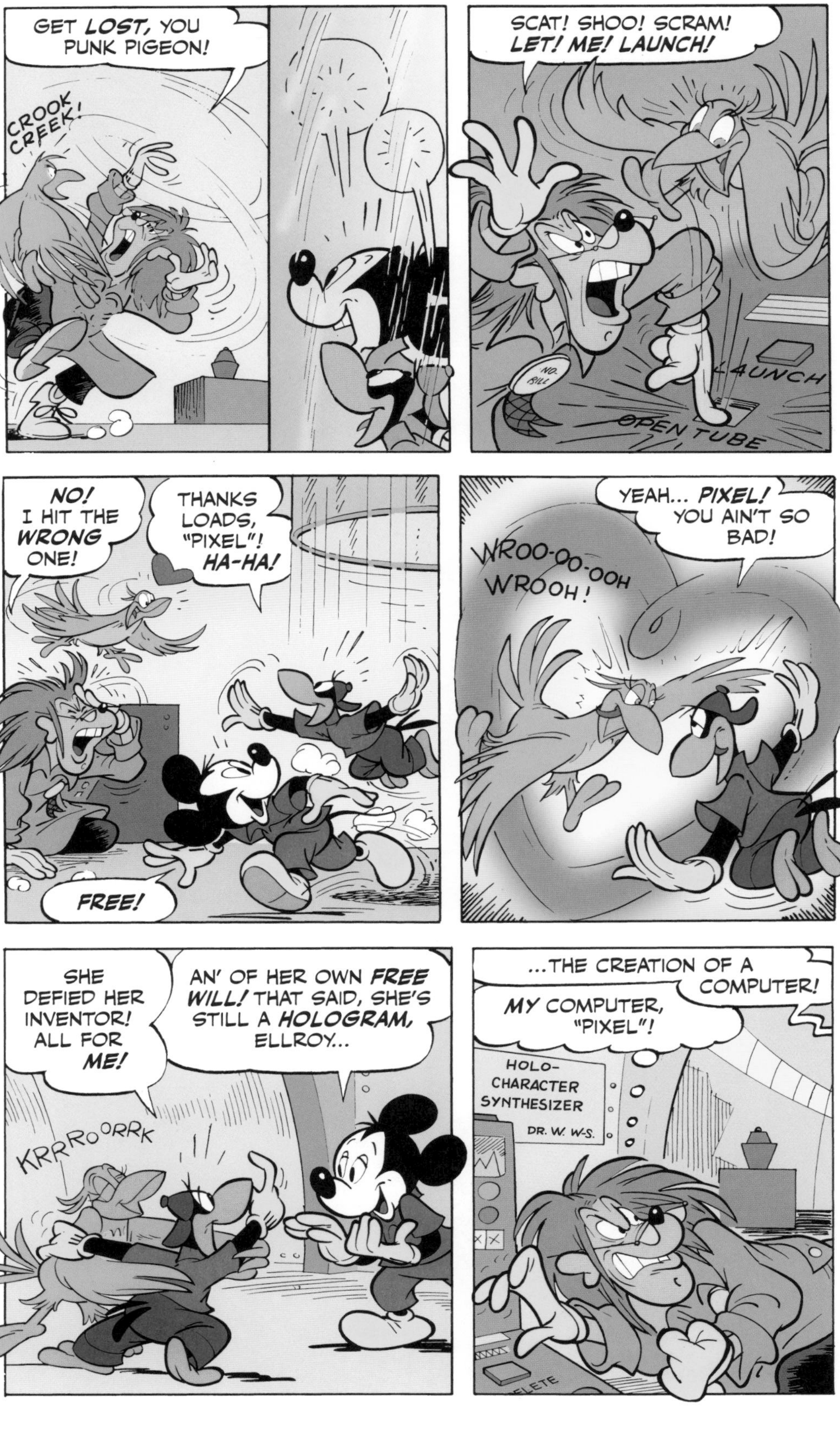
GET LOST, YOU PUNK PIGEON!
CROOK CREEK!
SCAT! SHOO! SCRAM! LET! ME! LAUNCH!
NO BILL
LAUNCH
OPEN TUBE
NO! I HIT THE WRONG ONE!
THANKS LOADS, "PIXEL"! HA-HA!
FREE!
YEAH... PIXEL! YOU AIN'T SO BAD!
WROO-OO-OOH WROOH!
SHE DEFIED HER INVENTOR! ALL FOR ME!
AN' OF HER OWN FREE WILL! THAT SAID, SHE'S STILL A HOLOGRAM, ELLROY...
KRRROORRK
...THE CREATION OF A COMPUTER!
MY COMPUTER, "PIXEL"!
HOLO-CHARACTER SYNTHESIZER
DR. W. W-S.

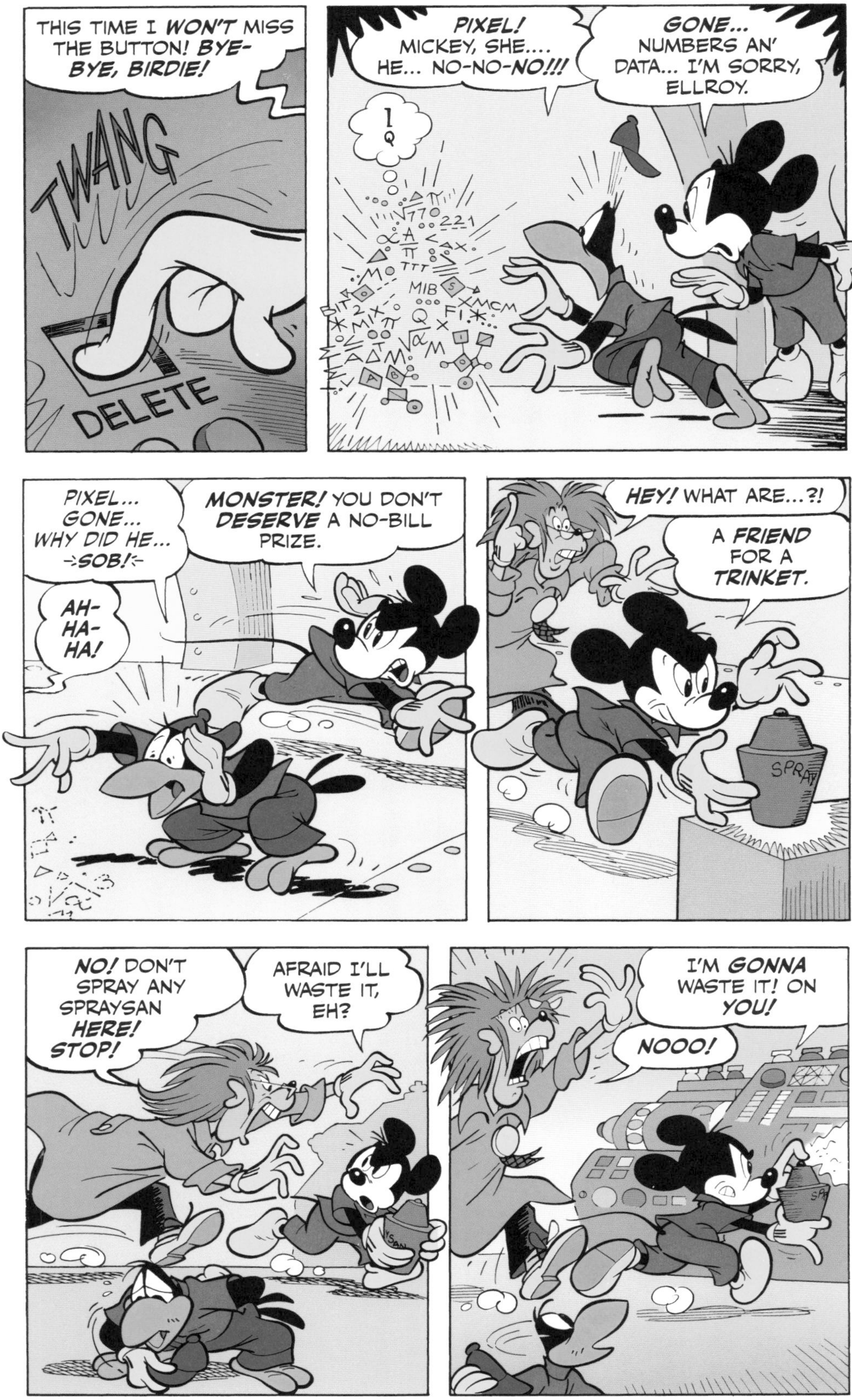
THIS TIME I **WON'T** MISS THE BUTTON! **BYE-BYE, BIRDIE!**
TWANG
DELETE
PIXEL! MICKEY, SHE.... HE... NO-NO-**NO!!!**
GONE... NUMBERS AN' DATA... I'M SORRY, ELLROY.
PIXEL... GONE... WHY DID HE... SOB!
MONSTER! YOU DON'T **DESERVE** A NO-BILL PRIZE.
AH-HA-HA!
HEY! WHAT ARE...?!
A **FRIEND** FOR A **TRINKET**.
SPRAY
NO! DON'T SPRAY ANY SPRAYSAN **HERE! STOP!**
AFRAID I'LL WASTE IT, EH?
I'M **GONNA** WASTE IT! ON **YOU!**
NOOO!

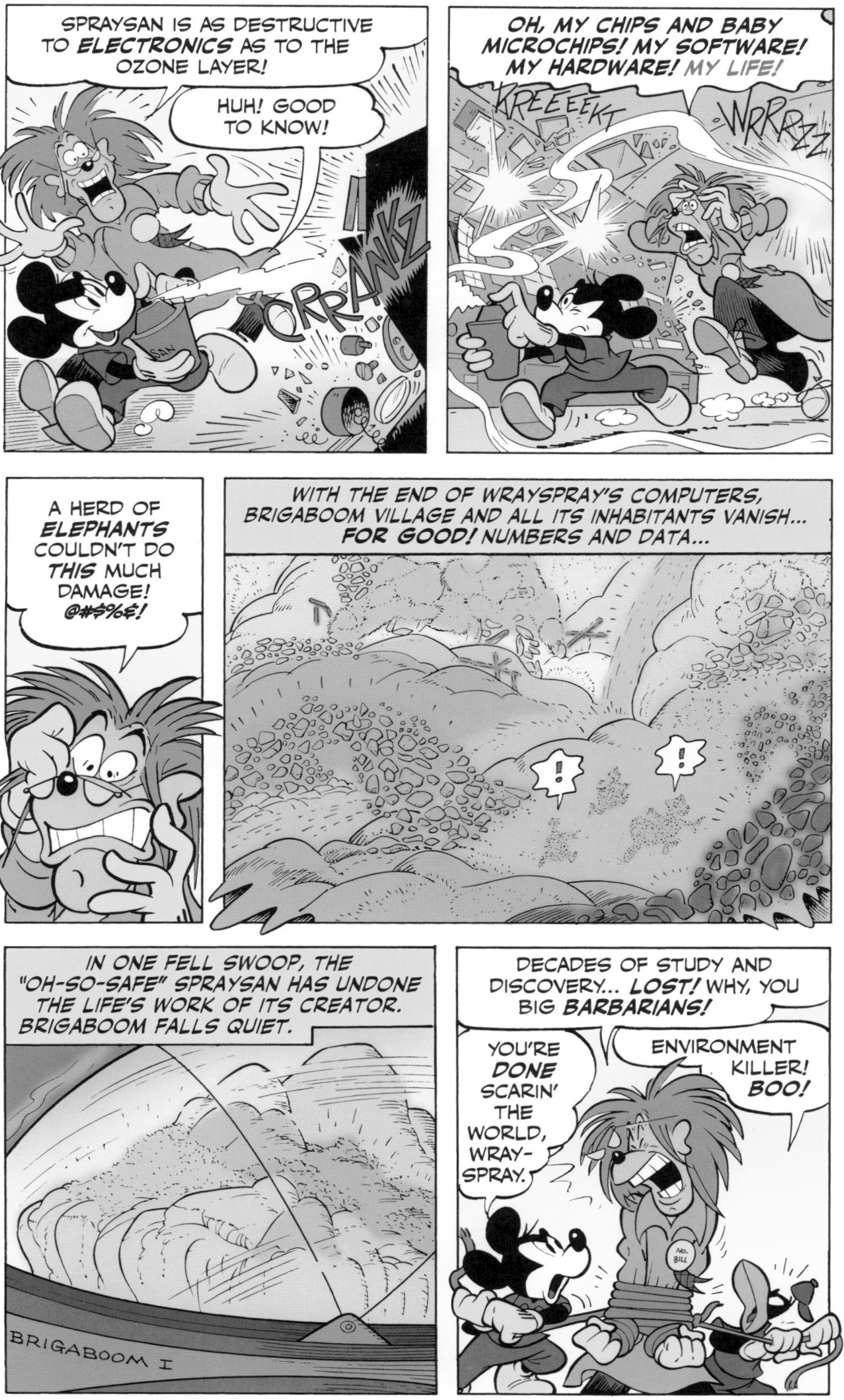

SPRAYSAN IS AS DESTRUCTIVE TO ELECTRONICS AS TO THE OZONE LAYER!
HUH! GOOD TO KNOW!
CRRANKZ
OH, MY CHIPS AND BABY MICROCHIPS! MY SOFTWARE! MY HARDWARE! MY LIFE!
KREEEEEKT
WRRRZZ
A HERD OF ELEPHANTS COULDN'T DO THIS MUCH DAMAGE! @#$%&!
WITH THE END OF WRAYSPRAY'S COMPUTERS, BRIGABOOM VILLAGE AND ALL ITS INHABITANTS VANISH... FOR GOOD! NUMBERS AND DATA...
!
!
IN ONE FELL SWOOP, THE "OH-SO-SAFE" SPRAYSAN HAS UNDONE THE LIFE'S WORK OF ITS CREATOR. BRIGABOOM FALLS QUIET.
BRIGABOOM I
DECADES OF STUDY AND DISCOVERY... LOST! WHY, YOU BIG BARBARIANS!
YOU'RE DONE SCARIN' THE WORLD, WRAY-SPRAY.
ENVIRONMENT KILLER! BOO!

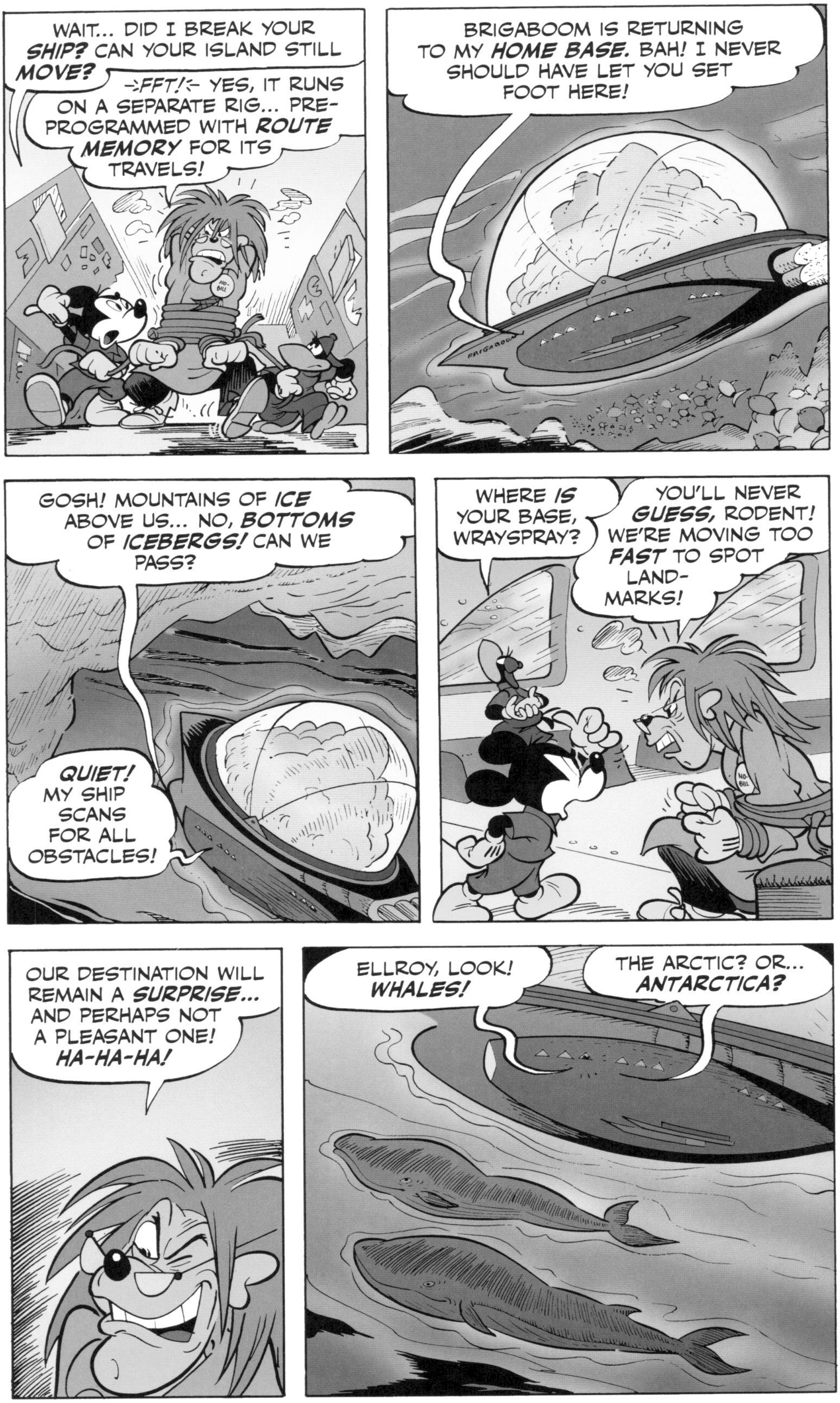
WAIT... DID I BREAK YOUR SHIP? CAN YOUR ISLAND STILL MOVE?
⇝FFT!⇜ YES, IT RUNS ON A SEPARATE RIG... PRE-PROGRAMMED WITH ROUTE MEMORY FOR ITS TRAVELS!
NO-BILL
BRIGABOOM IS RETURNING TO MY HOME BASE. BAH! I NEVER SHOULD HAVE LET YOU SET FOOT HERE!
BRIGABOOM
GOSH! MOUNTAINS OF ICE ABOVE US... NO, BOTTOMS OF ICEBERGS! CAN WE PASS?
QUIET! MY SHIP SCANS FOR ALL OBSTACLES!
WHERE IS YOUR BASE, WRAYSPRAY?
YOU'LL NEVER GUESS, RODENT! WE'RE MOVING TOO FAST TO SPOT LAND-MARKS!
NO-BILL
OUR DESTINATION WILL REMAIN A SURPRISE... AND PERHAPS NOT A PLEASANT ONE! HA-HA-HA!
ELLROY, LOOK! WHALES!
THE ARCTIC? OR... ANTARCTICA?

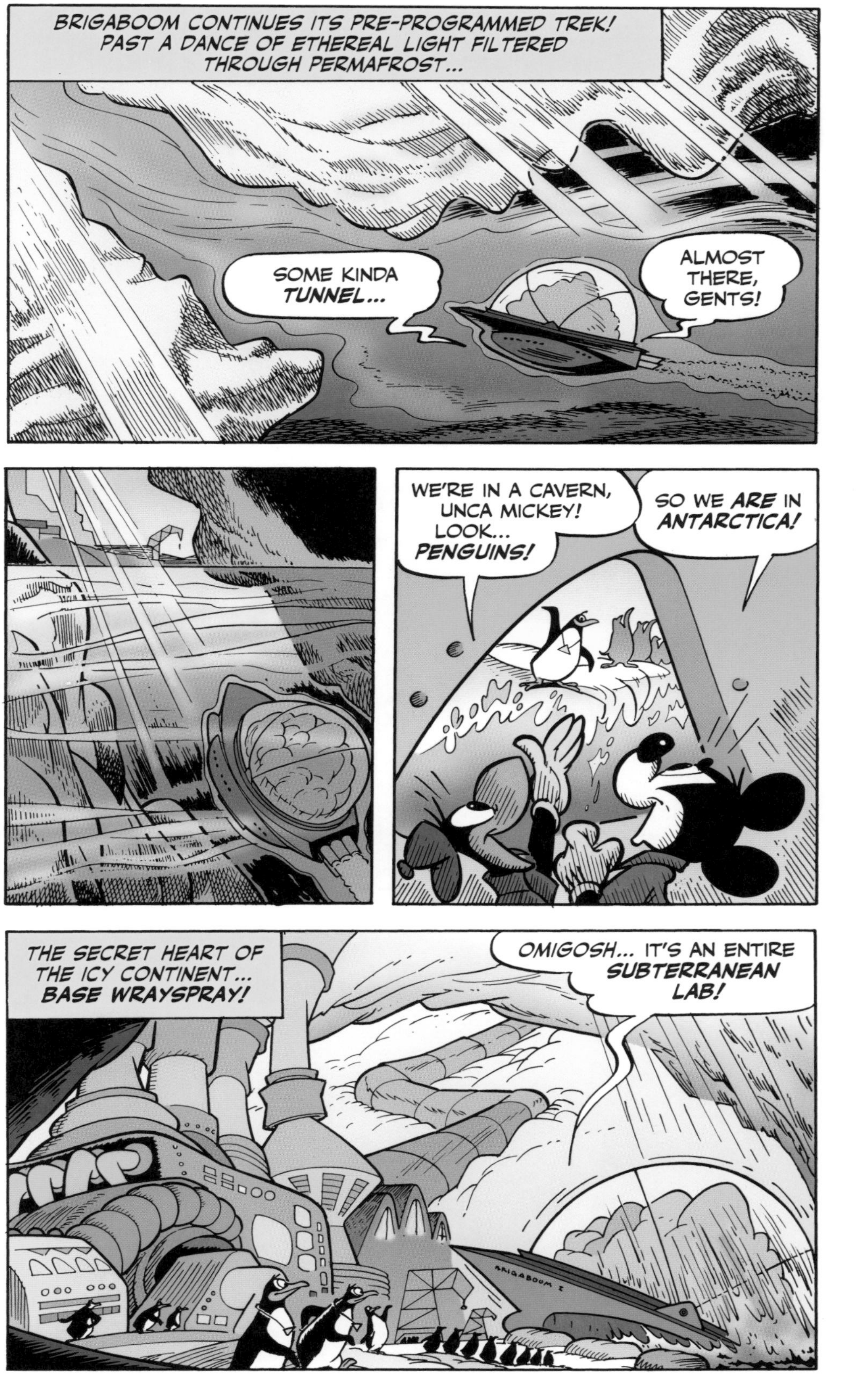
BRIGABOOM CONTINUES ITS PRE-PROGRAMMED TREK! PAST A DANCE OF ETHEREAL LIGHT FILTERED THROUGH PERMAFROST...
SOME KINDA TUNNEL...
ALMOST THERE, GENTS!
WE'RE IN A CAVERN, UNCA MICKEY! LOOK... PENGUINS!
SO WE ARE IN ANTARCTICA!
THE SECRET HEART OF THE ICY CONTINENT... BASE WRAYSPRAY!
OMIGOSH... IT'S AN ENTIRE SUBTERRANEAN LAB!

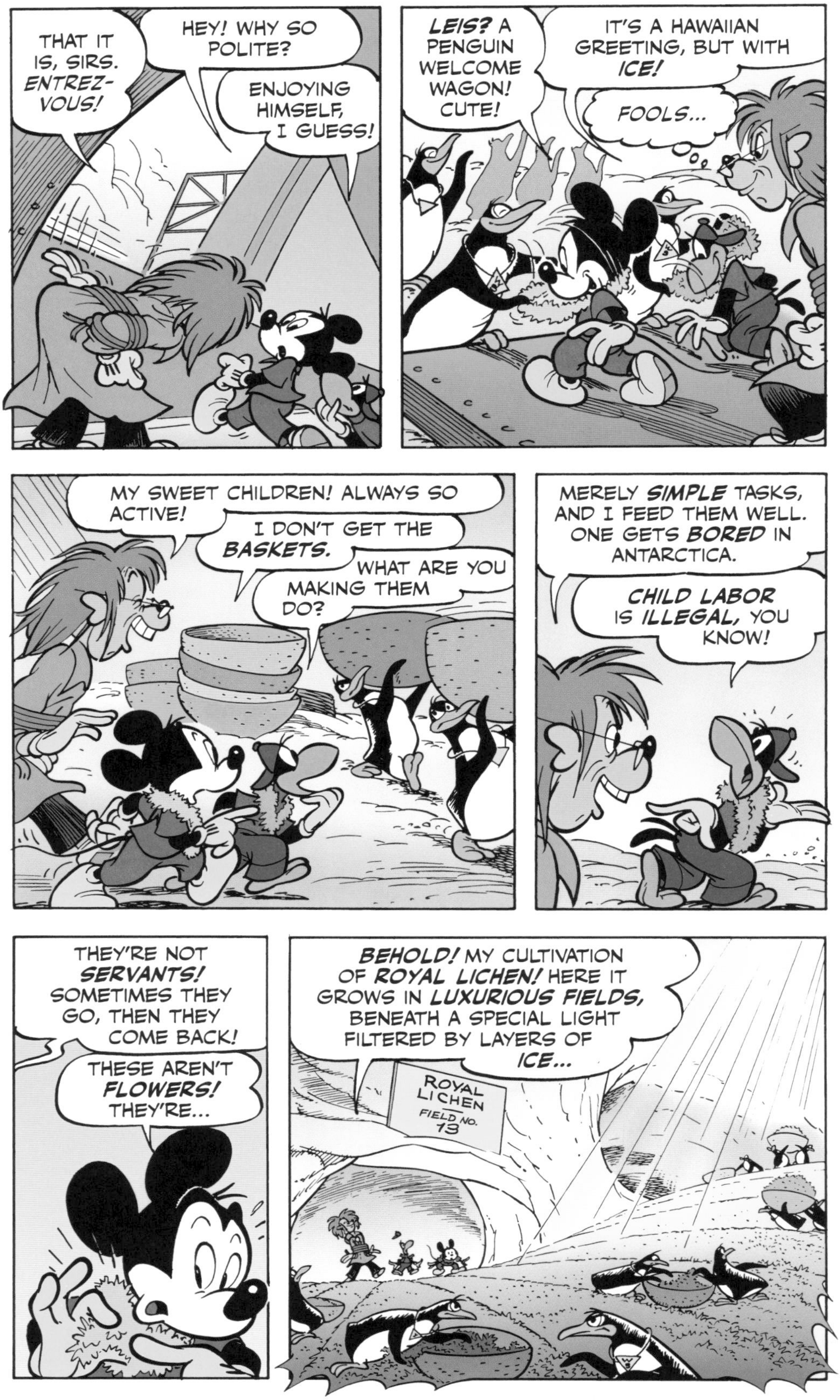
THAT IT IS, SIRS. ENTREZ-VOUS!
HEY! WHY SO POLITE?
ENJOYING HIMSELF, I GUESS!
LEIS? A PENGUIN WELCOME WAGON! CUTE!
IT'S A HAWAIIAN GREETING, BUT WITH ICE!
FOOLS...
MY SWEET CHILDREN! ALWAYS SO ACTIVE!
I DON'T GET THE BASKETS.
WHAT ARE YOU MAKING THEM DO?
MERELY SIMPLE TASKS, AND I FEED THEM WELL. ONE GETS BORED IN ANTARCTICA.
CHILD LABOR IS ILLEGAL, YOU KNOW!
THEY'RE NOT SERVANTS! SOMETIMES THEY GO, THEN THEY COME BACK!
THESE AREN'T FLOWERS! THEY'RE...
BEHOLD! MY CULTIVATION OF ROYAL LICHEN! HERE IT GROWS IN LUXURIOUS FIELDS, BENEATH A SPECIAL LIGHT FILTERED BY LAYERS OF ICE...
ROYAL LICHEN FIELD NO. 13

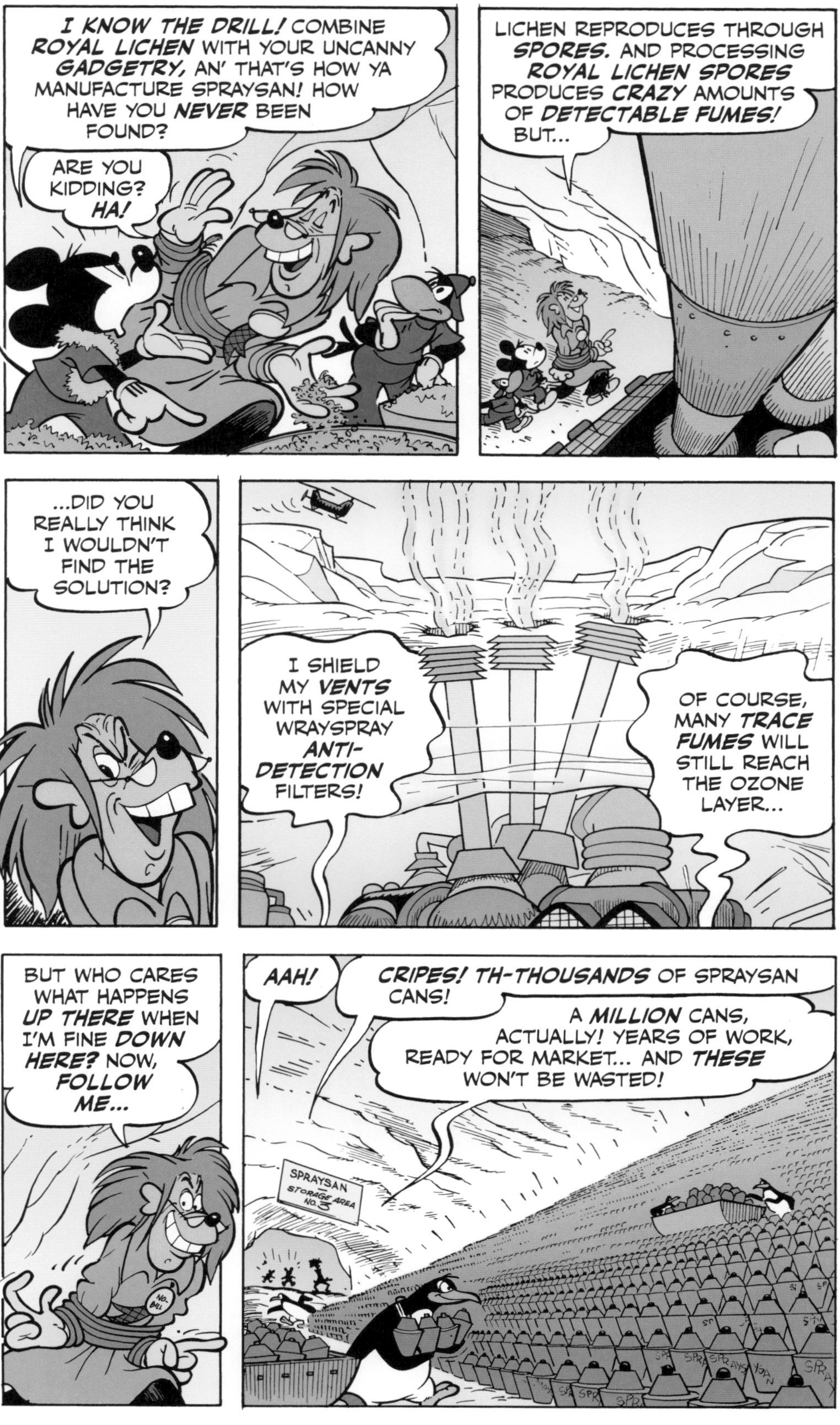
I KNOW THE DRILL! COMBINE ROYAL LICHEN WITH YOUR UNCANNY GADGETRY, AN' THAT'S HOW YA MANUFACTURE SPRAYSAN! HOW HAVE YOU NEVER BEEN FOUND?
ARE YOU KIDDING? HA!
LICHEN REPRODUCES THROUGH SPORES. AND PROCESSING ROYAL LICHEN SPORES PRODUCES CRAZY AMOUNTS OF DETECTABLE FUMES! BUT...
...DID YOU REALLY THINK I WOULDN'T FIND THE SOLUTION?
I SHIELD MY VENTS WITH SPECIAL WRAYSPRAY ANTI-DETECTION FILTERS!
OF COURSE, MANY TRACE FUMES WILL STILL REACH THE OZONE LAYER...
BUT WHO CARES WHAT HAPPENS UP THERE WHEN I'M FINE DOWN HERE? NOW, FOLLOW ME...
AAH!
CRIPES! TH-THOUSANDS OF SPRAYSAN CANS!
A MILLION CANS, ACTUALLY! YEARS OF WORK, READY FOR MARKET... AND THESE WON'T BE WASTED!
SPRAYSAN STORAGE AREA NO. 3

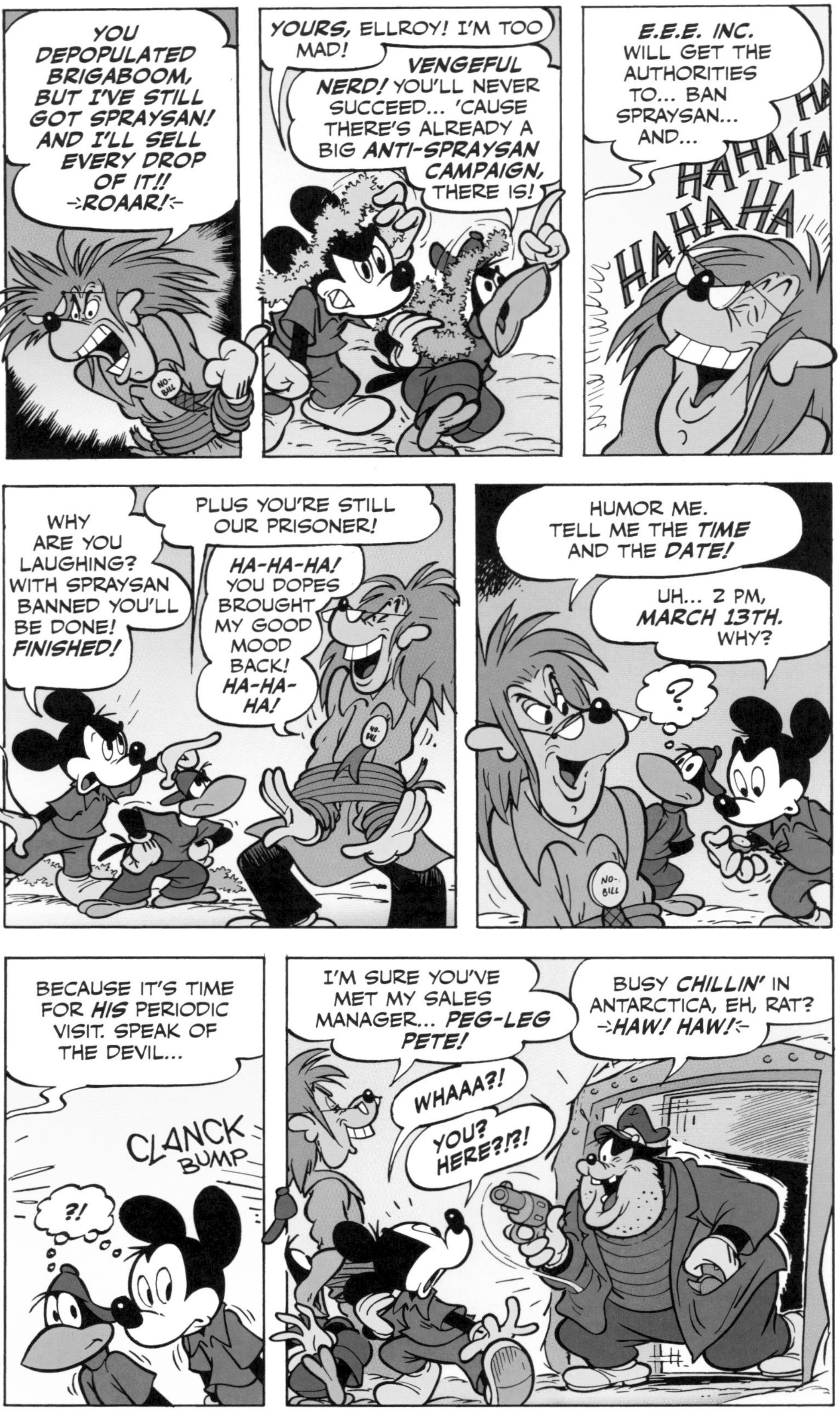
YOU DEPOPULATED BRIGABOOM, BUT I'VE STILL GOT SPRAYSAN! AND I'LL SELL EVERY DROP OF IT!! -ROAAR!-
YOURS, ELLROY! I'M TOO MAD!
VENGEFUL NERD! YOU'LL NEVER SUCCEED... 'CAUSE THERE'S ALREADY A BIG ANTI-SPRAYSAN CAMPAIGN, THERE IS!
E.E.E. INC. WILL GET THE AUTHORITIES TO... BAN SPRAYSAN... AND...
HAHAHAHAHAHAHAHA
WHY ARE YOU LAUGHING? WITH SPRAYSAN BANNED YOU'LL BE DONE! FINISHED!
PLUS YOU'RE STILL OUR PRISONER!
HA-HA-HA! YOU DOPES BROUGHT MY GOOD MOOD BACK! HA-HA-HA!
HUMOR ME. TELL ME THE TIME AND THE DATE!
UH... 2 PM, MARCH 13TH. WHY?
?
BECAUSE IT'S TIME FOR HIS PERIODIC VISIT. SPEAK OF THE DEVIL...
CLANCK
BUMP
?!
I'M SURE YOU'VE MET MY SALES MANAGER... PEG-LEG PETE!
BUSY CHILLIN' IN ANTARCTICA, EH, RAT? -HAW! HAW!-
WHAAA?!
YOU? HERE?!?!

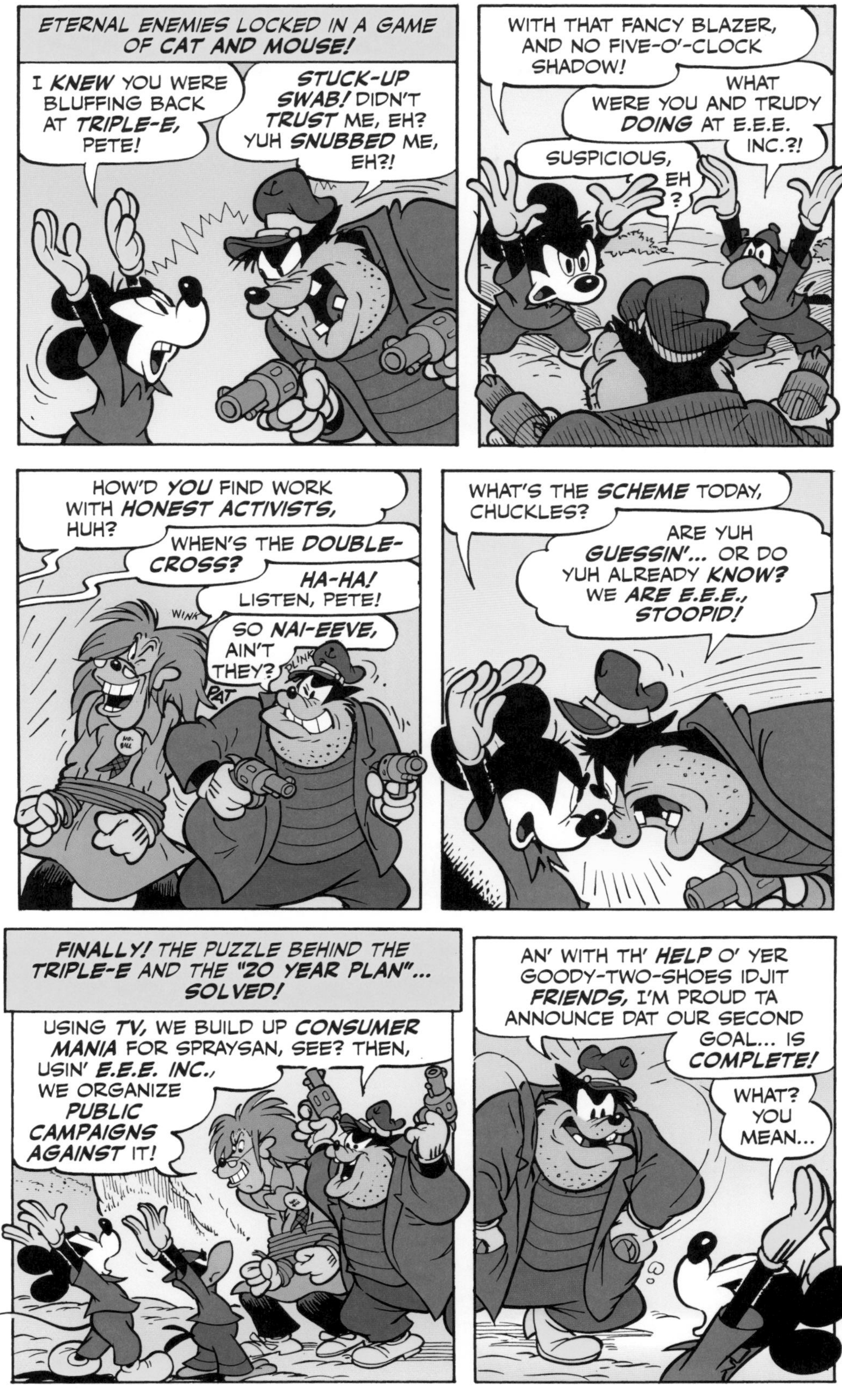
ETERNAL ENEMIES LOCKED IN A GAME OF CAT AND MOUSE!
I KNEW YOU WERE BLUFFING BACK AT TRIPLE-E, PETE!
STUCK-UP SWAB! DIDN'T TRUST ME, EH? YUH SNUBBED ME, EH?!
WITH THAT FANCY BLAZER, AND NO FIVE-O'-CLOCK SHADOW!
WHAT WERE YOU AND TRUDY DOING AT E.E.E. INC.?!
SUSPICIOUS, EH?
HOW'D YOU FIND WORK WITH HONEST ACTIVISTS, HUH?
WHEN'S THE DOUBLE-CROSS?
HA-HA! LISTEN, PETE!
SO NAI-EEVE, AIN'T THEY?
WINK
PAT
WHAT'S THE SCHEME TODAY, CHUCKLES?
ARE YUH GUESSIN'... OR DO YUH ALREADY KNOW? WE ARE E.E.E., STOOPID!
FINALLY! THE PUZZLE BEHIND THE TRIPLE-E AND THE "20 YEAR PLAN"... SOLVED!
USING TV, WE BUILD UP CONSUMER MANIA FOR SPRAYSAN, SEE? THEN, USIN' E.E.E. INC., WE ORGANIZE PUBLIC CAMPAIGNS AGAINST IT!
AN' WITH TH' HELP O' YER GOODY-TWO-SHOES IDJIT FRIENDS, I'M PROUD TA ANNOUNCE DAT OUR SECOND GOAL... IS COMPLETE!
WHAT? YOU MEAN...

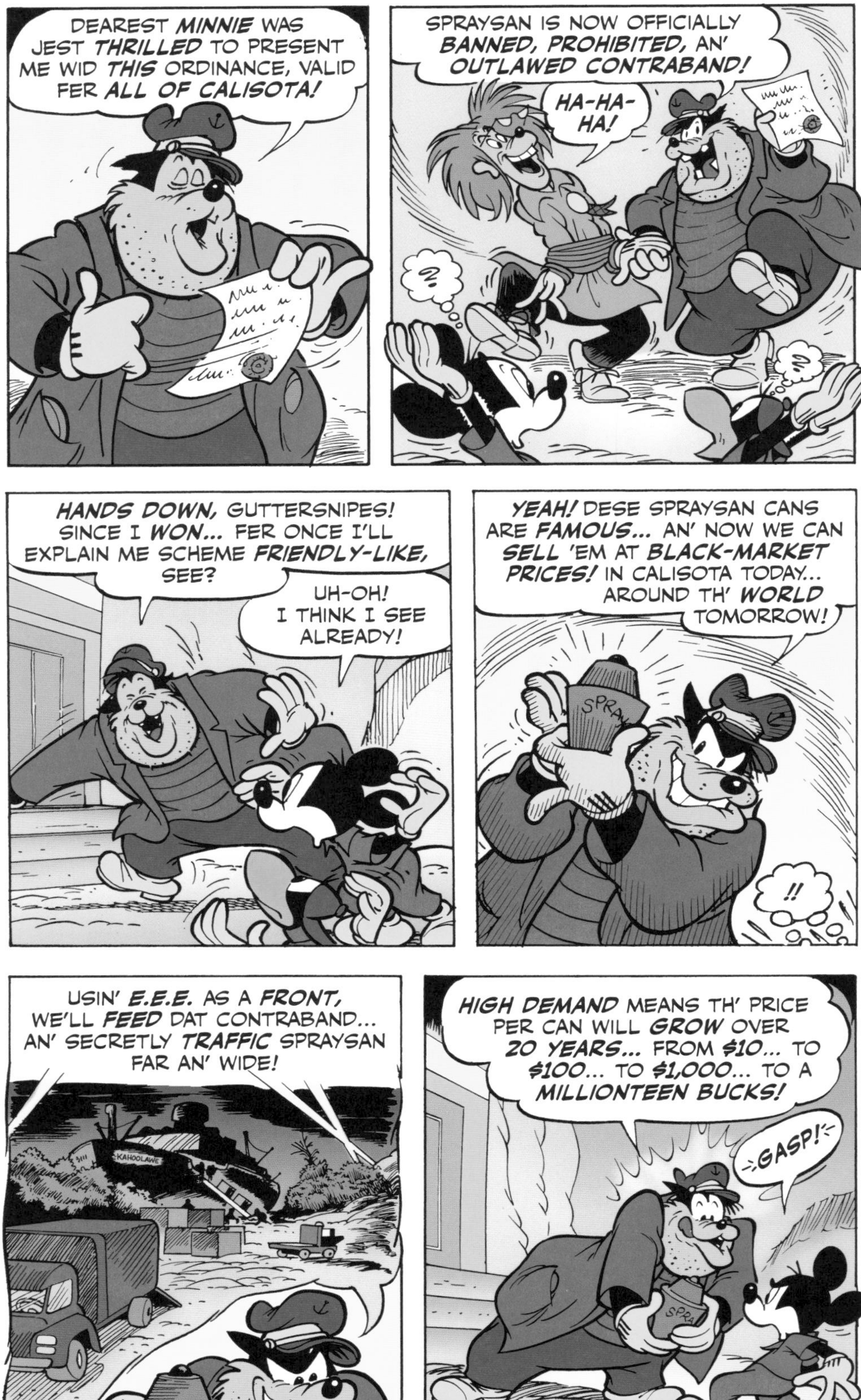
DEAREST MINNIE WAS JEST THRILLED TO PRESENT ME WID THIS ORDINANCE, VALID FER ALL OF CALISOTA!
SPRAYSAN IS NOW OFFICIALLY BANNED, PROHIBITED, AN' OUTLAWED CONTRABAND!
HA-HA-HA!
?
?
HANDS DOWN, GUTTERSNIPES! SINCE I WON... FER ONCE I'LL EXPLAIN ME SCHEME FRIENDLY-LIKE, SEE?
UH-OH! I THINK I SEE ALREADY!
YEAH! DESE SPRAYSAN CANS ARE FAMOUS... AN' NOW WE CAN SELL 'EM AT BLACK-MARKET PRICES! IN CALISOTA TODAY... AROUND TH' WORLD TOMORROW!
!!
USIN' E.E.E. AS A FRONT, WE'LL FEED DAT CONTRABAND... AN' SECRETLY TRAFFIC SPRAYSAN FAR AN' WIDE!
KAHOOLAWE
HIGH DEMAND MEANS TH' PRICE PER CAN WILL GROW OVER 20 YEARS... FROM $10... TO $100... TO $1,000... TO A MILLIONTEEN BUCKS!
GASP!

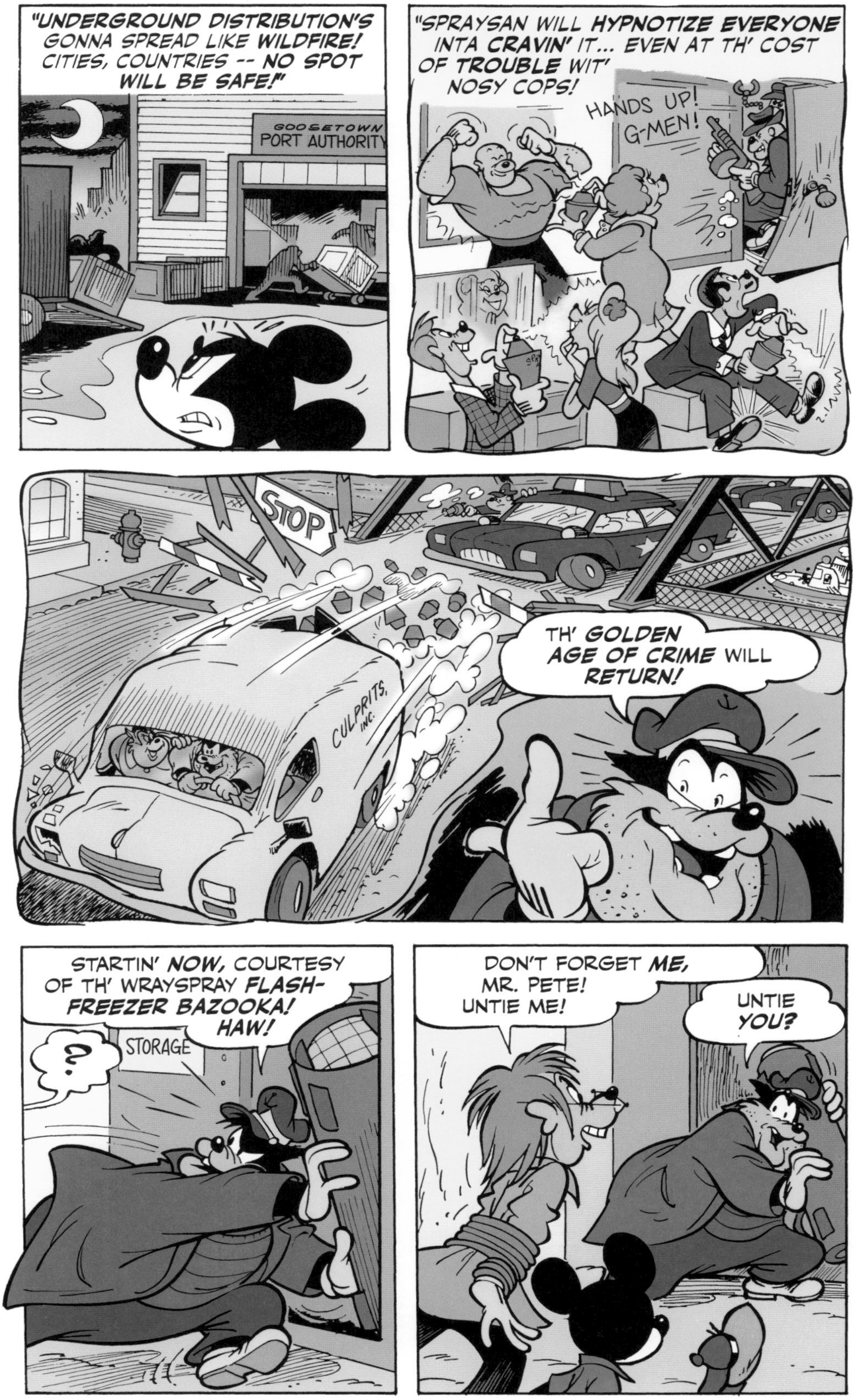
"UNDERGROUND DISTRIBUTION'S GONNA SPREAD LIKE WILDFIRE! CITIES, COUNTRIES -- NO SPOT WILL BE SAFE!"
GOOSETOWN PORT AUTHORITY
"SPRAYSAN WILL HYPNOTIZE EVERYONE INTA CRAVIN' IT... EVEN AT TH' COST OF TROUBLE WIT' NOSY COPS!
HANDS UP! G-MEN!
STOP
CULPRITS, INC.
TH' GOLDEN AGE OF CRIME WILL RETURN!
STARTIN' NOW, COURTESY OF TH' WRAYSPRAY FLASH-FREEZER BAZOOKA! HAW!
?
STORAGE
DON'T FORGET ME, MR. PETE! UNTIE ME!
UNTIE YOU?

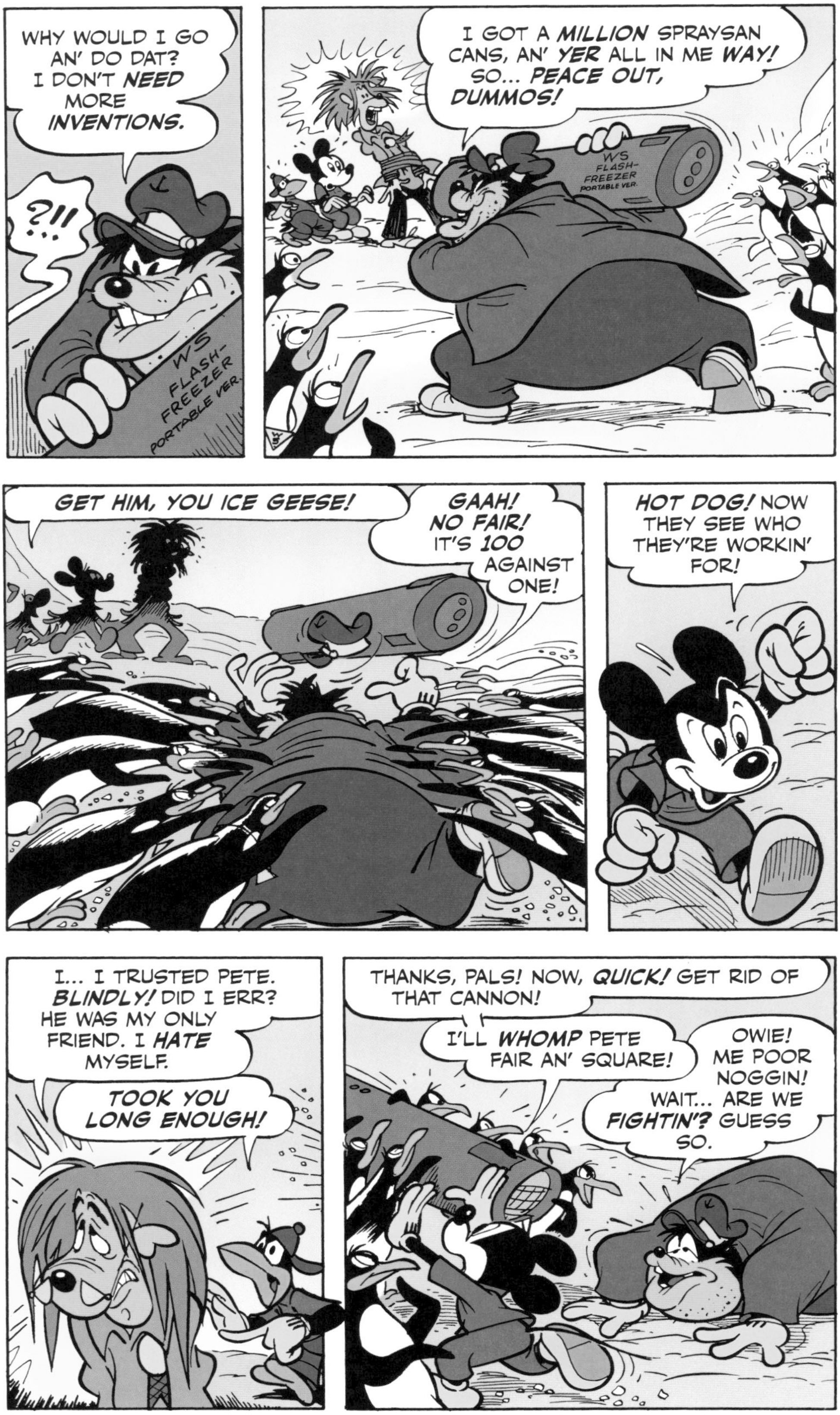
WHY WOULD I GO AN' DO DAT? I DON'T NEED MORE INVENTIONS.
?!!
I GOT A MILLION SPRAYSAN CANS, AN' YER ALL IN ME WAY! SO... PEACE OUT, DUMMOS!
WS FLASH-FREEZER PORTABLE VER.
GET HIM, YOU ICE GEESE!
GAAH! NO FAIR! IT'S 100 AGAINST ONE!
HOT DOG! NOW THEY SEE WHO THEY'RE WORKIN' FOR!
I... I TRUSTED PETE. BLINDLY! DID I ERR? HE WAS MY ONLY FRIEND. I HATE MYSELF.
TOOK YOU LONG ENOUGH!
THANKS, PALS! NOW, QUICK! GET RID OF THAT CANNON!
I'LL WHOMP PETE FAIR AN' SQUARE!
OWIE! ME POOR NOGGIN! WAIT... ARE WE FIGHTIN'? GUESS SO.

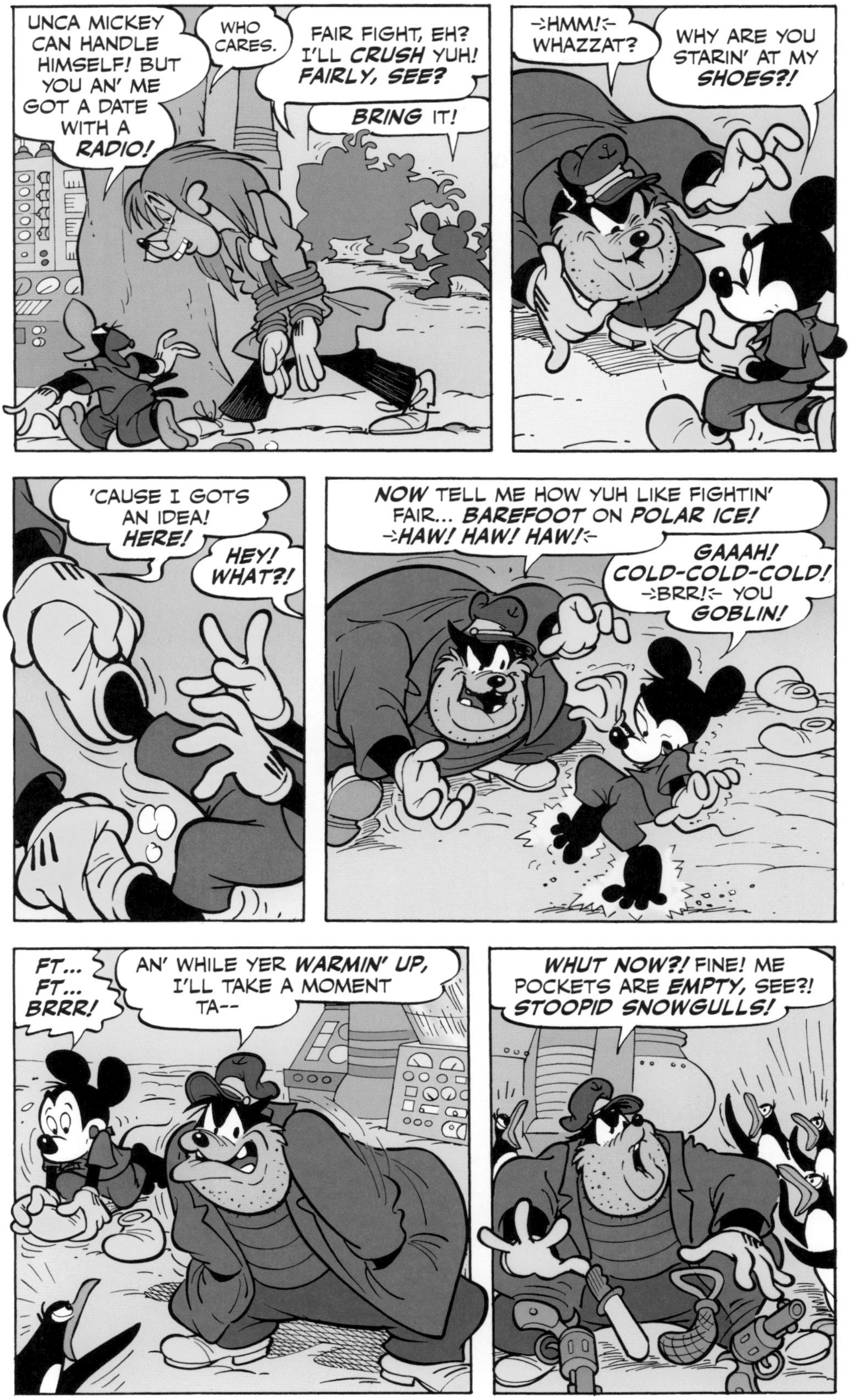
UNCA MICKEY CAN HANDLE HIMSELF! BUT YOU AN' ME GOT A DATE WITH A RADIO!
WHO CARES.
FAIR FIGHT, EH? I'LL CRUSH YUH! FAIRLY, SEE?
BRING IT!
->HMM!<- WHAZZAT?
WHY ARE YOU STARIN' AT MY SHOES?!
'CAUSE I GOTS AN IDEA! HERE!
HEY! WHAT?!
NOW TELL ME HOW YUH LIKE FIGHTIN' FAIR... BAREFOOT ON POLAR ICE! ->HAW! HAW! HAW!<-
GAAAH! COLD-COLD-COLD! ->BRR!<- YOU GOBLIN!
FT... FT... BRRR!
AN' WHILE YER WARMIN' UP, I'LL TAKE A MOMENT TA--
WHUT NOW?! FINE! ME POCKETS ARE EMPTY, SEE?! STOOPID SNOWGULLS!

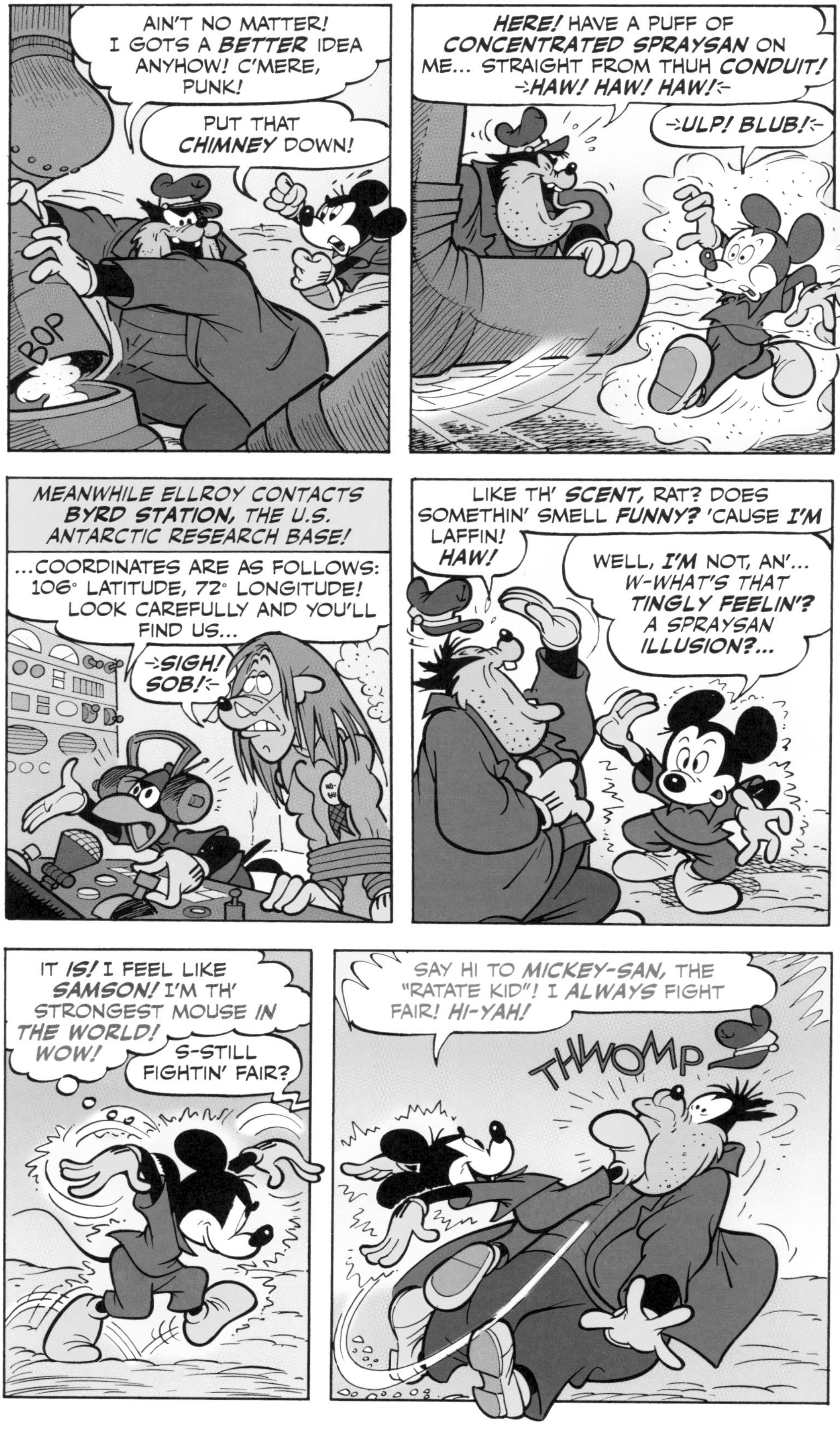
AIN'T NO MATTER! I GOTS A BETTER IDEA ANYHOW! C'MERE, PUNK!
PUT THAT CHIMNEY DOWN!
BOP
HERE! HAVE A PUFF OF CONCENTRATED SPRAYSAN ON ME... STRAIGHT FROM THUH CONDUIT! HAW! HAW! HAW!
ULP! BLUB!
MEANWHILE ELLROY CONTACTS BYRD STATION, THE U.S. ANTARCTIC RESEARCH BASE!
...COORDINATES ARE AS FOLLOWS: 106° LATITUDE, 72° LONGITUDE! LOOK CAREFULLY AND YOU'LL FIND US...
SIGH! SOB!
LIKE TH' SCENT, RAT? DOES SOMETHIN' SMELL FUNNY? 'CAUSE I'M LAFFIN! HAW!
WELL, I'M NOT, AN'... W-WHAT'S THAT TINGLY FEELIN'? A SPRAYSAN ILLUSION?...
IT IS! I FEEL LIKE SAMSON! I'M TH' STRONGEST MOUSE IN THE WORLD! WOW!
S-STILL FIGHTIN' FAIR?
SAY HI TO MICKEY-SAN, THE "RATATE KID"! I ALWAYS FIGHT FAIR! HI-YAH!
THWOMP

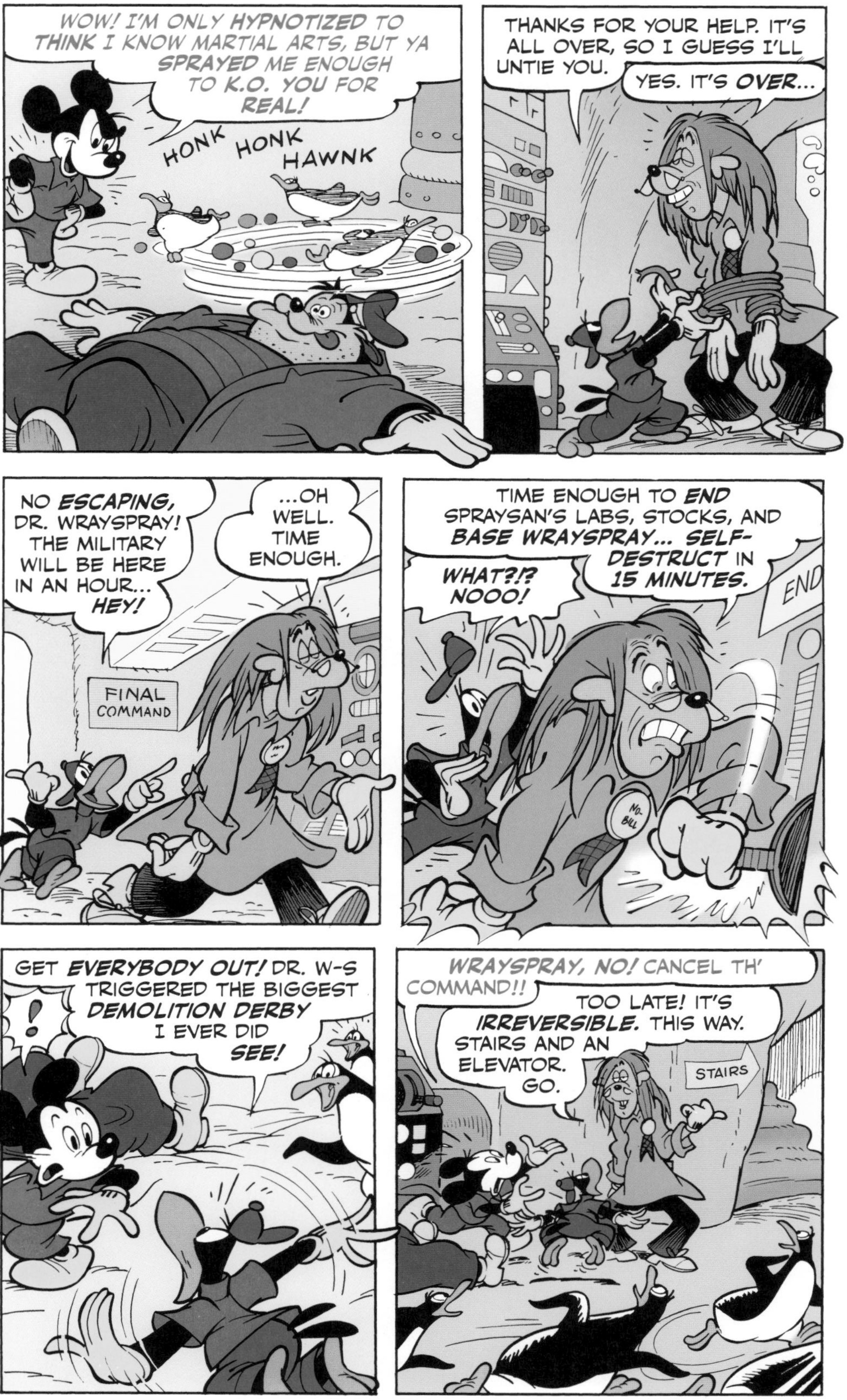
WOW! I'M ONLY HYPNOTIZED TO THINK I KNOW MARTIAL ARTS, BUT YA SPRAYED ME ENOUGH TO K.O. YOU FOR REAL!
HONK HONK HAWNK
THANKS FOR YOUR HELP. IT'S ALL OVER, SO I GUESS I'LL UNTIE YOU.
YES. IT'S OVER...
NO ESCAPING, DR. WRAYSPRAY! THE MILITARY WILL BE HERE IN AN HOUR... HEY!
...OH WELL. TIME ENOUGH.
FINAL COMMAND
TIME ENOUGH TO END SPRAYSAN'S LABS, STOCKS, AND BASE WRAYSPRAY... SELF-DESTRUCT IN 15 MINUTES.
WHAT?!? NOOO!
END
GET EVERYBODY OUT! DR. W-S TRIGGERED THE BIGGEST DEMOLITION DERBY I EVER DID SEE!
!
WRAYSPRAY, NO! CANCEL TH' COMMAND!!
TOO LATE! IT'S IRREVERSIBLE. THIS WAY. STAIRS AND AN ELEVATOR. GO.
STAIRS

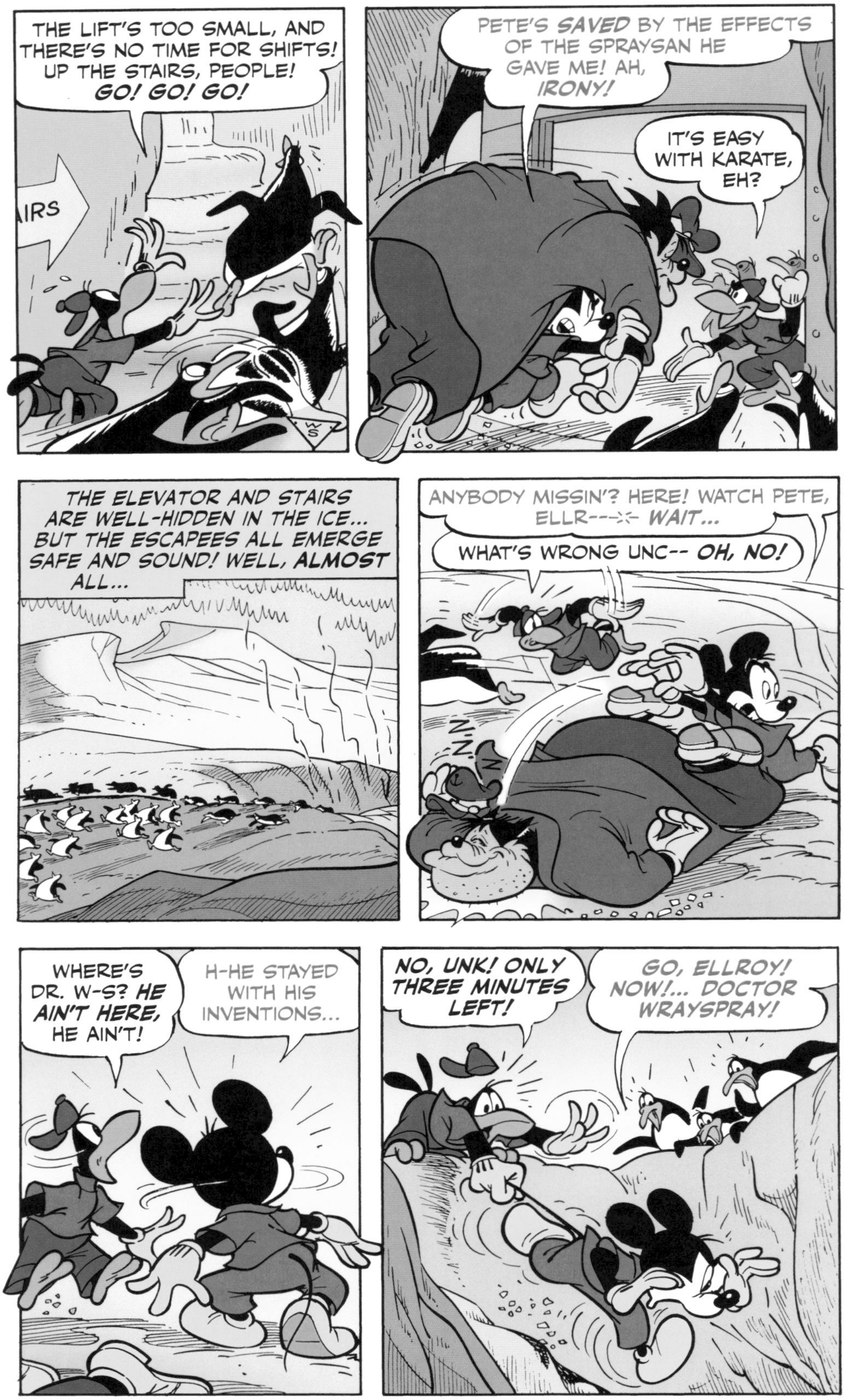
THE LIFT'S TOO SMALL, AND THERE'S NO TIME FOR SHIFTS! UP THE STAIRS, PEOPLE! GO! GO! GO!
AIRS
PETE'S SAVED BY THE EFFECTS OF THE SPRAYSAN HE GAVE ME! AH, IRONY!
IT'S EASY WITH KARATE, EH?
THE ELEVATOR AND STAIRS ARE WELL-HIDDEN IN THE ICE... BUT THE ESCAPEES ALL EMERGE SAFE AND SOUND! WELL, ALMOST ALL...
ANYBODY MISSIN'? HERE! WATCH PETE, ELLR--- WAIT...
WHAT'S WRONG UNC-- OH, NO!
WHERE'S DR. W-S? HE AIN'T HERE, HE AIN'T!
H-HE STAYED WITH HIS INVENTIONS...
NO, UNK! ONLY THREE MINUTES LEFT!
GO, ELLROY! NOW!... DOCTOR WRAYSPRAY!

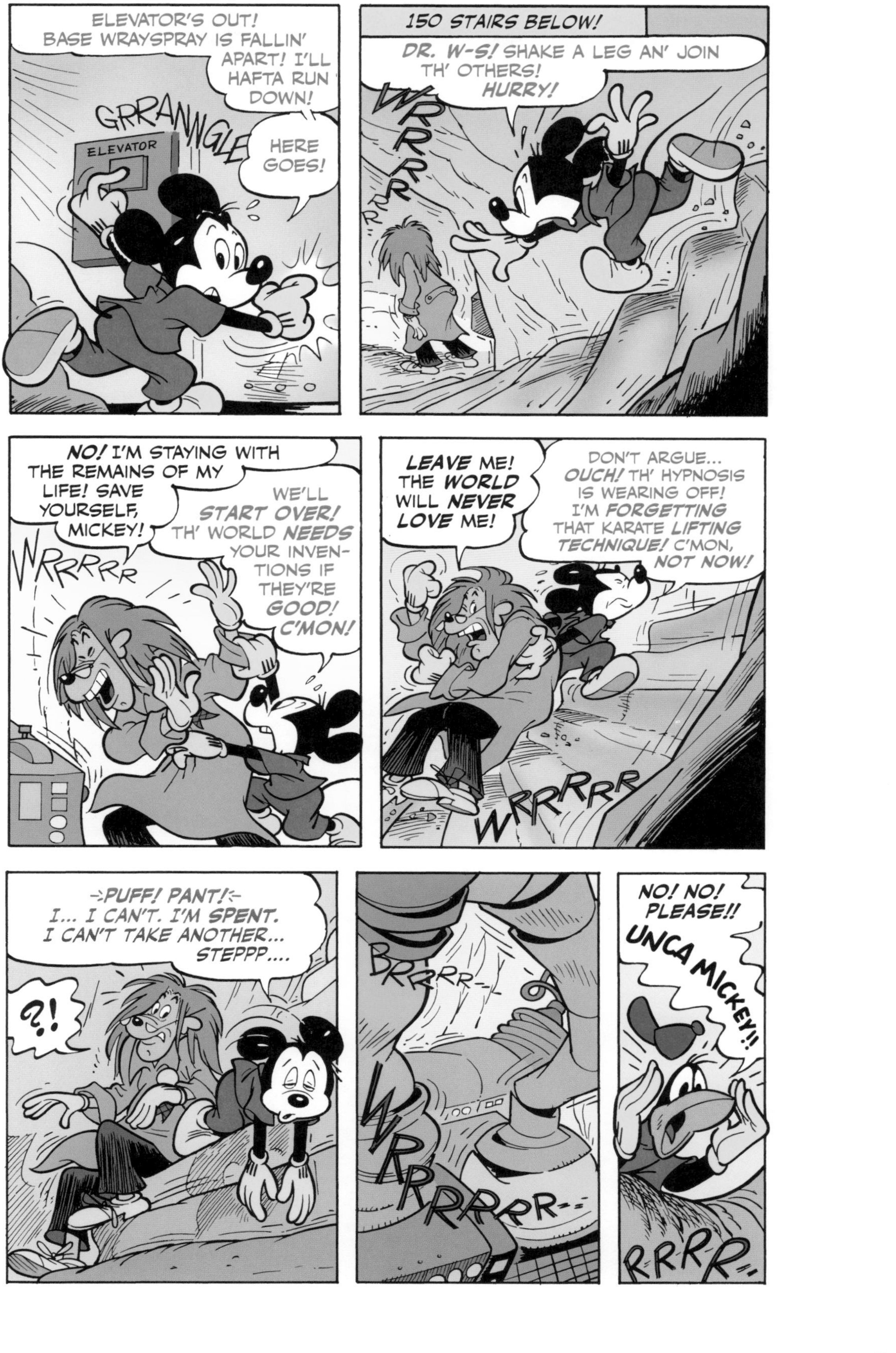
ELEVATOR'S OUT! BASE WRAYSPRAY IS FALLIN' APART! I'LL HAFTA RUN DOWN!
GRRANNGLE
ELEVATOR
HERE GOES!
150 STAIRS BELOW!
DR. W-S! SHAKE A LEG AN' JOIN TH' OTHERS! HURRY!
WRRRRR
NO! I'M STAYING WITH THE REMAINS OF MY LIFE! SAVE YOURSELF, MICKEY!
WE'LL START OVER! TH' WORLD NEEDS YOUR INVENTIONS IF THEY'RE GOOD! C'MON!
WRRRRR
LEAVE ME! THE WORLD WILL NEVER LOVE ME!
DON'T ARGUE... OUCH! TH' HYPNOSIS IS WEARING OFF! I'M FORGETTING THAT KARATE LIFTING TECHNIQUE! C'MON, NOT NOW!
WRRRRRR
-PUFF! PANT!- I... I CAN'T. I'M SPENT. I CAN'T TAKE ANOTHER... STEPPP....
?!
BRRRRR
WRRRRRRR
NO! NO! PLEASE!!
UNCA MICKEY!!
RRRRR

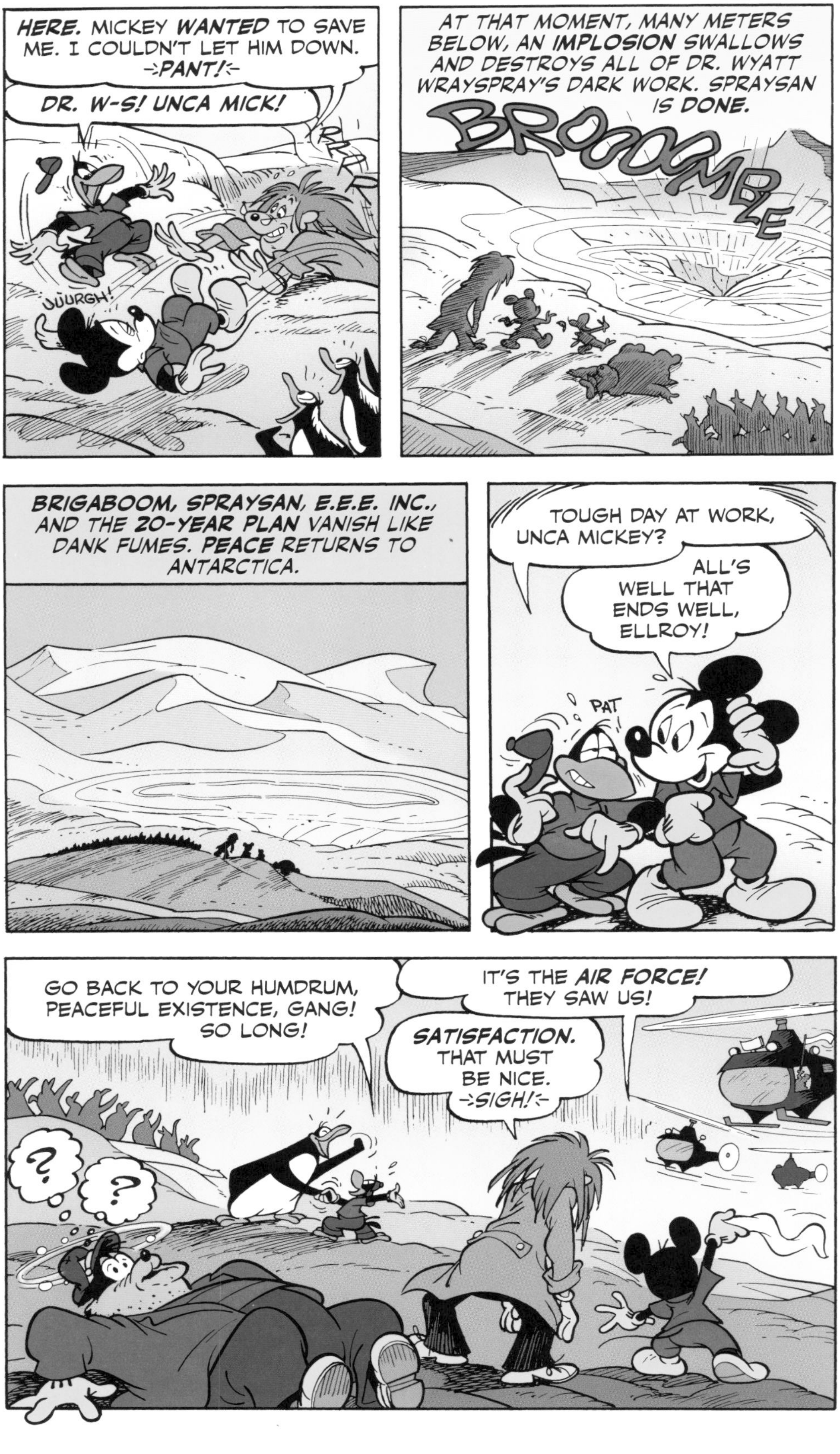
HERE. MICKEY WANTED TO SAVE ME. I COULDN'T LET HIM DOWN. -PANT!-
DR. W-S! UNCA MICK!
UUURGH!
AT THAT MOMENT, MANY METERS BELOW, AN IMPLOSION SWALLOWS AND DESTROYS ALL OF DR. WYATT WRAYSPRAY'S DARK WORK. SPRAYSAN IS DONE.
BROOOOOMBLE
BRIGABOOM, SPRAYSAN, E.E.E. INC., AND THE 20-YEAR PLAN VANISH LIKE DANK FUMES. PEACE RETURNS TO ANTARCTICA.
TOUGH DAY AT WORK, UNCA MICKEY?
ALL'S WELL THAT ENDS WELL, ELLROY!
PAT
GO BACK TO YOUR HUMDRUM, PEACEFUL EXISTENCE, GANG! SO LONG!
IT'S THE AIR FORCE! THEY SAW US!
SATISFACTION. THAT MUST BE NICE. -SIGH!-
?
?

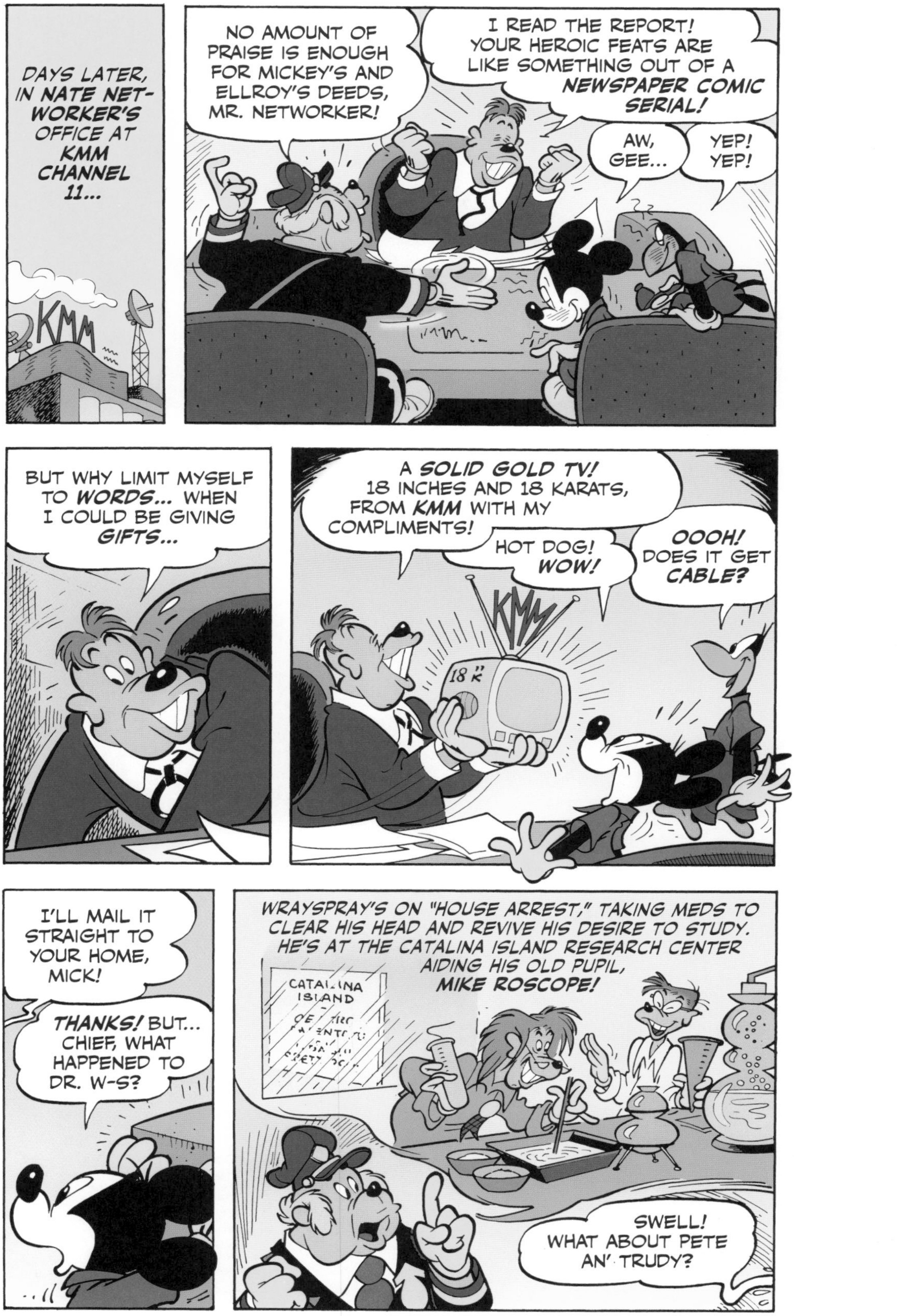
DAYS LATER, IN NATE NET-WORKER'S OFFICE AT KMM CHANNEL 11...
KMM
NO AMOUNT OF PRAISE IS ENOUGH FOR MICKEY'S AND ELLROY'S DEEDS, MR. NETWORKER!
I READ THE REPORT! YOUR HEROIC FEATS ARE LIKE SOMETHING OUT OF A NEWSPAPER COMIC SERIAL!
AW, GEE...
YEP! YEP!
BUT WHY LIMIT MYSELF TO WORDS... WHEN I COULD BE GIVING GIFTS...
A SOLID GOLD TV! 18 INCHES AND 18 KARATS, FROM KMM WITH MY COMPLIMENTS!
HOT DOG! WOW!
OOOH! DOES IT GET CABLE?
KMM
I'LL MAIL IT STRAIGHT TO YOUR HOME, MICK!
THANKS! BUT... CHIEF, WHAT HAPPENED TO DR. W-S?
WRAYSPRAY'S ON "HOUSE ARREST," TAKING MEDS TO CLEAR HIS HEAD AND REVIVE HIS DESIRE TO STUDY. HE'S AT THE CATALINA ISLAND RESEARCH CENTER AIDING HIS OLD PUPIL, MIKE ROSCOPE!
CATALINA ISLAND
SWELL! WHAT ABOUT PETE AN' TRUDY?

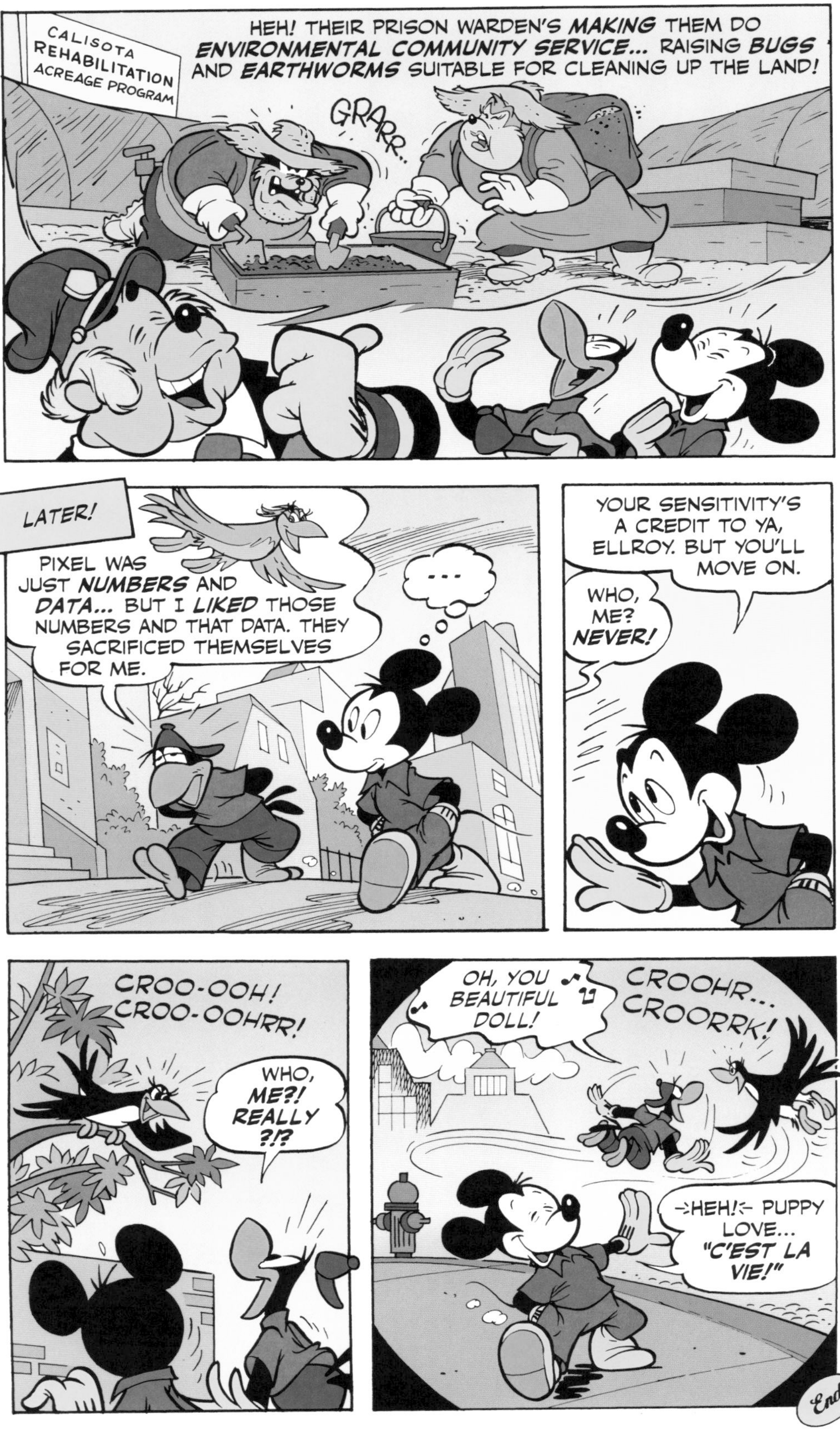

CALISOTA REHABILITATION ACREAGE PROGRAM
HEH! THEIR PRISON WARDEN'S MAKING THEM DO ENVIRONMENTAL COMMUNITY SERVICE... RAISING BUGS AND EARTHWORMS SUITABLE FOR CLEANING UP THE LAND!
GRARR...
LATER!
PIXEL WAS JUST NUMBERS AND DATA... BUT I LIKED THOSE NUMBERS AND THAT DATA. THEY SACRIFICED THEMSELVES FOR ME.
...
YOUR SENSITIVITY'S A CREDIT TO YA, ELLROY. BUT YOU'LL MOVE ON.
WHO, ME? NEVER!
CROO-OOH! CROO-OOHRR!
WHO, ME?! REALLY ?!?
OH, YOU BEAUTIFUL DOLL!
CROOHR... CROORRK!
→HEH!← PUPPY LOVE... "C'EST LA VIE!"
End

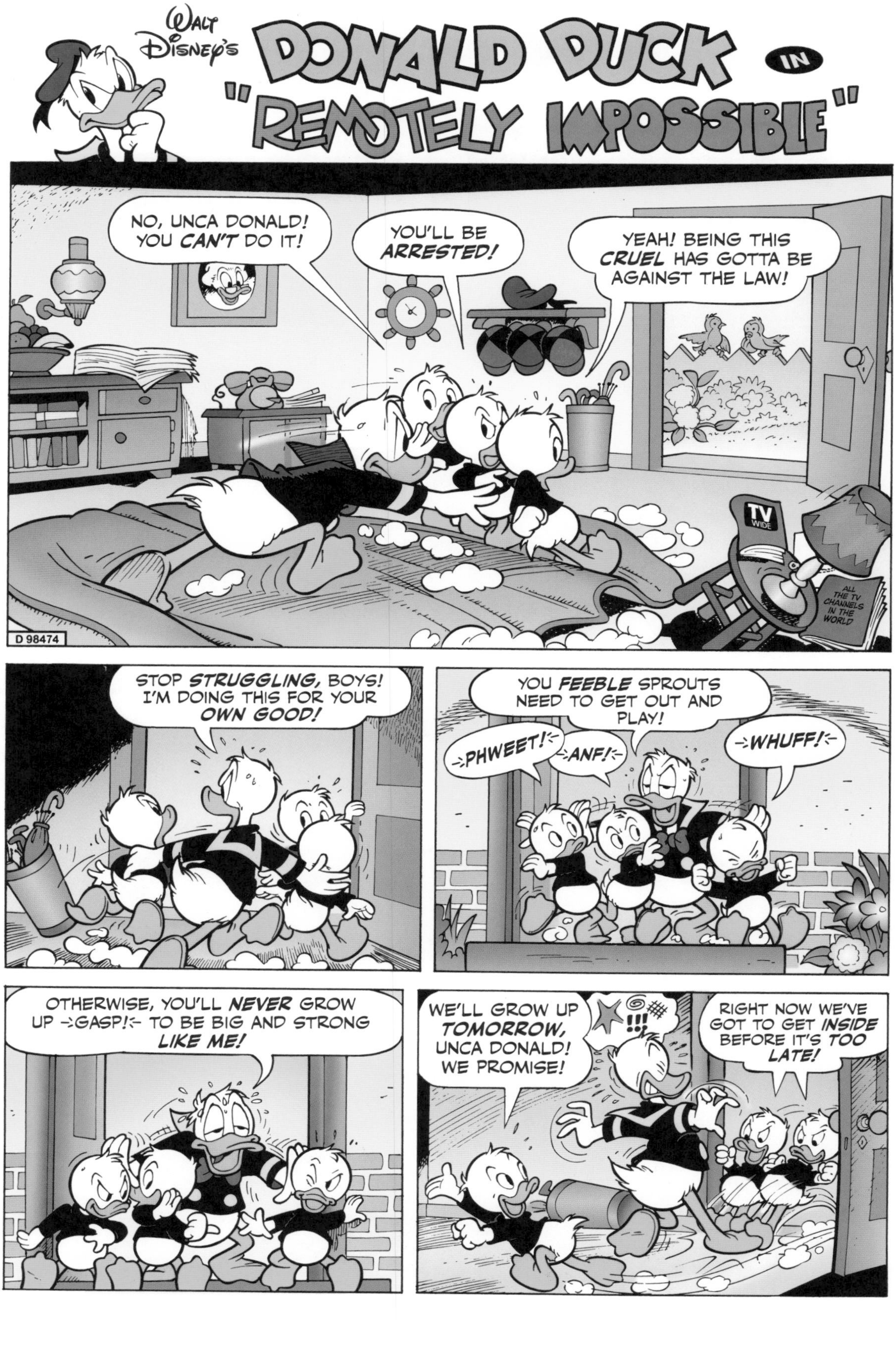

WALT DISNEY'S
DONALD DUCK IN
"REMOTELY IMPOSSIBLE"
NO, UNCA DONALD! YOU CAN'T DO IT!
YOU'LL BE ARRESTED!
YEAH! BEING THIS CRUEL HAS GOTTA BE AGAINST THE LAW!
TV WIDE
ALL THE TV CHANNELS IN THE WORLD
D 98474
STOP STRUGGLING, BOYS! I'M DOING THIS FOR YOUR OWN GOOD!
YOU FEEBLE SPROUTS NEED TO GET OUT AND PLAY!
PHWEET!
ANF!
WHUFF!
OTHERWISE, YOU'LL NEVER GROW UP -GASP!- TO BE BIG AND STRONG LIKE ME!
WE'LL GROW UP TOMORROW, UNCA DONALD! WE PROMISE!
!!!
RIGHT NOW WE'VE GOT TO GET INSIDE BEFORE IT'S TOO LATE!

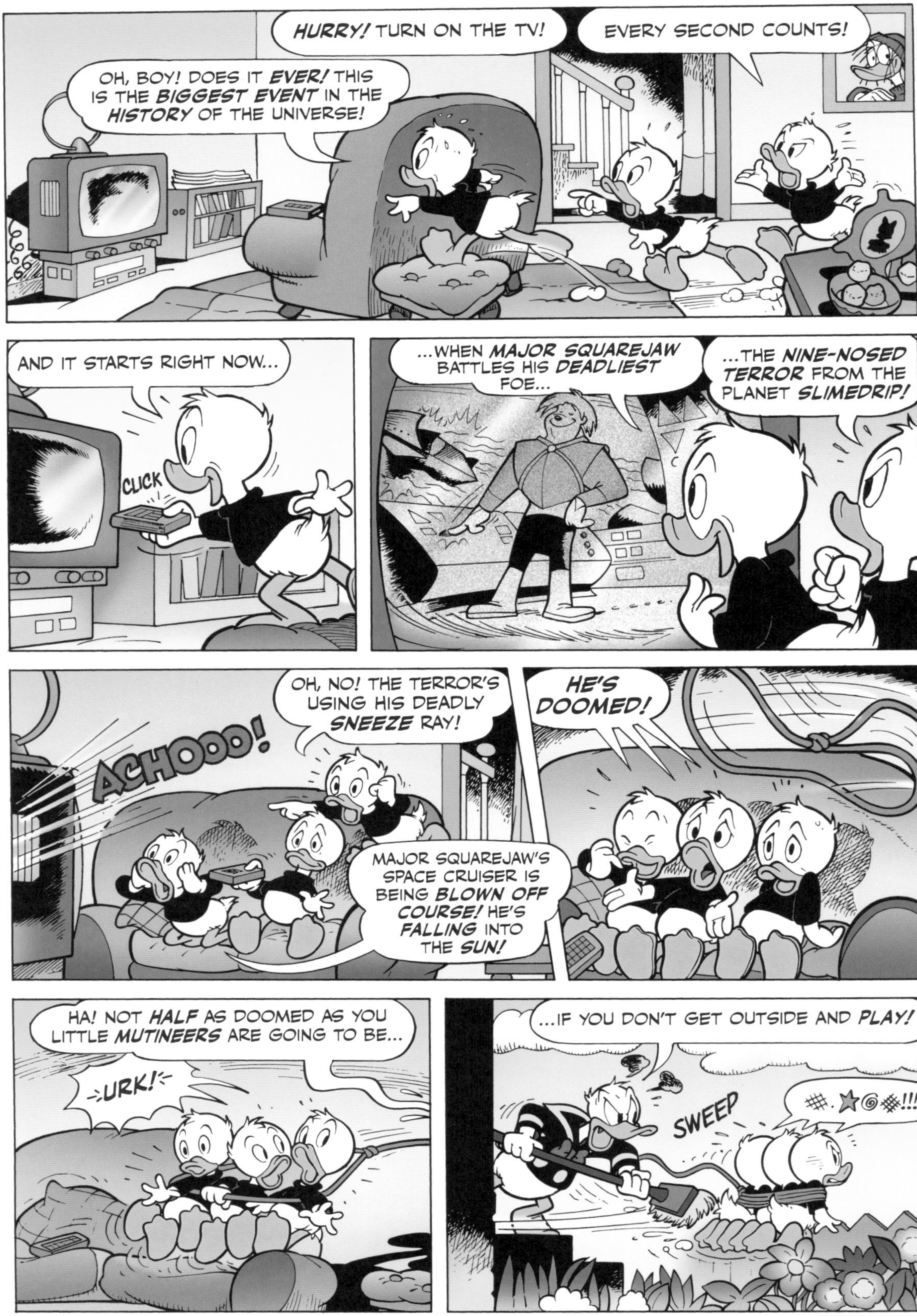
HURRY! TURN ON THE TV!
EVERY SECOND COUNTS!
OH, BOY! DOES IT EVER! THIS IS THE BIGGEST EVENT IN THE HISTORY OF THE UNIVERSE!
AND IT STARTS RIGHT NOW...
CLICK
...WHEN MAJOR SQUAREJAW BATTLES HIS DEADLIEST FOE...
...THE NINE-NOSED TERROR FROM THE PLANET SLIMEDRIP!
ACHOOO!
OH, NO! THE TERROR'S USING HIS DEADLY SNEEZE RAY!
MAJOR SQUAREJAW'S SPACE CRUISER IS BEING BLOWN OFF COURSE! HE'S FALLING INTO THE SUN!
HE'S DOOMED!
HA! NOT HALF AS DOOMED AS YOU LITTLE MUTINEERS ARE GOING TO BE...
URK!
...IF YOU DON'T GET OUTSIDE AND PLAY!
SWEEP

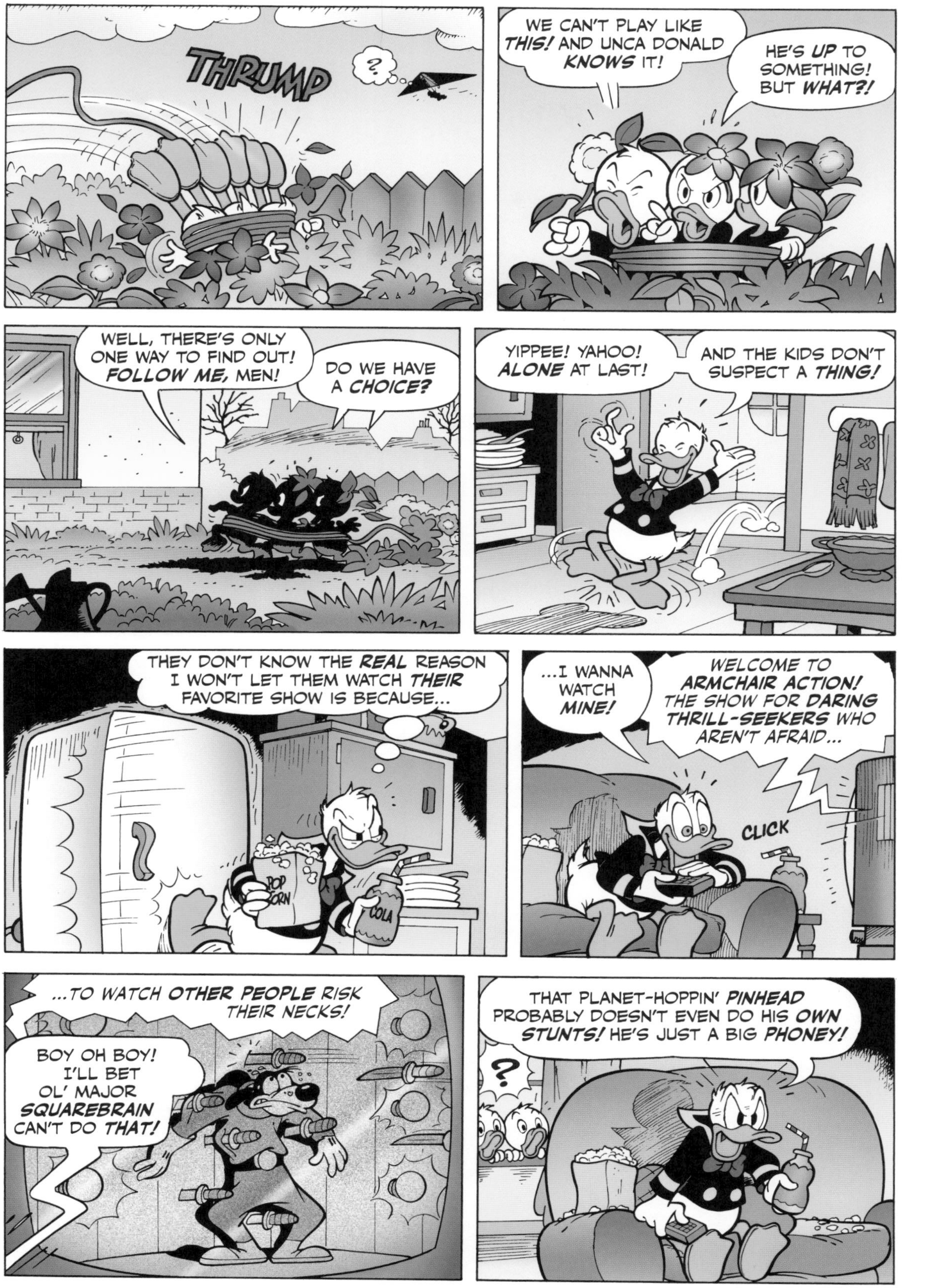
THRUMP
?
WE CAN'T PLAY LIKE THIS! AND UNCA DONALD KNOWS IT!
HE'S UP TO SOMETHING! BUT WHAT?!
WELL, THERE'S ONLY ONE WAY TO FIND OUT! FOLLOW ME, MEN!
DO WE HAVE A CHOICE?
YIPPEE! YAHOO! ALONE AT LAST!
AND THE KIDS DON'T SUSPECT A THING!
THEY DON'T KNOW THE REAL REASON I WON'T LET THEM WATCH THEIR FAVORITE SHOW IS BECAUSE...
POP CORN
COLA
...I WANNA WATCH MINE!
WELCOME TO ARMCHAIR ACTION! THE SHOW FOR DARING THRILL-SEEKERS WHO AREN'T AFRAID...
CLICK
...TO WATCH OTHER PEOPLE RISK THEIR NECKS!
BOY OH BOY! I'LL BET OL' MAJOR SQUAREBRAIN CAN'T DO THAT!
THAT PLANET-HOPPIN' PINHEAD PROBABLY DOESN'T EVEN DO HIS OWN STUNTS! HE'S JUST A BIG PHONEY!
?

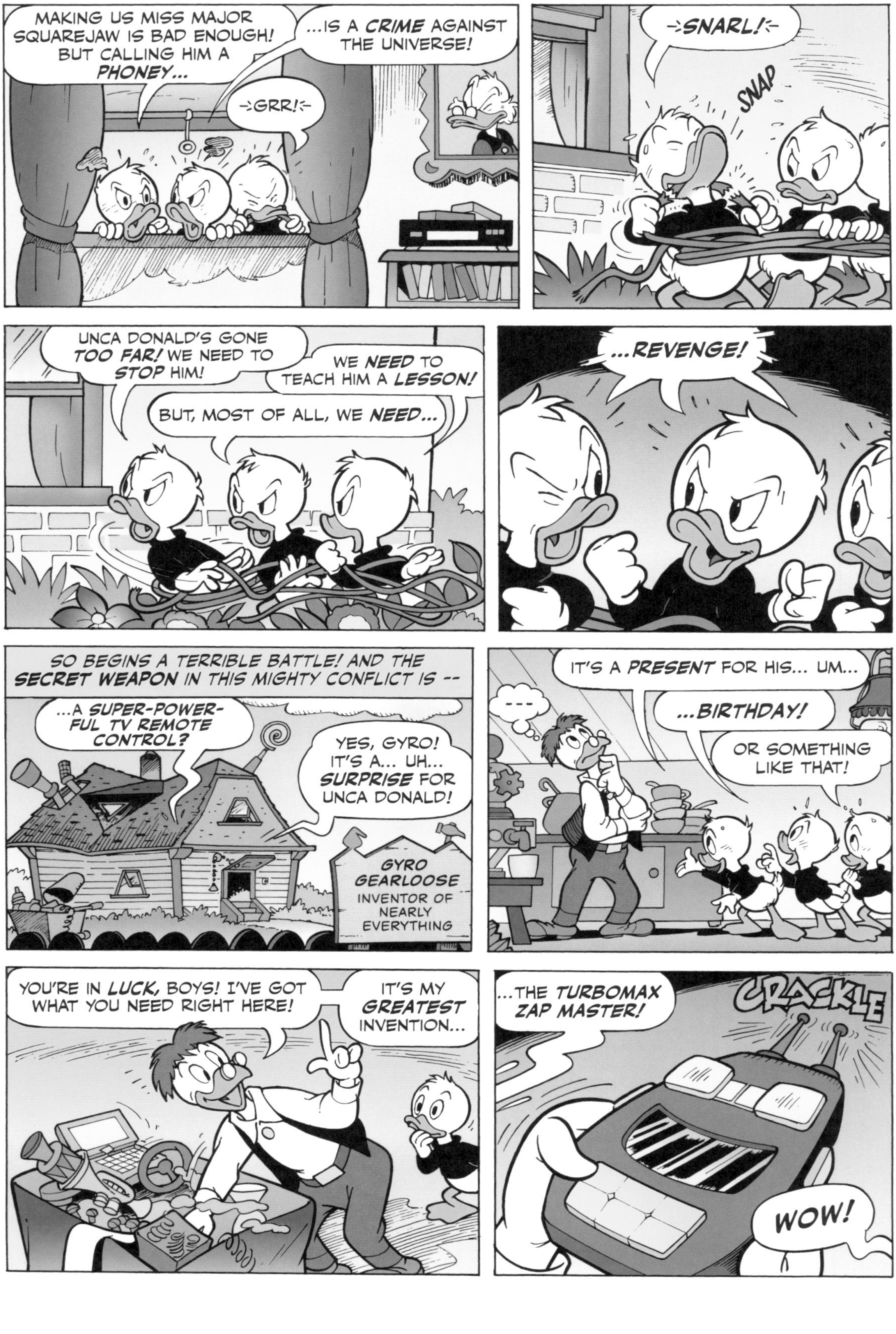
MAKING US MISS MAJOR SQUAREJAW IS BAD ENOUGH! BUT CALLING HIM A PHONEY...
...IS A CRIME AGAINST THE UNIVERSE!
-GRR!-
-SNARL!-
SNAP
UNCA DONALD'S GONE TOO FAR! WE NEED TO STOP HIM!
WE NEED TO TEACH HIM A LESSON!
BUT, MOST OF ALL, WE NEED...
...REVENGE!
SO BEGINS A TERRIBLE BATTLE! AND THE SECRET WEAPON IN THIS MIGHTY CONFLICT IS --
...A SUPER-POWERFUL TV REMOTE CONTROL?
YES, GYRO! IT'S A... UH... SURPRISE FOR UNCA DONALD!
GYRO GEARLOOSE INVENTOR OF NEARLY EVERYTHING
IT'S A PRESENT FOR HIS... UM...

...BIRTHDAY!
OR SOMETHING LIKE THAT!
YOU'RE IN LUCK, BOYS! I'VE GOT WHAT YOU NEED RIGHT HERE!
IT'S MY GREATEST INVENTION...
...THE TURBOMAX ZAP MASTER!
CRACKLE
WOW!

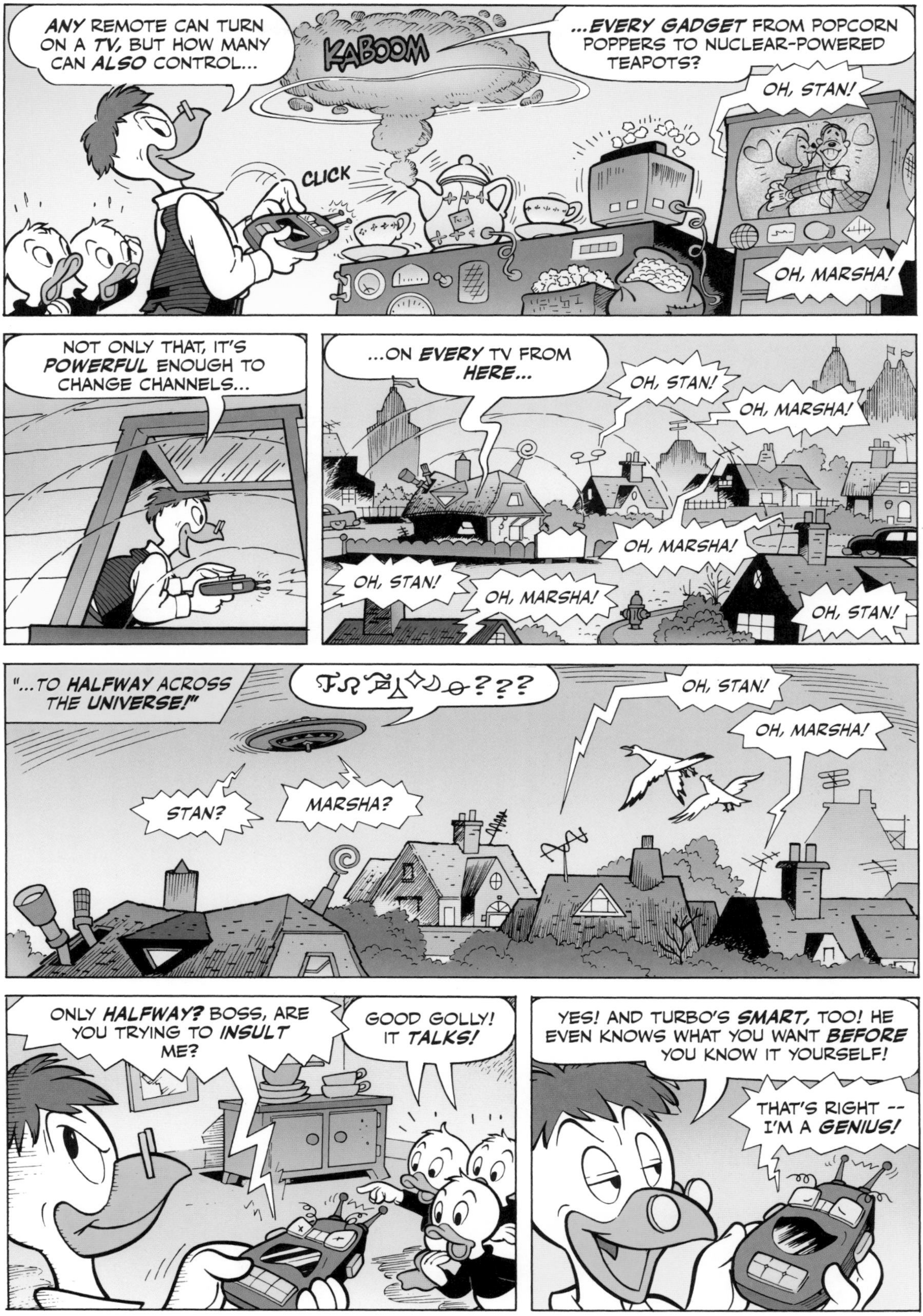
ANY REMOTE CAN TURN ON A TV, BUT HOW MANY CAN ALSO CONTROL...
KABOOM
...EVERY GADGET FROM POPCORN POPPERS TO NUCLEAR-POWERED TEAPOTS?
CLICK
OH, STAN!
OH, MARSHA!
NOT ONLY THAT, IT'S POWERFUL ENOUGH TO CHANGE CHANNELS...
...ON EVERY TV FROM HERE...
OH, STAN!
OH, MARSHA!
OH, MARSHA!
OH, STAN!
OH, MARSHA!
OH, STAN!
"...TO HALFWAY ACROSS THE UNIVERSE!"
???
OH, STAN!
OH, MARSHA!
STAN?
MARSHA?
ONLY HALFWAY? BOSS, ARE YOU TRYING TO INSULT ME?
GOOD GOLLY! IT TALKS!
YES! AND TURBO'S SMART, TOO! HE EVEN KNOWS WHAT YOU WANT BEFORE YOU KNOW IT YOURSELF!
THAT'S RIGHT -- I'M A GENIUS!

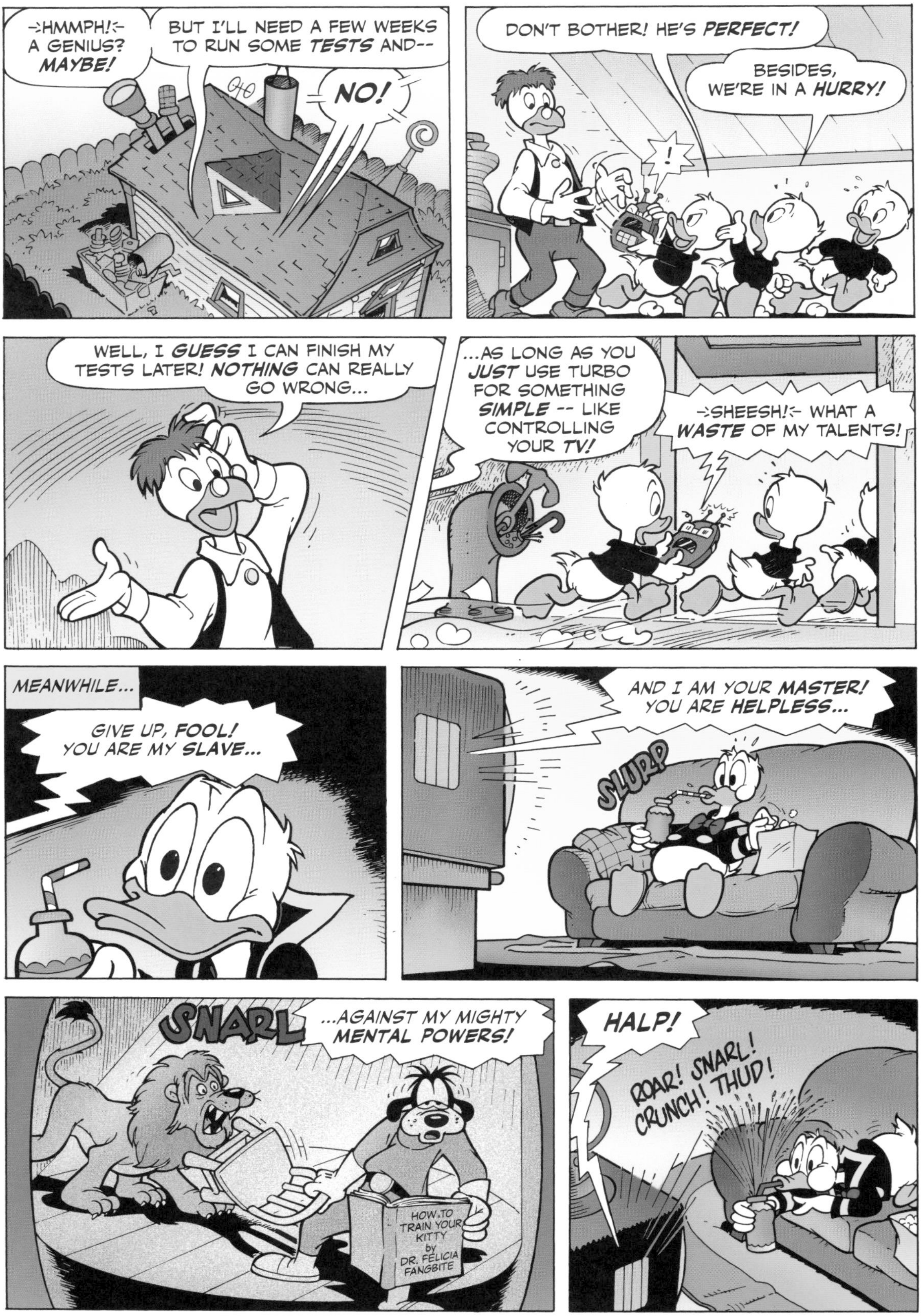
–HMMPH!– A GENIUS? MAYBE!
BUT I'LL NEED A FEW WEEKS TO RUN SOME TESTS AND--
NO!
DON'T BOTHER! HE'S PERFECT!
BESIDES, WE'RE IN A HURRY!
!
WELL, I GUESS I CAN FINISH MY TESTS LATER! NOTHING CAN REALLY GO WRONG...
...AS LONG AS YOU JUST USE TURBO FOR SOMETHING SIMPLE -- LIKE CONTROLLING YOUR TV!
–SHEESH!– WHAT A WASTE OF MY TALENTS!
MEANWHILE...
GIVE UP, FOOL! YOU ARE MY SLAVE...
AND I AM YOUR MASTER! YOU ARE HELPLESS...
SLURP
SNARL
...AGAINST MY MIGHTY MENTAL POWERS!
HOW TO TRAIN YOUR KITTY by DR. FELICIA FANGBITE
HALP!
ROAR! SNARL! CRUNCH! THUD!

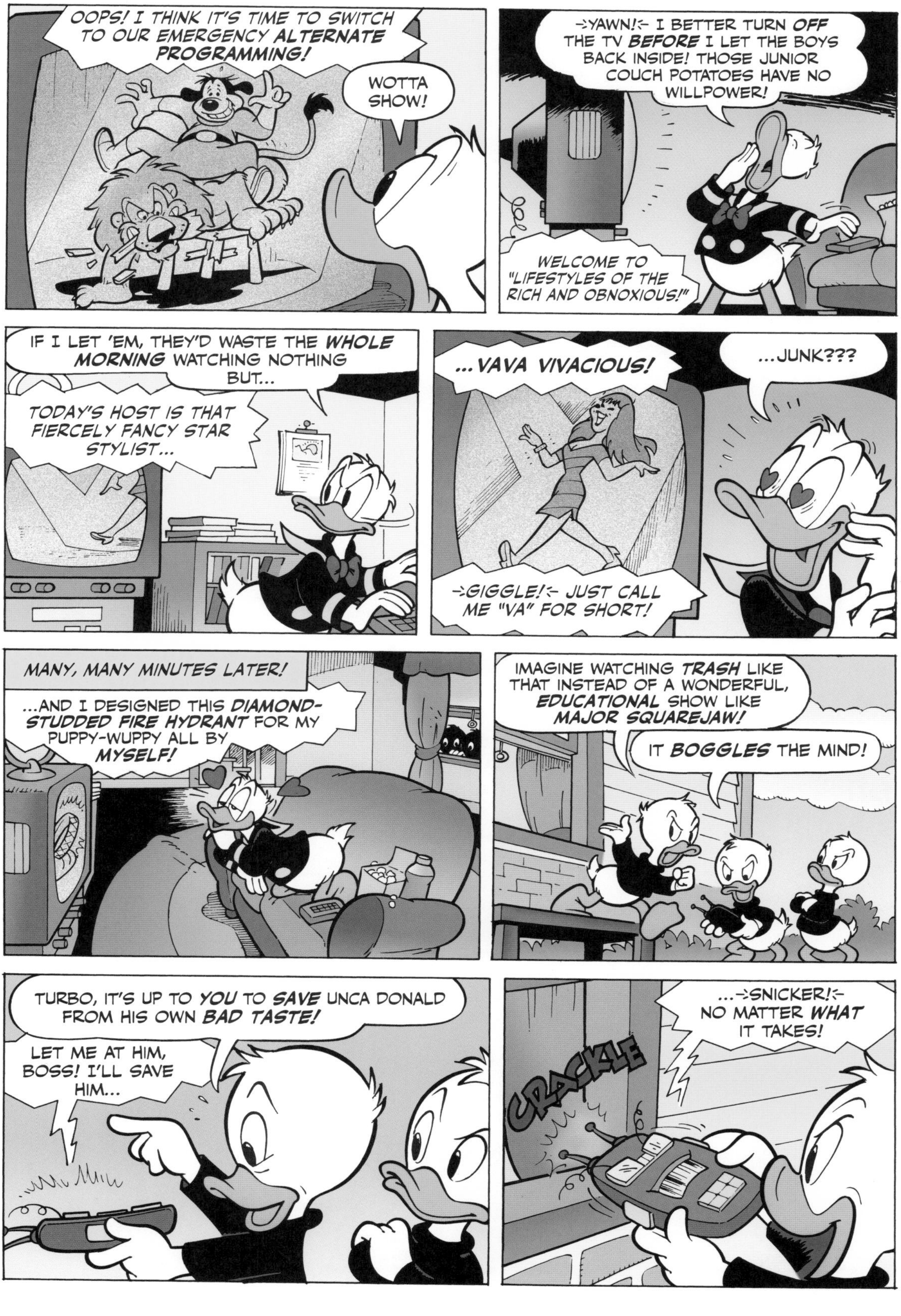
OOPS! I THINK IT'S TIME TO SWITCH TO OUR EMERGENCY ALTERNATE PROGRAMMING!
WOTTA SHOW!
->YAWN!<- I BETTER TURN OFF THE TV BEFORE I LET THE BOYS BACK INSIDE! THOSE JUNIOR COUCH POTATOES HAVE NO WILLPOWER!
WELCOME TO "LIFESTYLES OF THE RICH AND OBNOXIOUS!"
IF I LET 'EM, THEY'D WASTE THE WHOLE MORNING WATCHING NOTHING BUT...
TODAY'S HOST IS THAT FIERCELY FANCY STAR STYLIST...
...VAVA VIVACIOUS!
...JUNK???
->GIGGLE!<- JUST CALL ME "VA" FOR SHORT!
MANY, MANY MINUTES LATER!
...AND I DESIGNED THIS DIAMOND-STUDDED FIRE HYDRANT FOR MY PUPPY-WUPPY ALL BY MYSELF!
IMAGINE WATCHING TRASH LIKE THAT INSTEAD OF A WONDERFUL, EDUCATIONAL SHOW LIKE MAJOR SQUAREJAW!
IT BOGGLES THE MIND!
TURBO, IT'S UP TO YOU TO SAVE UNCA DONALD FROM HIS OWN BAD TASTE!
LET ME AT HIM, BOSS! I'LL SAVE HIM...
CRACKLE
...->SNICKER!<- NO MATTER WHAT IT TAKES!

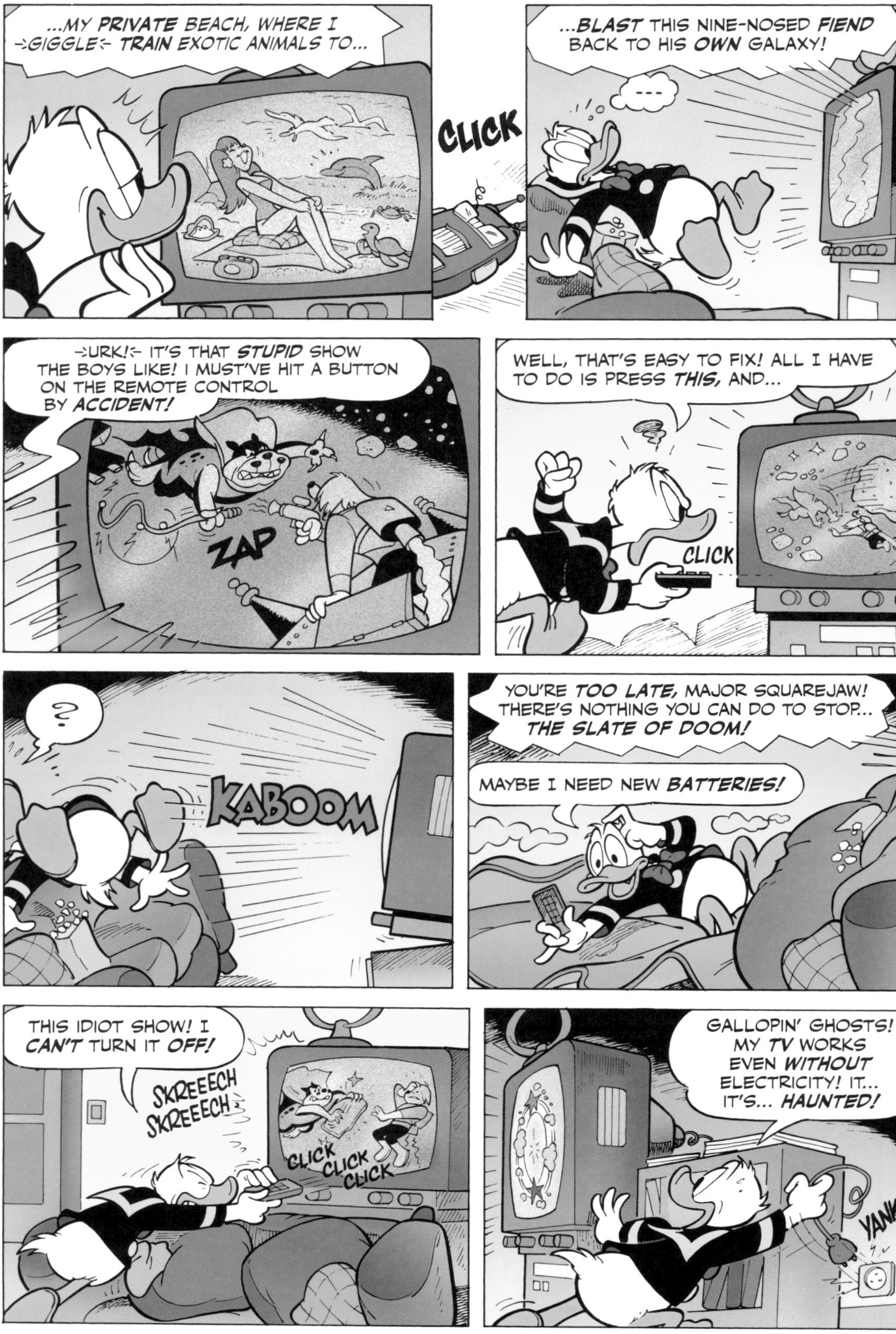
...MY PRIVATE BEACH, WHERE I ⇝GIGGLE⇜ TRAIN EXOTIC ANIMALS TO...
CLICK
...BLAST THIS NINE-NOSED FIEND BACK TO HIS OWN GALAXY!

⇝URK!⇜ IT'S THAT STUPID SHOW THE BOYS LIKE! I MUST'VE HIT A BUTTON ON THE REMOTE CONTROL BY ACCIDENT!
ZAP
WELL, THAT'S EASY TO FIX! ALL I HAVE TO DO IS PRESS THIS, AND...
CLICK
?
KABOOM
YOU'RE TOO LATE, MAJOR SQUAREJAW! THERE'S NOTHING YOU CAN DO TO STOP... THE SLATE OF DOOM!
MAYBE I NEED NEW BATTERIES!
THIS IDIOT SHOW! I CAN'T TURN IT OFF!
SKREEECH SKREEECH
CLICK CLICK CLICK
GALLOPIN' GHOSTS! MY TV WORKS EVEN WITHOUT ELECTRICITY! IT... IT'S... HAUNTED!
YANK

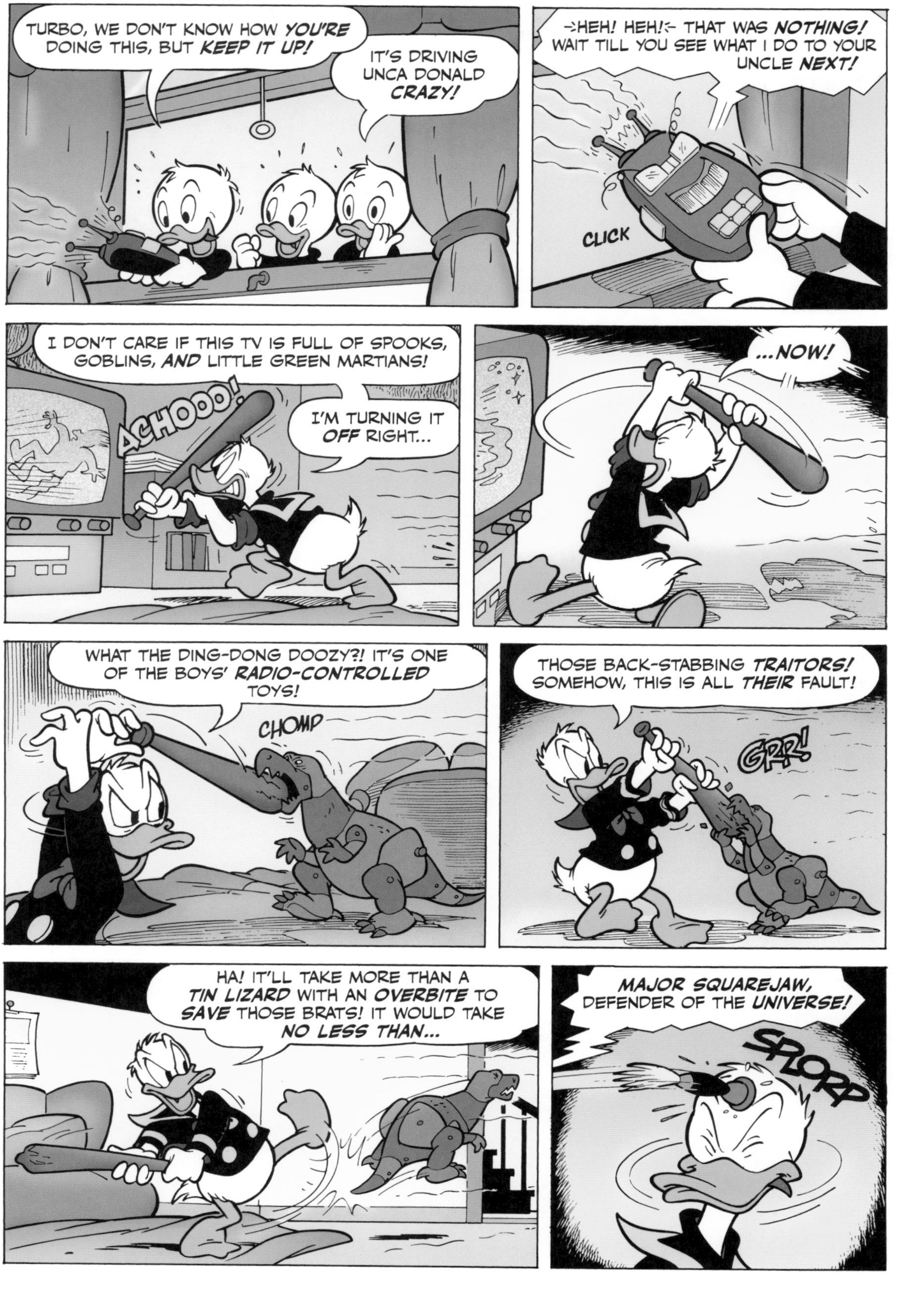
TURBO, WE DON'T KNOW HOW YOU'RE DOING THIS, BUT KEEP IT UP!
IT'S DRIVING UNCA DONALD CRAZY!
HEH! HEH! THAT WAS NOTHING! WAIT TILL YOU SEE WHAT I DO TO YOUR UNCLE NEXT!
CLICK
I DON'T CARE IF THIS TV IS FULL OF SPOOKS, GOBLINS, AND LITTLE GREEN MARTIANS!
ACHOOO!
I'M TURNING IT OFF RIGHT...
...NOW!
WHAT THE DING-DONG DOOZY?! IT'S ONE OF THE BOYS' RADIO-CONTROLLED TOYS!
CHOMP
THOSE BACK-STABBING TRAITORS! SOMEHOW, THIS IS ALL THEIR FAULT!
GRR!
HA! IT'LL TAKE MORE THAN A TIN LIZARD WITH AN OVERBITE TO SAVE THOSE BRATS! IT WOULD TAKE NO LESS THAN...
MAJOR SQUAREJAW, DEFENDER OF THE UNIVERSE!
SPLORP

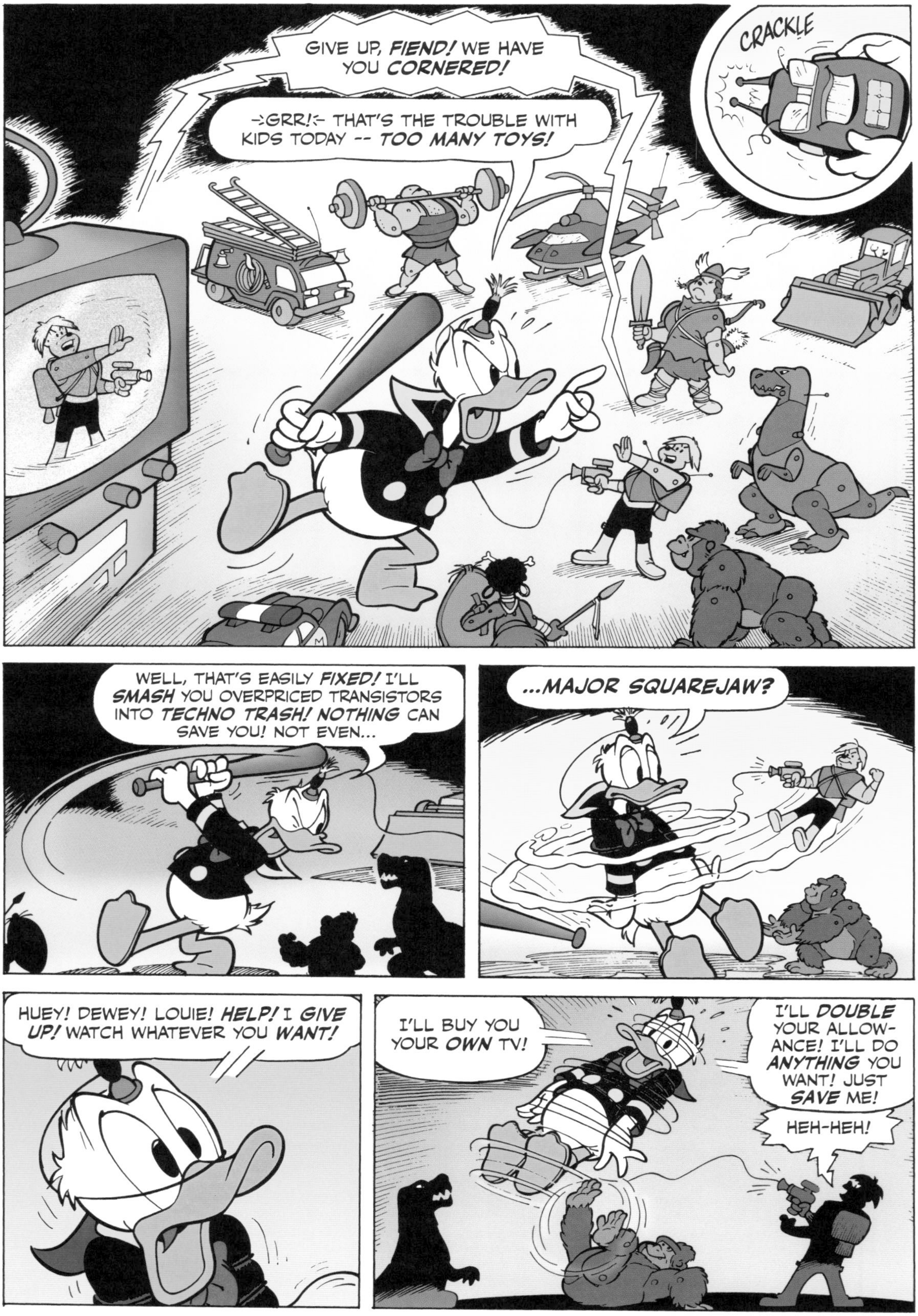
GIVE UP, FIEND! WE HAVE YOU CORNERED!
CRACKLE
-GRR!- THAT'S THE TROUBLE WITH KIDS TODAY -- TOO MANY TOYS!
WELL, THAT'S EASILY FIXED! I'LL SMASH YOU OVERPRICED TRANSISTORS INTO TECHNO TRASH! NOTHING CAN SAVE YOU! NOT EVEN...
...MAJOR SQUAREJAW?
HUEY! DEWEY! LOUIE! HELP! I GIVE UP! WATCH WHATEVER YOU WANT!
I'LL BUY YOU YOUR OWN TV!
I'LL DOUBLE YOUR ALLOWANCE! I'LL DO ANYTHING YOU WANT! JUST SAVE ME!
HEH-HEH!

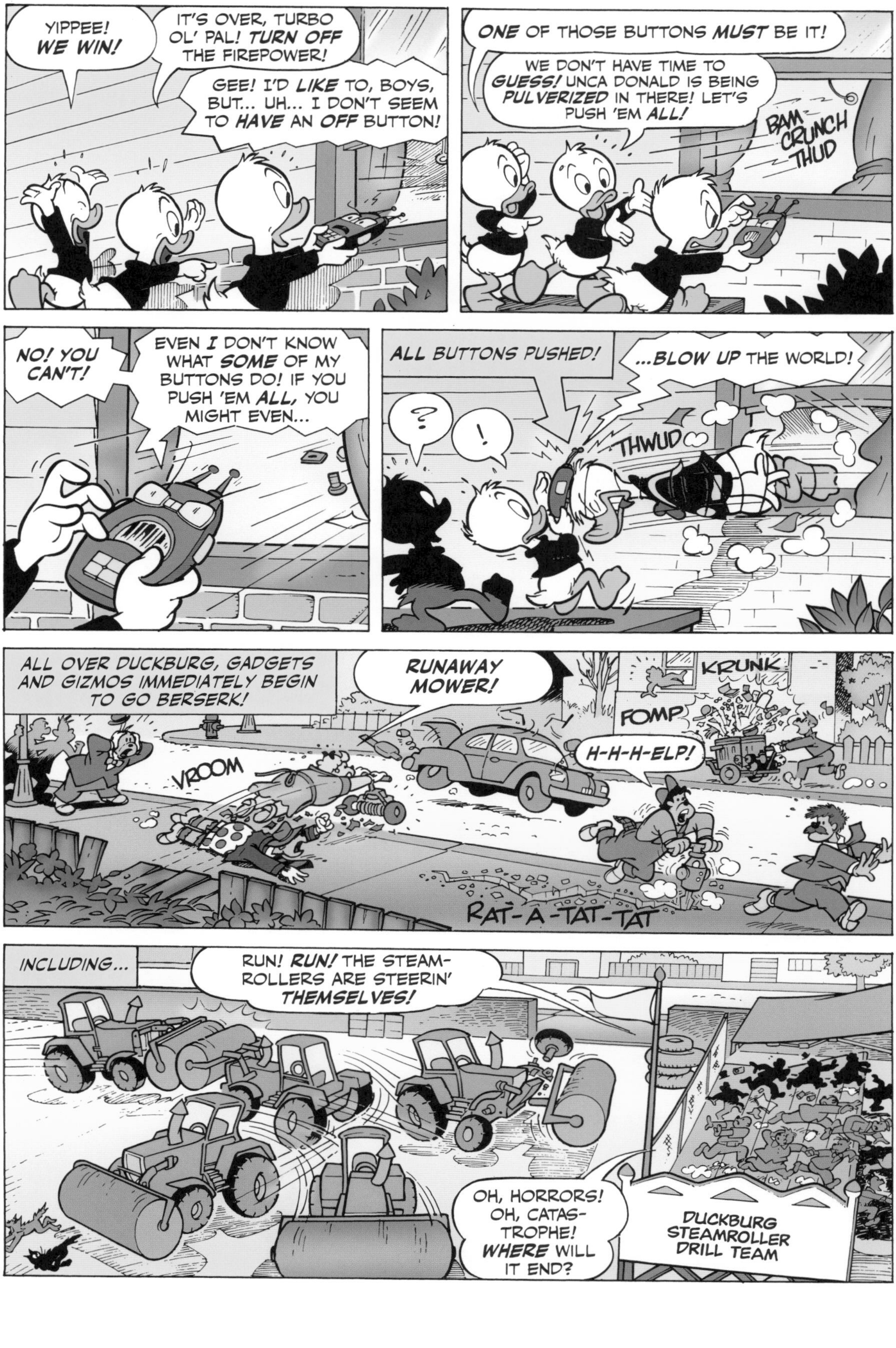
YIPPEE! WE WIN!
IT'S OVER, TURBO OL' PAL! TURN OFF THE FIREPOWER!
GEE! I'D LIKE TO, BOYS, BUT... UH... I DON'T SEEM TO HAVE AN OFF BUTTON!
ONE OF THOSE BUTTONS MUST BE IT!
WE DON'T HAVE TIME TO GUESS! UNCA DONALD IS BEING PULVERIZED IN THERE! LET'S PUSH 'EM ALL!
BAM
CRUNCH
THUD
NO! YOU CAN'T!
EVEN I DON'T KNOW WHAT SOME OF MY BUTTONS DO! IF YOU PUSH 'EM ALL, YOU MIGHT EVEN...
ALL BUTTONS PUSHED!
...BLOW UP THE WORLD!
?
!
THWUD
ALL OVER DUCKBURG, GADGETS AND GIZMOS IMMEDIATELY BEGIN TO GO BERSERK!
RUNAWAY MOWER!
KRUNK
FOMP
H-H-H-ELP!
VROOM
RAT-A-TAT-TAT
INCLUDING...
RUN! RUN! THE STEAM-ROLLERS ARE STEERIN' THEMSELVES!
OH, HORRORS! OH, CATAS-TROPHE! WHERE WILL IT END?
DUCKBURG STEAMROLLER DRILL TEAM

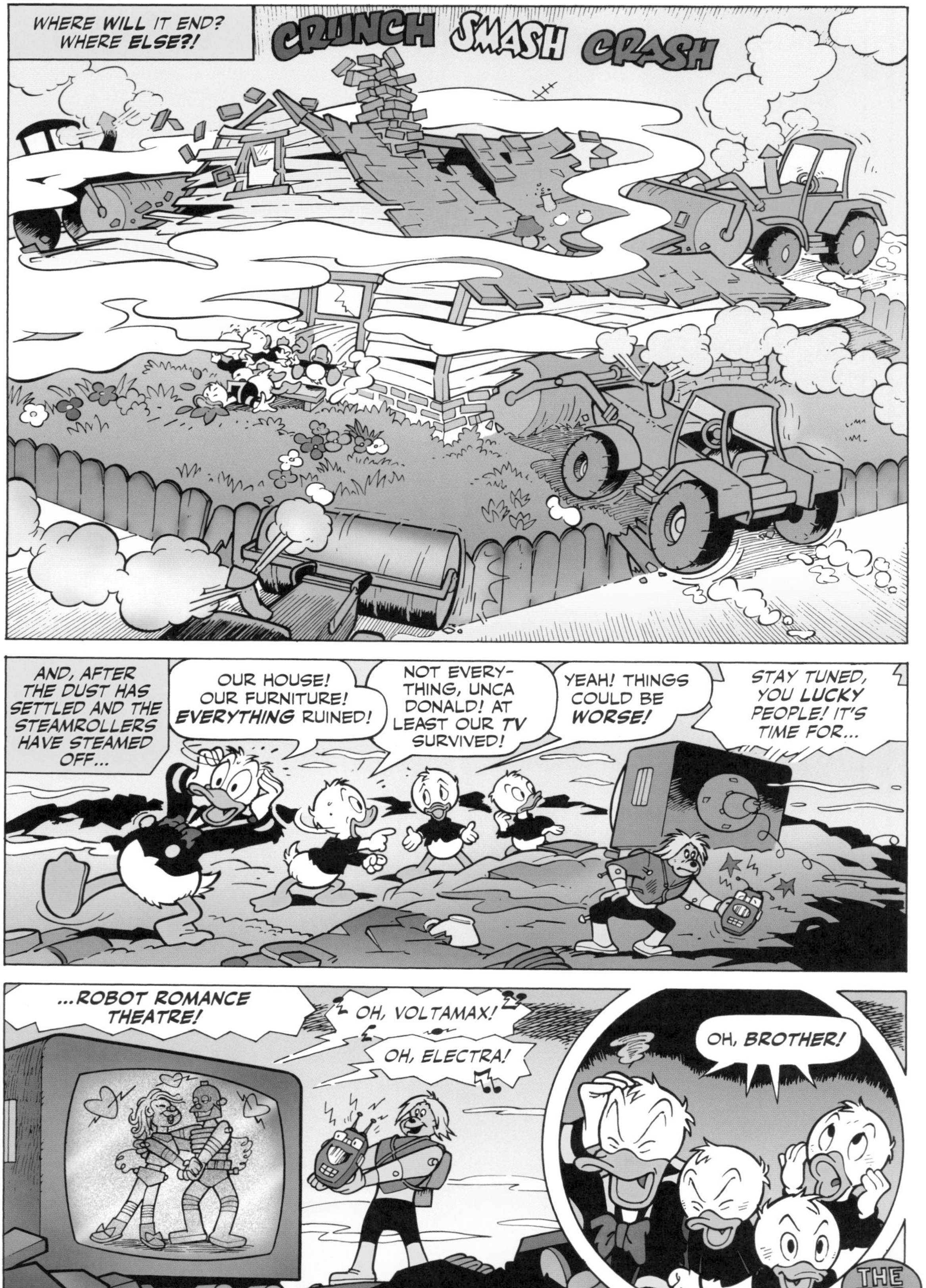
WHERE WILL IT END? WHERE ELSE?!
CRUNCH SMASH CRASH
AND, AFTER THE DUST HAS SETTLED AND THE STEAMROLLERS HAVE STEAMED OFF...
OUR HOUSE! OUR FURNITURE! EVERYTHING RUINED!
NOT EVERY-THING, UNCA DONALD! AT LEAST OUR TV SURVIVED!
YEAH! THINGS COULD BE WORSE!
STAY TUNED, YOU LUCKY PEOPLE! IT'S TIME FOR...
...ROBOT ROMANCE THEATRE!
OH, VOLTAMAX!
OH, ELECTRA!
OH, BROTHER!
THE END

Romano Scarpa: Mouse Maestro

by FRANCESCO STAJANO *and* LEONARDO GORI

AMERICAN COMICS FANS have long admired the work of Floyd Gottfredson (1905-1986), the celebrated "Mouse Man" who created decades' worth of great Mickey newspaper strip adventure stories. But it would be a sin of omission not to point out the special place held by Romano Scarpa (1927-2005) in the ranks of Gottfredson's successors, and as a pivotal figure in his own right. Among the comparatively few Disney comics talents who have both written and drawn their own material, Scarpa was the "maestro" who — better than any other — followed in Gottfredson's footsteps, closely recreating that unique atmosphere of "great adventure" for Mickey.

Born in Venice, Romano Scarpa was the son of an enlightened baker who, rather than forcing him to join the family business, allowed him to pursue his artistic dreams. As a child, Scarpa adored the Gottfredson strips printed in the newspaper-format Disney comic *Topolino* (Mickey Mouse); but he was perhaps even more fascinated by Walt Disney's film masterpiece, *Snow White and the Seven Dwarfs* (1937) — to the point that he decided to try his hand at animation. With his father's support, Scarpa outfitted a small animation studio and gathered a group of other young enthusiasts to work with him as artists, inkers, colorists and inbetweeners: among them Giorgio Bordini and Rodolfo Cimino, both of whom would later also draw and write Disney comics. In 1953, Scarpa's team produced an animated short, *La piccola fiammiferaia* ("The Little Match Girl"), based on the Hans Christian Andersen fairy tale.

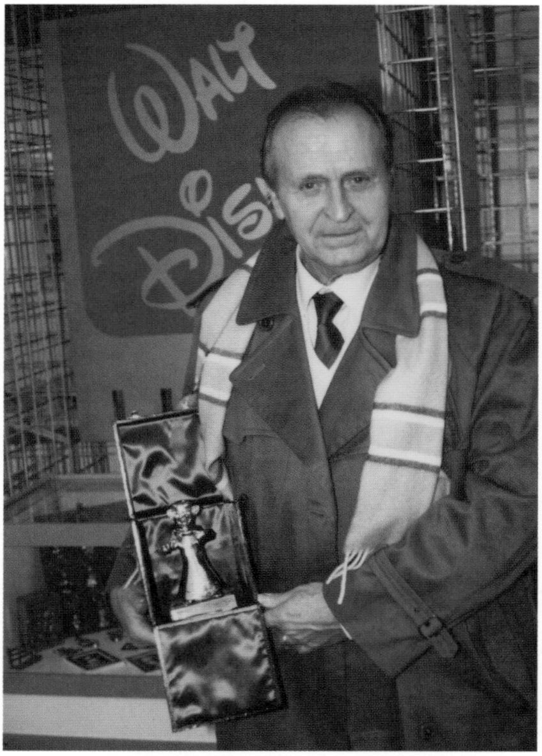
WALT DISNEY

Romano Scarpa receives the Yellow Kid Award, a major comics industry prize, at the Lucca Comics convention in Tuscany, 1990. Image © and courtesy Luca Boschi.

Alas, soon afterward a minor accident rendered Scarpa unable to stand for several months. Alongside market conditions, this handicap was a contributing factor in his decision to set animation aside for a while. He thus turned to comics. Having been accepted at Mondadori, the Italian Disney publisher, he soon found himself drawing a story written by Guido Martina featuring his beloved Snow White — for whom Scarpa's fiancée and later wife Sandra Zanardi posed as the model (U.S. printing in Fantagraphics' *The Return of Snow White and the Seven Dwarfs*). From the start, Scarpa's artwork owed much to Golden Age animation, and one can see echoes of Seven Dwarfs designer Fred Moore in his strokes — convenient for a Snow White artist but precipitous, too, for another reason. Master Disney animator Moore had famously streamlined Mickey Mouse throughout the 1930s. The better Scarpa learned to imitate Moore, the better he was also able to emulate Floyd Gottfredson.

Then Scarpa got the chance to step into Gottfredson's shoes. In 1955, when Gottfredson was forced by King Features Syndicate to stop making Mickey Mouse serials and switch to daily gags, the move cut Mondadori off from a major source of popular *Topolino* content. Noting Scarpa as an up-and-coming talent, the publisher drafted him first to draw new Mickey stories, then to write them too — and as a Gottfredson fan, Scarpa chose to mimic the Gottfredson style. The job was a labor of love. Many Italian readers of the time thought, to Scarpa's delight, that Scarpa's yarns were Gottfredson's latest output.

After initially working from Martina's scripts, Scarpa soon started writing his own stories, creating suspenseful, elaborate plots similar in feel to the best Gottfredson long adventures, such as "Mickey Mouse Outwits the Phantom Blot," "Monarch of Medioka," and "Island in the Sky." Scarpa's own stories in the same spirit, such as "Kali's Nail" (1958; U.S. printing in *Disney Masters* Vol. 17), "The Mystery of Tapiocus VI" (1956; U.S. printing in *Mickey Mouse* 256, 1990), and "The Delta Dimension" (1959; U.S. printing in *Disney Masters* Vol. 1) have equally powerful evocative imagery; each is characteristically built upon several intertwining subplots, which ultimately unravel in a dramatic conclusion.

Some Scarpa Mickey stories build new and original yarns atop plot devices, settings, or characters from the Gottfredson classics: the spy hides the secret formula inside an item that accidentally gets away from him; danger threatens either the weak sovereign of a faraway European kingdom or the enigmatic genius Dr. Einmug and his amazing scientific discoveries.

Other great Scarpa stories share no details with Gottfredson's tales, but still retain those tales' epic Disney spirit. "The Chirikawa Necklace" (1960; U.S. printing in *MM* 317-318, 2016) is a Freudian masterpiece worthy of Alfred Hitchcock — and, indeed, reminiscent of Hitchcock's *Vertigo* (1958) — in which Mickey must fight childhood nightmares and solve a long-ago crime in order to unravel a modern mystery. In the same story, Scarpa introduces Trudy Van Tubb, Peg-Leg Pete's brassy girlfriend, as the perfect companion for Mickey's archrival.

On that note, we should point out that Scarpa became, after Barks and Gottfredson, the most prolific creator of ongoing Disney characters for comics — and like almost no other writer-artist, Scarpa was equally at ease with both Mice and Ducks. From the aforementioned Trudy to Brigitta MacBridge and Jubal Pomp (respectively, Uncle Scrooge's hopeless love interest and his hapless business rival), Scarpa gave birth to an array of new characters who fit so naturally into Duckburg and Mouseton that other authors picked them up, regarding them as genuinely "Disney" as their Barks and Gottfredson forerunners.

Scarpa even created a figure in the mold of Eega Beeva, Gottfredson's wacky time traveler. Atomo Bleep-Bleep — originally an atom, but magnified to human proportions by Dr. Einmug — picked up where Eega left off in terms of acting as a "superhero sidekick" for Mickey on some of his most memorable adventures (see *Disney Masters* Vol. 1 for several of Atomo's first appearances).

Scarpa's "golden age" was arguably his first decade of activity: 1953 to 1963, during which time he spared no effort to build meticulously crafted plots as suspenseful and surprising as Gottfredson's. Unfortunately for his avid fans, Scarpa, having become dissatisfied with the inadequate financial reward for his own elaborate scripts, gradually switched to only illustrating the stories of other writers.

He did, however, return to storytelling in full glory near the end of his career, when — as an explicit homage to Gottfredson — he created four special Mickey "strip stories," such as this volume's "The Riddle of Brigaboom," that recreated not only the spirit but the layout and structure of Gottfredson's daily strips.

Romano Scarpa's legacy, as both a Gottfredson protégé and as a towering comics talent in his own right, remains unsurpassed.

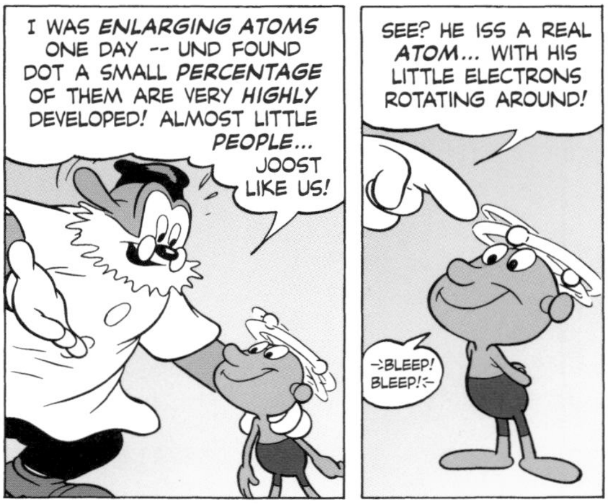
I WAS ENLARGING ATOMS ONE DAY -- UND FOUND DOT A SMALL PERCENTAGE OF THEM ARE VERY HIGHLY DEVELOPED! ALMOST LITTLE PEOPLE... JOOST LIKE US!
SEE? HE ISS A REAL ATOM... WITH HIS LITTLE ELECTRONS ROTATING AROUND!
BLEEP! BLEEP!

Mickey's Gottfredson-era friend and mentor, the brilliant atomic scientist Dr. Einmug, introduces Atomo Bleep-Bleep in Scarpa's "The Delta Dimension." Atomo continues to feature in new European Disney comics to this day.